J.M. Synge

Collected Works IV
PLAYS Book 2

THE PLAY BOY   JACK B YEATS

J. M. SYNGE: COLLECTED WORKS

General Editor: ROBIN SKELTON

———

PLAYS

BOOK II

J. M. SYNGE

COLLECTED WORKS

Volume IV

PLAYS

BOOK II

EDITED BY
ANN SADDLEMYER

1982
COLIN SMYTHE
GERRARDS CROSS, BUCKS

THE CATHOLIC UNIVERSITY OF
AMERICA PRESS
WASHINGTON, D.C.

Copyright © 1968 Oxford University Press

This edition published in 1982
by Colin Smythe Limited, Gerrards Cross,
Buckinghamshire

British Library Cataloguing in Publication Data

Synge, John Millington
   The collected works of J. M. Synge
   Vol. 4: Plays. Book 2
   I. Saddlemyer, Ann
   822'.9'12   PR5530

ISBN 0–86140–137–9
ISBN 0–86140–061–5 Pbk.

First published in North America in 1982
by The Catholic University of America Press, Washington, D.C.

ISBN 0–8132–0569–7
ISBN 0–8132–0568–9 Pbk.
Library of Congress Catalog Card No. 82–70364

Printed in Great Britain
Set by Oxford University Press
Printed from copy supplied, and bound by
Billing & Sons Ltd., Worcester and London

TO

LILO STEPHENS

CONTENTS

INTRODUCTION

'THERE is no work I ⟨believe⟩ that requires such slow care as
writing a play,' Synge wrote to the journalist Leon Brodzky on
10 December 1907. Certainly Synge's own slow progress over his
last three plays justifies that belief. *The Well of the Saints*, although
not produced until February 1905, had been completed by July of
the preceding year; yet *The Playboy of the Western World*, on which
he started work almost immediately, was not turned over to the
company until January 1907, less than a month before its first
production, and even during rehearsals and proof-reading Synge
was still making important alterations to the text. Similarly, *The
Tinker's Wedding*, begun while he was at work on *Riders to the Sea*
and *The Shadow of the Glen* in the summer of 1902, was not published until December 1907. And *Deirdre of the Sorrows*, well under
way by the autumn of 1907 but contemplated at least a year before
that, had received perhaps only half its intended revisions when
Synge died in March 1909.

This reluctance either to be satisfied or to discard can be seen
most clearly in his attitude to the unpublished play, *When the
Moon Has Set*; it also explains to a great extent his treatment of
The Tinker's Wedding, which more than any of his published plays
suffered from the author's keen awareness of its limitations. In
another letter to Brodzky he explained, 'Though I wrote 'Riders'
and 'The Shadow' for Fay's company, I had been out of Ireland
so much that I had never met any of the company or seen them
act, at that time.'[1] *The Tinker's Wedding*, conceived at the same
time, was to be twice rejected as 'too dangerous' to play in Ireland; yet for years it remained among his papers, unpublished and
therefore, in Synge's eyes, incomplete and challenging. It, like
The Shadow of the Glen and *The Well of the Saints*, was a translation
of his experiences in County Wicklow,[2] but unlike his later plays
it offered little scope for development of character or mood; the

[1] 12 December 1907. Both these letters are now in the Brodney papers, Trinity College,
Dublin. It was not until February 1903, after Synge's two one-act plays had been accepted,
that Willie Fay's company officially became the Irish National Theatre Society.
[2] In his notes to Brodzky, 10 December 1907, Synge wrote, 'In 1898 I went to the Aran
Islands—I had known the Co Wicklow peasantry—we always spend every summer there
—intimately for years—and found the subjects of most of my plays there.'

intractable plot forbade alteration in terms of ideas or theatrical experience, and so it remained simply an experiment in expansion.

Apart from the early draft in Notebook 'H' (summer 1902), the first reference to *The Tinker's Wedding* occurs in Synge's diary for 3 October 1903, crammed between a cycling journey through 'the Scalp' (a rocky valley in County Wicklow) and research on Petit de Julleville's *Théâtre en France* (where he found the plot for *The Well of the Saints*). It is the last entry in the last diary he preserved. By the end of 1903, however, the first draft appears to have been completed, for in a letter to Lady Gregory on 16 December concerning Elkin Mathews's projected Vigo edition of the two one-act plays he asks, 'Do you think if he brings out the plays in the spring I should add the tinkers?' Apparently he also consulted John Masefield, who was acting as go-between, for on 18 December Masefield replied, 'By all means add the abortive wedding play.'

Correspondence was not, however, resumed until over a year later, when Elkin Mathews himself wrote to Synge on 20 January 1905:

Did you tell me you had *three* plays for publication or is the idea due to my imagination? For I find that besides your Aranmor MS. I have only two plays, viz. 'In the Shadow of the Glen' (typed) and 'Riders to the Sea' (in *Samhain*).

These two would I think be just sufficient to make up a volume for the *Vigo Cabinet Series*. As I want to put the latter in Printers' hands will you kindly let me know from you?

An undated draft of Synge's reply is preserved:

Excuse delay in answering yours of the 20th. You are perfectly right about the 3rd play. You had another in two acts 'The Tinker's Wedding', but the day I called on you last spring you gave me back the MS. as I wanted to make some corrections in it. Being in two acts it is about as long as the other two plays together, so if they are long enough to fill your volume, I suppose you would hardly have room for 'The Tinkers' with them. As far as I am concerned I would rather have the two plays you have brought out now together, and hold over the third as a character in 'The Tinker's Wedding' is likely to displease⟨...⟩ a good many of our Dublin friends and would perhaps hinder the sale of the book in Ireland—[1]

[1] Unless otherwise stated all quotations come from papers in the Synge Estate.

Mathews's Vigo edition of the one-act plays appeared in May 1905, and the next suggestion concerning publication of *The Tinker's Wedding* came from Yeats, who wrote from Coole Park to Synge in Mountain Stage, County Kerry, on 9 September 1905:

Bring if you can, or have sent to me, the MS. of the Tinkers. I want to see if it would do for *Samhain*, if you don't object, and also to see whether we can discuss it for our winter session. We are rather hard up for new short pieces, and you have such a bad reputation now it can hardly do you any harm. But we may find it too dangerous for the Theatre at present. . . .

Synge replied on 12 September:

I cannot bring or send you the Tinker MS. I am sorry to say, as I have not got it with me, and I am afraid to set my pious relations to hunt for it among my papers for fear they would set fire to the whole. I can give it to you in Dublin if that will be time enough.[1]

Synge, Yeats, and W. G. Fay duly met in Dublin later that month, but Yeats reported to Lady Gregory that they decided performance and publication 'would be dangerous at present'.[2]

Still later in 1905 George Roberts of Maunsel and Company wrote to Synge about the publication of *The Aran Islands* and added, 'W.B. suggested we should put your tinker play in this Arrow but I think one play is enough for the publication—for other reasons I think this would be better as a separate book. I should like to have the MS. of this also. . . .'[3] Apparently Synge responded to Maunsel's overture, for a further letter from Roberts on 2 January 1906 commented, 'Glad to hear about the tinker play—hope arrangements will be completed. We can discuss your price for this book when I see you.'

The next day, encouraged by his correspondence with Roberts, Synge wrote to Max Meyerfeld, who had translated *The Well of the Saints* into German:

I am hard at work on my new play now—it was delayed by my illness—and I hope also to bring out a little two-act comedy—'The

---

[1] Original letter in the Gregory papers, Berg Collection, New York Public Library.

[2] Letter in the possession of Mrs. W. B. Yeats and quoted by David H. Greene and Edward M. Stephens, *J. M. Synge 1871–1909* (New York, Macmillan, 1959), p. 198.

[3] *The Arrow*, first appearing in October 1906, was an occasional pamphlet alternating with *Samhain*, its purpose to confound attackers of Abbey Theatre policy.

Tinker's Wedding'—very shortly which I wrote some time ago but quite forgot to mention to you. We have never played it here as they say it is too immoral for Dublin! There is however some talk of having it done in London before long though nothing is decided as yet. I am inclined to think it would do rather well in German, in any case if it is published I will have pleasure in sending you a copy. . . .

Meyerfeld expressed his interest by the next post, and Synge wrote again on 18 January 1906, 'I have a few changes to make in the "Tinker's Wedding" then—if you have still any wish to see it—I will be glad to send you a copy of the MS. to see what you think of it.' Another letter, on 10 March, made further apologies:

I am sorry for delay in sending you 'The Tinker's Wedding', I have had to revise it a little, and I have had influenza which has kept me back in all my work. I hope to send you the MS. to look at next week if possible. Remember it is a little play written before the 'Well of the Saints' but never played here because it is thought too immoral and anticlerical. My new play in 3 acts ⟨*The Playboy of the Western World*⟩ will not be finished for some time yet. We hope to play it here in the early autumn. . . .

Finally the MS. itself was posted in April, although Synge was still not happy with his work:

I have been revising it ever since, and only got the clean copy last night. So I send it to you now with very many apologies. I may work at it a little more still as in some ways I am not wholly satisfied with it, but it will not differ much from what I am sending you; please let me know when convenient if you think it would have any chance in Germany.

But Meyerfeld's reaction was a disappointment; he considered the play 'too undramatic and too Irish', and impossible for Germany. He advised Synge to give up writing peasant plays if he wished to achieve lasting fame. Synge waited a month before replying on 14 May 1906, 'I received the MS. of the Tinker and your kind letter. I am glad to hear your opinion about my "peasant" plays, though naturally I do not share it. . . .' Dr. Meyerfeld did not translate any other play by Synge.[1]

That the fears concerning the play were genuine is evident from Lady Gregory's comments in December 1906 concerning another

[1] Synge's letters to Max Meyerfeld are now in the National Library of Ireland. Meyerfeld edited the letters for the *Yale Review*, July 1924.

play submitted to the Abbey Theatre, 'I think it more capable than any new work that has been sent in, but I doubt its being any advantage to us, and a priest on the stage is risky.' However, it is likely that the next overture, this time from England, was due to Yeats's and Lady Gregory's continuing championship. On 7 August 1907 Synge wrote to Frank Sidgwick, at that time a partner with A. H. Bullen at the Shakespeare Head Press, Stratford, publishers of Yeats's work in England:

Many thanks for your letter of July 30th, which I would have answered sooner only that I have been away in the country—

I have a short play the 'Tinker's Wedding' which has never been produced and I will be very glad to show it to Mr. Granville Barker, but I would like to run through the MS. and make a few alterations before I do so—

We have never acted it here as it would have made a greater disturbance, if possible, than the 'Playboy'.

I do not think the 'T. Wedding' is altogether a satisfactory play and as what merits it has lie in a humorous dialogue that would have to be very richly and confidently spoken, I am not sure that it would be a very wise experiment for Mr. Barker to produce it. However as I said, I will be very glad to let him see it and then we can see what he thinks. I have promised to let Maunsel publish it in the autumn.

I suppose if I send the MS. to the Savoy and mention your name to Mr. Barker it will be all right, or shall I send it to you? I would be interested to know what you might think its chances would be with an English company and an English audience. . . .[1]

Harley Granville Barker himself replied on 18 September 1907, from the Savoy Theatre, which he and J. E. Vedrenne had taken over for a series of Shaw's plays after leaving the Court Theatre:

Three things about The Tinker's Wedding. I want my partner to see it. I want us to think whether we can really get the Irish atmosphere, without which it would be a cruelty to you to play it. And I want to see what sort of bill we could fit it into. If this delay is intolerable to you, please let me know.

And again on 2 December 1907:

I have kept your play a disgraceful time: your letter has remained unanswered a disgraceful time. I am very interested in 'The Tinker's Wedding'; whether Redford ⟨of the Lord Chamberlain's Office⟩

[1] Original letter in the possession of the Academic Center Library, University of Texas.

would pass it or not I don't know. I am unaware of his views on the Irish question, or whether he has any. Probably he regards Ireland as a benighted place, since it is not in his moral keeping. But one of my difficulties is that I doubt if we could do it here; I doubt if our actors could capture it. I want to look at the MS. again. I want to show it to some one if I may. Then I expect I'll be reluctantly returning it to you. . . .

Granville Barker's fears were realized, for when the play was finally produced by an English company (the Afternoon Theatre Company at His Majesty's Theatre, 11 November 1909), Yeats was so indignant that he walked out after the first act.[1] The reviewer for the London *Times* described it as 'less a play than a picture of Irish life in its more squalid aspects' and commented that 'the climax of the piece, in which the priest, in full canonicals, is gagged and put into a sack, seems a little far-fetched to English audiences, but the whole is a vivid and effective little work'.

Synge himself seems to have had an ambiguous attitude towards the play. On 28 November 1907 he wrote to his fiancée, Molly Allgood, 'I corrected the final first proofs of the Tinkers Wedding yesterday and this morning I have finished (?) the Preface to it. The play is good I think, but it looks mighty shocking in print.' To his Scottish friend James Paterson he wrote on 27 March 1908, 'I am sending you a little play which I wrote some years ago but did not publish till the other day—The Tinkers Wedding—as you will understand we think it too dangerous to put on in the Abbey —it is founded on a real incident that happened in Wicklow a few years ago.' And in a letter to Louis Untermeyer on 29 November 1908 he passed it off casually, calling it 'slight but may interest you'.[2]

It could well be that Synge's decision to publish *The Tinker's Wedding* was in part at least a result of the furore caused by the first production of *The Playboy of the Western World* in January 1907, and, as such, was an emphatic reiteration of his flustered reply to the press on that occasion, 'I don't care a rap.' That he did care deeply, however, is evident from the innumerable revisions and immense care devoted to the creation of *The Playboy*.

[1] See his letter to Lady Gregory, 26 November 1909, *The Letters of W. B. Yeats*, ed. Allan Wade (London, Rupert Hart-Davis, 1954), p. 538.

[2] Original in the possession of the Lilly Library, Indiana University. Untermeyer quoted from this letter in his article 'The Late J. M. Synge' in the *New York Times*, 17 April 1909.

As early as 8 July 1905 Yeats wrote from London, 'I am looking forward to your new play with great expectations. There are very stirring rumours about your first act.' But early struggles with *The Playboy* alternated with bouts of sickness. Synge went to Kerry to recover from influenza, and it was not until late September that he could write to Lady Gregory, 'I am trying not very successfully to pick up the threads of my play. It is hard to begin again after such a long holiday.' On 16 February 1906 he reported, 'My play has made practically no way since as I have been down for ten days with bronchitis and not able to work.' Finally by 5 August of that year he could write, 'I am pleased with the way my play is going but I find it is quite impossible to rush through with it now. So I rather think I shall take it and the typewriter to Kerry where I could work. By doing so I would get some sort of holiday and still avoid dropping the play again—which is a rather dangerous process.' On 12 August he wrote again, 'I shall be very glad, thanks to go down and read you my play if it is finished in time, but there is still a great deal to do. I have had a very steady week's work since last Sunday and have made good way, but my head is getting very tired, working in hot weather takes a lot out of me.' And on 22 August, still in Dublin, he wrote wistfully of Kerry, 'I want to be among peasants for a while, and it is a good mountainy place for this hot weather.'[1]

When he finally did get to County Kerry, he stayed less than three weeks and worked little on *The Playboy*, although much of the flavour of his visits to Mountain Stage and the Blasket Islands entered the play.[2] Back in Dublin on 14 September he wrote to Meyerfeld:

I hope to have my new play ready in a few weeks' time, and I will send you a copy as soon as possible. I have been working at it most of the summer—except for a few weeks which I spent in Kerry—but as you know play writing is slow work. I think it will be a much better *acting* play than the 'Well of the Saints' and I hope you will think it suitable for translation.

Originally the first production was scheduled for 19 December, but on 4 October Synge wrote to Yeats:

My play, though in its last agony, is not finished and I cannot promise it for any definite day. It is more than likely that when I read it to

---

[1] Original letters to Lady Gregory in the Berg Collection, New York Public Library.
[2] See Greene and Stephens, *J. M. Synge*, p. 214.

you and Fay ⟨. . .⟩ there will be little things to alter that have escaped me. And with my stuff it takes time to get even half a page of new dialogue fully into key with what goes before it. The play, I think, will be one of the longest we have done, and in places extremely difficult. If we said the nineteenth ⟨. . .⟩ I could only have some six or seven full rehearsals, which would not I am quite sure be enough. We could not rehearse it in the evening till the Mineral Workers ⟨a play by William Boyle⟩ are done with, then ⟨W. G.⟩ Fay goes to Scotland to get married, and however speedy he is one cannot hope to get much work out of him that week. So there would be only a fortnight (6 rehearsals) over. In the Playboy he has a very big part and I do not see that the thing can be managed. I am very sorry, but what is to be done? ⟨. . .⟩ If F. Fay could play my playboy there might be some chance of being ready as he learns quickly but I fear some of it would be altogether out of his range⟨. . . .⟩ My difficulty is that I can only have full rehearsals —with my big cast—*three nights* in the week (and of course W. G. Fay's memory).

On 5 November he wrote to Lady Gregory, 'I have only very little now to do to the Playboy to get him *provisionally* finished', but two days later he confessed in a letter to Yeats, 'I would have been in during the week but I could not leave the Play-Boy. I am nearly in distraction with him, and consequently am very unwell.' However, the next day, 8 November, he wrote to Lady Gregory, 'May I read the Playboy to you and Yeats and Fay some time tomorrow, Saturday or Monday according as it suits you all. A little verbal correction is still necessary and one or two structural points may need—I fancy do need—revision, but I would like to have your opinions on it before I go further.'[1] And the same day he wrote to Molly Allgood: 'The Playboy is very nearly ready. I am writing to Lady Gregory by this post to ask her to fix a time for me to read it to them. Then there will be the job of making a clean copy. My MS. at present could not be read by anyone but myself, it is all written over and corrected and pulled to bits. . . .'[2] The proposed reading took place on 13 November, but of Acts I and II only, and on 16 November Lady Gregory wrote, 'We are longing to have last act of *Playboy*. We were both immensely impressed and delighted with the play. . . .'[3]

[1] Original letters to Yeats and Lady Gregory in the Berg Collection, New York Public Library.

[2] Original letter in the possession of A. Saddlemyer.

[3] See Greene and Stephens, *J. M. Synge*, p. 225. Original letter in the possession of the Synge Estate.

But there were still further delays, and Synge wrote to Lady Gregory on 25 November:

I have had rather a worse attack than I expected when I wrote my last note, but I am much better now, and out as usual. One of my lungs however has been a little touched so I shall have to be careful for a while. Would it be possible to put off the Playboy for a couple of weeks? I am afraid if I went to work at him again now, and then rehearsed all December I would be very likely to knock up badly before I was done with him. My doctor says I may do it, if it is *necessary*, but he advises me to take a couple of weeks rest if it can be managed. A cousin of mine who etches is over here now and he wants me to go and stay with him for a fortnight in a sort of country house he has in Surrey, so if you think the Playboy can be put off I will go across Thursday or Friday and get back in time to see the Shadowy Waters and get the Playboy under way for January. What do you think? If I go I would like to read the third act of Playboy to you before I go, and then make final changes while I am away as I shall have a quiet time. . . .

A further postponement was arranged, and the reading of Act III took place on 28 November. On 1 December Synge wrote to Lady Gregory from Edward Synge's Surrey home, 'I think the change of place and ideas will help me to finish the Playboy.'[1] To Molly on 5 December he reported, 'I've been through Act I. It is good I think and only needs a little more revision. I wish I could say the same for Act III!'

Back in Dublin he handed over Acts I and II on 31 December and the next day wrote to Molly, 'The III Act is coming out all right and all will be well I hope.'[2] A letter to Professor H. J. C. Grierson on 7 January, thanking him for hospitality the previous summer during the company's visit to Aberdeen, adds, 'I have been very hard at work ever since at a new comedy—The Playboy of the Western World—which goes into rehearsal tomorrow, for production on the 26th of this month, so you can imagine that I am in an anxious state.'[3]

Synge's uneasiness about his play continued into rehearsals, affected in part by Miss Horniman's hiring, over Willie Fay's head, of Ben Iden Payne as general manager. Synge wrote to

[1] Original letters to Lady Gregory in the Berg Collection, New York Public Library.

[2] Unless otherwise stated, Synge's letters to Molly are in the possession of Mrs. L. M. Stephens. Portions of many are quoted by Greene and Stephens, *J. M. Synge.*

[3] Original letter in the possession of Mr. James A. Healy of New York.

Yeats, 'The Playboy is going very well in rehearsal and for the time all is smooth. Please *do not* bring or send over new man till the Playboy is over as it is *absolutely* essential that Fay should be undisturbed till he has got through this big part.'[1] Furthermore, anxiety was expressed by both directors and cast over the strong language in the play. Synge made cuts in rehearsals and apparently complained to Jack Yeats, who replied prophetically in his letter of 11 January 1907 (enclosing designs for Christy's jockey costume in the third act):

If you don't want to have to leave out all the coloured language in your play you'll have to station a drummer in the wings, to welt the drums every time the language gets too high for the stomachs of the audience. They used to do this in the old Music Halls.
Thus
   get out of that ye son of a—rub, a dub, dub, dub—

But it is clear from the early drafts and many scenarios that Synge's concern was also due to the deliberately mannered production his concept of the play demanded and his doubts as to the capacity of the players. He conducted rehearsals so painstakingly that Lady Gregory remarked in a letter to Yeats, 'The Playboy will I think be very fine indeed, though I only saw the last act. . . . You have never looked like a tiger with its cub as Synge did last night with Playboy.'[2] To Synge she wrote encouragingly, 'I thought Playboy very fine indeed, and very well acted. It made me a little sad to think how long it will be before the verse plays can get anything like as good an all round show', and, just before opening night, 'I am sure Playboy will go all right. One always gets nervous towards the end—They seemed to me as if they could not go wrong in it.'[3]
Synge replied on 26 January, the day of the performance:

Thanks for your note. Yeats wired in favour of Riders so it goes on with Playboy though I think the Pot[4] would have made a better bill. I do not know how things will go tonight, the day company are all

---

[1] Quoted by Gerard Fay in *The Abbey Theatre: Cradle of Genius* (Dublin, Clonmore and Reynolds, 1958), p. 111. Cf. Greene and Stephens, *J. M. Synge*, pp. 231–6.

[2] Original in the Berg Collection, New York Public Library.

[3] Original letters in the Synge Estate. Lady Gregory quoted much of this correspondence in *Our Irish Theatre* (London, Putnam, 1913), pp. 130–2.

[4] *The Pot of Broth*, a one-act farce by Yeats and Lady Gregory, which Synge wanted as curtain-raiser.

very steady, but Power is in a most deplorable state of uncertainty. Miss O'Sullivan and ⟨Miss⟩ Craig are very shaky also on the few words they have to speak.

Many thanks for your good wishes for P. Boy. I have a sort ⟨of⟩ second edition of influenza, and I am looking gloomily at everything. Fay has worked very hard all through and everything has gone smoothly.[1]

But no one could have been prepared for the uproar, now almost legendary, that Synge's play created.[2] The first-night audience, already made uneasy by the disturbing rumours circulating about the play, erupted at the word 'shifts', the line being made even more explosive by Willie Fay's substitution of 'Mayo girls' for Christy's 'drift of chosen females standing in their shifts'. For the second performance on Monday the 28th an angry audience forced Lady Gregory to call in the police and the actors were reduced to performing in dumb show. The following day, when Yeats returned from lecturing in Scotland, the three directors decided as a matter of policy to continue the performances for the rest of the week, under police protection, until Synge's play was given its fair hearing. By the end of the week the players had earned their first uninterrupted performance and on the following Monday Yeats invited those interested to a public debate on 'the freedom of the theatre'. Dissent spread further than Dublin; Lady Gregory reported that district councils in Clare and Kerry 'are cheerfully passing resolutions against the French Government and the Playboy',[3] the Gort Board of Guardians prohibited workhouse children from picnics at Coole Park,[4] and among Synge's papers is the following resolution:

That this meeting of the Federated Irish Societies of the Liverpool District places on record its high appreciation of the gallant stand made by the Irish men and Irish women of Dublin in their defence of the Pure, Honest and Noble Characteristics of their people at home.

And they further desire to express their disgust and abhorence ⟨sic⟩ of such productions as 'The Playboy of the West', and will by every means within their power prevent any such production being given in the Liverpool District.

[1] Original in the Berg Collection, New York Public Library.
[2] See Greene and Stephens, *J. M. Synge*, chapter 13; Walter Starkie, 'The Playboy Riots', *Irish Times*, 7 October 1963.
[3] Original in the Berg Collection, New York Public Library.
[4] According to Yeats, the most painful slight of all for Lady Gregory; letter to John Quinn, 18 February 1907, in the Manuscript Division, New York Public Library.

It is clear from Synge's letter to Molly after the first performance that he did not realize the extent to which he had offended
his audience:

I wish I had you here to talk over the whole show last night. W.G.
⟨Fay⟩ was pretty bluffy, and Power was very confused in places. Then
the crowd was wretched and Mrs. W. G. ⟨Brigit O'Dempsey⟩ missed
the new cue we gave, though she can hardly be blamed for that. I think
with a better Mahon and crowd and a few slight cuts the play would
be thoroughly sound. I feel like old Maurya today, 'It's four fine plays
I have, though it was a hard birth I had with every one of them and
they coming to the world.'

It is better any day to have the row we had last night, than to have
your play fizzling out in half-hearted applause. Now we'll be talked
about. We're an event in the history of the Irish stage.

That he blamed part of the trouble on the actors' inability to
express the 'subtleties' of his play is evident in his letter to M. J.
Nolan, quoted below, and six months later in a letter to Lady
Gregory he claimed that the company acted Yeats's verse plays
better than they did *The Playboy*. But with their experience of his
earlier plays, the actors could hardly be blamed if, on such short
notice, they interpreted Synge's wishes during rehearsals as merely
a demand for more realism in what appeared to be simply a
peasant satire on the Irish love of hero-worship and the debilita-
tion caused by emigration, both subjects already exploited by
Lady Gregory. The further cutting that took place after the first
night's performance tended in fact to make the production even
more realistic.[1]

That Synge himself did not look upon his play in this light is
evident also from his statements of defence, both public (see
Appendix B) and private. To the press he had indicated that his
play was 'a comedy, an extravaganza, made to amuse' and in a
later interview admitted that the idea of the play had been suggested both by the incident recorded in *The Aran Islands* and by
the case of James Lynchehaun, who, like the Aran refugee, had
been harboured by peasants even though convicted of a brutal
murder.[2] His letter to the *Irish Times* accepted, further, an inter-

[1] See *Our Irish Theatre*, pp. 133–4. The copy registered by the Lord Chamberlain's
Office on 27 April 1907 shows cuts and emendations to over fifty speeches, which can be
directly attributed to the company's censorship of the play.

[2] *The Freeman's Journal*, 30 January 1907. The same interview quotes Synge as describing 'shift' as 'an everyday word in the West of Ireland, which could not be taken offence at

pretation offered by 'Pat' ⟨Patrick Kenny, author of *Economics for Irishmen*⟩ that the play forecasts the doom of a nation forced to export the strong and healthy and subsist by loveless arranged marriages.

Privately he explained to Stephen MacKenna,

> It isn't accurate to say, I think, that the thing is a generalization from a single case. *If* the idea had occurred to me I could and would just as readily have written the thing, as it stands, without the Lynchehaun case or the Aran case. The story—in its *essence*—is probable given the psychic state of the locality. I used the cases afterwards to controvert critics who said it was *impossible*.[1]

On 19 February he replied to M. J. Nolan, a young aspiring playwright who had sent him an 'interesting and clearheaded' essay on *The Playboy*:

> With a great deal of what you say I am most heartily in agreement— as where you see that I wrote the P.B. directly, as a piece of life, without thinking, or caring to think, whether it was a comedy tragedy or extravaganza, or whether it would be held to have, or not to have, a purpose—also where you speak very accurately and rightly about Shakespere's 'mirror'. In the same way you see—what it seems so impossible to get our Dublin people to see, obvious as it is—that the wildness and, if you will, vices of the Irish peasantry are due, like their extraordinary good points of all kinds, to the *richness* of their nature—a thing that is priceless beyond words.
>
> I fancy when you read the play—or see it performed in more possible conditions—you will find Christy Mahon more interesting than you are inclined to do now. Remember on the first production of a play the most subtle characters always tend to come out less strongly than the simple characters, because those who act the subtle parts can do no more than feel their way till they have acted the whole play a number of times. Whether or not I agree with your final interpretation of the whole play is my secret. I follow Goethe's rule to tell no one what one means in one's writings. I am sure you will agree that the rule is a good one.[2]

there, and might be used differently by people in Dublin. It was used without any objection in Douglas Hyde's *Songs of Connaught*, in the Irish, but what could be published in Irish perhaps could not be published in English!'

[1] 'Synge to MacKenna: The Mature Years', *Irish Renaissance*, ed. Robin Skelton and David R. Clark (Dublin, Dolmen, 1966), p. 75. See also Greene and Stephens, *J. M. Synge*, pp. 265–7.

[2] Original in Trinity College, Dublin. This letter was published as 'A Letter to a Young Man' in the 1932 edition of the plays.

On 12 March he wrote to his Scottish friend James Paterson:

I am extremely glad to hear that the play interested you. As to the point you raise as to a possible want of contrast in the moral attitude of my people, I am doubtful myself. I feel the want, and yet my instinct when I am working is always towards keeping my characters bound together as far as possible in one mood. One gains perhaps as much as one loses. The storm has quite blown over here now, but I do not know what reception the play will get when we revive it. There have been several very intelligent and favourable articles in the papers recently, so the Dublin public may come round to understand it better by degrees.

Further, two fragments from early drafts of his essays on the people and places of Wicklow express his attitude towards the Irish peasant portrayed in his plays; both extracts were omitted from his final revisions:

The younger people of these glens are not so interesting as the old men and women, and, though there are still many fine young men to be met with among them who are extraordinarily gifted and agile, it too often happens, especially in the more lonely places, that the men under thirty are badly built, shy and despondent. Even among the old people, whose singular charm I have tried to interpret, it should perhaps be added that it is possible to find many individuals who are far from admirable either in body or mind. One would hardly stop to assert a fact so obvious if it had not become the fashion in Dublin, quite recently, to reject a fundamental doctrine of theology, and to exalt the Irish peasant into a type of almost absolute virtue, frugal, self-sacrificing, valiant, and I know not what. There is some truth in this estimate, yet it is safer to hold with the theologians that, even west of the Shannon, the heart of man is not spotless, for though the Irish peasant has many beautiful virtues, it is idle to assert that he ⟨is⟩ totally unacquainted with the deadly sins, and many minor rogueries. He has however, it should never be forgotten, a fine sense of humour, and the greatest courtesy. When a benevolent visitor comes to his cottage, seeing a sort of holy family, the man of the house, his wife, and all their infants, too courteous to disappoint him, play their parts with delight. When the amiable visitor, however, is out once more in the boreen, a storm of good-tempered irony breaks out behind him, that would surprise him could he hear it. This irony I have met with many times, in places where I have been intimate with the people and have always been overjoyed to hear it. It shows that, in spite of relief-works, commissions, and patronizing philanthropy—that sickly thing—the Irish peasant, in his own mind, is neither abject nor servile.[1]

.   .   .   .   .

There has been some discussion recently in Dublin on the character of the Irish peasantry. The controversy is a futile one. The crimeless virtuous side of Irish life is well known and cannot be disputed. The wilder—the Rabelaisian side of the Irish temperament is so wild it cannot be dealt with in book or periodical that is intended for Irish readers. I have come across a great deal of this side of the life in the months and months that I have spent in living among the people or wandering about the roads of Ireland. During the controversy that ⟨has⟩ followed the production of one or two of my plays a number of people who ⟨mourn the passing⟩[2]

Nor do his letters betray any of the doubts harboured over *The Tinker's Wedding*; with *The Playboy* he at last felt secure in his own judgement and craftsmanship. On 4 May he wrote to Meyerfeld:

I hope you were interested in my new play. It is certainly a much stronger *stage-play* than the 'Well of the Saints' or any of my other work. If it was translated for the German—or any foreign stage—a few incidents such as the talk of the 'bona fides' would of course have to be adapted in some way to make them comprehensible, but the main line of the story I imagine would be clear enough anywhere.

And to a criticism forwarded by John Quinn from New York he replied on 5 September 1907:

He is quite right that early work, like 'Riders to the Sea', has a certain quality that more mature work is without. People who prefer the early quality are quite free to do so. When he blames the 'coarseness', however, I don't think he sees that the romantic note and a Rabelaisian note are working to a climax through a great part of the play, and that the Rabelaisian note, the 'gross' note, if you will, *must* have its climax no matter who may be shocked.[3]

[1] A slightly different version of this paragraph is published in his article 'The People of the Glens', *The Shanachie* (March 1907), but is not included in the 1910 edition.
[2] Perhaps intended for 'The People of the Glens' also; see his letters to Stephen MacKenna in *Irish Renaissance*, pp. 66–74.
[3] Original in the Quinn Papers, Manuscript Division, New York Public Library. In a letter dated 29 November 1907 to Lady Gregory (now in the Berg Collection, New York Public Library) he wrote of a submitted play, 'It has real dramatic gifts of characterization and arrangement, and general power of building up something that can stand by itself, but the treatment of the hero at the end is so sentimental and foolish I hardly see how we can stage it.' See Appendix B, Section II, A for Synge's own careful planning of *The Playboy*.

It is the lack of this 'Rabelaisian note' in his final play, *Deirdre of the Sorrows,* that prompted Synge to suggest that Yeats and Lady Gregory should complete the play, as Yeats recounts in his essays and preface to the first edition. In other ways, however, this next play was to be a new departure. 'I wanted a change from Peasant Comedy—or thought I did,' he wrote to Louis Untermeyer on 29 November 1908.[1] And to John Quinn, in a letter enclosing his *Playboy* manuscript, he enlarged on the difficulties of a new medium:

I am glad to say that, since the operation, I have been as well as possible, walking a great deal, and very hard at work. I don't know whether I told you that I am trying a three-act prose 'Deirdre', to change my hand. I am not sure yet whether I shall be able to make a satisfactory play out of it. These saga people, when one comes to deal with them, seem very remote; one does not know what they thought or what they are or where they went to sleep, so one is apt to fall into rhetoric. In any case, I find it an interesting experiment, full of new difficulties, and I shall be the better, I think, for the change.[2]

Although he constantly emphasized that *Deirdre of the Sorrows* was being written as 'an experiment chiefly to change my hand',[3] the saga of the Irish Helen had evidently intrigued Synge for some time. In a letter to Lady Gregory in 1904 he wrote, 'Your Cuchulain is still a part of my daily bread',[4] and he had himself attempted a rough translation of the Irish text while on Aran in 1900 or 1901.[5] But it was not until *The Playboy* was almost completed that he allowed his mind to stray to another plot. He sent a copy of Lady Gregory's *Cuchulain of Muirthemne* to Molly early in November 1906 and advised her to read 'The Sons of Usnach', commenting, 'It is charming.' And in a theatre memorandum in December of that year he mentions 'an historical play of mine which I might think Fay would understand better ⟨than the new manager⟩'. However, concentrated work does not appear to have

---

[1] Original in the Lilly Library, Indiana University.

[2] Original letter, dated 4 January 1908, in the Manuscript Division, New York Public Library.

[3] Letter to Brodzky, 10 December 1907, now in Trinity College, Dublin. See his letter to Stephen MacKenna concerning 'unmodern, ideal, breezy, springdayish Cuchulainoid National Theatre', *Irish Renaissance*, p. 67.

[4] Of her *Cuchulain of Muirthemne*, published in 1902, quoted by Lady Gregory in *Our Irish Theatre*, p. 124.

[5] See Appendix C, Section I, c.

begun until almost a year later. 'I have play ideas at the back of my mind,' he wrote to Lady Gregory from County Wicklow on 12 July 1907, 'but I'm not doing anything yet, as I want to get well first.'[1] And to Frederick J. Gregg, the Irish-American journalist, who had written sympathetically of his work, he wrote on 12 September 1907:

I am particularly grateful for any outlying friendship that the 'Playboy' has been able to win for himself, as although our actual 'row' in the Abbey was invigorating, the peculiarly ignorant malignity of some ⟨of⟩ the articles and letters that followed it—in the Irish Press—gave one a sort of disgust for the whole business. I hope to be at work again in a few weeks, but I do not quite know what my next play will be like. The 'Playboy' affair brought so much unpopularity on my friends Lady Gregory, Mr. Yeats and the individual players of our company that I am placed in rather a delicate position. I am half inclined to try a play on 'Deirdre'—it would be amusing to compare it with Yeats' and Russell's ⟨Æ⟩—but I am a little afraid that the 'Saga' people might loosen my grip on reality.[2]

In his daily letters to Molly Allgood, Synge records his struggles with the new play. In December 1906 he had written, 'My next play must be quite different from the P. Boy. I want to do something quiet and stately and restrained and I want you to act in it.' Now, on 9 November 1907, almost a year later, he reported,

I have been working at Deirdre till my head is going round. I was too taken up with her yesterday to write to you—I got her into such a mess as I think I'd have put her into the fire, only that I want to write a part for *you*, so you mustn't be jealous of her—Since yesterday I have pulled two acts into one, so that, if I can work it, the play will have three acts instead of four, and that has of course given me many problems to think out. As it is, I am not sure that the plan I have is a good one. Ideas seem admirable when they occur to you, and then they get so doubtful when you have thought over them for a while.

Later the same day he wrote, 'I finished a second rough draft of the Sons of Usna today. So I have the whole thing now under my hand to work at next week.' On 14 November, 'I am working myself sick with Deirdre or whatever you call it. It is a very anxious job. I don't want to make a failure.' And two days later,

[1] Original in the Berg Collection, New York Public Library.
[2] Original in the Lilly Library, Indiana University.

'I did a good deal of work on Deirdre, not on the MS. but just notes for a new scene in it. I'm going to Lady G. at five.' Then again on 27 November, 'My dear dear child, I'm at my wit's end to know what to do—I'm squirming and thrilling and quivering with the excitement of writing Deirdre and I *daren't* break the thread of composition by going out to look for digs and moving into them at this moment.⟨. . .⟩ Let me get Deirdre out of danger —she may be safe in a week—then marriage in God's name.' And finally, on 1 December, 'I finished the G, i.e. the 8th revision or re-writing of Act III yesterday. It goes all through—the Act III I mean—but it wants a good deal of strengthening, of making personal, still before it will satisfy me.' The next day he told Yeats the story of the play and reported to Molly, 'He was very much pleased with it I think.'

Still the play was not 'personal' enough, and on 7 January 1908 he wrote to Molly,

I am working at Deirdre—I can't keep away from her till I get her right. I have changed the first half of the first Act a good deal, by making Fergus go into the inner room instead of Conchubar, and giving C. an important scene with Lav. Then D. comes in and Lav. goes out and D and C have an important scene together. That—when it is done—will make the whole thing drama instead of narrative and there will be a good contrast between the scenes of Deirdre and Conchubar and Deirdre & Naisi. It is quite useless trying to rush it. I must take my time and let them all grow by degrees.[1]

But the last draft of Act I is dated 7 March 1908, and on 29 April he wrote to Yeats, 'I go into hospital tomorrow.⟨. . .⟩ I will not be able to have Deirdre for your sister ⟨for publication by the Cuala Press⟩ and have written to tell her.'[2] On 4 May Synge was operated on, and on 16 June he wrote to John Quinn from the hospital, 'I will be very glad that you should have the MS. of "Deirdre" whenever it is finished to my satisfaction. I suppose after the summer I'll get to work on it again. It is difficult picking up work after such a complete break in one's ideas, but, in the end, one often gains in richness.'[3]

[1] In a letter to Lady Gregory of 20 August 1905, he wrote of her play *The White Cockade*, 'once or twice I felt doubtful if there was quite current enough in a scene'. In a letter to Nolan of 7 December 1908 he wrote, 'one has to interlace one's characters—a first Act A & B, with a second act all A & C is not satisfactory'.

[2] Original in the Synge Estate.

[3] Original in the Quinn Papers, Manuscript Division, New York Public Library.

It was not until August that he was once more well enough to resume work on the play. In a letter to Molly on the 24th of that month he wrote, 'I've decided to cut off the second act—you remember Jesus Christ says if the second act offend thee pluck it out; but I forget you're a heathen, and there's no use quoting Holy Scriptures to you.' Five days later he reported to Lady Gregory, 'I have been fiddling with Deirdre a little. I think I'll have to cut it down to two longish acts. The middle act in Scotland is impossible.'

But again ill health intervened, followed by the sorrow of his mother's death. In October Synge had travelled to Germany in the hope of recovering, but wrote little, although as with his trips to Kerry during the writing of *The Playboy* he hoped 'this knocking about in the woods may help me with Deirdre in a way'.[1] Back in Dublin in November Molly helped him by reading passages aloud, and on 22 December he wrote to her, 'I've pretty nearly gone on to the end of Deirdre and cut it down a little. It is delicate work—a scene is so easily spoiled. I am anxious to hear you read it to me.' On 3 January 1909 he reported to Lady Gregory,

I have done a great deal to Deirdre since I saw you,—chiefly in the way of strengthening motives ⟨motifs?⟩ and recasting the general scenario—but there is still a good deal to be done with the dialogue, and some scenes in the first Act must be re-written to make them fit in with the new parts I have added. I only work a little every day as I suffer more than I like with indigestion and general uneasiness inside—I hope it is only because I haven't quite got over the shock of the operation— the doctors are vague and don't say much that is definite.[2]

A month later he was back in hospital; he died there on 24 March. On the back of a fragment of Deirdre's keen over the grave of Naisi are scribbled the words, 'Unfinish⟨ed⟩ play of "Deirdre"', can be sent if desired to Mr. W. B. Yeats'.

This was not the first time Synge had expressed concern about his play. Before his operation the preceding year he had suggested in a letter to Yeats that Acts I and III of *Deirdre* would be worth preserving; according to Yeats, Synge several times during his final illness asked that his fellow directors should 'finish' the play.

---

[1] Original letter to Molly now in the Academic Center Library, University of Texas.
[2] Original in the Berg Collection, New York Public Library. Extracts from many of these letters were quoted by Lady Gregory in *Our Irish Theatre*, pp. 136-8.

During the summer of 1909 Yeats, Lady Gregory, and Molly Allgood worked on the manuscript, trying to determine some order and form from the thousand typescript pages, although apparently they were ignorant of the additional notebook material. An undated fragment of a letter from Lady Gregory to Yeats may refer to their early attempts to write in stage directions and linking passages according to Synge's instructions: 'I am more hopeful of Deirdre now, I have got Conchubor and Fergus off at the last, in Deirdre's long speech, and that makes an immense improvement. She ⟨looks⟩ lonely and pathetic with the other two women crouching and rocking themselves on the floor.'[1] But according to Yeats, the editors finally decided to produce the play without any additional material or alterations, and the same assemblage of manuscripts was used by the Cuala Press for their edition of April 1910. Although notes to the present edition suggest that alterations have been made by an unknown hand, especially to Deirdre's final speeches, it is conceivable that these were written in by Molly during Synge's final frantic revisions. The only definite allocations that can be made to others occur in minor stage directions, and here again they were probably determined by Molly, who directed the first production.

The year 1907, which saw the publication of both *The Tinker's Wedding* and *The Playboy*, found Synge confident at last in his method and his material. Just as important, by that year he felt confident of his own role in the new dramatic movement of Ireland. An entry in Notebook 30, written about 1904, records his early reaction to the literary renaissance:

Dramatic literature relatively much more mature ⟨than poetry?⟩. Hence the intellectual maturity of most races is marked by a definite moment of dramatic creation. Greece, England, Spain, Germany, France, Norway, and Ireland. The same impulse is now felt in Ireland. Lyrical art, is the art of a national adolescence. Dramatic art is first of all a childish art—a reproduction of external experience—without form or philosophy—then after a lyrical interval we have it as mature drama dealing with the deeper truth of general life in a perfect form and with mature philosophy. ⟨. . .⟩ Journalism may be literary, literature is always scriptural.

[1] Original in the Berg Collection, New York Public Library. Lady Gregory quotes part of this in *Our Irish Theatre*, pp. 138-9.

Over two years later, as a Director of the Abbey Theatre, he stated in firmer tones his own stand on the future of Irish drama, in a reply to a memorandum from Yeats suggesting enlargement of method and aims:

I think we should be mistaken in taking the continental Municipal Theatre as the pattern of what we wish to attain as our 'final object' even in a fairly remote future. A dramatic movement is either (a) a creation of a new dramatic literature where the interest is in the novelty and power of the new work rather than in the quality of the execution, or (b) a highly organized executive undertaking where the interest lies in the more and more perfect interpretation of works that are already received as classics. A movement of this kind is chiefly useful in a country where there has been a successful *creative movement*. So far our movement has been entirely creative—the only movement of the kind I think now existing—and it is for this reason that it has attracted so much attention. To turn this movement now—for what are to some extent extrinsic reasons—into an executive movement for the production of a great number of foreign plays of many types would be, I cannot but think, a disastrous policy. None of us are suited for such an undertaking,—it will be done in good time by a dramatic Hugh Lane when Ireland is ripe for it. I think Yeats's view that it would be a good thing for Irish audiences—*our* audiences—or young writers is mistaken. Goethe at the end of his life said that he and Schiller had failed to found a German drama a⟨t⟩ Weimar because they had confused the public mind by giving one day Shakespere, one day Calderon, one day Sophocles and so on. Whether he is right or not we can see that none of the 'Municip⟨al⟩ Theatres' that are all over Europe are creating or helping to create a new stage-literature. We are right to do work like the 'Doctor ⟨in Spite of Himself', Lady Gregory's Kiltartan translation⟩ and Oedipus because they illuminate our work but for that reason only. Our supply of native plays is very small and we should go on I think for a long time with a very small company so that the mature work may go a long way towards keeping it occupied.
⟨. . .⟩ Now for the practical matters.

W. Fay must be freed, that I think is urgently necessary if he is to keep up the quality of his acting. An Assistant Stage Manager as we agreed will do this if we can find the right man. For the verse plays—Yeats's plays—I am ready to agree to almost any experiment that he thinks desirable in order to ensure good performances. Mrs. Emery ⟨Florence Farr⟩—as you suggest—might be of great use. At the same time I think he is possibly mistaken in looking on the English stage for the people that are needed. Looking back from here with the sort of perspective that distance gives I greatly dislike the impression that

⟨Yeats's⟩ 'Deirdre' or rather Miss Darragh has left on me. Emotion— if it cannot be given with some trace of distinction or nobility—is best left to the imagination of the audience. Did not Cleopatra, and Lady Macbeth, and Miranda make more impression when they were played by small boys than when they are done by Mrs. P⟨atrick⟩ Campbell. ⟨...⟩ I would rather go on trying our own people for ten years, than bring in this readymade style that is so likely to destroy the sort of distinction everyone recognises in our own company. Still that is only my personal feeling and, as I said, I think it essential that Yeats should be able to try anything that seems at all likely to help on his work, which requires much skill.[1]

Later, while in Kerry in August 1907, he added a private post-script in Notebook 44, suggested perhaps by his experiences with the *Playboy* audiences:

This scene last night of story-telling and old-fashioned dignity and this outside pageant of curiously winning magnificence make me shudder to think of the smug vulgarity of the town life most of us are condemned to. I think especially of the theatre, the commercial theatre with its hateful vulgar managers and clientele and its whole atmo-sphere without a gleam of the light of the world. It is not impossible in Ireland to get a company of people who have no vulgarity and a few plays that are uncorrupted also but it is not proved that such work can bring together a few people to listen and look on.

As I explained in my Introduction to Book One, each play has demanded special editorial treatment, although again I have tried to impose certain guiding principles. Synge's own descrip-tion of his working methods, in his letter of 5 September 1907 to John Quinn about the *Playboy* manuscript, illuminates the major problem facing an editor of his plays:

As to my manuscript, I work always with a typewriter—typing myself—so I suppose it has no value? I make a rough draft first and then work over it with a pen till it is nearly unreadable; then I make a clean draft again, adding whatever seems wanting, and so on. My final drafts—I letter them as I go along—were 'G' for the first act, 'I' for the second, and 'K' for the third! I really wrote parts of the last act more than eleven times, as I often took out individual scenes and worked at them separately. The MS., as it now stands, is a good deal

---

[1] December 1906. Original in the Berg Collection, New York Public Library; slightly different versions exist in the Synge Estate and the Yeats papers.

written over, and some of it is in slips or strips only, cut from the earlier versions—so I do not know whether it has any interest for the collector.[1]

Every available draft has been consulted for each of the plays and Synge's marginalia and striking variations in text or stage directions are noted. Detailed descriptions of manuscript material and earliest drafts, as well as related passages from the notebooks, are included in the appendixes. Because of the wealth of material available, I have been able to document Synge's working methods for *The Playboy of the Western World* and *Deirdre of the Sorrows* more thoroughly than was possible for the earlier plays. In both appendixes and text, spelling and presentation of dialogue have been made consistent, but Synge's own punctuation is scrupulously followed wherever possible in order to indicate his suggested rhythms.

[1] Original in the Quinn Papers, Manuscript Division, New York Public Library.

ACKNOWLEDGEMENTS

AGAIN I am indebted to so many individuals and institutions on two continents over such a long period of time that it is impossible to thank by name each person who has made this edition possible. As always, my gratitude to Mrs. Lilo Stephens is unbounded and I greatly appreciate the encouragement and help given by Mrs. W. B. Yeats. Again, Miss Anne Yeats provided a new drawing of Synge by Jack B. Yeats. Mr. Austin Clarke gave freely of his advice and help in constructing the glossary and guide to pronunciation. Miss Mary Pollard and Mr. Liam Miller have throughout offered their support and advice. In New York Mr. James A. Healy placed his massive store of manuscripts and letters at my disposal; and once more I have been helped by the valuable biography of Synge by David Greene and E. M. Stephens. Professor R. K. Alspach kindly read both volumes in proof and asked many shrewd questions. The executors and trustees of the J. M. Synge Estate made all material in their possession available to me.

Further material was provided by Mrs. Mary Hirth of the Academic Center Library, University of Texas; Mr. David Randall of the Lilly Library, Indiana University; Dr. John Gordan, Curator of the Berg Collection, and Mr. Robert W. Hill, Keeper of the Manuscript Room, both of the New York Public Library; Mr. F. J. Hurst of the Library, Trinity College, Dublin; the Trustees of the National Library of Ireland; Miss Ria Mooney and the Directors of the Abbey Theatre, Dublin; the Office of the Lord Chamberlain, St. James's Palace.

Permission to quote has been graciously granted by Mrs. W. B. Yeats for her husband's letters to John Quinn, Lady Gregory, and Synge; Miss Anne Yeats and Mr. M. B. Yeats for Jack Yeats's letter to Synge; Major Richard Gregory for Lady Gregory's letters to Synge and W. B. Yeats; Messrs. Field, Roscoe, and Co. Ltd. for Granville Barker's letters to Synge; Messrs. Allen and Unwin for Elkin Mathews's letters to Synge; Messrs. Rupert Hart-Davis for excerpts from *The Letters of W. B. Yeats*, edited by Allan Wade; Miss Anne Yeats and Macmillan & Co. Ltd. for W. B. Yeats's Preface to *Deirdre of the Sorrows*; Messrs. Rich and Cowan for *The Fays of the Abbey Theatre*, by W. G. Fay and Catherine Carswell.

Again I must thank the staff of the National City Bank, Dublin, for their kindness; Mr. Robin Skelton for his constant encouragement; and Miss Joan Coldwell for her helpful criticism.

ANN SADDLEMYER

University of Victoria,
Victoria, British Columbia,
Canada

GLOSSARY AND
GUIDE TO PRONUNCIATION

agents—landlord representatives empowered to evict tenants failing to pay their rent

agradh—*pr.* u′grah; oh love

Alban—Scotland, from the genitive form of Alba

Annagolan—*pr.* Annagoulan, as in out

banbhs—*pr.* bannuvs, or bonnivs; young pigs

black hags—cormorants

blackthorn—walking-stick made from stem of the blackthorn shrub

blather—foolish talk, nonsense

bona fides—*pr.* as in sides; genuine travellers exempt from licensing hours

boreen—narrow lane or passage between stone walls or high earth banks

Bride—*pr.* Bridee; version of the name Bridget

butt—bottom or end (of his tailpocket, of the ditch, of a rope, etc.)

Cearneach—*pr.* Carnah

cholera morbus—bilious diarrhoea and stomach cramps

cleeve—basket or hamper

cnuceen—*pr.* knockeen; a little hill

cockshot-man—man at fair whose blackened face is the target for wooden balls thrown by competitors

conceit—liking or preference

Conchubor—*pr.* Connahar or, more often by Synge, Conor

creel cart—turf-cart with open or grated sides

curagh—small canoe made of wickerwork covered with hides (by Synge's time with tarred canvas), the shape varying from district to district

Deirdre—*pr.* Dare′dra

destroyed—bothered or exhausted, not necessarily as in *The Playboy*, killed

Doul—*pr.* as in out

dreepiness—described by Synge as that red-nosed look people get when they have a bad cold in the head

dun—hill-fort, often in ancient times a royal residence

-een—*pr.* yeen; diminutive suffix, e.g. houseen, Shaneen, supeen

Emain Macha—*pr.* Evin Vaha; fort near Armagh

Emer—*pr.* Eemer

felts—thrushes

frish-frash—Indian meal and raw cabbage boiled down as thin as gruel

from the licence—to avoid paying for a dog licence

gallous—mischievous, spirited, plucky

gob—mouth

gripe of the ditch—grasp or hollow of the ditch

griseldy—grisly

haggard—farmyard, or walled field next to farmyard

hooshing—lifting up or removing

jobber—livestock dealer

jobbing jockies—men who travel about breaking in horses

keen—a lament for the dead

Kilmainham—a large prison in Dublin

knacky fancier—ingenious or artful chooser
Lavarcham—*pr.* Lower'kem (as in allow)
letting on—pretending
loy—a long narrow spade
lug—ear
madder and stone-crop—vegetable dyes of red and orange
mitch off—play truant
Naisi—*pr.* Nee'shi
the old hen—influenza
parish public—licensed public-house
parlatic—paralytic from drink
paters—the Lord's Prayer
peelers—policemen, nicknamed after Sir Robert Peel
polis—the police
pot-boy—serving-man
poteen—*pr.* potyeen; illegally distilled whisky
a power of—many, a great deal of
Samhain—*pr.* sow'in (as in allow); All Souls' Day, 1 November, the beginning
    of winter
scribes of bog—long stretches of wasteland, where turf-cutting took place
shebeen—usually an unlicensed house selling poteen; in *The Playboy* used more
    generally as a low wayside public-house
shift—chemise, a woman's undergarment like a slip, worn next to the skin and
    reaching to the knees
skelping—beating
Slieve Fuadh—*pr.* Sleeve Foo'a
sluig—ditch or piece of muddy ground
small farmers—poor farmers possessing very small farms, as opposed to strong
    farmers
sop of grass tobacco—tuft of uncured tobacco leaf
spancelled—tied together
spavindy—lame or halting from the spavin, a disease of the hock-joint
streeleen—trail or stream of talk
streeler—loiterer, slovenly person
swiggling—swaying and wriggling
thraneen—withered stalk of grass, i.e. a worthless thing
tight—well-made and healthy
trick-o'-the-loop—game at the fair in which spectator must guess centre loop
    in a leather belt
turbary—the right of cutting peat
union—the workhouse
Usna—*pr.* Uish'na
wake—the watching of the dead' before burial, frequently an occasion for all-
    night social gatherings
warrant—a certainty
wattle—a small switch
winkered mule—mule with blinkers

THE TINKER'S WEDDING

A COMEDY IN TWO ACTS

PREFACE

THE drama is made serious—in the French sense of the word—not by the degree in which it is taken up with problems that are serious in themselves, but by the degree in which it gives the nourishment, not very easy to define, on which our imaginations live. We should not go to the theatre as we go to a chemist's, or a dram-shop, but as we go to a dinner, where the food we need is taken with pleasure and excitement. This was nearly always so in Spain and England and France when the drama was at its richest—the infancy and decay of the drama tend to be didactic—but in these days the playhouse is too often stocked with the drugs of many seedy problems, or with the absinthe or vermouth of the last musical comedy.[1]

The drama, like the symphony, does not teach or prove anything. Analysts with their problems, and teachers with their systems, are soon as old-fashioned as the pharmacopoeia of Galen,—look at Ibsen and the Germans[2]—but the best plays of Ben Jonson and Molière can no more go out of fashion than the blackberries on the hedges.

Of the things which nourish the imagination humour is one of the most needful, and it is dangerous to limit or destroy it. Baudelaire calls laughter the greatest sign of the Satanic element in man; and where a country loses its humour, as some towns in Ireland[3] are doing, there will be morbidity of mind, as Baudelaire's mind was morbid.

In the greater part of Ireland, however, the whole people, from the tinkers to the clergy, have still a life, and view of life, that are rich and genial and humorous. I do not think that these country people, who have so much humour themselves, will mind being laughed at without malice, as the people in every country have been laughed at in their own comedies.[4]

J. M. S.

December 2nd, 1907.

---

[1] See Appendix A, Section IV for earlier versions of this Preface.

[2] The typescript draft dated 20 November 1907 originally read 'look at Ibsen and Pinero'; Synge then struck out 'Pinero' and added 'the Germans and their power'.

[3] The TS. draft dated 20 November 1907 originally read 'some towns and lonely places in Ireland' etc.

[4] The TS. draft dated 20 November 1907 reads, 'I do not think these country clergy, who have so much humour—and so much heroism that everyone who has seen them facing typhus or dangerous seas for the comfort of their people on the coasts of the west

NOTE.—'The Tinker's Wedding' was first written a few years ago, about the time I was working at 'Riders to the Sea', and 'In the Shadow of the Glen'. I have re-written it since.

J. M. S.

must acknowledge—will mind being laughed at for half an hour without malice, as the clergy in every Roman Catholic country were laughed at through the ages that had real religion.'

An earlier undated manuscript (now in item 52) reads, 'This play was first written four or five years ago, but it has been rewritten not long ago. In all Roman Catholic countr⟨ies⟩ the cleric has been made fun of with good humour from the early ages down and there is no reason why the same thing should not be done in Ireland where the clerics with all their fine qualities are humorous and genial also beyond any that I have met in Europe.'

PERSONS

MICHAEL BYRNE, a tinker

MARY BYRNE, an old woman, his mother

SARAH CASEY, a young tinker woman

A PRIEST

SCENE

A road-side near a village[1]

---

[1] Description taken from earlier drafts. See Appendix A, Section II for the earliest description of scene and persons. Two tinker children, Micky and Nanny, and some village children are not omitted until TS. 'D'. The earliest title-page gives the alternative title *Movements of May*, and even at the galley stage Synge was considering describing his play as a one-act comedy in two scenes.

¹ See Appendix A for TS. 'A'. TS. 'B' reads *A village roadside after nightfall. A fire is burning near the ditch*; MICHEAL BYRNE *is working beside it, and* NORA CASEY *is sitting close to him, keeping the fire bright by throwing on it dry twigs from a withered furze-bush which she holds on her lap. An unyoked donkey cart is seen in the shadow behind them, and further off there is a cottage with a light seen above the half-door. They work for a moment without speaking.* TS. 'C' replaces the cart with a tent. Not until TS. 'D' does the play open with Sarah coming in hurriedly on the right. In TS. 'C' Nora becomes Sarah and in TS. 'D' the spelling of Michael's name is altered to the English form.

² TS. 'D' reads 'and not be wasting your senses making lamentations that would choke a fool.' This is questioned by Synge in the margin of TS. 'E' and then altered to the final form.

³ TS. 'D' reads 'and not a mortal knowing what may ail you now.' This is altered in MS. in TS. 'E' to final form.

⁴ This direction is not added until the final draft; TS. 'C' has *hums tune* added in MS.

⁵ Not until the galley stage does Synge alter 'at the present day' to 'since the moon did change'.

⁶ All early drafts read [*indifferently*] instead of [*musingly*].

ACT I

After nightfall. A fire of sticks is burning near the ditch a little to the right. MICHAEL *is working beside it. In the background, on the left, a sort of tent and ragged clothes drying on the hedge. On the right a chapel-gate.*[1]

SARAH CASEY [*coming in on right, eagerly*]. We'll see his reverence this place, Michael Byrne, and he passing backward to his house to-night.

MICHAEL [*grimly*]. That'll be a sacred and a sainted joy!

SARAH [*sharply*]. It'll be small joy for yourself if you aren't ready with my wedding ring. [*She goes over to him.*] Is it near done this time, or what way is it at all?

MICHAEL. A poor way only, Sarah Casey, for it's the divil's job making a ring, and you'll be having my hands destroyed in a short while the way I'll not be able to make a tin can at all maybe at the dawn of day.

SARAH [*sitting down beside him and throwing sticks on the fire*]. If it's the divil's job, let you mind it, and leave your speeches that would choke a fool.[2]

MICHAEL [*slowly and glumly*]. And it's you'll go talking of fools, Sarah Casey, when no man did ever hear a lying story even of your like unto this mortal day. You to be going beside me a great while, and rearing a lot of them, and then to be setting off with your talk of getting married, and your driving me to it, and I not asking it at all.[3]

[SARAH *turns her back to him and arranges something in the ditch.*][4]

MICHAEL [*angrily*]. Can't you speak a word when I'm asking what is it ails you since the moon did change?[5]

SARAH [*musingly*].[6] I'm thinking there isn't anything ails me, Michael Byrne; but the spring-time is a queer time, and it's queer thoughts maybe I do think at whiles.

MICHAEL. It's hard set you'd be to think queerer than welcome, Sarah Casey; but what will you gain dragging me to the priest this night, I'm saying, when it's new thoughts you'll be thinking at the dawn of day?

[1] Early drafts enlarge on this distinction: 'to be driving east and west in a flat country with young Walking Jim in a place where there wouldn't be' etc.

[2] TS. 'B' has 'white trees' for 'thorn trees'.

[3] Synge records 'wary' meaning 'careful' among phrases in Notebook 28, in use in Kerry in September 1903.

[4] Struck out of TS. 'E' is the following exchange:

SARAH [*indifferently*]. It's a clumsy man you are this night, I'm thinking, and let you make haste now, or herself will be coming with the porter. [*Raising her voice.*] For I'm thinking you wouldn't have me make her drink the whole of it the way she'ld be falling asleep and knowing nothing of our job.

MICHAEL [*angrily*]. I would not, Sarah Casey, and if she comes before it's fixed on us, I'll fling your ring into the gripe, I'm thinking, and not marry you at all. [*He puts down the soldering iron and lights his pipe.*] It's that sign we'll have.

SARAH [*shouting at him*]. Let you make haste now or pray the divil to defend your head.

[5] TS. 'E' adds the direction *nursing his finger*.

[6] TS. 'B' reads 'Rathdangan' for 'Rathvanna'.

SARAH [*teasingly*]. It's at the dawn of day I do be thinking I'd have a right to be going off to the rich tinkers do be travelling from Tibradden to the Tara Hill; for it'd be a fine life to be driving with young Jaunting Jim, where there wouldn't be any big hills to break the back of you, with walking up and walking down.[1]

MICHAEL [*with dismay*]. It's the like of that you do be thinking!

SARAH. The like of that, Michael Byrne, when there is a bit of sun in it, and a kind air, and a great smell coming from the thorn trees[2] is above your head.

MICHAEL [*looks at her for a moment with horror, and then hands her the ring*]. Will that fit you now?

SARAH [*trying it on*]. It's making it tight you are, and the edges sharp on the tin.

MICHAEL [*looking at it carefully*]. It's the fat of your own finger, Sarah Casey; and isn't it a mad thing I'm saying again that you'd be asking marriage of me, or making a talk of going away from me, and you thriving and getting your good health by the grace of the Almighty God?

SARAH [*giving it back to him*]. Fix it now, and it'll do, if you're wary[3] you don't squeeze it again.

MICHAEL [*moodily, working again*]. It's easy saying be wary; there's many things easy said, Sarah Casey, you'd wonder a fool even would be saying at all. [*He starts violently.*] The divil mend you, I'm scalded again!

SARAH [*scornfully*]. If you are, it's a clumsy man you are this night, Michael Byrne [*raising her voice*]; and let you make haste now, or herself will be coming with the porter.[4]

MICHAEL [*defiantly, raising his voice[5]*]. Let me make haste? I'll be making haste maybe to hit you a great clout; for I'm thinking it's the like of that you want. I'm thinking on the day I got you above at Rathvanna,[6] and the way you began crying out and we coming down off the hill, crying out and saying, 'I'll go back to my ma,' and I'm thinking on the way I came behind you that time, and hit you a great clout in the lug, and how quiet and easy it was you came along with me from that hour to this present day.

¹ TS. 'B' reads [NORA *throws the whole furze-bush into the fire with an angry gesture, and stands up just as the fire flares for a moment and shows her as a tall fine looking woman.*] TS. 'C' adds [*very provocatively*].

² TS. 'B' reads 'by the Aughavanna stream' for 'in Ballinaclash'.

³ TS. 'C' reads [*working again with impatient gestures*].

⁴ Struck out of TSS. 'D' and 'E' is the introductory comment 'It's jealous you are, I'm thinking and you've a right too maybe for he's' etc.

⁵ Synge gradually cut this speech down. TS. 'B' reads:

NORA. Didn't you hear the grand word a gentleman said behind me this day and I leaving the Dargle? Didn't you ever hear tell of the peelers followed me ten miles along the Glen Malure, and they talking love to me in the dark night? And of the ladies by the sea-shore do be running this way and that way with their boxes and their pencils and their bits of paint, trying would they sketch my face and I letting on I wouldn't see them at all?

MICHEAL [*scornfully*]. Did ever you hear of the quality, or the peelers with them, doing a thing, or saying a thing wouldn't make Tom Daly, the fool of tinkers, ashamed?

⁶ TS. 'B' adds the direction [*contemptuously*].

⁷ TSS. 'B' and 'C' include a scene here with the two children, Micky and Nanny, beginning 'Let you whisht now . . .'. See Appendix A, Section II.

SARAH [*standing up and throwing all her sticks into the fire*].[1] And a big
fool I was too, maybe; but we'll be seeing Jaunting Jim to-morrow in
Ballinaclash,[2] and he after getting a great price for his white foal in
the horse-fair of Wicklow, the way it'll be a great sight to see him
squandering his share of gold, and he with a grand eye for a fine
horse, and a grand eye for a woman.

MICHAEL [*working again with impatience*][3]. The divil do him good with
the two of them.

SARAH [*kicking up the ashes with her foot*]. Ah,[4] he's a great lad, I'm
telling you, and it's proud and happy I'll be to see him, and he the
first one called me the Beauty of Ballinacree, a fine name for a
woman.

MICHAEL [*with contempt*]. It's the like of that name they do be putting
on the horses they have below racing in Arklow. It's easy pleased
you are, Sarah Casey, easy pleased with a big word, or the liar speaks
it.

SARAH. Liar!

MICHAEL. Liar, surely.

SARAH [*indignantly*]. Liar, is it? Didn't you ever hear tell of the peelers
followed me ten miles along the Glen Malure, and they talking love
to me in the dark night,[5] or of the children you'll meet coming from
school and they saying one to the other, 'It's this day we seen Sarah
Casey, the Beauty of Ballinacree, a great sight surely.'

MICHAEL.[6] God help the lot of them!

SARAH. It's yourself you'll be calling God to help, in two weeks or
three, when you'll be waking up in the dark night and thinking you
see me coming with the sun on me, and I driving a high cart with
Jaunting Jim going behind. It's lonesome and cold you'll be feeling
the ditch where you'll be lying down that night, I'm telling you,
and you hearing the old woman making a great noise in her sleep,
and the bats squeaking in the trees.

MICHAEL. Whisht. I hear some one coming the road.[7]

SARAH [*looking out right*]. It's some one coming forward from the
doctor's door.

[1] In a notebook he had in Kerry in September 1903 (No. 28), Synge records having heard the phrase 'a big boast of a man'.

[2] TS. 'D' reads 'There it is, fit for the finger of a sainted queen' etc.

[3] Struck out of TS. 'D' is the remark 'And they think they've great simplicity when they ask the prices on the weight of tins'.

[4] TS. 'C' reads [PRIEST *comes in mumbling Latin.*

MICHAEL. It's often his reverence does be in there playing cards, or drinking a sup, or singing songs, until the dawn of day.

SARAH. It's a big boast of a man[1] with a long step on him and a trumpeting voice. It's his reverence surely; and if you have the ring done, it's a great bargain we'll make now and he after drinking his glass.

MICHAEL [*going to her and giving her the ring*]. There's your ring, Sarah Casey;[2] but I'm thinking he'll walk by and not stop to speak with the like of us at all.

SARAH [*tidying herself, in great excitement*]. Let you be sitting here and keeping a great blaze, the way he can look on my face; and let you seem to be working, for it's great love the like of him have to talk of work.

MICHAEL [*moodily, sitting down and beginning to work at a tin can*]. Great love surely.[3]

SARAH [*eagerly*]. Make a great blaze now, Michael Byrne.

[*The* PRIEST *comes in on right;[4] she comes forward in front of him.*]

SARAH [*in a very plausible voice*]. Good evening, your reverence. It's a grand fine night, by the grace of God.

PRIEST. The Lord have mercy on us! What kind of a living woman is it that you are at all?

SARAH. It's Sarah Casey I am, your reverence, the Beauty of Ballinacree, and it's Michael Byrne is below in the ditch.

PRIEST. A holy pair, surely! Let you get out of my way. [*He tries to pass by.*]

SARAH [*keeping in front of him*]. We are wanting a little word with your reverence.

PRIEST. I haven't a halfpenny at all. Leave the road I'm saying.

SARAH. It isn't a halfpenny we're asking, holy father; but we were thinking maybe we'd have a right to be getting married; and we were thinking it's yourself would marry us for not a halfpenny at all; for you're a kind man, your reverence, a kind man with the poor.

PRIEST [*with astonishment*]. Is it marry you for nothing at all?

¹ Earlier drafts add the words 'a wedding present I'm told they call it'.

² TS. 'B' reads 'the Carlow plain' for 'the county Meath'. The question mark is not added until the final page proofs.

³ TS. 'B' reads [*going over and sitting down on the shaft of the cart*]; TS. 'C' reads [*goes over and sits down on a bough at the tent*].

⁴ TS. 'E' questions and then strikes out 'a heathen tinker of the roads'. TS. 'D' adds an exclamation mark.

SARAH. It is, your reverence; and we were thinking maybe you'd give us a little small bit of silver to pay for the ring.[1]

PRIEST [*loudly*]. Let you hold your tongue; let you be quiet, Sarah Casey. I've no silver at all for the like of you; and if you want to be married, let you pay your pound. I'd do it for a pound only, and that's making it a sight cheaper than I'd make it for one of my own pairs is living here in the place.

SARAH. Where would the like of us get a pound, your reverence?

PRIEST. Wouldn't you easy get it with your selling asses, and making cans, and your stealing east and west in Wicklow and Wexford and the county Meath?[2] [*He tries to pass her.*] Let you leave the road, and not be plaguing me more.

SARAH [*pleadingly, taking money from her pocket*]. Wouldn't you have a little mercy on us, your reverence? [*Holding out money.*] Wouldn't you marry us for a half a sovereign, and it a nice shiny one with a view on it of the living king's mamma?

PRIEST. If it's ten shillings you have, let you get ten more the same way, and I'll marry you then.

SARAH [*whining*]. It's two years we are getting that bit, your reverence, with our pence and our halfpence and an odd threepenny bit; and if you don't marry us now, himself and the old woman, who has a great drouth, will be drinking it to-morrow in the fair [*she puts her apron to her eyes, half sobbing*], and then I won't be married any time, and I'll be saying till I'm an old woman: 'It's a cruel and a wicked thing to be bred poor.'

PRIEST [*turning up towards the fire*].[3] Let you not be crying, Sarah Casey. It's a queer woman you are to be crying at the like of that, and you your whole life walking the roads.[4]

SARAH [*sobbing*]. It's two years we are getting the gold, your reverence, and now you won't marry us for that bit, and we hard-working poor people do be making cans in the dark night, and blinding our eyes with the black smoke from the bits of twigs we do be burning.

[*An old woman is heard singing tipsily on the left.*]

PRIEST [*looking at the can* MICHAEL *is making*]. When will you have that can done, Michael Byrne?

[1] In all the earlier drafts Micheal sends Nora/Sarah off to rescue the jug of porter from Mary while he explains his mother's thirst to the Priest: 'a hard woman to keep in food and drink'.

[2] TS. 'B' adds *in front of the fire.*

MICHAEL. In a short space only, your reverence, for I'm putting the last dab of solder on the rim.

PRIEST. Let you get a crown along with the ten shillings and the gallon can, Sarah Casey, and I will wed you so.

MARY [*suddenly shouting behind, tipsily*]. Larry was a fine lad, I'm saying; Larry was a fine lad, Sarah Casey—

MICHAEL. Whisht, now, the two of you. There's my mother coming, and she'd have us destroyed if she heard the like of that talk the time she's been drinking her fill.[1]

MARY [*comes in singing*]—
And when we asked him what way he'd die,
  And he hanging unrepented,
'Begob,' says Larry, 'that's all in my eye,
  By the clergy first invented.'

SARAH. Give me the jug now, or you'll have it spilt in the ditch.

MARY [*holding the jug with both her hands, in a stilted voice*]. Let you leave me easy, Sarah Casey. I won't spill it, I'm saying. God help you; are you thinking it's frothing full to the brim it is at this hour of the night, and I after carrying it in my two hands a long step from Jemmy Neill's?

MICHAEL [*anxiously*]. Is there a sup left at all?

SARAH [*looking into the jug*]. A little small sup only I'm thinking.

MARY [*sees the priest, and holds out jug towards him*]. God save your reverence. I'm after bringing down a smart drop; and let you drink it up now, for it's a middling drouthy man you are at all times, God forgive you, and this night is cruel dry. [*She tries to go towards him.*[2] SARAH *holds her back.*]

PRIEST [*waving her away*]. Let you not be falling to the flames. Keep off, I'm saying.

MARY [*persuasively*]. Let you not be shy of us, your reverence. Aren't we all sinners, God help us! Drink a sup now, I'm telling you; and we won't let on a word about it till the Judgment Day. [*She takes up a tin mug, pours some porter into it, and gives it to him.*]

[1] TS. 'B' gives a slightly different version of Mary's song:

> A lonesome ditch in Bally-na-quin
> The time you'ld be drinking a tight drop in,
> A lonesome ditch in Bally-na-gan
> The time you'ld be making a ten-penny can.
>
> A lonesome bank in Ballyduff
> The time . . . [*She breaks off.*]

[2] TSS. 'B' and 'D' add the stage direction [*lighting his pipe*].

[3] TS. 'B' reads [*pensively*] instead of [*with compassion*]; TS. 'C' reads [*with sympathy*] and adds an exclamation mark at the end of Mary's speech.

[4] TS. 'B' reads 'an old bitter man'.

[5] TS. 'B' adds '& when the bishop comes itself, let you give him a little sup and he won't mind you at all . . .
[*she sings*]—

> When an old one is lonesome, age making her sick,
> And she walking the world with a bit of a stick,
> Then give her a jugful of Jameson's best,
> And she'll see a grand gold-house built up for her rest.'

This was then struck out of TS. 'C'.

MARY [*singing, and holding the jug in her hand*]—

> A lonesome ditch in Ballygan
> The day you're beating a tenpenny can;
> A lonesome bank in Ballyduff
> The time . . . [*She breaks off.*][1]

It's a bad, wicked song, Sarah Casey; and let you put me down now in the ditch, and I won't sing it till himself will be gone; for it's bad enough he is, I'm thinking, without ourselves making him worse.

SARAH [*putting her down, to the* PRIEST, *half laughing*]. Don't mind her at all, your reverence. She's no shame the time she's a drop taken; and if it was the Holy Father from Rome was in it, she'd give him a little sup out of her mug, and say the same as she'd say to yourself.

MARY [*to the* PRIEST]. Let you drink it up, holy father. Let you drink it up, I'm saying, and not be letting on you wouldn't do the like of it, and you with a stack of pint bottles above, reaching the sky.

PRIEST [*with resignation*]. Well, here's to your good health, and God forgive us all. [*He drinks.*]

MARY. That's right now, your reverence, and the blessing of God be on you. Isn't it a grand thing to see you sitting down, with no pride in you, and drinking a sup with the like of us, and we the poorest, wretched, starving creatures you'd see any place on the earth?

PRIEST.[2] If it's starving you are itself, I'm thinking it's well for the like of you that do be drinking when there's drouth on you, and lying down to sleep when your legs are stiff. [*He sighs gloomily.*] What would you do if it was the like of myself you were, saying Mass with your mouth dry, and running east and west for a sick call maybe, and hearing the rural people again and they saying their sins?

MARY [*with compassion*].[3] It's destroyed you must be hearing the sins of the rural people on a fine spring.

PRIEST [*with despondency*]. It's a hard life I'm telling you, a hard life, Mary Byrne; and there's the bishop coming in the morning, and he an old man,[4] would have you destroyed if he seen a thing at all.

MARY [*with great sympathy*]. It'd break my heart to hear you talking and sighing the like of that, your reverence. [*She pats him on the knee.*] Let you rouse up, now, if it's a poor, single man you are itself, and I'll be singing you songs unto the dawn of day.[5]

¹ TS. 'B' adds the direction [*she gabbles with her mouth*].

² Earlier drafts read 'a fatted scholar', which Synge finally altered in the galley proof.

³ Synge altered in the galley proof the words 'a little tasty prayer, I'm telling you, and I'll give you a hugeen, or the last sup' etc.

⁴ Synge had considerable trouble with the Priest's exit. TS. 'B' adds the following exchange in a much emended passage:

NORA [*to the* PRIEST, *in a low voice*]. Do it your reverence. Say a prayer now, the way we'll know the thing we'll hear the time we're married in the church.

MARY [*nudging* MICHEAL, *in a loud whisper*]. Do you see that Micheal? Didn't you hear me saying to you it's flighty she is since the change in the moon, and she making whisper talk with one man and another man along by the road?

MICHEAL [*not minding her*]. Say it your reverence. It'd be a grand thing to hear a prayer said all for ourselves.

PRIEST. What kind of a prayer would I say with the like of you?

NORA [*whispering*]. A marriage prayer your reverence. . . .

[*A clock strikes in the chapel ten o'clock a ray of moonlight falls on them slanting across into the ditch.*]

PRIEST [*stands up quickly*]. There's the moon rising, God help me, and the clock striking and I must be walking up now, and not making myself a fool with the like of you, the way I'll be stirring early and getting ready for the bishop at the dawn of day—[*he stretches himself wearily*]—and isn't it great trouble and worry to be living at all the time, there's great heat rising from the earth, and you killed working?

[*He goes up the scene a few paces to right,* NORA *follows him.*]

MARY. Well the blessing of God on your ⟨reverence⟩ and that we may have a long life and meet in Heaven.

On the back of a page of TS. 'C' Synge tries another approach:

MARY [*getting up on her knees*]. It's little I want with prayers, your reverence, but whisper till I tell you holy father that young woman is gone crazy with her talking of priests and prayers and prayers and the marriage vow. You're a wise man your reverence and maybe you'd learn us of some mixture that would cure her now, for it's hard set I am to know what ails her if it's wind within her belly or the strengthening sun.

⁵ Synge apparently added the question mark in the final page proofs; earlier drafts have either a comma or a semicolon.

PRIEST [*interrupting her*]. What is it I want with your songs when it'd be better for the like of you, that'll soon die, to be down on your two knees saying prayers to the Almighty God?

MARY. If it's prayers I want, you'd have a right to say one yourself, holy father; for we don't have them at all, and I've heard tell a power of times it's that you're for. Say one now, your reverence; for I've heard a power of queer things and I walking the world, but there's one thing I never heard any time, and that's a real priest saying a prayer.

PRIEST. The Lord protect us!

MARY. It's no lie, holy father. I often heard the rural people making a queer noise[1] and they going to rest; but who'd mind the like of them? And I'm thinking it should be great game to hear a scholar,[2] the like of you, speaking Latin to the saints above.

PRIEST [*scandalized*]. Stop your talking, Mary Byrne; you're an old flagrant heathen, and I'll stay no more with the lot of you. [*He rises.*]

MARY [*catching hold of him*]. Stop till you say a prayer, your reverence; stop till you say a little prayer, I'm telling you, and I'll give you my blessing and the last sup[3] from the jug.

PRIEST [*breaking away*]. Leave me go, Mary Byrne; for I never met your like for hard abominations the score and two years I'm living in the place.

MARY [*innocently*]. Is that the truth?

PRIEST. It is, then, and God have mercy on your soul.[4]

[*The PRIEST goes towards the left, and SARAH follows him.*]

SARAH [*in a low voice*]. And what time will you do the thing I'm asking, holy father?[5] for I'm thinking you'll do it surely, and not have me growing into an old wicked heathen like herself.

MARY [*calling out shrilly*]. Let you be walking back here, Sarah Casey, and not be talking whisper-talk with the like of him in the face of the Almighty God.

SARAH [*to the PRIEST*]. Do you hear her now, your reverence? Isn't it true, surely, she's an old, flagrant heathen, would destroy the world?

[1] This question mark was apparently added in page proof; in TS. 'C' a question mark is altered to an exclamation mark.

[2] TS. 'C' adds 'and they with grins on them would scare the world'.

[3] Earlier drafts begin Mary's speech with the words 'It'd not be the first time if she did [*shaking her head*'] and break up the discussion between the Priest and Sarah, placing their final speeches at this point.

PRIEST [*to* SARAH, *moving off*]. Well, I'll be coming down early to the chapel, and let you come to me a while after you see me passing, and bring the bit of gold along with you, and the tin can. I'll marry you for them two, though it's a pitiful small sum; for I wouldn't be easy in my soul if I left you growing into an old, wicked heathen the like of her.

SARAH [*following him out*]. The blessing of the Almighty God be on you, holy father, and that He may reward and watch you from this present day.

MARY [*nudging* MICHAEL]. Did you see that, Michael Byrne?[1] Didn't you hear me telling you she's flighty a while back since the change of the moon? With her fussing for marriage, and she making whisper-talk with one man or another man along by the road.[2]

MICHAEL. Whisht now, or she'll knock the head of you the time she comes back.

MARY. Ah, it's a bad, wicked way the world is this night, if there's a fine air in it itself. You'd never have seen me, and I a young woman, making whisper-talk with the like of him, and he the fearfullest old fellow you'd see any place walking the world.[3]

[SARAH *comes back quickly*.]

MARY [*calling out to her*]. What is it you're after whispering above with himself?

SARAH [*exultingly*]. Lie down, and leave us in peace. [*She whispers with* MICHAEL.]

MARY [*poking out her pipe with a straw, sings*]—
   She'd whisper with one, and she'd whisper with two—
[*She breaks off coughing*.] My singing voice is gone for this night, Sarah Casey. [*She lights her pipe*.] But if it's flighty you are itself, you're a grand handsome woman, the glory of tinkers, the pride of Wicklow, the Beauty of Ballinacree. I wouldn't have you lying down and you lonesome to sleep this night in a dark ditch when the spring is coming in the trees; so let you sit down there by the big bough, and I'll be telling you the finest story you'd hear any place from Dundalk to Ballinacree, with great queens in it, making themselves matches from the start to the end, and they with shiny silks on them the length of the day, and white shifts for the night.

¹ TS. 'C' adds the direction *and putting away his tools*. TS. 'B' reads just *threateningly*.

² TS. 'C' adds the direction *but watching them warily*.

³ In TS. 'B' Micheal promises Nora he will 'end the can' in good time the next morning.

⁴ TS. 'B' reads [*sinking gradually to sleep under the cart*].

⁵ In Notebook 29, in use in 1903, Synge records the phrase 'does be stretched back sleeping'.

MICHAEL [*standing up with the tin can in his hand*[1]]. Let you go asleep, and not have us destroyed.

MARY [*lying back sleepily*[2]]. Don't mind him, Sarah Casey. Sit down now, and I'll be telling you a story would be fit to tell a woman the like of you in the spring-time of the year.

SARAH [*taking the can from* MICHAEL, *and tying it up in a piece of sacking*]. That'll not be rusting now in the dews of night. I'll put it up in the ditch the way it will be handy in the morning; and now we've that done, Michael Byrne,[3] I'll go along with you and welcome for Tim Flaherty's hens. [*She puts the can in the ditch.*]

MARY [*sleepily*].[4] I've a grand story of the great queens of Ireland with white necks on them the like of Sarah Casey, and fine arms would hit you a slap the way Sarah Casey would hit you.

SARAH [*beckoning on the left*]. Come along now, Michael, while she's falling asleep.

[*He goes towards left.* MARY *sees that they are going, starts up suddenly, and turns over on her hands and knees.*]

MARY [*piteously*]. Where is it you're going? Let you walk back here, and not be leaving me lonesome when the night is fine.

SARAH. Don't be waking the world with your talk when we're going up through the back wood to get two of Tim Flaherty's hens are roosting in the ash-tree above at the well.

MARY. And it's leaving me lone you are? Come back here, Sarah Casey. Come back here, I'm saying; or if it's off you must go, leave me the two little coppers you have, the way I can walk up in a short while, and get another pint for my sleep.

SARAH. It's too much you have taken. Let you stretch yourself out and take a long sleep;[5] for isn't that the best thing any woman can do, and she an old drinking heathen like yourself.

[*She and* MICHAEL *go out left.*]

MARY [*standing up slowly*]. It's gone they are, and I with my feet that weak under me you'd knock me down with a rush, and my head with a noise in it the like of what you'd hear in a stream and it running between two rocks and rain falling. [*She goes over to the ditch where*

¹ It was not until TS. 'C' that Synge thought of making Mary Byrne steal the can. TS. 'B' offers a different ending to her long speech, which otherwise varies little:

[*The fire sinks again.*] What's stories God help me, when it's young you are and the night is fine? It's a little short while they have only, and let them walk out while they may. [*She reaches out the jug and drains it.*]

> [*Sings.*] And I'll have a jugful of Jameson's best
> Till I see a black coffin built up for my rest.
> [*She leans back again and the curtain falls.*]

Notebook 31 contains two speeches, directly following dialogue for *The Well of the Saints*, Act III, 'B', 4 (May 1904). The first of these speeches appears to be a transcription of an actual incident, while the other, a variation on Mary Byrne's final speech, is on the same page:

Drunken man (to correct G⟨entleman⟩) Well, we re both gentlemen and I hope we'll meet again in Heaven.

What is it I am this night God help me? With my feet that weak you'd throw me over like a man tossing hay if you'ld raise up that little rush in your hand to me, and what is my head at all? Isn't there a noise in it the like ⟨of⟩ the noise of a river going in a low place between two black rocks when the great rain is falling?

A recently discovered fragment of manuscript (now in Envelope 50) contains the following speech which appears to have been written about the time of TS. 'B':

I do be thinking and I drinking a sup of water out of a well the like of that well, or washing my feet in it maybe, or my old shift itself, that it's a power of cows have been coming to it and a power of fine tinkers have drunk from the sides of it, and gone on passing on again and getting old, the way it's old I'm getting, and dying one day or the next.

the can is tied in sacking, and takes it down.] What good am I this night, God help me? What good are the grand stories I have when it's few would listen to an old woman, few but a girl maybe would be in great fear the time her hour was come, or a little child wouldn't be sleeping with the hunger on a cold night? [*She takes the can from the sacking, and fits in three empty bottles and straw in its place, and ties them up.*] Maybe the two of them have a good right to be walking out the little short while they'd be young; but if they have itself, they'll not keep Mary Byrne from her full pint when the night's fine, and there's a dry moon in the sky. [*She takes up the can, and puts the package back in the ditch.*] Jemmy Neill's a decent lad; and he'll give me a good drop for the can; and maybe if I keep near the peelers to-morrow for the first bit of the fair, herself won't strike me at all; and if she does itself, what's a little stroke on your head beside sitting lonesome on a fine night, hearing the dogs barking, and the bats squeaking, and you saying over, it's a short while only till you die. [*She goes out singing 'The night before Larry was stretched'.*][1]

CURTAIN

¹ In TS. 'B' a hawthorn tree is in full flower over Nora Casey's head. Struck out of TS. 'C' is the description *Ragged clothes are drying on the bushes.*

² In Notebook 28, in use in Kerry in September 1903, Synge twice records the phrase 'to tackle' meaning 'to tie up'.

³ TS. 'C' adds the following speech:

MICHEAL [*gloomily*]. God help them that do have this trouble and messing every week of the year. You'd as lief be shut up in the Union I'm thinking, or in the Gaol of Kilmainham itself, as be washing and fooling every Sunday, and walking to mass.

⁴ See Appendix A, Section II for the additional scene in TS. 'B' with the little girls from the village. In TS. 'C' Synge makes Micheal speak directly to the children.

ACT II

The same. Early morning. SARAH *is washing her face in an old bucket;
then plaits her hair.* MICHAEL *is tidying himself also.* MARY BYRNE
is asleep against the ditch.[1]

SARAH [*to* MICHAEL, *with pleased excitement*]. Go over, now, to the
bundle beyond, and you'll find a kind of a red handkerchief to put
upon your neck, and a green one for myself.

MICHAEL [*getting them*]. You're after spending more money on the like
of them. Well, it's a power we're losing this time, and we not gaining
a thing at all. [*With the handkerchiefs.*] Is it them two?

SARAH. It is, Michael. [*She takes one of them.*] Let you tackle[2] that one
round under your chin; and let you not forget to take your hat from
your head when we go up into the church. I asked Biddy Flynn
below, that's after marrying her second man, and she told me it's
the like of that they do.[3]

[MARY *yawns, and turns over in her sleep.*]

SARAH [*with anxiety*]. There she is waking up on us, and I thinking we'd
have the job done before she'd know of it at all.

MICHAEL. She'll be crying out now, and making game of us, and
saying it's fools we are surely.

SARAH. I'll send her to her sleep again, or get her out of it one way or
another; for it'd be a bad case to have a divil's scholar the like of her
turning the priest against us maybe with her godless talk.

MARY [*waking up, and looking at them with curiosity, blandly*].[4] That's
fine things you have on you, Sarah Casey; and it's a great stir you're
making this day, washing your face. I'm that used to the hammer, I
wouldn't hear it at all, but washing is a rare thing, and you're after
waking me up, and I having a great sleep in the sun. [*She looks around
cautiously at the bundle in which she has hidden the bottles.*]

SARAH [*coaxingly*]. Let you stretch out again for a sleep, Mary Byrne,
for it'll be a middling time yet before we go to the fair.

¹ TS. 'C' adds the direction [*She settles herself comfortably in the ditch.*]

² TS. 'C' adds the words 'a bit to the cross roads of Grianan'.

³ Synge added the question mark in the final page proofs, but apparently did not wish to lose the rhythm of the entire sentence and therefore retained the small 'a' in 'and'.

⁴ Early drafts added the words 'for I'd sell it a sight better than the likes of her'.

⁵ Early drafts read 'a lovely harmless poor creature would fill your hand with shillings for a leaky can'.

MARY [*with suspicion*]. That's a sweet tongue you have, Sarah Casey; but if sleep's a grand thing, it's a grand thing to be waking up a day the like of this, when there's a warm sun in it, and a kind air, and you'll hear the cuckoos singing and crying out on the top of the hills.[1]

SARAH. If it's that gay you are, you'd have a right to walk down[2] and see would you get a few halfpence from the rich men do be driving early to the fair.

MARY. When rich men do be driving early, it's queer tempers they have, the Lord forgive them; the way it's little but bad words and swearing out you'd get from them all.

SARAH [*losing her temper and breaking out fiercely*]. Then if you'll neither beg nor sleep, let you walk off from this place where you're not wanted, and not have us waiting for you maybe at the turn of day.

MARY [*rather uneasy, turning to* MICHAEL]. God help our spirits, Michael; there she is again rousing cranky from the break of dawn. Oh! isn't she a terror since the moon did change [*she gets up slowly*]?[3] and I'd best be going forward to sell the gallon can.[4] [*She goes over and takes up the bundle.*]

SARAH [*crying out angrily*]. Leave that down, Mary Byrne. Oh! aren't you the scorn of women to think that you'd have that drouth and roguery on you that you'd go drinking the can and the dew not dried from the grass?

MARY [*in a feigned tone of pacification, with the bundle still in her hand*]. It's not a drouth but a heartburn I have this day, Sarah Casey, so I'm going down to cool my gullet at the blessed well; and I'll sell the can to the parson's daughter below, a harmless poor creature would fill your hand with shillings for a brace of lies.[5]

SARAH. Leave down the tin can, Mary Byrne, for I hear the drouth upon your tongue to-day.

MARY. There's not a drink-house from this place to the fair, Sarah Casey; the way you'll find me below with the full price, and not a farthing gone. [*She turns to go off left.*]

SARAH [*jumping up, and picking up the hammer threateningly*]. Put down that can, I'm saying.

[1] Synge's final typescript originally read 'gag of women'.

[2] TS. 'D' reads 'It's staring mad you're going, Sarah Casey. Oh, but it's a mortal warning when a woman begins talking of marriage ever and always the way yourself does be talking of the skinny-looking poor female we seen a while since walking up with a white veil on her to be wedded in the chapel of Bray.' This is questioned, then struck out of TS. 'E'.

[3] The galley proofs originally read 'shift' for 'clothes'.

[4] Early drafts read *up stage* in place of *up towards the ditch*.

MARY [*looking at her for a moment in terror, and putting down the bundle in the ditch*]. Is it raving mad you're going, Sarah Casey, and you the pride of women[1] to destroy the world?[2]

SARAH [*going up to her, and giving her a push off left*]. I'll show you if it's raving mad I am. Go on from this place, I'm saying, and be wary now.

MARY [*turning back after her*]. If I go, I'll be telling old and young you're a weathered heathen savage, Sarah Casey, the one did put down a head of the parson's cabbage to boil in the pot with your clothes[3] [*the priest comes in behind her on the left, and listens*], and quenched the flaming candles on the throne of God the time your shadow fell within the pillars of the chapel door.

[SARAH *turns on her, and she springs round nearly into the* PRIEST's *arms. When she sees him, she claps her shawl over her mouth, and goes up towards the ditch,[4] laughing to herself.*]

PRIEST [*going to* SARAH, *half terrified at the language that he has heard*]. Well, aren't you a fearful lot? I'm thinking it's only humbug you were making at the fall of night, and you won't need me at all.

SARAH [*with anger still in her voice*]. Humbug is it! would you be turning back upon your spoken promise in the face of God!

PRIEST [*dubiously*]. I'm thinking you were never christened, Sarah Casey; and it would be a queer job to go dealing Christian sacraments unto the like of you. [*Persuasively, feeling in his pocket.*] So it would be best, maybe, I'd give you a shilling for to drink my health, and let you walk on, and not trouble me at all.

SARAH. That's your talking, is it? If you don't stand to your spoken word, holy father, I'll make my own complaint to the mitred bishop in the face of all.

PRIEST. You'd do that!

SARAH. I would surely, holy father, if I walked to the city of Dublin with blood and blisters on my naked feet.

PRIEST [*uneasily scratching his ear*]. I wish this day was done, Sarah Casey; for I'm thinking it's a risky thing getting mixed in any matters with the like of you.

¹ Early drafts add the words *on the right.*

² TS. 'D' reads 'horses will be passing the wind'.

³ TS. 'C' reads 'in the bits of black styes you see there beyond in the street'. TS. 'D' develops this exchange further:

SARAH [*angrily*]. Let you not be destroying us with your talk when I've as good a right as another to make myself safe from the Almighty God.

MARY [*sitting down and leaning back against the ditch*]. Safe from the Almighty God is it! What is it he'd care for the like of you. You wouldn't see the Almighty God going up into the sky after the larks and swallows and the swift birds, or after the hares do be racing above on a fine Spring, and what would he want following us and we not troubling him at all.

SARAH. If he doesn't itself I'll wed this day, I'm telling you, for I've as good a right to a decent marriage as any speckled female bastard does be sleeping in the black hovels above would choke a rat.

Notebook 28, in use during Synge's visit to Kerry in September 1903, records the following description of a 'Turkish gypsy woman': 'an old speckled looking Kruger of a woman'.

SARAH. Be hasty then, and you'll have us done with before you'd think at all.

PRIEST [*giving in*]. Well, maybe it's right you are, and let you come up to the chapel when you see me looking from the door. [*He goes up into the chapel.*[1]]

SARAH [*calling after him*]. We will, and God preserve you, holy father.

MARY [*coming down to them, speaking with amazement and consternation, but without anger*]. Going to the chapel! It's at marriage you're fooling again, maybe? [SARAH *turns her back on her.*] It was for that you were washing your face, and you after sending me for porter at the fall of night the way I'd drink a good half from the jug? [*Going round in front of* SARAH.] Is it at marriage you're fooling again?

SARAH [*triumphantly*]. It is, Mary Byrne. I'll be married now in a short while; and from this day there will no one have a right to call me a dirty name and I selling cans in Wicklow or Wexford or the city of Dublin itself.

MARY [*turning to* MICHAEL]. And it's yourself is wedding her, Michael Byrne?

MICHAEL [*gloomily*]. It is, God spare us.

MARY [*looks at* SARAH *for a moment, and then bursts out into a laugh of derision*]. Well, she's a tight, hardy girl, and it's no lie; but I never knew till this day it was a black born fool I had for a son. You'll breed asses, I've heard them say, and poaching dogs, and horses'd go licking the wind,[2] but it's a hard thing, God help me, to breed sense in a son.

MICHAEL [*gloomily*]. If I didn't marry her, she'd be walking off to Jaunting Jim maybe at the fall of night; and it's well yourself knows there isn't the like of her for getting money and selling songs to the men.

MARY. And you're thinking it's paying gold to his reverence would make a woman stop when she's a mind to go?

SARAH [*angrily*]. Let you not be destroying us with your talk when I've as good a right to a decent marriage as any speckled female does be sleeping in the black hovels above, would choke a mule.[3]

¹ TS. 'C' adds the words 'as good a call as the divil maybe to be damned to hell and it isn't the like of that would distress me at all for it's well used I am to seeing a power of big fools every place walking the world. [*Sarah has finished dressing and is trying the ring on her finger.*] But if you have itself what good'll it do?'

² TS. 'B' adds further material with the tinker children and contrasts them with the little girls from the village. See Appendix A, Section II.

MARY [*soothingly*]. It's as good a right you have surely, Sarah Casey,[1] but what good will it do? Is it putting that ring on your finger will keep you from getting an aged woman and losing the fine face you have, or be easing your pains, when it's the grand ladies do be married in silk dresses, with rings of gold, that do pass any woman with their share of torment in the hour of birth, and do be paying the doctors in the city of Dublin a great price at that time, the like of what you'd pay for a good ass and a cart? [*She sits down.*]

SARAH [*puzzled*]. Is that the truth?

MARY [*pleased with the point she has made*]. Wouldn't any know it's the truth? Ah, it's few short years you are yet in the world, Sarah Casey, and it's little or nothing at all maybe you know about it.

SARAH [*vehement but uneasy*]. What is it yourself knows of the fine ladies when they wouldn't let the like of you go near to them at all?

MARY. If you do be drinking a little sup in one town and another town, it's soon you get great knowledge and a great sight into the world. You'll see men there, and women there, sitting up on the ends of barrels in the dark night, and they making great talk would soon have the like of you, Sarah Casey, as wise as a March hare.[2]

MICHAEL [*to* SARAH]. That's the truth she's saying, and maybe if you've sense in you at all, you'd have a right still to leave your fooling, and not be wasting our gold.

SARAH [*decisively*]. If it's wise or fool I am, I've made a good bargain and I'll stand to it now.

MARY. What is it he's making you give?

MICHAEL. The ten shillings in gold, and the tin can is above tied in the sack.

MARY [*looking at the bundle with surprise and dread*]. The bit of gold and the tin can, is it?

MICHAEL. The half a sovereign, and the gallon can.

MARY [*scrambling to her feet quickly*]. Well, I think I'll be walking off the road to the fair the way you won't be destroying me going too fast on the hills. [*She goes a few steps towards the left, then turns and speaks to* SARAH *very persuasively.*] Let you not take the can from the

¹ TS. 'C' spells 'Grianane' in the customary form; other drafts alter the spelling to give a more accurate pronunciation, as in the final text.

² Earlier drafts add commas after 'it now' and 'of us'.

sack, Sarah Casey; for the people is coming above would be making game of you, and pointing their fingers if they seen you do the like of that. Let you leave it safe in the bag, I'm saying, Sarah darling. It's that way will be best. [*She goes towards left, and pauses for a moment, looking about her with embarrassment.*]

MICHAEL [*in a low voice*]. What ails her at all?

SARAH [*anxiously*]. It's real wicked she does be when you hear her speaking as easy as that.

MARY [*to herself*]. I'd be safer in the chapel, I'm thinking; for if she caught me after on the road, maybe she would kill me then. [*She comes hobbling back towards the right.*]

SARAH. Where is it you're going? It isn't that way we'll be walking to the fair.

MARY. I'm going up into the chapel to give you my blessing and hear the priest saying his prayers. It's a lonesome road is running below to Greenane,[1] and a woman would never know the things might happen her and she walking single in a lonesome place.

[*As she reaches the chapel-gate, the* PRIEST *comes to it in his surplice.*]

PRIEST [*crying out*]. Come along now. Is it the whole day you'd keep me here saying my prayers, and I getting my death with not a bit in my stomach, and my breakfast in ruins, and the Lord Bishop maybe driving on the road to-day?

SARAH. We're coming now, holy father.

PRIEST. Give me the bit of gold into my hand.

SARAH. It's here, holy father.

[*She gives it to him.* MICHAEL *takes the bundle from the ditch and brings it over, standing a little behind* SARAH. *He feels the bundle, and looks at* MARY *with a meaning look.*]

PRIEST [*looking at the gold*]. It's a good one I'm thinking wherever you got it. And where is the can?

SARAH [*taking the bundle*]. We have it here in a bit of clean sack, your reverence. We tied it up in the inside of that to keep it from rusting in the dews of night, and let you not open it now or you'll have the people making game of us[2] and telling the story on us, east and west to the butt of the hills.

¹ TS. 'C' adds the direction SARAH *looks at her suspiciously.*

² Synge struck out of TS. 'C' the additional comment 'If it was the like of us all she was she'd never have the bit of gold saved or be making her fuss with the ring, but she's' etc.

³ TS. 'C' adds the direction [MICHEAL *takes the red handkerchief from his neck, folds it up and puts it in his pocket. Sits down a little behind* SARAH *& lights his pipe.*]
A fragment of an unnumbered early draft adds the following exchange:

PRIEST [*shouting at her*]. Would you have me curse you I'm saying?

MARY [*putting up her head over the wall*]. He's a grand man to talk, God bless him, and there's a fine blessing surely for a young pair would be making themselves Christians at the dawn of day.

⁴ In the margin above this speech in TS. 'C' Synge has written 'Make plead more with priest and so make Sarah suspicious'.

PRIEST [*taking the bundle*]. Give it here into my hand, Sarah Casey. What is it any person would think of a tinker making a can? [*He begins opening the bundle.*]

SARAH. It's a fine can, your reverence, for if it's poor simple people we are, it's fine cans we can make, and himself, God help him, is a great man surely at the trade.

[PRIEST *opens the bundle; the three empty bottles fall out.*]

SARAH. Glory to the saints of joy!

PRIEST. Did ever any man see the like of that? To think you'd be putting deceit on me, and telling lies to me, and I going to marry you for a little sum wouldn't marry a child.

SARAH [*crestfallen and astonished*]. It's the divil did it, your reverence, and I wouldn't tell you a lie. [*Raising her hands.*] May the Lord Almighty strike me dead if the divil isn't after hooshing the tin can from the bag.

PRIEST [*vehemently*]. Go along now, and don't be swearing your lies. Go along now, and let you not be thinking I'm big fool enough to believe the like of that, when it's after selling it you are or making a swap for drink of it, maybe, in the darkness of the night.

MARY [*in a peacemaking voice, putting her hand on the* PRIEST's *left arm*[1]]. She wouldn't do the like of that, your reverence, when she hasn't a decent standing drouth on her at all;[2] and she's setting great store on her marriage the way you'd have a right to be taking her easy, and not minding the can. What differ would an empty can make with a fine, rich, hardy man the like of you?

SARAH [*imploringly*]. Marry us, your reverence, for the ten shillings in gold, and we'll make you a grand can in the evening—a can would be fit to carry water for the holy man of God. Marry us now and I'll be saying fine prayers for you, morning and night, if it'd be raining itself, and it'd be in two black pools I'd be setting my knees.

PRIEST [*loudly*]. It's a wicked, thieving, lying, scheming lot you are, the pack of you. Let you walk off now and take every stinking rag you have there from the ditch.[3]

MARY [*putting her shawl over her head*]. Marry her, your reverence, for the love of God, for there'll be queer doings below if you send her off the like of that and she swearing crazy on the road.[4]

[1] TS. 'C' reads *keeping* for *waving*.

[2] TS. 'C' reads 'I've bet peelers and pub-men, and a power of strong lads'. This is not struck out until after TS. 'F'.

[3] TS. 'C' adds 'and leave me in peace for my work when the Lord Bishop's coming on the road.—[*Looking up the road and nearly crying with desperation.*]—Let you walk off I'm saying.'

SARAH [*angrily*]. It's the truth she's saying; for it's herself, I'm thinking, is after swapping the tin can for a pint, the time she was raging mad with the drouth, and ourselves above walking the hill.

MARY [*crying out with indignation*]. Have you no shame, Sarah Casey, to tell lies unto a holy man?

SARAH [*to* MARY, *working herself into a rage*]. It's making game of me you'd be, and putting a fool's head on me in the face of the world; but if you were thinking to be mighty cute walking off, or going up to hide in the church, I've got you this time, and you'll not run from me now. [*She seizes up one of the bottles.*]

MARY [*hiding behind the* PRIEST]. Keep her off, your reverence, keep her off for the love of the Almighty God. What at all would the Lord Bishop say if he found me here lying with my head broken across, or the two of yous maybe digging a bloody grave for me at the door of the church?

PRIEST [*waving*[1] SARAH *off*]. Go along, Sarah Casey. Would you be doing murder at my feet? Go along from me now, and wasn't I a big fool to have to do with you when it's nothing but distraction and torment I get from the kindness of my heart?

SARAH [*shouting*]. I've bet a power of strong lads[2] cast and west through the world, and are you thinking I'd turn back from a priest? Leave the road now, or maybe I would strike yourself.

PRIEST. You would not, Sarah Casey. I've no fear for the lot of you; but let you walk off I'm saying,[3] and not be coming where you've no business, and screeching tumult and murder at the doorway of the church.

SARAH. I'll not go a step till I have her head broke, or till I'm wed with himself. If you want to get shut of us, let you marry us now, for I'm thinking the ten shillings in gold is a good price for the like of you, and you near burst with the fat.

PRIEST. I wouldn't have you coming in on me and soiling my church; for there's nothing at all, I'm thinking, would keep the like of you from hell. [*He throws down the ten shillings on the ground.*] Gather up your gold now, and begone from my sight, for if ever I set an eye on you again you'll hear me telling the peelers who it was stole the black

¹ At this point TS. 'C' adds the directions MICHEAL *begins bundling up the tent etc. while the* PRIEST *shades his eyes with his hand & looks up the road.* From here on TS. 'C' is similar in action to TSS. 'A' and 'B', but Synge has expanded the dialogue and, still dissatisfied, writes in the margin 'Rewrite from here giving Michael a part'.

² TS. 'D' gives this first part of Sarah's speech to Michael. Originally Synge had 'looking at', which was altered in TS. 'F' to 'winking on' and presumably in the page proofs to 'blinking at'.

³ Early drafts read 'barracks' for 'shanty'.

⁴ Synge altered 'coast' to 'coasts' in TS. 'D' but this alteration was not made to TSS. 'E' or 'F'.

⁵ Early drafts read 'blast' for 'blight' in both speeches.

⁶ In the margin of TS. 'D' Synge queries the original direction [*He beats him with a stick.*]

⁷ The galley proofs still read *up stage* for *up to ditch.* Synge questioned, then struck out of TS. 'F' the words 'The Lord in Glory spare us, I'm destroyed today' before 'There are' etc.

ass belonging to Philly O'Cullen, and whose hay it is the grey ass does be eating.

SARAH. You'd do that?

PRIEST. I would, surely.[1]

SARAH. If you do, you'll be getting all the tinkers from Wicklow and Wexford, and the County Meath, to put up block tin in the place of glass to shield your windows where you do be looking out and blinking at[2] the girls. It's hard set you'll be that time, I'm telling you, to fill the depth of your belly the long days of Lent; for we wouldn't leave a laying pullet in your yard at all.

PRIEST [*losing his temper finally*]. Go on, now, or I'll send the Lords of Justice a dated story of your villainies—burning, stealing, robbing, raping to this mortal day. Go on now, I'm saying, if you'd run from Kilmainham or the rope itself.

MICHAEL [*taking off his coat*]. Is it run from the like of you, holy father? Go up to your own shanty,[3] or I'll beat you with the ass's reins till the world would hear you roaring from this place to the coast[4] of Clare.

PRIEST. Is it lift your hand upon myself when the Lord would blight your members if you'd touch me now? Go on from this. [*He gives him a shove.*]

MICHAEL. Blight[5] me is it? Take it then, your reverence, and God help you so. [*He runs at him with the reins.*][6]

PRIEST [*runs up to ditch, crying out*].[7] There are the peelers passing by the grace of God—hey, below!

MARY [*clapping her hand over his mouth*]. Knock him down on the road; they didn't hear him at all.

[MICHAEL *pulls him down.*]

SARAH. Gag his jaws.

MARY. Stuff the sacking in his teeth.

[*They gag him with the sack that had the can in it.*]

SARAH. Tie the bag around his head, and if the peelers come, we'll put him headfirst in the boghole is beyond the ditch.

[*They tie him up in some sacking.*]

[1] All earlier drafts including the galley proofs read 'squirming' for 'wrigglings'.

[2] Struck out of TS. 'D', which in general follows the final ending, is the sentence, 'That's it. Let you not be walloping the earth for fatness is a nasty thing, your reverence, and the sweat out of you would stink the nation with your struggling now.'

[3] TS. 'D' originally read 'the gaols of God' for 'a church'.

[4] TS. 'D' originally read 'in the hailstone showers of the days of Lent' for 'in rains falling'.

[5] In the galley proofs Synge altered 'with the poor fellow, and he' etc. to 'with him, Sarah Casey'.

[6] The phrase 'upon the gate of hell' is struck out of TS. 'D'.

MICHAEL [*to* MARY]. Keep him quiet, and the rags tight on him for fear he'd screech. [*He goes back to their camp.*] Hurry with the things, Sarah Casey. The peelers aren't coming this way, and maybe we'll get off from them now.

[*They bundle the things together in wild haste, the* PRIEST *wriggling and struggling about on the ground, with old* MARY *trying to keep him quiet.*]

MARY [*patting his head*]. Be quiet, your reverence. What is it ails you, with your wrigglings[1] now? Is it choking maybe? [*She puts her hand under the sack, and feels his mouth, patting him on the back.*] It's only letting on you are, holy father, for your nose is blowing back and forward as easy as an east wind on an April day. [*In a soothing voice.*] There now, holy father, let you stay easy, I'm telling you, and learn a little sense and patience, the way you'll not be so airy again going to rob poor sinners of their scraps of gold. [*He gets quieter.*][2] That's a good boy you are now, your reverence, and let you not be uneasy, for we wouldn't hurt you at all. It's sick and sorry we are to tease you; but what did you want meddling with the like of us, when it's a long time we are going our own ways—father and son, and his son after him, or mother and daughter, and her own daughter again—and it's little need we ever had of going up into a church[3] and swearing— I'm told there's swearing with it—a word no man would believe, or with drawing rings on our fingers, would be cutting our skins maybe when we'd be taking the ass from the shafts, and pulling the straps the time they'd be slippy with going around beneath the heavens in rains falling.[4]

MICHAEL [*who has finished bundling up the things, comes over with* SARAH]. We're fixed now; and I have a mind to run him in a bog-hole the way he'll not be tattling to the peelers of our games to-day.

SARAH. You'd have a right too, I'm thinking.

MARY [*soothingly*]. Let you not be rough with him, Sarah Casey,[5] and he after drinking his sup of porter with us at the fall of night. Maybe he'd swear a mighty oath[6] he wouldn't harm us, and then we'd safer loose him; for if we went to drown him, they'd maybe hang the batch of us, man and child and woman, and the ass itself.

MICHAEL. What would he care for an oath?

1 TS. 'D' originally read 'are fearful cowards of' etc.

2 TSS. 'B' and 'C' add at this point the words 'and the young don't know any time the thing they want. But I've had one man, and another man, and a power of children, and it's little need we had of your swearing, or your rings with it, to get us our bit to eat,'.

3 TS. 'B' adds the following speech by Mary: 'We're coming surely and it's a great story I'll ⟨be⟩ telling this night and in the long nights of the year of the way Micheal Byrne wasn't married at all to Nora Casey, the beauty of Ballinacree, on a grand morning, and we driving down the grey ass to the fair.'

MARY. Don't you know his like do live in terror of [1] the wrath of God? [*Putting her mouth to the* PRIEST'S *ear in the sacking.*] Would you swear an oath, holy father, to leave us in our freedom, and not talk at all? [PRIEST *nods in sacking.*] Didn't I tell you? Look at the poor fellow nodding his head off in the bias of the sacks. Strip them off from him, and he'll be easy now.

MICHAEL [*as if speaking to a horse*]. Hold up, holy father.

[*He pulls the sacking off, and shows the* PRIEST *with his hair on end. They free his mouth.*]

MARY. Hold him till he swears.

PRIEST [*in a faint voice*]. I swear surely. If you let me go in peace, I'll not inform against you or say a thing at all, and may God forgive me for giving heed unto your like to-day.

SARAH [*puts the ring on his finger*]. There's the ring, holy father, to keep you minding of your oath until the end of time; for my heart's scalded with your fooling; and it'll be a long day till I go making talk of marriage or the like of that.

MARY [*complacently, standing up slowly*]. She's vexed now, your reverence; and let you not mind her at all,[2] for she's right surely, and it's little need we ever had of the like of you to get us our bit to eat, and our bit to drink, and our time of love when we were young men and women, and were fine to look at.

MICHAEL. Hurry on now. He's a great man to have kept us from fooling our gold; and we'll have a great time drinking that bit with the trampers on the green of Clash.[3]

[*They gather up their things. The* PRIEST *stands up.*]

PRIEST [*lifting up his hand*]. I've sworn not to call the hand of man upon your crimes to-day; but I haven't sworn I wouldn't call the fire of heaven from the hand of the Almighty God. [*He begins saying a Latin malediction in a loud ecclesiastical voice.*]

MARY. There's an old villain.

ALL [*together*]. Run, run. Run for your lives.

[*They rush out, leaving the* PRIEST *master of the situation.*]

CURTAIN

THE PLAYBOY OF THE WESTERN WORLD[1]

A COMEDY IN THREE ACTS

[1] Originally Synge entitled his play 'The Murderer (a Farce)' and opened it in the potato garden. Subsequent drafts, some in four acts, were headed 'Murder Will Out', 'The Fool of the Family', 'The Fool of Farnham', 'Christy Mahon', and, finally, 'The Playboy of the Western World'.

PREFACE

IN writing *The Playboy of the Western World*, as in my other plays, I have used one or two words only, that I have not heard among the country people of Ireland, or spoken in my own nursery before I could read the newspapers.[1] A certain number of the phrases I employ I have heard also from herds and fishermen along the coast from Kerry to Mayo, or from beggar-women and ballad-singers nearer Dublin; and I am glad to acknowledge how much I owe to the folk-imagination of these fine people. Anyone who has lived in real intimacy with the Irish peasantry will know that the wildest sayings and ideas in this play are tame indeed compared with the fancies one may hear in any little hill-side cabin in Geesala, or Carraroe, or Dingle Bay. All art is a collabora-tion; and there is little doubt that in the happy ages of literature striking and beautiful phrases were as ready to the story-teller's or the play-wright's hand as the rich cloaks and dresses of his time.[2] It is probable that when the Elizabethan dramatist took his ink-horn and sat down to his work he used many phrases that he had just heard, as he sat at dinner, from his mother or his children. In Ireland those of us who know the people have the same privilege. When I was writing *The Shadow of the Glen*, some years ago, I got more aid than any learning could have given me, from a chink in the floor of the old Wicklow house where I was staying, that let me hear what was being said by the servant girls in the kitchen. This matter, I think, is of importance, for in countries where the imagination of the people, and the language they use, is rich and living, it is possible for a writer to be rich and copious in his words, and at the same time to give the reality which is the root of all poetry, in a comprehensive and natural form. In the modern literature of towns, however, richness is found only in sonnets, or prose poems, or in one or two elaborate books that are far away from the profound and com-mon interests of life. One has, on one side, Mallarmé and Huysmans producing this literature; and on the other Ibsen and Zola dealing with the reality of life in joyless and pallid words. On the stage one must have

[1] A draft in Notebook 34 reads: 'It may be said that my rule in these plays has been to use no word that I have not heard among illiterate people or used myself before I read the newspapers a great deal or Macaulay's Essays.'

[2] The draft in Notebook 34 reads: 'I have no doubt at all that in all the great literary moments the living speech that was in the ears of Cervantes and Ben Jonson teemed with phrases that pass anything produced by the Goncourts.'

reality, and one must have joy, and that is why the intellectual modern drama has failed, and people have grown sick of the false joy of the musical comedy, that has been given them in place of the rich joy found only in[1] what is superb and wild in reality. In a good play every speech should be as fully flavoured as a nut or apple, and such speeches cannot be written by anyone who works among people who have shut their lips on poetry. In Ireland, for a few years more, we have a popular imagination that is fiery and magnificent, and tender; so that those of us who wish to write start with a chance that is not given to writers in places where the springtime of the local life has been forgotten, and the harvest is a memory only, and the straw has been turned into bricks.[2]

J. M. S.

January 21st, 1907.

[1] The typescript sent to the printers reads 'the rich joy of what is superb and wild', etc.
[2] See Appendix B for Synge's various public defences of *The Playboy*.

PERSONS[1]

CHRISTOPHER MAHON

OLD MAHON, his father, a squatter

MICHAEL JAMES FLAHERTY (called MICHAEL JAMES), a publican

MARGARET FLAHERTY (called PEGEEN MIKE), his daughter

SHAWN KEOGH, her second cousin, a young farmer

PHILLY O'CULLEN, \
JIMMY FARRELL, } small farmers

WIDOW QUIN

SARA TANSEY, \
SUSAN BRADY, \
HONOR BLAKE, } village girls \
NELLY McLAUGHLIN, /

A BELLMAN

SOME PEASANTS

SCENE

The action takes place near a village, on a wild coast of Mayo. The first Act passes on a dark evening of autumn, the other two Acts on the following day.

1. Synge's final typescript omits the Widow Quin from the list of persons; when added (presumably at the proof stage) her name was placed before Shawn Keogh. This inadvertently obscured the blood relationship between Shawn and Pegeen (and the need for a dispensation enabling them to marry) and made Shawn and the Widow Quin cousins by mistake, an error which was perpetrated in all ensuing editions of the play, although corrected in the Abbey programme. A further omission from the list of persons is the fourth village girl, Nelly McLaughlin, who appears in all earlier drafts of the play but in the later drafts lost many of her speeches to a new character, Sara Tansey; Nelly is given only three speeches in the first scene of Act II of the printed text and her name does not appear in the programme of the first performance. According to alterations made in the copy registered by the Lord Chamberlain's Office on 27 April 1907, Nelly's speeches were given to Honor Blake in the first production.

[1] Various drafts add different details to this picture of Pegeen: TS. 'A' describes her as a 'tall girl of about 25, good-humoured and sympathetic but masterful and rather impetuous'; the list of 'Types' in Notebook 28 characterizes her as 'contented and goodfeathering but haughty and quick-tempered . . . interested in her hope of marriage and ambitious in all ways hence her taking of Christy'; TS. 'G' adds the word 'untidy'.

[2] Synge originally planned his play in three acts, the first act showing the 'murder' in the potato garden, the second act beginning with the action here. Later drafts indicate a four-act scheme, but all succeeding drafts give this as the opening act. (See Appendix B.)

[3] The earliest drafts of this act open with Pegeen sweeping the floor with 'a homemade brush ⟨of⟩ twig⟨s⟩'. The 'Fool of Farnham' draft in Notebook 31 opens with Pegeen briefly ordering 'three barrels of porter with the best compliments of the season'; in drafts 'D' and 'E' this order is enlarged to 'Two dozens of Powers Whiskey. Three barrels of porter. And soda as before', with reference to the coming fair. Finally, in the margin of draft 'E' (23 May 1905), Synge suggested 'Open out? Try making her order her trousseau?'

[4] Early drafts describe Shawn as 'a tall loutish young man, fair hair' and 'innately slow awkward and helpless'.

[5] Draft 'F' originally read, 'You'd want cat's eyes to see the length of your leg this night, Shaneen Keogh.'

[6] Included among a list of phrases jotted down in Notebook 32 is the version 'hearing the cows breathing and sighing like Christian sinners in the white light of the moon'. Notebook 31 provides another variation: 'as when you'd hear on a drouthy day the west or south wind sighing with its weight of rain'.

ACT I

Country public house or shebeen, very rough and untidy. There is a sort of counter on the right with shelves, holding many bottles and jugs, just seen above it. Empty barrels stand near the counter. At back, a little to left of counter, there is a door into the open air; then, more to the left, there is a settle with shelves above it, with more jugs, and a table beneath a window. At the left there is a large open fire-place, with turf fire, and a small door into inner room. PEGEEN, *a wild-looking but fine girl of about twenty,*[1] *is writing at table. She is dressed in the usual peasant dress.*[2]

PEGEEN [*slowly, as she writes*]. Six yards of stuff for to make a yellow gown. A pair of lace boots with lengthy heels on them and brassy eyes. A hat is suited for a wedding-day. A fine tooth comb. To be sent with three barrels of porter in Jimmy Farrell's creel cart on the evening of the coming Fair to Mister Michael James Flaherty. With the best compliments of this season: Margaret Flaherty.[3]

SHAWN KEOGH [*a fat and fair young man comes in down right centre as she signs and looks round awkwardly, when he sees she is alone*[4]]. Where's himself?

PEGEEN [*without looking at him*]. He's coming. [*She directs letter.*] To Mister Sheamus Mulroy, Wine and Spirit Dealer, Castlebar.

SHAWN [*uneasily*]. I didn't see him on the road.

PEGEEN. How would you see him [*licks stamp and puts it on letter*] and it dark night this half an hour gone by?[5]

SHAWN [*turning towards door again*]. I stood a while outside wondering would I have a right to pass on or to walk in and see you, Pegeen Mike [*comes to the fire*], and I could hear the cows breathing, and sighing in the stillness of the air,[6] and not a step moving any place from this gate to the bridge.

PEGEEN [*putting letter in envelope*]. It's above at the cross-roads he is, meeting Philly O'Cullen and a couple more are going along with him to Kate Cassidy's wake.

¹ An early draft includes the marginal note 'strengthen scene between P and S so as to use P's vacillations as a motif?'

² The 'Fool of the Family' draft includes the marginal note 'make Shawn's marriage depend on meeting of fathers which is to take place after wake'. The 'Fool of Farnham' draft in Notebook 31 uses this suggestion:

PEGEEN. And you're thinking we'll wed? Surely?

SHAWN. Didn't you ⟨say⟩ at the turn of day you were after bidding himself to take the bargain with myself.

This idea is developed further by draft 'E' (23 May 1905):

SHAWN. I am making sure, and I've bought the ring this day, for didn't I hear you bidding himself make a good bargain with my father?

PEGEEN [*taking ring from him and trying it*]. It fits on surely, and what was it you paid for that?

SHAWN. Five shillings to a tinker man, and I'm told it was cheap. You'll be bound now to wed me by the honour of your soul, for where would I get my five shillings again for a thing the like of that.

PEGEEN. You'll do maybe as well as any young lad is left in the parish for it's a flat place this last while, where you'll meet none but the like of Jimmy Farrell is losing his teeth, or Patcheen is lame in his heel, or the two young lads is come home from California and they lost in their wits.

³ An early version of Shawn's reply explains the need for a dispensation: 'If he didn't send his dispensation what way at all would we live a decent life and we all second cousins for five miles around.'

In TS. 'F' Shawn interjects here: 'Amn't I as well worthy of his notice as any young lad in the place?'

⁴ In his final typescript Synge contemplated altering this to 'their high graces on their sacred seats'.

⁵ TS. 'G' originally read 'bit the ear from a peeler'. Notebook 29 includes the definition 'guff—a great warrant to tell a story'.

SHAWN [*looking at her blankly*]. And he's going that length in the dark night?

PEGEEN [*impatiently*]. He is surely, and leaving me lonesome on the scruff of the hill. [*She gets up and puts envelope on dresser, then winds clock.*] Isn't it long the nights are now, Shawn Keogh, to be leaving a poor girl with her own self counting the hours to the dawn of day?

SHAWN [*with awkward humour*]. If it is, when we're wedded in a short while you'll have no call to complain, for I've little will to be walking off to wakes or weddings in the darkness of the night.

PEGEEN [*with rather scornful good humour*]. You're making mighty certain, Shaneen, that I'll wed you now.[1]

SHAWN. Aren't we after making a good bargain, the way we're only waiting these days on Father Reilly's dispensation from the bishops or the Court of Rome?[2]

PEGEEN [*looking at him teasingly, washing up at dresser*]. It's a wonder, Shaneen, the Holy Father'd be taking notice of the likes of you,[3] for if I was him, I wouldn't bother with this place where you'll meet none but Red Linahan, has a squint in his eye, and Patcheen is lame in his heel, or the mad Mulrannies were driven from California and they lost in their wits. We're a queer lot these times to go troubling the Holy Father on his sacred seat.[4]

SHAWN [*scandalized*]. If we are, we're as good this place as another, maybe, and as good these times as we were for ever.

PEGEEN [*with scorn*]. As good, is it? Where now will you meet the like of Daneen Sullivan knocked the eye from a peeler, or Marcus Quin, God rest him, got six months for maiming ewes, and he a great warrant to tell stories[5] of holy Ireland till he'd have the old women shedding down tears about their feet. Where will you find the like of them, I'm saying?

SHAWN [*timidly*]. If you don't, it's a good job, maybe, for [*with peculiar emphasis on the words*] Father Reilly has small conceit to have that kind walking around and talking to the girls.

PEGEEN [*impatiently, throwing water from basin out of the door*]. Stop tormenting me with Father Reilly [*imitating his voice*], when I'm

¹ Notebook 31 reads:

SHAWN. I'm thinking you'd easy go further than myself maybe and fare the worse.

PEGEEN. If I would itself don't be bothering me this night when I'm asking how I'll pass these twelve hours of dark and not get my death with the fear?

Struck out of TS. 'E' is yet another reply from Pegeen: 'A good job is it? A good job to be living with no fighting or dancing or good works at all, and hardly a fellow left in it with the heart in him to make a keg of poteen and to dare the law.'

² In place of [*timidly*] earlier drafts read [*in an unsuccessful wheedling tone*].

³ Synge's final typescripts include the stage direction [*turning her head towards him*].

⁴ An early typescript includes the following exchange:

PEGEEN. Is it a fat man like him stay back from a wake?

SHAWN. Would I have a right to tell him the priest's after routing them out of it, and there's no decent wake holding at all.

⁵ A variation of this occurs in Notebook 32: 'Lowing and moaning like six heifers you'd see looking out through a gate in the wet mud, and they seeking their food in the cold evenings of the year.'

⁶ TS. 'F' adds the direction [*proud of his prudence*].

⁷ Struck out of draft 'G' is the following exchange:

SHAWN. . . . Don't tell the men, I'm saying, for it's a bad case to go mixing yourself up with the queer dark deeds or the dead men of the world.

PEGEEN [*contemptuously*]. I'm thinking maybe the dead men itself is better company than the like of you, Shaneen Keogh, who'd quit the harps of Heaven for to save your skin.

SHAWN [*impatiently*]. Don't be talking. I hear their voices on the road, and if they heard that story they'd have great blabbing this night at the wake.

⁸ An early typescript includes the following admonition from Pegeen: 'And let you mind you don't go along with them. I'll not have you learning to drink, and all the queer ways of the wake.'

⁹ Earlier drafts describe Philly as 'a thin political pauper' and 'elderly, thin and political'.

¹⁰ Draft 'F' describes Jimmy as 'forty-five, amorous in his thoughts and as fat as working men can grow in Mayo'. Originally Jimmy was 'Timmy', then 'Jimmy Laughlin'.

asking only what way I'll pass these twelve hours of dark, and not take my death with the fear.[1] [*Looking out of door.*]

SHAWN [*timidly*].[2] Would I fetch you the Widow Quin, maybe.

PEGEEN.[3] Is it the like of that murderer? You'll not, surely.

SHAWN [*going to her, soothingly*]. Then I'm thinking himself will stop along with you when he sees you taking on,[4] for it'll be a long night and with great darkness, and I'm after feeling a kind of fellow above in the furzy ditch, groaning wicked like a maddening dog,[5] the way it's good cause you have, maybe, to be fearing now.

PEGEEN [*turning on him sharply*]. What's that? Is it a man you seen?

SHAWN [*retreating*]. I couldn't see him at all, but I heard him groaning out and breaking his heart. It should have been a young man from his words speaking.

PEGEEN [*going after him*]. And you never went near to see was he hurted or what ailed him at all?

SHAWN.[6] I did not, Pegeen Mike. It was a dark lonesome place to be hearing the like of him.

PEGEEN. Well, you're a daring fellow! And if they find his corpse stretched above in the dews of dawn, what'll you say then to the peelers or the Justice of the Peace?

SHAWN [*thunderstruck*]. I wasn't thinking of that. For the love of God, Pegeen Mike, don't let on I was speaking of him. Don't tell your father and the men is coming above, for if they heard that story they'd have great blabbing this night at the wake.[7]

PEGEEN. I'll maybe tell them, and I'll maybe not.

SHAWN. They are coming at the door. Will you whisht, I'm saying.

PEGEEN. Whisht yourself.[8]

[*She goes behind counter.* MICHAEL JAMES, *fat jovial publican, comes in down right centre followed by* PHILLY O' CULLEN, *who is thin and mistrusting,*[9] *and* JIMMY FARRELL, *who is fat and amorous, about forty-five.*[10]]

MEN [*together*]. God bless you. The blessing of God on this place.

¹ An earlier draft adds the direction [*foolishly*]. The earliest drafts make the men's entrance much more abrupt; beside the margin of 'Murder Will Out II' Synge has written 'expand and link'.

² Additional stage directions from TS. 'G' read [*where she is standing with the men*].

³ Struck out of draft 'F' is an additional speech by Jimmy Farrell: '[*trying to laugh her off*]. The last wake we were coming from himself took a boghole with the stars shining out for the door of a house, and "God save all here", says he, walking into it.' Pegeen replies, 'Let you make none of your game Jimmy Farrell. . . .'

⁴ Direction taken from TS. 'G'.

⁵ Struck out of the printer's typescript is the direction [SHAWN *watches her with anxiety to see if she will tell of young man, then he tries to creep off.*]

PEGEEN. God bless you kindly.

MICHAEL [*to men, who go to the counter right*]. Sit down now, and take your rest. [*Crosses to* SHAWN *at the fire left.*] And how is it you are, Shawn Keogh? Are you coming over the sands to Kate Cassidy's wake?

SHAWN.¹ I am not, Michael James. I'm going home the short-cut to my bed.

PEGEEN [*speaking across from counter*].² He's right too, and have you no shame, Michael James, to be quitting off for the whole night and leaving myself lonesome in the shop?

MICHAEL [*good-humouredly*]. Isn't it the same whether I go for the whole night or a part only? and I'm thinking it's a queer daughter you are if you'd have me crossing backward through the Stooks of the Dead Women, with a drop taken.³

PEGEEN [*angrily*].⁴ If I am a queer daughter, it's a queer father'd be leaving me lonesome these twelve hours of dark, and I piling the turf with the dogs barking, and the calves mooing, and my own teeth rattling with the fear.

JIMMY [*flatteringly*]. What is there to hurt you and you a fine, hardy girl would knock the head of any two men in the place.

PEGEEN [*working herself up*]. Isn't there the harvest boys with their tongues red for drink, and the ten tinkers is camped in the east glen, and the thousand militia—bad cess to them!—walking idle through the land?⁵ There's lots surely to hurt me, and I won't stop alone in it, let himself do what he will.

MICHAEL. If you're that afeard, let Shawn Keogh stop along with you. It's the will of God, I'm thinking, himself should be seeing to you now. [*They all turn on* SHAWN.]

SHAWN [*in horrified confusion*]. I would and welcome, Michael James; but I'm afeard of Father Reilly, and what at all would the Holy Father and the Cardinals of Rome be saying if they heard I did the like of that?

MICHAEL [*with contempt*]. God help you! Can't you sit in by the hearth with the light lit and herself beyond in the room? You'll do that

¹ Struck out of draft 'G' is the additional speech by Michael James, 'There would be a fine lad to swear again the poteen in a court of law.'

² The 'Fool of the Family' draft, which does not include any 'business' with Shawn's coat, has the marginal direction 'Strengthen exit of Sh.' Draft 'F' enlarges on the stage directions here: *Just as he gets it open* MICHAEL *catches him by the coat and drags him back into the room backwards* ⟨*amid*⟩ *roars of laughter from the men*: PEGEEN *as black as hell.*

³ Struck out of an intermediate draft (about 'C') is more business with Shawn's coat:

MICHAEL JAMES [*taking things from his pocket*]. Rabbit snares. A corkscrew, a bad shilling, the *Leader* of Dublin, well there's sainted glory in the lonesome west, . . .

⁴ A marginal note to an early draft reads 'work through piece Shawn's righteousness in contrast with Christy'.

surely, for I've heard tell there's a queer fellow above going mad or getting his death, maybe, in the gripe of the ditch, so she'd be safer this night with a person here.

SHAWN [*with plaintive despair*]. I'm afeard of Father Reilly, I'm saying. Let you not be tempting me and we near married itself.

PHILLY [*with cold contempt*]. Lock him in the west room. He'll stay then and have no sin to be telling to the priest.

MICHAEL [*to* SHAWN, *getting between him and the door*]. Go up now.

SHAWN [*at the top of his voice*]. Don't stop me, Michael James. Let me out of the door, I'm saying, for the love of the Almighty God. Let me out [*trying to dodge past him*]. Let me out of it and may God grant you His indulgence in the hour of need.

MICHAEL [*loudly*]. Stop your noising and sit down by the hearth. [*Gives him a push and goes to counter laughing.*]

SHAWN [*turning back, wringing his hands*]. Oh, Father Reilly and the saints of God, where will I hide myself today? Oh, St. Joseph and St. Patrick and St. Brigid and St. James, have mercy on me now![1] [*He turns round, sees door clear and makes a rush for it.*]

MICHAEL [*catching him by the coat-tail*]. You'd be going, is it?

SHAWN [*screaming*]. Leave me go, Michael James, leave me go, you old Pagan, leave me go or I'll get the curse of the priests on you, and of the scarlet-coated bishops of the courts of Rome. [*With a sudden movement he pulls himself out of his coat and disappears out of the door, leaving his coat in* MICHAEL's *hands.*[2]]

MICHAEL [*turning round, and holding up coat*]. Well, there's the coat of a Christian man. Oh, there's sainted glory this day in the lonesome west,[3] and by the will of God I've got you a decent man, Pegeen, you'll have no call to be spying after if you've a score of young girls, maybe, weeding in your fields.

PEGEEN [*taking up the defence of her property*]. What right have you to be making game of a poor fellow for minding the priest[4] when it's your own the fault is, not paying a penny pot-boy to stand along with me and give me courage in the doing of my work? [*She snaps the coat away from him, and goes behind counter with it.*]

[1] A very early draft reads 'I'd pay a pot-boy and welcome, but where would I get one unless I sent the Town Crier shouting through the streets of New York?'

[2] Draft 'E' gives the direction [*with mock tenderness*].

[3] One of the earliest typescript drafts adds the words *but more like a farmer than a tramp*. In his analysis of 'Types' in Notebook 28 Synge describes Christy as 'small short and dark'; in an early draft of Act II he tells Pegeen, 'I'm four and twenty years of age and five months a Tuesday'.

[4] Draft 'F' adds the direction *on the threshold*.

[5] Not until draft 'E' (23 May 1905) is the phrase 'saving one widow alone' added in manuscript.

MICHAEL [*taken aback*]. Where would I get a pot-boy? Would you have me send the bell-man screaming in the streets of Castlebar?[1]

SHAWN [*opening the door a chink and putting in his head, in a small voice*]. Michael James!

MICHAEL [*imitating him*].[2] What ails you?

SHAWN. The queer dying fellow's beyond looking over the ditch. He's come up, I'm thinking, stealing your hens. [*Looks over his shoulder.*] God help me, he's following me now [*he runs into room*], and if he's heard what I said, he'll be having my life and I going home lonesome in the darkness of the night.

[*For a perceptible moment they watch the door with curiosity. Someone coughs outside. Then* CHRISTY MAHON, *a slight young man, comes in, very tired and frightened and dirty.*[3]]

CHRISTY [*in a small voice*][4]. God save all here!

MEN. God save you kindly.

CHRISTY [*going to counter*]. I'd trouble you for a glass of porter, woman of the house. [*He puts down coin.*]

PEGEEN [*serving him*]. You're one of the tinkers, young fellow, is beyond camped in the glen?

CHRISTY. I am not; but I'm destroyed walking.

MICHAEL [*patronizingly*]. Let you come up then to the fire. You're looking famished with the cold.

CHRISTY. God reward you. [*He takes up his glass, and goes a little way across to the left, then stops and looks about him.*] Is it often the polis do be coming into this place, master of the house?

MICHAEL. If you'd come in better hours, you'd have seen 'Licensed for the Sale of Beer and Spirits, to be consumed on the Premises,' written in white letters above the door, and what would the polis want spying on me, and not a decent house within four miles, the way every living Christian is a bona fide saving one widow alone?[5]

CHRISTY [*with relief*]. It's a safe house, so. [*He goes over to the fire, sighing and moaning. Then he sits down putting his glass beside him and begins gnawing a turnip, too miserable to feel the others staring at him with curiosity.*]

¹ An early draft reads, 'Were you never in school, young fellow, or the Petty Sessions, itself? What do you say at confession if you don't know the names of your sins?'

² TS. 'B' reads [*revealing his vanity*].

³ An early typescript has the marginal note 'work motif of continual argument between Philly and Timmy ⟨Jimmy⟩'.

MICHAEL [*going after him*]. Is it yourself is fearing the polis? You're wanting, maybe?

CHRISTY. There's many wanting.

MICHAEL. Many surely, with the broken harvest and the ended wars. [*He picks up some stockings etc. that are near the fire, and carries them away furtively.*] It should be larceny, I'm thinking?

CHRISTY [*dolefully*]. I had it in my mind it was a different word and a bigger.

PEGEEN. There's a queer lad! Were you never slapped in school, young fellow, that you don't know the name of your deed?[1]

CHRISTY [*bashfully*]. I'm slow at learning, a middling scholar only.

MICHAEL. If you're a dunce itself, you'd have a right to know that larceny's robbing and stealing. Is it for the like of that you're wanting?

CHRISTY [*with a flash of family pride*].[2] And I the son of a strong farmer [*with a sudden qualm*], God rest his soul, could have bought up the whole of your old house a while since from the butt of his tail-pocket and not have missed the weight of it gone.

MICHAEL [*impressed*]. If it's not stealing, it's maybe something big.

CHRISTY [*flattered*]. Aye; it's maybe something big.

JIMMY. He's a wicked-looking young fellow. Maybe he followed after a young woman on a lonesome night.

CHRISTY [*shocked*]. Oh, the saints forbid, mister. I was all times a decent lad.

PHILLY [*turning on* JIMMY][3]. You're a silly man, Jimmy Farrell. He said his father was a farmer a while since, and there's himself now in a poor state. Maybe the land was grabbed from him, and he did what any decent man would do.

MICHAEL [*to* CHRISTY, *mysteriously*]. Was it bailiffs?

CHRISTY. The divil a one.

MICHAEL. Agents?

CHRISTY. The divil a one.

¹ TS. 'F' elaborates Michael's questions: 'Was it bailiffs the like of MacSheehan?' 'Agents the like of Hickey of Kenmare?' 'Landlords the like of great Clanricard or an earl itself?'

² One of the earliest drafts reads [*Michael fills his glass and they all crowd round him with great curiosity. It must be made very plain that Christy is continually growing in his own estimation as the interest in him increases.*]

³ TS. 'F' reads 'or the prayers of Lent'. In TS. 'G' the word 'missioners' is substituted, possibly by another hand, for the original 'Brotherhoods'.

⁴ Early drafts read 'the Orange of the north'.

⁵ A very early typescript reads, 'Maybe he went fighting for the Boers the like of Major MacBride, God shield him, who's afeard to put the tip of his nose into Ireland fearing he'd be hanged, quartered, and drawn.' Presumably the reference is to John MacBride who married Maud Gonne.

⁶ Struck out of the printer's typescript is the additional phrase in Pegeen's list, 'or sheep-stealing'.
⁷ The Maunsel edition adds the word 'that' before 'would', but there is no indication of this in any of the drafts, and the construction is common elsewhere in Synge's work.

MICHAEL. Landlords?[1]

CHRISTY [*peevishly*]. Ah, not at all, I'm saying. You'd see the like of them stories on any little paper of a Munster town. But I'm not calling to mind any person, gentle, simple, judge or jury, did the like of me.

[*They all draw nearer with delighted curiosity.*][2]

PHILLY. Well that lad's a puzzle-the-world.

JIMMY. He'd beat Dan Davies' Circus or the holy missioners making sermons on the villainy of man.[3] Try him again, Philly.

PHILLY. Did you strike golden guineas out of solder, young fellow, or shilling coins itself?

CHRISTY. I did not mister, not sixpence nor a farthing coin.

JIMMY. Did you marry three wives maybe? I'm told there's a sprinkling have done that among the holy Luthers of the preaching North.[4]

CHRISTY [*shyly*]. I never married with one, let alone with a couple or three.

PHILLY. Maybe he went fighting for the Boers, the like of the man beyond, was judged to be hanged, quartered, and drawn. Were you off east, young fellow, fighting bloody wars for Kruger and the freedom of the Boers?[5]

CHRISTY. I never left my own parish till Tuesday was a week.

PEGEEN [*coming from counter*]. He's done nothing, so. [*To* CHRISTY.] If you didn't commit murder or a bad nasty thing, or false coining,[6] or robbery, or butchery or the like of them, there isn't anything[7] would be worth your troubling for to run from now. You did nothing at all.

CHRISTY [*his feelings hurt*]. That's an unkindly thing to be saying to a poor orphaned traveller, has a prison behind him, and hanging before, and hell's gap gaping below.

PEGEEN [*with a sign to the men to be quiet*]. You're only saying it. You did nothing at all. A soft lad the like of you wouldn't slit the windpipe of a screeching sow.

¹ Draft 'F' further emphasizes Christy's small size by adding the word 'little' before 'head'.

² Earlier drafts add the speech:

SHAWN [*pushing the men from the door*]. He should be a dangerous fellow. Will you open the latch Philly Cullen?

³ Notebook 29 records the incident 'man hangs his dog and you hear it screeching half the day and it hanging from the head of a ditch'.

⁴ An early draft adds the exchange:

PEGEEN. That should be a droughty thing to have weighing on your mind.

CHRISTY. Oh, it is surely, I've my tongue cracking, and throat cracked, and I after drinking the brown streams dry on the plains of Ireland.

CHRISTY [*offended*]. You're not speaking the truth.

PEGEEN [*in mock rage*]. Not speaking the truth, is it? Would you have me knock the head[1] of you with the butt of the broom?

CHRISTY [*twisting round on her with a sharp cry of horror*]. Don't strike me. . . . I killed my poor father, Tuesday was a week, for doing the like of that.

PEGEEN [*with blank amazement*]. Is it killed your father?

CHRISTY [*subsiding*]. With the help of God I did surely, and that the Holy Immaculate Mother may intercede for his soul.[2]

PHILLY [*retreating with* JIMMY]. There's a daring fellow.

JIMMY. Oh, glory be to God!

MICHAEL [*with great respect*]. That was a hanging crime, mister honey. You should have had good reason for doing the like of that.

CHRISTY [*in a very reasonable tone*]. He was a dirty man, God forgive him, and he getting old and crusty, the way I couldn't put up with him at all.

PEGEEN. And you shot him dead?

CHRISTY [*shaking his head*]. I never used weapons. I've no licence, and I'm a law-fearing man.

MICHAEL. It was with a hilted knife maybe? I'm told, in the big world, it's bloody knives they use.

CHRISTY [*loudly, scandalized*]. Do you take me for a slaughter-boy?

PEGEEN. You never hanged him, the way Jimmy Farrell hanged his dog from the licence and had it screeching and wriggling three hours at the butt of a string, and himself swearing it was a dead dog, and the peelers swearing it had life?[3]

CHRISTY. I did not then. I just riz the loy and let fall the edge of it on the ridge of his skull, and he went down at my feet like an empty sack, and never let a grunt or groan from him at all.[4]

MICHAEL [*making a sign to* PEGEEN *to fill* CHRISTY'*s glass*]. And what way weren't you hanged, mister? Did you bury him then?

¹ TS. 'F' adds the direction *He goes to counter after his glass, the men making room for him.*

² Early drafts give Philly the additional speech, 'Sure they never laid a hand to Lynche-haun from the day they knew the kind he was. It's only with a common weekday' etc. A marginal note to one draft of this scene reads 'strengthen transition', presumably referring to the emphasis in later drafts on Christy's bravery and suitability as pot-boy.

³ TS. 'F' reads 'Well isn't it a great story to think of you that length walking the world. You should have great courage to be going that way facing the roads, and where at all . . .'.

⁴ In the margin of TS. 'E' beside the speeches discussing Christy's bravery Synge has written the direction 'ornament', which is carried out in succeeding drafts.

CHRISTY [*considering*[1]]. Aye. I buried him then. Wasn't I digging spuds in the field?

MICHAEL. And the peelers never followed after you the eleven days that you're out?

CHRISTY [*shaking his head*]. Never a one of them and I walking forward facing hog, dog, or divil on the highway of the road.

PHILLY [*nodding wisely*].[2] It's only with a common week-day kind of a murderer them lads would be trusting their carcase, and that man should be a great terror when his temper's roused.

MICHAEL. He should then.[3] [*To* CHRISTY.] And where was it, mister honey, that you did the deed?

CHRISTY [*looking at him with suspicion*]. Oh, a distant place, master of the house, a windy corner of high distant hills.

PHILLY [*nodding with approval*]. He's a close man and he's right surely.

PEGEEN. That'd be a lad with the sense of Solomon to have for a pot-boy, Michael James, if it's the truth you're seeking one at all.[4]

PHILLY. The peelers is fearing him, and if you'd that lad in the house there isn't one of them would come smelling around if the dogs itself were lapping poteen from the dung-pit of the yard.

JIMMY. Bravery's a treasure in a lonesome place, and a lad would kill his father, I'm thinking, would face a foxy divil with a pitchpike on the flags of hell.

PEGEEN. It's the truth they're saying, and if I'd that lad in the house, I wouldn't be fearing the loosèd khaki cut-throats, or the walking dead.

CHRISTY [*swelling with surprise and triumph*]. Well, glory be to God!

MICHAEL [*with deference*]. Would you think well to stop here and be pot-boy, mister honey, if we gave you good wages, and didn't destroy you with the weight of work?

SHAWN [*coming forward uneasily*]. That'd be a queer kind to bring into a decent quiet household with the like of Pegeen Mike.

PEGEEN [*very sharply*]. Will you whisht. Who's speaking to you?

¹ A marginal note to the second draft reads 'Let Shawn oppose?', presumably leading to the reading in the final typescripts and galley proofs: 'with the like of her [*with a gesture towards* PEGEEN].'

² Earlier typescripts add the words 'if you were the second cousin of the queen of Spain'.

³ Draft 'F' (1 January 1906) tries developing the theme of Christy's clothes, presumably in preparation for Shawn's attempted bribery in Act II:

CHRISTY [*looking round him*]. It's a nice room. [*To* MICHAEL, *nervously uncertain.*] Is it not humbugging me you are and I in poor rags as I am?

MICHAEL. I'd be afeard to make games of the like of you, and let you give her your old clothes when you strip off and she'll have them grand in the morning.

CHRISTY [*looking round naïvely*]. I'm thinking I'll stay.

⁴ In draft 'A' Christy gives the false name of 'Ned Mulvaney', which Synge then altered in manuscript to 'Simon Fitzhenry' and 'Fitzsimon Henry'. An early draft of the final act (then Act IV) mentions the name 'John Doyle', and other drafts read 'Christy Sheehan'. Not until draft 'E' (23 May 1905) does Christy give his own name, which was originally 'Christy Flaherty', but earlier drafts have Pegeen coaxing him to confide his real name to her during the curtain scene. See below.

⁵ In one of the early drafts Shawn hesitates, then sits down and says,

. . . You'll likely be feeling strange and queer in your mind young fellow sitting here with a woman you never set your eyes on till half an hour gone by?

PEGEEN [*interrupting him*]. Are you thinking him as big a fool as yourself, Shawn Keogh Do you think a man has killed his father and walked round the width of Ireland fearing neither peeler nor priest would be shying off from a girl?

CHRISTY [*taking his cue gladly*]. That's the truth.

SHAWN [*retreating*]. A bloody-handed murderer the like of. . . .[1]

PEGEEN [*snapping at him*]. Whisht, I'm saying, we'll take no fooling from your like at all.[2] [*To* CHRISTY *with a honeyed voice*.] And you, young fellow, you'd have a right to stop I'm thinking, for we'd do our all and utmost to content your needs.

CHRISTY [*overcome with wonder*]. And I'd be safe this place from the searching law?

MICHAEL. You would surely. If they're not fearing you itself, the peelers in this place is decent, droughty poor fellows, wouldn't touch a cur dog and not give warning in the dead of night.

PEGEEN [*very kindly and persuasively*]. Let you stop a short while anyhow. Aren't you destroyed walking with your feet in bleeding blisters, and your whole skin needing washing like a Wicklow sheep.

CHRISTY [*looking round with satisfaction*]. It's a nice room, and if it's not humbugging me you are, I'm thinking that I'll surely stay.[3]

JIMMY [*jumps up*]. Now, by the grace of God, herself will be safe this night, with a man killed his father holding danger from the door, and let you come on, Michael James, or they'll have the best stuff drunk at the wake.

MICHAEL [*going to the door with* MEN]. And begging your pardon, mister, what name will we call you for we'd like to know.

CHRISTY. Christopher Mahon.[4]

MICHAEL. Well, God bless you Christy, and a good rest till we meet again when the sun'll be rising to the noon of day.

CHRISTY. God bless you all.

MEN. God bless you. [*They go out except* SHAWN *who lingers at door*.][5]

SHAWN [*to* PEGEEN]. Are you wanting me to stop along with you and keep you from harm?

PEGEEN [*gruffly*]. Didn't you say you were fearing Father Reilly?

SHAWN. There'd be no harm staying now, I'm thinking, and himself in it too.

¹ In draft 'D' Pegeen replies scornfully, 'Will you send me Satan's ma.'

² This direction is added in manuscript to draft 'E'. See Oxford, *Prose*, p. 249.

³ An early typescript develops the motif of the false name:

PEGEEN [*very kindly*]. You should have fine people in your family, for I'm thinking Fitzsimon Henry is a kind of a quality name people do have who are driving and hunting and having great times in the land.

CHRISTY [*looking at her with wonder and admiration*]. Can a man get married when he has a wrong name on him, Pegeen Mike?

PEGEEN. Oh ho, it's a wrong name you've given is it? And you're wanting to wed in this place? You're a gamey lad surely.

CHRISTY. It'd be a dangerous thing to tell me name to those lads I'm thinking and have it spreading round through the land.

⁴ Earlier drafts read [*sitting bolt up with astonishment*].

⁵ TS. 'F' adds the direction [*skittishly*]. A marginal note to TS. 'E' reads 'note write up s.d.', and in TS. 'F' Synge introduces a hamper or cleeve of clothes which Pegeen tries on Christy throughout their scene. In TS. 'G' Synge rejects this idea and has Pegeen preparing Christy's supper of bread and milk before filling the sack for his bed.

PEGEEN. You wouldn't stay when there was need for you, and let you step off nimble this time when there's none.

SHAWN. Didn't I say it was Father Reilly. . . .

PEGEEN. Go on then to Father Reilly [*in a jeering tone*], and let him put you in the holy brotherhoods and leave that lad to me.

SHAWN. If I meet the Widow Quin. . . .

PEGEEN. Go on, I'm saying, and don't be waking this place with your noise.[1] [*She hustles him out and bolts door.*] That lad would wear the spirits from the saints of peace. [*Bustles about, then takes off her apron and pins it up in the window as a blind,[2] CHRISTY watching her timidly. Then she comes to him and speaks with bland good humour.*] Let you stretch out now by the fire, young fellow. You should be destroyed travelling.

CHRISTY [*shyly again, drawing off his boots*]. I'm tired surely, walking wild eleven days and waking fearful in the night. [*He holds up one of his feet, feeling his blisters and looking at it with compassion.*]

PEGEEN [*standing beside him, watching him with delight*]. You should have had great people in your family, I'm thinking, with the little small feet you have, and you with a kind of a quality name, the like of what you'd find on the great powers and potentates of France and Spain.[3]

CHRISTY [*with pride*]. We were great surely, with wide and windy acres of rich Munster land.

PEGEEN. Wasn't I telling you, and you a fine, handsome young fellow with a noble brow.

CHRISTY [*with a flash of delighted surprise*].[4] Is it me?

PEGEEN.[5] Aye. Did you never hear that from the young girls where you come from in the west or south?

CHRISTY [*with venom*]. I did not then. . . . Oh, they're bloody liars in the naked parish where I grew a man.

PEGEEN. If they are itself, you've heard it these days, I'm thinking, and you walking the world telling out your story to young girls or old.

¹ Additional stage directions from draft 'G'.

² TS. 'C' has the word 'crescendo' here, and in the margin the note 'make Christy stretch out on floor before coming of Widow Quin, to help sleeping motif'.

³ Earlier drafts add the word 'long' after 'eleven'.

⁴ A fragment in Notebook 32 may have been intended here: 'hearing a bloody souper saying "To hell with the Pope" and "That's the best talk I ever had in my life" says . . .'.

⁵ Stage direction from earlier drafts.

⁶ Notebook 29 includes the phrases 'Paddy from Clare with as much streeleen as a poet' and 'fiery patriots'.

⁷ TS. 'F' gives additional stage directions to Christy: [*draws a little towards her and stops, draws nearer again, sinking his voice to a whisper*], and to Pegeen: [*leading him off subject*].

⁸ TS. 'D' adds the marginal note to this scene 'talk with Ch. and Pegeen, make vanity felt in Christy'.

A marginal note to a very early draft suggests 'Try letting P know C's ⟨tale?⟩ a fake and get effect from it at Climax II'.

⁹ The draft entitled 'Murder Will Out' (B) (End)' continues with information Synge later worked into the conversation between Old Mahon and the Widow in Act II:

PEGEEN. A hard woman's a bad thing, but what was it she did to you then?

CHRISTY. She sat herself down at the side of me father, and there they were making great talk of the ill-deeds of my youth, he telling the way I built a hay-cock with no belly in it, till it was scattered all ways with the wind, and telling the way I broke the leg of the one cow alone we had, and buried it after with its skin on it because I didn't want it cut up. Then says she 'It's that lad has brought ill luck on you,'—my father'd a decree for debt again him from the shop—'for your family's after living in this place' says she, 'since the days of the fire worshipper and pagans and the high times of Ireland and they never troubled till this day the way it's plain surely it's that lad'—meaning myself—'has brought ill luck upon your race.'

At one time (draft 'D') Synge contemplated introducing the Widow Quin here: [*The Widow Quin's head is seen listening at window.*] Notebook 28 makes Christy a ballad-singer (see Appendix B).

CHRISTY. I've told my story no place till this night, Pegeen Mike, and it's foolish I was here, maybe, to be talking free, but you're decent people, I'm thinking, and yourself a kindly woman, the way I wasn't fearing you at all.

PEGEEN [*filling a sack with straw, right*].[1] You've said the like of that, maybe, in every cot and cabin where you've met a young girl on your way.

CHRISTY [*going over to her, gradually raising his voice*].[2] I've said it nowhere till this night, I'm telling you, for I've seen none the like of you the eleven[3] days I am walking the world, looking over a low ditch or a high ditch on my north or south, into stony scattered fields, or scribes of bog, where you'd see young limber girls, and fine prancing women making laughter with the men.[4]

PEGEEN [*nodding with approval[5]*]. If you weren't destroyed travelling you'd have as much talk and streeleen, I'm thinking, as Owen Roe O'Sullivan or the poets of the Dingle Bay, and I've heard all times it's the poets are your like, fine fiery fellows with great rages when their temper's roused.[6]

CHRISTY [*drawing a little nearer to her*]. You've a power of rings, God bless you, and would there be any offence if I was asking are you single now?

PEGEEN.[7] What would I want wedding so young?

CHRISTY [*with relief*]. We're alike, so.

PEGEEN [*putting sack on settle and beating it up*]. I never killed my father. I'd be afeard to do that, except I was the like of yourself with blind rages tearing me within, for I'm thinking you should have had great tussling when the end was come.

CHRISTY [*expanding with delight at the first confidential talk he has ever had with a woman[8]*]. We had not then. It was a hard woman was come over the hill, and if he was always a crusty kind, when he'd a hard woman setting him on, not the divil himself or his four fathers could put up with him at all.[9]

PEGEEN [*with curiosity*]. And isn't it a great wonder that one wasn't fearing you?

¹ Intermediate drafts include the following exchange, which is finally struck out, with the marginal note 'Reserve this lonesome motif for II (2) (b)':

PEGEEN. There's many lonesome places I'm thinking in the width of Ireland now.

CHRISTY. It was lonesome surely. . . .

² Throughout all the early drafts Synge toyed with the idea of developing the motif of Christy's clothing, an idea which remains in the final draft only with Shawn's attempted bribery and the Jockey costume. On the back of an early draft he suggested an incident borrowed from his notebooks on Wicklow: 'Ch. talks of washing his shirt in a stream. P. offers to wash it, will give him one of her father's in the morning.' A slightly later draft combines this with another early motif, Christy's dislike of women: Christy says, 'I washed my old shirt yesterday in a kind of a pool and didn't two girls come and make game of me, and I there washing with my coat buttoned over my skin.'

Finally, in draft 'F', Synge makes Pegeen during the following speeches try different coats on Christy from a hamper of clothing; the first coat is far too big for him and provokes comments from Pegeen on his small size, but a second one meets with her approval.

³ Draft 'D' (probably winter 1905) includes the following scene, with the marginal comment 'climax?':

CHRISTY. What would the king of Heaven do itself and he pitted against an old man and hard woman with eleven children alive.

PEGEEN. If they were that bad, you'd a good right to strike them before you struck your father if it was bad he was itself, women is worst young fellow, any fool knows that.

CHRISTY. It's the truth you're saying surely, and it's often I'd have liked to cut their bloody throats, to throw them down again the ground in a stony place the way I'd blacken their giggling eyes and break their necks.

PEGEEN [*pityingly*]. You should have had a hard life young fellow, to have that rage in you now, and you tired with your walk. Let you not take on now, I'm telling ⟨you⟩ for there's not a hard woman within ten miles will come to you here, and there isn't one of them will mind you from this day, but when they hear the story of you there won't be a young girl in the parish won't be asking a sweet look from your eye.

CHRISTY [*touched and brightening*]. Is that the truth?

PEGEEN. It's the truth I'm telling you, my poor man. Don't you see how I'm sitting up here beside ⟨you⟩ and holding your hand when it's time I was taking my rest.

⁴ Synge wrote many different versions of this speech. 'The Fool of Farnham' draft in Notebook 28 reads:

There's many a night I was out poaching on the hills beyond—I'm a great divil to poach—snaring rabbits and I looking up at the stars and moon the time there'd be a white fog spread on the bog and you wouldn't see a thing but a bit of a chimney maybe in this or the bough of an old ash tree beyond in another and I'd hear a rabbit beginning to scream God help it and I hard set to know what kind of walking sinner I was at all.

Notebook 31 reads:

And it's many a time when I'd be abroad the like of that seeing a light shining in this place and a light shining beyond I'd be asking myself if I'd ever my own self ⟨be⟩ sitting the way I'm sitting this night with a kind lovely girl and. . . .

⁵ In his final drafts Synge was still not satisfied with this exchange. TS. 'G' strikes out the stage direction for Pegeen [*with a shade of contempt*], then suggests and strikes out her reply, 'If I wasn't scared I'd be like you too, maybe, for it should be great. . . .'

⁶ Struck out of TS. 'G' is the direction [*with enthusiasm*]. An earlier draft has the marginal note 'Increase climaxes of first duo?'

⁷ Notebook 28 includes among scattered passages of dialogue, 'As naked as an ash tree in the moon of March (JMS)'. The initials indicate that Synge invented the phrase.

CHRISTY [*very confidentially*]. Up to the day I killed my father, there wasn't a person in Ireland knew the kind I was, and I there drinking, waking, eating, sleeping, a quiet, simple poor fellow with no man giving me heed.

PEGEEN [*getting a quilt out of cupboard and putting it on the sack*]. It was the girls were giving you heed maybe, and I'm thinking it's most conceit you'd have to be gaming with their like.

CHRISTY [*shaking his head, with simplicity*]. Not the girls itself, and I won't tell you a lie. There wasn't anyone heeding me in that place saving only the dumb beasts of the field.[1] [*He sits down at fire.*]

PEGEEN [*with disappointment*]. And I thinking you should have been living the like of a king of Norway or the Eastern world. [*She comes and sits beside him after placing bread and mug of milk on the table.*][2]

CHRISTY [*laughing piteously*]. The like of a king, is it![3] And I after toiling, moiling, digging, dodging from the dawn till dusk with never a sight of joy or sport saving only when I'd be abroad in the dark night poaching rabbits on hills, for I was a divil to poach, God forgive me [*very naïvely*], and I near got six months for going with a dung-fork and stabbing a fish.[4]

PEGEEN.[5] And it's that you'd call sport is it, to be abroad in the darkness with yourself alone?

CHRISTY.[6] I did, God help me, and there I'd be as happy as the sunshine of St. Martin's Day, watching the light passing the north or the patches of fog, till I'd hear a rabbit starting to screech and I'd go running in the furze. Then when I'd my full share I'd come walking down where you'd see the ducks and geese stretched sleeping on the highway of the road, and before I'd pass the dunghill, I'd hear himself snoring out, a loud lonesome snore he'd be making all times, the while he was sleeping, and he a man'd be raging all times the while he was waking, like a gaudy officer you'd hear cursing and damning and swearing oaths.

PEGEEN. Providence and Mercy, spare us all!

CHRISTY. It's that you'd say surely if you seen him and he after drinking for weeks, rising up in the red dawn, or before it maybe, and going out into the yard as naked as an ash tree in the moon of May,[7]

¹ Earlier drafts read [*he wipes a tear*]. A marginal note to draft 'D' reads 'strengthen and characterise Peg. in duo'.

² A very early sketch in Notebook 28 tries other responses:

CHRISTY. Why would you curse your father etc. but my own didn't ever leave me etc. men [*with family pride*] for he was a gallous lad I'm told and he a young man the way there wasn't the like of him for romping and roaring in the length of the South, though there he is now stretched—God rest him—and it was myself that did the deed. [*He nods his head in meditation.*]

PEGEEN. Well don't fret, God help you.

CHRISTY. I was thinking it'd be well for me to be back there bad as it was with my father live, . . .—for his soul for it's a strange thing I'm telling you to have ⟨the⟩ death of the man reared you weighing on your mind.

CHRISTY [*exalts his father with a share of his vanity*]. And he with a big voice the like you'd ⟨be⟩ thinking was a gaudy officer swearing an oath.

³ Earlier drafts are more explicit: [*clinging round Pegeen's waist*].

⁴ In draft 'C' Christy hides and the Widow Quin goes away disappointed without entering; this is then revised so that she enters but does not talk to Christy who pretends to be asleep. In draft 'D' Christy again pretends to sleep while Pegeen and the Widow raise their voices in argument over the proposed match between Pegeen and Shawn, which Pegeen denies:

WIDOW QUIN [*ironically*]. Isn't that a great lad for sleeping. You roaring out and not a budge from him at all. [*She stirs up* CHRISTY *with her foot.*] Get up from that, don't I know you're letting on and I after looking in at that window and seeing you sitting up and hearing you gabbing away in little whispered talk.

[CHRISTY *sits up doubtfully and looks foolishly at* PEGEEN *for his cue.*]

PEGEEN. And what right have you to ⟨go⟩ prying at my window when the night is down?

WIDOW QUIN. What would I want knocking if you were already in your sleep?

PEGEEN. I don't know what you wanted knocking and I sitting awake. Let you stroll off now to your old hut, and not be plaguing us more.

WIDOW QUIN [*turning to* CHRISTY]. Well isn't a new young lad a great treasure for a flighty girl. I wasn't thinking you'd be so huffy Pegeen Mike, and I ax your pardon for coming round to you at all. [*She goes out.*]

A fragment about this time has Christy ask, 'Do I look now that I'm sleeping?' to which Pegeen replies, 'Your eyes is too shut. Stay now the way you are.'

and shying clods again the visage of the stars till he'd put the fear of
death into the banbhs and the screeching sows.

PEGEEN. I'd be well-nigh afeard of that lad myself, I'm thinking. And
there was no one in it but the two of you alone?

CHRISTY. The divil a one, though he'd sons and daughters walking all
great states and territories of the world, and not a one of them to this
day but would say their seven curses on him, and they rousing up
to let a cough or sneeze, maybe, in the deadness of the night.

PEGEEN [*nodding her head*]. Well, you should have been a queer lot.
. . . I never cursed my father the like of that though I'm twenty and
more years of age.

CHRISTY. Then you'd have cursed mine, I'm telling you, and he a man
never gave peace to any saving when he'd get two months or three,
or be locked in the asylum for battering peelers or assaulting men
[*with depression*],[1] the way it was a bitter life he led me till I did up a
Tuesday and halve his skull.[2]

PEGEEN [*putting her hand on his shoulder*]. Well, you'll have peace in this
place, Christy Mahon, and none to trouble you, and it's near time a
fine lad the like of you should have your good share of the earth.

CHRISTY. It's time surely, and I a seemly fellow with great strength in
me and bravery of. . . . [*Some one knocks.*]

CHRISTY [*clinging to* PEGEEN].[3] Oh, glory! it's late for knocking, and
this last while I'm in terror of the peelers, and the walking dead. . . .
[*Knocking again.*]

PEGEEN. Who's there?

VOICE [*outside*]. Me.

PEGEEN. Who's me?

VOICE. The Widow Quin.

PEGEEN [*jumping up and giving him the bread and milk*]. Go on now with
your supper, and let on to be sleepy, for if she found you were such
a warrant to talk, she'd be stringing gabble till the dawn of day.

[CHRISTY *takes bread and sits shyly with his back to the door.*][4]

¹ The Widow Quin does not appear at all in the earliest drafts of the play, but gradually develops out of Sally Quin, one of the village girls who visits Christy in the second act, when Synge discovered he needed a foil to Christy and a transition into Old Mahon's appearance. Apparently he then decided to develop the character as a foil to Pegeen also, and so she appears first in the early drafts of TS. 'C'. In his note on 'Types' in Notebook 28, Synge describes one of his first concepts of the Widow: '(thirty dark) not gloomy but rather stiff in her relations with villagers very poor and very proud and very cynical (give her rich father in North that she will not write to because of her pride) so indifferent that she has no ambition—hence her taking Christy'. At this early stage he also contemplated making her the widow of a judge, but as the characterization deepened in Act II he retained the pride and cynicism and sense of isolation from the villagers and reduced her social status. (See notes to Act II and Appendix B.)

² Not until he revised draft 'F' (after January 1906) did Synge think of adding the priest's instructions. TS. 'F' originally read:

WIDOW QUIN. I'll not see them again for it's late night, and my breath's gone mounting the hill in great haste and I lonesome in the darkness of the glen.

PEGEEN. It's queer you'd be lonesome and you all times straying abroad.

WIDOW QUIN [*crossing to* CHRISTY]. God save you, young fellow, it's not yourself I'm thinking would say the like of that.

³ Draft 'F' reads 'sitting on your — so simple' etc.

⁴ Synge drafted several variations of this scene between Pegeen and the Widow Quin in Notebook 28 (see Appendix B for the ballad-singing scene). One version has them discussing Christy, who pretends to sleep:

WIDOW QUIN [*looking at* CHRISTY]. Look at him there sleeping as quiet as a calf, and no stir from him at all. He should be bet up travelling.

PEGEEN. He should be surely! Hasn't he the great courage to go walking this world and he not fear the hang-man's hand hitching a black knot to the gullet of his neck?

PEGEEN [*opening door, with temper*]. What ails you, or what is it you're wanting at this hour of the night?

WIDOW QUIN[1] [*coming in a step and peering at* CHRISTY]. I'm after meeting Shawn Keogh and Father Reilly below, who told me of your curiosity man, and they fearing by this time he was maybe roaring, romping on your hands with drink.

PEGEEN [*pointing to* CHRISTY]. Look now, is he roaring, and he stretched out drowsy with his supper, and his mug of milk. Walk down and tell that to Father Reilly and to Shaneen Keogh.

WIDOW QUIN [*coming forward*]. I'll not see them again, for I've their word to lead that lad forward for to lodge with me.

PEGEEN [*in blank amazement*]. This night, is it?

WIDOW QUIN[*going over*]. This night. 'It isn't fitting,' says the priesteen, 'to have his likeness lodging with an orphaned girl.' [*To* CHRISTY.] God save you, mister![2]

CHRISTY [*shyly*]. God save you kindly.

WIDOW QUIN [*looking at him with half-amused curiosity*]. Well, aren't you a little smiling fellow? It should have been great and bitter torments did rouse your spirits to a deed of blood.

CHRISTY [*doubtfully*]. It should, maybe.

WIDOW QUIN. It's more than 'maybe' I'm saying, and it'd soften my heart to see you sitting so simple[3] with your cup and cake, and you fitter to be saying your catechism than slaying your da.

PEGEEN [*at counter, washing glasses*]. There's talking when any'd see he's fit to be holding his head high with the wonders of the world.[4] Walk on from this, for I'll not have him tormented and he destroyed travelling since Tuesday was a week.

WIDOW QUIN [*peaceably*]. We'll be walking surely when his supper's done, and you'll find we're great company, young fellow, when it's of the like of you and me you'd hear the penny poets singing in an August Fair.

CHRISTY [*innocently*]. Did you kill your father?

¹ Earlier drafts including 'F' added further details to the Widow's 'murder':

WIDOW QUIN. I did not but if you'd come a while since you'd have heard the lads telling a great story of the way I killed himself—God rest him—a fine strappy fellow of the name of Marcus Quin. Ask Pegeen and she'll tell you it is true.

PEGEEN. She hit him a blow with a rusted pick the way she had him with a blue bruised back on him stretched out three weeks on the broad of his belly, and in the long run the rusted poison did corrode his blood the way he never overed at it and died after. That was a sneaky kind of a murder did breed small glory in the place at all.

WIDOW QUIN. I could string you better records if I'd patience now.

Many of the drafts add Christy's reaction, '[*jealous of his reputation*]. And I thinking it was myself only in this place had ever done the like of that.'

² An early draft includes the direction [*coaxingly to* CHRISTY *her mouth at his ear and her eyes on* PEGEEN MIKE].

³ Earlier stage directions are more explicit, with Pegeen pushing Christy down while the Widow Quin tries to pull him up.

⁴ Early drafts add the word 'lousy' before 'buck goat'.

⁵ Earlier drafts add the direction [*quietly*].

⁶ Struck out of draft 'E' (23 May 1905) is Pegeen's opening line: 'It isn't to the like of her you'd trust your soul young fellow if you've sense in you at all.'

⁷ Practically all of Pegeen's references in this speech have their origin in notes Synge made of his visit to the Dingle peninsula and Mountain Stage, Co. Kerry, August–September 1905. Notebook 38 records a story he heard at Philly Harris's cottage in Mountain Stage: 'woman suckles lamb in which doctor detects the elements of a Christian in Cahirciveen'. Other Kerry notes refer to the French fishermen from Fécamp and their 'grass tobacco'. (See Greene and Stephens, *J. M. Synge*, ch. 11.) This speech was altered during the first production of the play.

PEGEEN [*contemptuously*]. She did not. She hit himself with a worn pick, and the rusted poison did corrode his blood the way he never overed it and died after. That was a sneaky kind of murder did win small glory with the boys itself.[1] [*She crosses to* CHRISTY's *left.*]

WIDOW QUIN [*with good-humour*].[2] If it didn't, maybe all knows a widow woman has buried her children and destroyed her man is a wiser comrade for a young lad than a girl the like of you who'd go helter-skeltering after any man would let you a wink upon the road.

PEGEEN [*breaking out into wild rage*]. And you'll say that, Widow Quin, and you gasping with the rage you had racing the hill beyond to look on his face.

WIDOW QUIN [*laughing derisively*]. Me, is it! Well, Father Reilly has cuteness to divide you now. [*She pulls* CHRISTY *up.*] There's great temptation in a man did slay his da, and we'd best be going, young fellow; so rise up and come with me.

PEGEEN [*seizing his arm*].[3] He'll not stir. He's pot-boy in this place and I'll not have him stolen off and kidnabbed while himself's abroad.

WIDOW QUIN. It'd be a crazy pot-boy'd lodge him in the shebeen where he works by day, so you'd have a right to come on, young fellow, till you see my little houseen, a perch off on the rising hill.

PEGEEN. Wait till morning, Christy Mahon, wait till you lay eyes on her leaky thatch is growing more pasture for her buck goat[4] than her square of fields, and she without a tramp itself to keep in order her place at all.

WIDOW QUIN.[5] When you see me contriving in my little gardens, Christy Mahon, you'll swear the Lord God formed me to be living lone and that there isn't my match in Mayo for thatching or mowing or shearing a sheep.

PEGEEN [*with noisy scorn*].[6] It's true the Lord God formed you to contrive indeed! Doesn't the world know you reared a black ram at your own breast, so that the Lord Bishop of Connaught felt the elements of a Christian, and he eating it after in a kidney stew? Doesn't the world know you've been seen shaving the foxy skipper from France for a threepenny bit and a sop of grass tobacco would wring the liver from a mountain goat you'd meet lepping the hills?[7]

¹ A late draft adds the line, 'For the love of God young fellow I'd have you wary of them that's flighty fidgets at the age of her, and you'd do well now to rise up on your feet and come with ⟨me⟩ for I'm a quiet grown woman does be pitying the world.'

² The final draft considers and then rejects 'wormy shed' and 'kind of ass's pigsty'.

³ Draft 'F' gives Pegeen the additional arguments, 'It's better sport you'll have this place I'm telling you, where there'll be pipes and fiddlers playing, and you dancing polkas with my own hand till the dawn of day', and later, 'You're like to be the talk and terror of Mayo for ten years to come, but if you go along with her there isn't one in this place will give a thought to you at all.'

Synge reworked this scene with the Widow Quin more often than any other scene in Act I, gradually building up the Widow's character until she becomes a strong foil to Pegeen. The following notes and speeches are jotted down on the back of draft 'F' (1 January 1906):

'Make W.Q. pity stronger and Pegeen's admiration throughout III and II.'

'Make Widow's entry more *dramatic* more abrupt in a sense, slightly *emphastze* W.Q.'s wish to take him with her.'

'Make W.Q. take possession of the settle and her expulsion bring on curtain.'

w.q. Who'd blame a lively playboy if he rose his hand itself upon the pope of Rome?

w.q. You'll find maybe that those who do take pity on the poor lads of the world will stand you a sight longer than those who go romancing with their praising lies.

A fairly late draft includes the note 'work at contrast between Widow and Pegeen more fully'. However, apparently even in his final draft Synge was still not completely happy with the scene; on the back of the last page he has written, then struck out, 'Revise Exit of W.Q.'

⁴ Draft 'F' reads: '[*triumphantly*]. Do you hear that Widow Quin. [*She goes up to her defiantly.*] Go on now and be keeping company with aged trampers or what kind you will isn't me is the right company for the like of him and I a young and lively person with no records of distress.'

⁵ Draft 'F' gives the Widow Quin the following final speech:

[*with a touch of sadness*]. You've killed your father, and faced the peelers and shivered trembling through long nights abroad, but I'm thinking there's a store of greater torment will await you now if you go romancing on the blather of the likes of her and she waiting only on a sheepskin parchment from the Court of Rome to be wedded to Shawn Keogh of Killikeen.

⁶ All earlier drafts read 'the pope' for 'a bishop'.

⁷ Written at the bottom of the page of draft 'D' is the note 'Use as structural motif for act end Christy's knowledge of proposed match between S and P and by his reception of it a suggestion of his falling for Pegeen.'

WIDOW QUIN [*with amusement*]. Do you hear her now, young fellow? Do you hear the way she'll be rating at your own self when a week is by?[1]

PEGEEN [*to* CHRISTY]. Don't heed her. Tell her to go on into her pigsty[2] and not plague us here.[3]

WIDOW QUIN. I'm going; but he'll come with me.

PEGEEN [*shaking him*]. Are you dumb, young fellow?

CHRISTY [*timidly to* WIDOW QUIN]. God increase you; but I'm pot-boy in this place, and it's here I'd liefer stay.

PEGEEN [*triumphantly*]. Now you've heard him, and go on from this.[4]

WIDOW QUIN [*looking round the room*]. It's lonesome this hour crossing the hill, and if he won't come along with me, I'd have a right maybe to stop this night with yourselves. Let me stretch out on the settle, Pegeen Mike, and himself can lie by the hearth.

PEGEEN [*short and fiercely*]. Faith I won't. Quit off or I will send you now.

WIDOW QUIN [*gathering her shawl up*]. Well, it's a terror to be aged a score! [*To* CHRISTY.] God bless you now, young fellow, and let you be wary, or there's right torment will await you here if you go romancing with her like, and she waiting only, as they bade me say, on a sheep-skin parchment to be wed with Shawn Keogh of Killakeen.[5] [*She goes out.*]

CHRISTY [*going to* PEGEEN, *as she bolts door*]. What's that she's after saying?

PEGEEN. Lies and blather, you've no call to mind. Well isn't Shawn Keogh an impudent fellow to send up spying on me? Wait till I lay hands on him. Let him wait, I'm saying.

CHRISTY. And you're not wedding him at all?

PEGEEN. I wouldn't wed him if a bishop[6] came walking for to join us here.

CHRISTY. That God in glory may be thanked for that.[7]

PEGEEN. There's your bed now. I've put a quilt upon you I'm after quilting a while since with my own two hands, and you'd best

¹ Draft 'F' expands on Christy's interest in Pegeen:

PEGEEN [*brusquely*]. Set out that sop of straw beyond on the bench, for it's time you were going to rest.

CHRISTY [*relieved*]. I will then; but I wouldn't rest at all if I was thinking that you'd wed with him. . . .

PEGEEN [*bringing him a red quilt*]. Put that blather from your head I'm saying, and take that to lay upon you. A quilt I'm after quilting with my own two hands.

In the margin of this draft Synge has written 'work in clothes again', but he apparently changed his mind before draft 'G'. Originally Pegeen gave Christy a big shawl; draft 'E' enlarged on Christy's reaction to the quilt: 'The king of England would be proud to stretch himself out beneath the like of that, and isn't it great ease and quietness I'll have this night to rest and yawn and stretch me till the light of day.'

² Before the inclusion of the Widow Quin Synge included the following exchange here:

PEGEEN: You should have slept queer places the days you were out?

CHRISTY. Most times in deep ditches and under haystacks and deep beds of fern, but one night there was great rain I went into ⟨a⟩ place with walking trampers and women and children, and I'm telling you there is great villainy walking the world; there's fearful people living surely.

³ An early draft adds the direction *takes up a rosary*.
⁴ See Appendix B for earliest draft of the curtain scene. Another early draft in Notebook 32 ends with Christy questioning Pegeen's attitude towards his crime:

C.M. Whisper now P.M. if I'd come in at that door and said I'd never done anything worse than stealing a pen'orth of salt would you have spoken that gentle in me ear?

PEGEEN. Troth I would not Mister couldn't any fool steal a pinch of salt.

CHRISTY [*scratching his head*]. Well the Almighty was wise surely and He writing in the Holy Scriptures it was a queer terrible world.

Curtain

Christy's final sentiment, 'Oh wasn't I a foolish fellow' etc., occurs originally in Act II after Pegeen relents and tells him he can stay. It first appears here in draft 'D' (spring 1905).

stretch out now for your sleep, and may God give you a good rest till I call you in the morning when the cocks will crow.[1]

CHRISTY [*as she goes to inner room*]. May God and Mary and St. Patrick bless you and reward you for your kindly talk.[2] [*She shuts the door behind her. He settles his bed slowly, feeling the quilt with immense satisfaction.*[3]] Well it's a clean bed and soft with it, and it's great luck and company I've won me in the end of time—two fine women fighting for the likes of me—, till I'm thinking this night wasn't I a foolish fellow not to kill my father in the years gone by.[4]

CURTAIN

¹ The earliest draft of this scene ('Murder Will Out III') opens with Christy washing glasses as Kitty enters and introduces herself as Shawn's sister. (See Appendix B.) Synge apparently next contemplated opening on an empty stage ('Murder Will Out Act II'), but on the back of this second typescript draft he wrote, 'Try opening with looking-glass Christy admiring himself', and the notes: 'Christy behind counter. After a moment looks at himself in looking-glass, then brings it over to window and practises sad and ogling faces, looks from window and rushes into room. Girls come in see straw examine boots etc. Christy puts head in—.'

By draft 'C' the scene begins with Christy counting the jugs; on the back of draft 'D' Synge suggests the boot-polishing. A marginal note to draft 'C' reads 'work from start the tension of Ch.'; a note to draft 'E' (24 May 1905) reads 'Bring out Christy's new mood and cause of it.' However, the general tenor of Christy's speech varies little from the early drafts.

² Until the final typescript Christy counts seventy jugs, not eighty.

³ Draft 'H' (10 August 1906) reads [*He puts down her boots carefully in cupboard.*]

⁴ A marginal note to draft 'C' reads 'strengthen obliquely his hopes in the future', but there is no direct reference to marriage in any of the drafts of this speech.

⁵ After he determined the opening to this scene Synge changed his mind several times about the details of Christy's monologue and flight. Apparently he discarded the idea of the looking-glass for a time, for he writes in Notebook 34 (November 1906) 'Restore looking-glass making Christy hang it up at her command.' For some time too he considered making Christy hide behind the counter instead of in the inner room; on the back of draft 'E' (24 May 1905) he writes,

'Trying to open inner door—oh she's taken out the spoon she had lifting the latch. She's put it in the pig's mess maybe or let it fall in the yard. Oh where's the iron spoon where's the iron spoon? (running round the room). They're coming now and I as good as naked with the buttons fallen from my shirt (he darts in behind something as the door is pushed open).'

No draft examined contains the reference to the spoon being used as a latch (an incident Synge noted on his visit to the Blaskets in August 1905, see Oxford, *Prose*, p. 249), but draft 'F' does have Christy popping up from behind the counter, an action which is paralleled by Old Mahon in one of the intermediate drafts of the next act.

⁶ Kitty Kinsella appears in the first draft only (although a note to an early draft of TS. 'C' does contemplate making Sally Quin, one of the village girls, Shawn's sister). The next drafts have Susan Brady and Nell (or Ellen) McLaughlin entering together, Honor Blake arriving after the first two have already presented their gifts, followed still later by Sally Quin. A revision of draft 'G' (after July 1906) first introduces Sara Tansey and from then on the four girls arrive together with their gifts. (See note to list of persons, p. 55.)

⁷ Draft 'B' adds the reply, 'He's no sense for making game.'

ACT II

Scene as before. Brilliant morning light. CHRISTY, *looking bright and cheerful, is cleaning a girl's boot.*

CHRISTY [*to himself, counting jugs on dresser*].[1] Half a hundred beyond. Ten there. A score that's above. Eighty[2] jugs. Six cups and a broken one. Two plates. A power of glasses. Bottles, a school-master'd be hard set to count, and enough in them, I'm thinking, to drunken all the wealth and wisdom of the County Clare. [*He puts down the boot carefully.*][3] There's her boots now, nice and decent for her evening use, and isn't it grand brushes she has? [*He puts them down and goes by degrees to the looking-glass.*] Well, this'd be a fine place to be my whole life talking out with swearing Christians in place of my old dogs and cat, and I stalking around, smoking my pipe and drinking my fill, and never a day's work but drawing a cork an odd time, or wiping a glass, or rinsing out a shiny tumbler for a decent man. [*He takes the looking-glass from the wall and puts it on the back of a chair; then sits down in front of it and begins washing his face.*] Didn't I know rightly I was handsome, though it was the divil's own mirror we had beyond, would twist a squint across an angel's brow, and I'll be growing fine from this day, the way I'll have a soft lovely skin on me and won't be the like of the clumsy young fellows do be ploughing all times in the earth and dung.[4] [*He starts.*] Is she coming again? [*He looks out.*] Stranger girls. God help me, where'll I hide myself away and my long neck naked to the world. [*He looks out.*] I'd best go to the room maybe till I'm dressed again.

[*He gathers up his coat and the looking-glass, and runs into the inner room.*[5] *The door is pushed open, and* SUSAN BRADY *looks in, and knocks on door.*]

SUSAN. There's nobody in it. [*Knocks again.*]

NELLY [*pushing her in and following her, with* HONOR BLAKE *and* SARA TANSEY].[6] It'd be early for them both to be out walking the hill.

SUSAN. I'm thinking Shawn Keogh was making game of us and there's no such man in it at all.[7]

¹ The following exchange is not struck out until draft 'F' (9 January 1906):

NELL. Oh, isn't Pegeen a lucky girl to have passed the whole night talking with the like of him?

SUSAN. She is then. And I'd think little to put a bag on my back and go walking the flinty ways of the world till I'd set my eyes on the like of him, for he should have great height I'm thinking and a fine leg on him, and a smile would knock a lep out of St. Martin's moon.

² Not until after November 1906 (Notebook 34) does Synge think of making one of the girls put on Christy's boots. In this same notebook Synge writes, 'Write up Sara Tansey' and 'Sara Tansey is the character of this scene'; he also suggests further speeches for her: 'There's not another girl in Mayo has had her foot in the boot of a man had killed his da.'

³ Notebook 34 contains further instructions concerning the village girls: 'Strengthen girls' scene.'

'Sara I walked five miles one time to see a man had fired at an agent he was a nice lad but this man should beat him out.'

'I yoked the ass-cart and drove to Keel to see the lad slit the lady's nose in Achill. He was a great devil.'

'I wonder if he's married. Hasn't Pegeen great chance lodging in the house with him.'

'Make them take liberties with Pegeen's shawl or hats?'

'Make Widow and Christy drink together arms linked (as P enters).'

'I wonder would he have songs I heard a man singing Munster songs one time, gallant songs I tell you the way I had to do a penance for every single line.'

⁴ Notebook 34 also suggests, 'Should girls see Mahon from window in scene 1st II?' and draft 'H' (10 August 1906) includes the following scene:

HONOR [*at window*]. . . . . There's a fellow in the furze beyond. That's him maybe.

SARA [*running up to window with one boot in her hand*]. Is it there stretched back in the furze? That old-looking warrior with the bandaged head? Stop your talking and we fooled today. [*Comes down stage putting on boot, singing, and clasping her hands in mock misery.*]

> One shoe off and one shoe on
> Oh it's the devil's luck our man's gone [*admiring boots*]

There's a great pair.

SUSAN [*sneeringly*]. You think you're a wonder Sara Tansey, and you in the boots of a man has killed his da.

SARA [*putting on other boot*]. And you're thinking you'd give your life and all to have the strings out of them itself to lace your Sunday stays. [*Walking across admiring the boots.*] They fit me well and I'm thinking I'll keep them. . . .

⁵ The version in Notebook 34 reads, 'This place you'd be ashamed going to confession without a thing at all but what a child might do—'.

⁶ Draft 'D' reads *as meek as a two-year-old infant.*

HONOR [*pointing to straw and quilt*]. Look at that. He's been sleeping there in the night. Well, it'll be a hard case if he's gone off now, the way we'll never set our eyes on a man killed his father, and we after rising early and destroying ourselves running fast on the hill.[1]

NELLY. Are you thinking them's his boots?

SARA [*taking them up*]. If they are, there should be his father's track on them. Did you never read in the papers the way murdered men do bleed and drip?

SUSAN. Is that blood there, Sara Tansey?

SARA [*smelling it*]. That's bog water, I'm thinking, but it's his own they are surely, for I never seen the like of them for whity mud, and red mud, and turf on them, and the fine sands of the sea. That man's been walking, I'm telling you. [*She goes down right, putting on one of his boots.*][2]

SUSAN [*going to window*]. Maybe he's stolen off to Belmullet with the boots of Michael James, and you'd have a right so to follow after him, Sara Tansey, and you the one yoked the ass cart and drove ten miles to set your eyes on the man bit the yellow lady's nostril on the northern shore.[3] [*She looks out.*][4]

SARA [*running to window, with one boot on*]. Don't be talking, and we fooled to-day. [*Putting on other boot.*] There's a pair do fit me well, and I'll be keeping them for walking to the priest, when you'd be ashamed this place, going up winter and summer with nothing worth while to confess at all.[5]

HONOR [*who has been listening at inner door*]. Whisht! there's some one inside the room. [*She pushes door a chink open.*] It's a man.

[SARA *kicks off boots and puts them where they were. They all stand in a line looking through chink.*]

SARA. I'll call him. Mister! Mister! [*He puts in his head.*] Is Pegeen within?

CHRISTY [*coming in as meek as a mouse,[6] with the looking-glass held behind his back.*] She's above on the cnuceen, seeking the nanny goats, the way she'd have a sup of goat's milk for to colour my tea.

SARA. And asking your pardon, is it you's the man killed his father?

¹ Late drafts read [*picking package from table*].

² Except for the first draft when Ellen brings a dictionary instead of the laying pullet (see Appendix B), the gifts remain the same although their order varies. Until Sara Tansey appears, the Widow Quin brings in the cake, explaining that Pegeen's cakes are always mouldy and old.

³ In draft 'K' the direction reads [*coming in quickly on his speech*]. Originally the Widow was simply Sally Quin, another village girl, bringing a piece of cake as her gift to Christy. In one of the earliest drafts ('A'?) Sally is described as 'a voluble girl' and greets Christy: '[*holding out her hand to him over the counter*]. My thousand welcomes to you, Mister——If you're a great terror itself. We do be quiet in this place without a lad in it would raise his hand on anything but an old ass or a dog, and it'll be grand for boys and girls I'm thinking to be talking with yourself.' In the margin of this scene Synge has written 'test speed', and on the back of the page the note 'work up whole scene with girls and if possible get Sally Quin into story'. Draft 'B' still retains Sally Quin in this scene but references in Synge's notes to revisions of 'B' are made to a Widow Porter, in revisions of 'C' to a Widow O'Flinn who becomes the Widow Quin and takes over Sally's role before TS. 'D'. By this time (draft 'C' of Act I) the Widow had also been incorporated into the first act.

⁴ Draft 'E' (24 May 1905) has the marginal note '(Make her flatter and compliment Christy because of the girls who have come in) Strengthen whole scene and her part in particular.' A late fragment (possibly 'K') adds the words 'the way we'll see if he's a hero or what kind at all'. Synge does not appear to have thought of the sports until the late drafts (possibly 'J', November 1906).

CHRISTY [*sidling toward the nail where the glass was hanging*]. I am, God help me!

SARA [*taking eggs she has brought*].[1] Then my thousand welcomes to you, and I've run up with a brace of duck's eggs for your food to-day. Pegeen's ducks is no use, but these are the real rich sort. Hold out your hand and you'll see it's no lie I'm telling you.

CHRISTY [*coming forward shyly, and holding out his left hand*]. They're a great and weighty size.

SUSAN. And I run up with a pat of butter, for it'd be a poor thing to have you eating your spuds dry, and you after running a great way since you did destroy your da.

CHRISTY. Thank you kindly.

HONOR. And I brought you a little cut of a cake, for you should have a thin stomach on you and you that length walking the world.

NELLY. And I brought you a little laying pullet—boiled and all she is— was crushed at the fall of night by the curate's car. Feel the fat of that breast, Mister.[2]

CHRISTY. It's bursting, surely. [*He feels it with the back of his left hand, in which he holds the presents.*]

SARA. Will you pinch it? Is your right hand too sacred for to use at all? [*She slips round behind him.*] It's a glass he has. Well I never seen to this day, a man with a looking-glass held to his back. Them that kills their fathers is a vain lot surely.

[GIRLS *giggle.*]

CHRISTY [*smiling innocently and piling presents on glass*]. I'm very thankful to you all to-day. . . .

WIDOW QUIN [*coming in quickly, at door*]. Sara Tansey, Susan Brady, Honor Blake! What in glory has you here at this hour of day?[3]

GIRLS [*giggling*]. That's the man killed his father.

WIDOW QUIN [*coming to them*]. I know well it's the man; and I'm after putting him down in the sports below for racing, lepping, pitching, and the Lord knows what.[4]

[1] In the margin of draft 'C' Synge suggested 'cut out breakfast?' but in all the early drafts the scene is expanded, as in draft 'E' below:

CHRISTY. Fasting if you please. . . . Waiting for herself is above milking the goats.

WIDOW QUIN. You'd as well wait for her to go milking the crows. [*She takes a jug from counter and smells it.*] There's a sup of milk is only sour a trifle. Sit down now and we'll make you a bit of a breakfast while herself's out racing on the hill.

CHRISTY. I'd liefer wait.

WIDOW QUIN. There's bosh from an empty man! For why would you wait?

CHRISTY. I'd liefer wait for Pegeen I'm saying and thank you kindly for your care.

WIDOW QUIN [*pushing him over to the bench left*]. Sit down then and talk to us, and don't be grinning your ears off didn't you hear me say.

[2] An early draft of 'Murder Will Out' ('A'?) describes the breakfast scene in more detail:

CHRISTY [*coming from behind counter*]. Well, I'll have a small bit with you now. [*He sits down at a low table and they crowd round him giving him his breakfast. One butters the bread and cuts it, holding the loaf against her body and cutting towards herself. Another pours out the tea and puts in milk and sugar stirring it herself. Another brings over the salt.*]

[3] Early drafts give a different direction, [*struggling with fears*].

[4] The first edition has a semicolon after 'story'; the unpunctuated version given here follows all the drafts. Earlier drafts give Christy the reply '[*shyly*]. Is it the story of my young life, or my walking the world?'

[5] Stage direction taken from earlier drafts.

SARA [*exuberantly*]. That's right, Widow Quin. I'll bet my dowry that he'll lick the world.

WIDOW QUIN. If you will, you'd have a right to have him fresh and nourished in place of nursing a feast. [*Taking presents.*] Are you fasting or fed, young fellow?

CHRISTY. Fasting, if you please.[1]

WIDOW QUIN [*loudly*]. Well, you're the lot. Stir up now and give him his breakfast. [*To* CHRISTY.] Come here to me [*she puts him on bench beside her while the* GIRLS *make tea and get his breakfast*] and let you tell us your story before Pegeen will come, in place of grinning your ears off like the moon of May.[2]

CHRISTY [*beginning to be pleased*].[3] It's a long story[4] you'd be destroyed listening.

WIDOW QUIN. Don't be letting on to be shy, a fine, gamey, treacherous lad the like of you. Was it in your house beyond you cracked his skull?

CHRISTY [*shy, but flattered*]. It was not. We were digging spuds in his cold, sloping, stony divil's patch of a field.

WIDOW QUIN. And you went asking money of him, or making talk of getting a wife would drive him from his farm?

CHRISTY. I did not, then; but there I was, digging and digging, and 'You squinting idiot,' says he, 'let you walk down now and tell the priest you'll wed the Widow Casey in a score of days.'

WIDOW QUIN. And what kind was she?

CHRISTY [*with horror*]. A walking terror from beyond the hills, and she two score and five years, and two hundredweights and five pounds in the weighing scales, with a limping leg on her, and a blinded eye, and she a woman of noted misbehaviour with the old and young. [*He begins gnawing a chicken leg.*][5]

GIRLS [*clustering round him, serving him*]. Glory be!

WIDOW QUIN. And what did he want driving you to wed with her? [*She takes a bit of the chicken.*]

¹ In draft 'I' 'divil' is struck out and 'angels' written in above. Notebook 29 records the phrase 'pigs make garters of shirt'.

² Additional stage direction from draft 'I'.

³ Not until October–November 1906 does the story of the fight take on its final form with the description of the Widow Casey. A marginal note to draft 'C' reads 'give folk-political basis to murder quarrel?' but with one exception the story follows the lines of the earliest drafts:

SALLY QUIN [*putting her hand on his shoulder*]. Tell us now my darling boy. . . . We never seen a man before that killed his father.

NELL. It's in a wild bewildered country we do live Mister, the way it's little at all we do hear of the wonders of the world.

HONOR. Let you tell us now Mister we're all safe girls. [*Giggles.*]

CHRISTY [*wiping his mouth with his sleeve*]. Me father was a big terrible man and he came down on me with a great thorn branch in his hand [*he pauses and nods*]—I was digging spuds in the garden. It was an east windy day, and the sun was sinking out of the sky [*he scratches his head*]—'The next spud you split' says he, 'I'll split your skull.' 'You will not, if I can help it,' says I. 'The next spud you stand on,' says he, 'I'll flatten you out, like an egg that's passed under a dray.' 'You will not, if I can help it,' says I. Then the sun come out then between the cloud and the clift in the hill, and it shining green in my face, I drove down the loy into the earth and when I riz it there was two split spuds on the tip. 'God have mercy on your soul,' says he, raising his tree. 'Amen for your own,' says I, lifting the loy. [*He pauses for applause.*]

A slightly different version in Notebook 28 incorporates the ballad-singing motif (see Appendix B); it occurs on the same page as the scenario 'Deaf Mutes for Ireland' (See *Plays, Book One*):

I was sitting out under a tree singing of songs and I thinking of the lost glory of Ireland and the bloody Saxons and the like of that. It was a silent kind of a day when you'd hear a man walking across the width of a glen and you'd see the smoke rising twisting from the burning furze. Well the old boy was rising ⟨over⟩ the road with a hard woman and they heard me singing and were swearing out. Then he come up where I was and when I heard him coming I began digging and digging and I thinking how well I was doing it in his cold sloping stony divil's patch of a field.

CHRISTY [*eating with growing satisfaction*]. He was letting on I was wanting a protector from the harshness of the world, and he without a thought the whole while but how he'd have her hut to live in and her gold to drink.

WIDOW QUIN. There's maybe worse than a dry hearth and a widow woman and your glass at night. So you hit him then?

CHRISTY [*getting almost excited*]. I did not. 'I won't wed her,' says I, 'when all know she did suckle me for six weeks when I came into the world, and she a hag this day with a tongue on her has the crows and seabirds scattered, the way they wouldn't cast a shadow on her garden with the dread of her curse.'

WIDOW QUIN [*teasingly*]. That one should be right company!

SARA [*eagerly*]. Don't mind her. Did you kill him then?

CHRISTY. 'She's too good for the like of you,' says he, 'and go on now or I'll flatten you out like a crawling beast has passed under a dray.' 'You will not if I can help it,' says I. 'Go on,' says he, 'or I'll have the divil making garters of your limbs to-night.'[1] 'You will not if I can help it,' says I. [*He sits bolt up, brandishing his mug.*][2]

SARA. You were right surely.

CHRISTY [*impressively*]. With that the sun came out between the cloud and the hill, and it shining green in my face. 'God have mercy on your soul,' says he, lifting a scythe; 'or on your own,' says I, raising the loy.[3]

SUSAN. That's a grand story.

HONOR. He tells it lovely.

CHRISTY [*flattered and confident, waving bone*]. He gave a drive with the scythe, and I gave a lep to the east. Then I turned around with my back to the north, and I hit a blow on the ridge of his skull, laid him stretched out, and he split to the knob of his gullet. [*He raises the chicken bone to his Adam's apple.*]

GIRLS [*together*]. Well, you're a marvel! Oh, God bless you! You're the lad surely!

SUSAN. I'm thinking the Lord God sent him this road to make a second husband to the Widow Quin, and she with a great yearning to be

¹ Early drafts ('A' and 'B'), before the introduction of Sara Tansey, add further dialogue which is not completely eliminated until draft 'F':

SALLY QUIN. Would you do the like of that if you had a wife, Mister.

CHRISTY [*looking round with triumph*]. My wife'd want to mind.

SUSAN. Maybe you've a wife already beyond in the south?

CHRISTY. If I have itself I'm thinking I'll be needing another from this day.

NELL [*pushing* SALLY *forward so that she sits on his knee*]. There's a girl is wanting to wed.

CHRISTY [*putting his arm round her*]. Let you not be shy, God help you.

[PEGEEN *comes in and stands aghast.*]

Intermediate drafts, such as draft 'C', have the Widow Quin pushing Nell down on Christy's knee:

NELL [*holding on to his neck*]. Will you behave yourself Widow Quin. There's no girl in the parish so eager as you for to wed, and maybe he'd do you now.

² Struck out of a fragment from draft 'K' is the following speech:

WIDOW QUIN [*putting her arm round him*]. Don't tease him for I've a mind to keep him and protect him from the torments of the world or his father's ghost when it's often those that have a great story do have hell's terrors hid within.

³ This speech originally had 'priests' for 'preachers' and 'bellies' for 'stomachs'; the final alterations are made to TS. 'I', perhaps by another hand. According to the copy registered by the Lord Chamberlain's Office, this speech was cut in the first production.

⁴ In his notes for this scene in Notebook 34 Synge wrote on 2 November ⟨1906⟩ 'Give W.Q. speech as she drinks with him. Revise II . . . and one speech to Widow? giving S.T. one speech at end.' On 6 November he wrote, in the same Notebook, 'Give Sara Tansey one characteristic speech at II's end.'

⁵ Synge's notes in Notebook 34 read 'Make girls interesting. Sportive breakfast scene. Christy is drinking with the Widow Quin on his left and Sara on his right when Pegeen comes in.'

⁶ Apparently the Widow Quin does not mention the sports until TS. 'G' (28 July 1906). An early draft has the exit line:

SALLY QUIN. When you're wearied talking with herself come down across the village, young fellow and there'll be a welcome before you. [PEGEEN *goes towards her, but she slips out and* PEGEEN *slams the door shut, then goes to counter and arranges some things, while* CHRISTY *wriggles about uneasily not knowing what to do, watching her out of the corner of his eyes.*]

⁷ On the back of the early 'Murder Will Out' draft Synge has scribbled,

PEGEEN [*simply*]. Eggs, fresh butter, chickens, cock you up indeed! If the lads heard tell the way you are there wouldn't be left a father living in Kilamuck at the fall of night.

wedded though all dread her here. Lift him on her knee, Sara Tansey.[1]

WIDOW QUIN. Don't tease him.[2]

SARA [*going over to dresser and counter very quickly, and getting two glasses and porter*]. You're heroes surely, and let you drink a supeen with your arms linked like the outlandish lovers in the sailor's song. [*She links their arms and gives them the glasses.*] There now. Drink a health to the wonders of the western world, the pirates, preachers, poteen-makers, with the jobbing jockies, parching peelers, and the juries fill their stomachs[3] selling judgments of the English law. [*Brandishing the bottle.*]

WIDOW QUIN. That's a right toast, Sara Tansey. Now Christy.[4]

[*They drink with their arms linked, he drinking with his left hand, she with her right. As they are drinking,* PEGEEN MIKE *comes in with a milk can and stands aghast.*[5] *They all spring away from* CHRISTY. *He goes down left.* WIDOW QUIN *remains seated.*]

PEGEEN [*angrily*]. What is it you're wanting [*to* SARA]?

SARA [*twisting her apron*]. An ounce of tobacco.

PEGEEN. Have you tuppence?

SARA. I've forgotten my purse.

PEGEEN. Then you'd best be getting it and not be fooling us here. [*To the* WIDOW QUIN, *with more elaborate scorn.*] And what is it you're wanting, Widow Quin?

WIDOW QUIN [*insolently*]. A penn'orth of starch.

PEGEEN [*breaking out*]. And you without a white shift or a shirt in your whole family since the drying of the flood. I've no starch for the like of you, and let you walk on now to Killamuck.

WIDOW QUIN [*turning to* CHRISTY, *as she goes out with the* GIRLS]. Well, you're mighty huffy this day, Pegeen Mike, and you young fellow, let you not forget the sports and racing when the noon is by.[6] [*They go out.*]

PEGEEN [*imperiously*]. Fling out that rubbish and put them cups away.[7] [CHRISTY *tidies away in great haste.*] Shove in the bench by the wall. [*He does so.*] And hang that glass on the nail. What disturbed it at all?

¹ Draft 'F' reads [*cajolingly*] for [*very meekly*]. Draft 'G' offers a slightly different apology from Christy, 'decent only and squeezing blackheads from my skin'. A fragment of draft 'I' makes Pegeen reply, 'And why couldn't you leave it hanging? You think you're a great beauty maybe but there's light that corner to show what share of good looks you can boast at all.'

² A marginal note to draft 'F' reads 'Add speech for Christy'. Struck out of draft 'K' are additional directions for Pegeen: 'Whisht I'm saying, and let you mind your business or quit off from this. [*She sings a verse from 'Larry'* ⟨'The Night before Larry was Stretched'⟩. *He comes across with a loy in his hand, then when she pauses*].' Notebook 34 suggests [*sings the Croppy Boy in snatches to irritate him*]. Not until draft 'I' (November 1906) does Synge strike out the instruction [PEGEEN *sings a hanging ballad through this scene*].

³ Draft 'F' adds the direction [*With a cry of horror*]. Not until the galley proofs did Synge alter 'pa' to 'da'.

⁴ The earliest draft of this incident ('A'?) is more explicit: 'It was a fine story of a man was hanged for killing his wife.'

⁵ A list of phrases in Notebook 28 includes the note 'Greek sailors eating a sort of "frish-frash" Indian meal, raw cabbage, boiled down as thin as gruel', evidently a description Synge overheard during his travels in the west.

CHRISTY [*very meekly*]. I was making myself decent only, and this a fine country for young lovely girls.¹

PEGEEN [*sharply*]. Whisht your talking of girls. [*Goes to counter right.*]

CHRISTY. Wouldn't any wish to be decent in a place. . . .

PEGEEN. Whisht, I'm saying.²

CHRISTY [*looks at her face for a moment with great misgivings, then as a last effort, takes up a loy, and goes towards her, with feigned assurance*]. It was with a loy the like of that I killed my father.

PEGEEN [*still sharply*]. You've told me that story six times since the dawn of day.

CHRISTY [*reproachfully*]. It's a queer thing you wouldn't care to be hearing it and them girls after walking four miles to be listening to me now.

PEGEEN [*turning round astonished*]. Four miles!

CHRISTY [*apologetically*]. Didn't himself say there were only bona fides living in the place?

PEGEEN. It's bona fides by the road they are, but that lot come over the river lepping the stones. It's not three perches when you go like that and I was down this morning looking on the papers the post-boy does have in his bag [*with meaning and emphasis*], for there was great news this day, Christopher Mahon. [*She goes into room left.*]

CHRISTY [*suspiciously*]. Is it news of my murder?

PEGEEN [*inside*]. Murder indeed!

CHRISTY [*loudly*]. A murdered da?³

PEGEEN [*coming in again and crossing right*]. There was not, but a story filled half a page of the hanging of a man.⁴ Ah, that should be a fearful end, young fellow, and it worst of all for a man destroyed his da, for the like of him would get small mercies, and when it's dead he is, they'd put him in a narrow grave, with cheap sacking wrapping him round, and pour down quicklime on his head, the way you'd see a woman pouring any frish-frash⁵ from a cup.

¹ Early drafts add the direction [*she pats him on the neck*]. Notebook 29 first records the speech, 'it'd make the green stones cry to think of it'.

² A late fragment gives the alternative direction [*finally terrified*].

³ The marginal note to an early draft reads 'make P. frighten him more definitely to motive his attempted retreat'. Early drafts include an additional speech by Pegeen here: '[*triumphant still beginning to play with him*]. On your naked feet is it?'

⁴ On the same page of Notebook 28 listing phrases overheard in Mayo and directly following the description of 'frish-frash' is the sentence, 'Seals crying in the bay a "lonesome sound"'.

⁵ Early drafts (before 'G') include variations on themes which Synge finally restricted or eliminated altogether:

CHRISTY [*getting his boots and realizing the situation as he puts them on*]. I'm thinking it's my own bloody destiny this day is making circuit here, and I after thinking last night as I sat on this stool I was shut of the great lonesomeness of the world, and there I am now starting again to be looking out on women and on girls the like of you—the way the needy fallen spirits do be looking on the Lord.

PEGEEN. With your fine story and your share of talk you should have girls and plenty.

CHRISTY. It's easy for the like of you to be talking of plenty and you with your shape and shop-stores and your share of gold, but there's great lonesomeness for a poor man is passing pauper on the highways of the world.

PEGEEN. I do be thinking odd times it is the whole world is lacking decent company and not poor men only would be lonesome and they great thousands in north Mayo now.

CHRISTY. And are you thinking thousands isn't lonesome at all?

PEGEEN. Odd times I do be thinking it's the whole world is lacking decent company for I've heard the poets to say the heart itself is lonesome in the lover's kiss.

CHRISTY [*bitterly*]. The poets will be talking surely but it's little they know maybe of tramping abroad when you'll be passing small towns. . . .

Draft 'I' still retains a form of Pegeen's comment on the lonesomeness of the lover's kiss and a rejected remnant of a later draft (possibly 'K', late November 1906) reads:

PEGEEN [*half playfully*]. It's a queer thing poor men would be lonesome and they great thousands in North Mayo now.

CHRISTY [*reproachfully*]. Is it with a kind of gaming that you'd meet my words and walking round beneath a desolation would strike terror in the demons held the seventh seal of Hell?

PEGEEN [*sadly*]. It is not Christy Mahon, for I'm thinking all souls are lacking decent fellowship since Eve and Adam did despise the law, and I've heard poets to say the heart itself is lonesome in the lover's kiss.

⁶ Notebook 34 contains the passage 'And you going forward till you'd take a mighty oath you could hear the North wind making whistles of your ribs within. 14/1/06'. Just below it, on the same page of dialogue, is another speech which may have been intended for the same passage: 'the roads stretching before you and they shining with their depth of water and the glimmer of the sky'.

CHRISTY [*very miserably*]. Oh, God help me. Are you thinking I'm safe? You were saying at the fall of night, I was shut of jeopardy and I here with yourselves.

PEGEEN [*severely*]. You'll be shut of jeopardy no place if you go talking with a pack of wild girls the like of them, do be walking abroad with the peelers, talking whispers at the fall of night.

CHRISTY [*with terror*]. And you're thinking they'd tell?

PEGEEN [*with mock sympathy*]. Who knows, God help you.

CHRISTY [*loudly*]. What joy would they have to bring hanging to the likes of me?

PEGEEN. It's queer joys they have, and who knows the thing they'd do, if it'd make the green stones cry itself to think of you swaying and swiggling at the butt of a rope,[1] and you with a fine, stout neck, God bless you! the way you'd be a half an hour, in great anguish, getting your death.

CHRISTY [*getting his boots and putting them on*].[2] If there's that terror of them, it'd be best, maybe, I went on wandering like Esau or Cain and Abel on the sides of Neifin or the Erris Plain.

PEGEEN [*beginning to play with him*]. It would, maybe, for I've heard the Circuit Judges this place is a heartless crew.[3]

CHRISTY [*bitterly*]. It's more than judges this place is a heartless crew. [*Looking up at her.*] And isn't it a poor thing to be starting again and I a lonesome fellow[4] will be looking out on women and girls the way the needy fallen spirits do be looking on the Lord?

PEGEEN. What call have you to be that lonesome when there's poor girls walking Mayo in their thousands now?

CHRISTY [*grimly*]. It's well you know what call I have. It's well you know it's a lonesome thing to be passing small towns[5] with the lights shining sideways when the night is down, or going in strange places with a dog nosing before you and a dog nosing behind, or drawn to the cities where you'd hear a voice kissing and talking deep love in every shadow of the ditch, and you passing on with an empty hungry stomach failing from your heart.[6]

[1] The early 'Murder Will Out' drafts add the exchange:

PEGEEN. You're talking as if you were after being a tramp from your birth, when you said last night it was a week only since you'd quit the place where you were reared.

CHRISTY. I'll be a tramp I'm thinking from this day to my death and hasn't a man a right to look before him, when he's sickened with looking behind?

[2] The early 'Murder Will Out' draft (TS. 'A'?) includes an incident which early in 1903 Synge had considered using for a one-act play (see 'Aughavanna Play', *Plays*, Book One):

PEGEEN. How many girls had you beyond in the south?

CHRISTY. There was Kitty Kinsella, I rarely even spoke to and there was his Lordship's daughter a rich lovely lady had a big window with a yellow blind in it looking out on the park. And it was a great light she had behind her, the way I used to sit out in the park at the butt of the trees and be looking on her lovely shadow the time she'd be combing her hair.

PEGEEN. God help you. And what was it came out of that.

CHRISTY [*with a painful recollection*]. I was charged for poaching, and the keeper shot at a fine lurching cur I had a very divil for running with hares, and put two grains of swan-drop behind in his rump.

[3] This exchange, heavily revised in draft 'C', reads:

CHRISTY. I wished to God I was letting on, but I'm telling you it's lonesome I was in my own land and lonesome walking the world.

PEGEEN. Well it's a story I'm not understanding at all that you'd be lonesome and you a fine lad with the great swaggery to raise your hand against the kings of the world and the great judgments of Eternal Law—

Still dissatisfied, Synge added the marginal note 'strengthen and tune', and tried several variations of Christy's reply on the back of the page:

An odd time I'd ⟨be⟩ taking on, an odd time I'd be
  in great spirit   in fair spirits and joy
  and an odd time   and an odd time again
  I'd be asking myself   I'd be asking myself
    if I'd grow an old   would I grow in ⟨the⟩ end
    divil like himself—   of time a swearing divil
    and I three score   like my murdered pa?
    and ten—

[4] Early drafts add the direction [*looking at her intently*].

[5] On the back of draft 'B' Synge has scribbled a slightly different ending to this scene:

CHRISTY [*looks at her then looks away rubs his eyes and looks at her again, then in a small intense voice with a new hope*]—You've a kind lovely look in your eyes Pegeen Mike a look I'm not dreading to quit this day if it'd. . . .

PEGEEN. Think what it'll be feeling the hangman knotting and hitching his hitches round the butt of your neck.

   [CHRISTY *goes to the door. She calls him back then a moment after entry of* SALLY—]

PEGEEN. I'm thinking you're an odd man, Christy Mahon. The oddest walking fellow I ever set my eyes on to this hour to-day.[1]

CHRISTY. What would any be but odd men and they living lonesome in the world?

PEGEEN. I'm not odd, and I'm my whole life with my father only.

CHRISTY [*with infinite admiration*]. How would a lovely handsome woman the like of you be lonesome when all men should be thronging around to hear the sweetness of your voice, and the little infant children should be pestering your steps I'm thinking, and you walking the roads.

PEGEEN. I'm hard set to know what way a coaxing fellow the like of yourself should be lonesome either.

CHRISTY. Coaxing!

PEGEEN. Would you have me think a man never talked with the girls would have the words you've spoken to-day? It's only letting on you are to be lonesome, the way you'd get around me now.[2]

CHRISTY. I wish to God I was letting on; but I was lonesome all times and born lonesome, I'm thinking, as the moon of dawn. [*Going to door.*]

PEGEEN [*puzzled by his talk*]. Well, it's a story I'm not understanding at all why you'd be worse than another, Christy Mahon, and you a fine lad with the great savagery to destroy your da.[3]

CHRISTY.[4] It's little I'm understanding myself, saving only that my heart's scalded this day, and I going off stretching out the earth between us, the way I'll not be waking near you another dawn of the year till the two of us do arise to hope or judgment with the saints of God, and now I'd best be going with my wattle in my hand, for hanging is a poor thing [*turning to go*], and it's little welcome only is left me in this house to-day.[5]

PEGEEN [*sharply*]. Christy! [*He turns round.*] Come here to me. [*He goes towards her.*] Lay down that switch and throw some sods on the fire. You're pot-boy in this place, and I'll not have you mitch off from us now.

CHRISTY. You were saying I'd be hanged if I stay.

¹ The early 'Murder Will Out' draft ('A'?) includes the following exchange, which Synge heavily questioned in the margin:

CHRISTY. Would you think bad to marry a poor lad ⟨the⟩ like of me?

PEGEEN. Did ever anyone see the like of you? Can you not say three words without talking of being wed?

CHRISTY. I was only thinking if I was here in this house seeing you combing your hair and washing your feet maybe at the fall of night, it'll not be a great while till I'd be crying out after your shadow and it passing the hill.

PEGEEN. And wouldn't you be hard set to cry louder than welcome? We'd put you to scare off the scald crows do come eating chickens in the month of May.

CHRISTY [*going a step or two towards door*]. I'm best maybe going forward seeking a quiet place where there won't be girls the like of you putting red rage in my heart.

² Earlier drafts read [*first with uncertainty*] in place of this direction.

³ A marginal note to the revised draft 'C' reads 'give rapturous speech to Christy'. An early fragment may relate to this time:

CHRISTY [*with a shriek of delight*]. Well then glory be to praises be to God and the saints and the glory of Heaven and wasn't I a foolish fellow not to kill my father in the years gone by?

[PEGEEN *watching him with interest. He flings turf on the fire, and then runs across right and vaults up on the counter beside her and begins polishing glasses. He flings up a glass into the air and catches it again, it is not quite empty and some dregs of porter fall over him.*]

PEGEEN [*laughing*]. Are you going mad young fellow, let you not be breaking our glasses. God knows when the crockery woman will come passing again.

CHRISTY. God help the crockery woman and the glasses too. [*He dries his face with ⟨the towel⟩ then holds it in his hand during following scene.*]

[*As he talks she pulls away along the counter as far as she ⟨can⟩ and he sidles along counter till he pins her into the corner next dresser, where scene ends.*]

CHRISTY. Won't it be grand now I'm saying sitting here and lying down with me fill eaten, and looking on yourself and no old father snuffling and snarling close to my heels? Oh, was it well I did turning in here, and I nearly dead with wishing for death.

PEGEEN. It was a queer-looking fright you were and it's no lie. If it hadn't been for the fine story you had we'd have turned you off walking in a bit of a jiffy I'm telling you.

CHRISTY. And small blame it'd have been to you and ⟨me⟩ the like of a tramp.

PEGEEN. Small blame surely, yet when I heard your story I liked you then for I've a soft heart though it's myself says it that shouldn't.

CHRISTY. Isn't it a great joy for a man to have a story to be telling to the girls? I'll be grand now I'm thinking. . . .

⁴ Not until the final typescript did Synge strike out the additional phrase 'or combing your hair'.

⁵ Originally Synge had planned to include the love-scene between Christy and Pegeen here. A note on the back of draft 'B' reads 'Make the Widow overhear at window the love-scene between Christy and Pegeen (?) so as in conjunction with—'. In a remnant marked 'J. II' Christy asks Pegeen not to marry Shawn, and she replies, 'I will maybe and I'll maybe not. If you're such a hero, let us see you doing wonders in the races and the sports below.'

A fragment marked 'Remnants II K' develops this further:

CHRISTY [*looking at her intently*]. And to think I'm waking and not dreaming at all.

[*Notes continued on pp. 114 and 116.*]

PEGEEN [*quite kindly at last*]. I'm after going down and reading the fearful crimes of Ireland for two weeks or three, and there wasn't a word of your murder. [*Getting up and going over to the counter.*] They've likely not found the body. You're safe so with ourselves.¹

CHRISTY [*astonished, slowly*]. It's making game of me you were [*following her with fearful joy*],² and I can stay so, working at your side, and I not lonesome from this mortal day.

PEGEEN. What's to hinder you staying, except the widow woman or the young girls would inveigle you off?³

CHRISTY [*with rapture*]. And I'll have your words from this day filling my ears, and that look is come upon you meeting my two eyes, and I watching you loafing around in the warm sun, or rinsing your ankles when the night is come.⁴

PEGEEN [*kindly, but a little embarrassed*]. I'm thinking you'll be a loyal young lad to have working around, and if you vexed me a while since with your leaguing with the girls, I wouldn't give a thraneen for a lad hadn't a mighty spirit in him and a gamey heart.⁵

[SHAWN KEOGH *runs in carrying a cleeve on his back, followed by the* WIDOW QUIN.]⁶

SHAWN [*to* PEGEEN]. I was passing below and I seen your mountainy sheep eating cabbages in Jimmy's field. Run up or they'll be bursting surely.

PEGEEN. Oh, God mend them! [*She puts a shawl over her head and runs out.*]

CHRISTY [*looking from one to the other, still in high spirits*]. I'd best go to her aid maybe. I'm handy with ewes.

WIDOW QUIN [*closing the door*]. She can do that much, and there is Shaneen has long speeches for to tell you now. [*She sits down with an amused⁷ smile.*]

SHAWN [*taking something from his pocket and offering it to* CHRISTY]. Do you see that, Mister?

CHRISTY [*looking at it*]. The half of a ticket to the Western States!

SHAWN [*trembling with anxiety*]. I'll give it to you and my new hat [*pulling it out of hamper*]; and my breeches with the double seat

¹ Struck out of a late fragment is the interjection by a puzzled Christy, 'And you're giving me that lot is it because I did destroy my da?'

² Draft 'I' originally read 'the holy peace'. Struck out of a late fragment '(J'?) after this speech of Shawn's is a comment by the Widow Quin: '[*chuckling*]. That's spoken like a scholar Shaneen Keogh. Faith we'll have you joining the holy brotherhoods if you're jilted now!'

Notes (cont.), p. 112.

PEGEEN. You'll have small space for dreaming this day, and the sports opening beyond where my heart will be back and forward watching out to see you doing the wonders of the world and all.

CHRISTY [*radiant with delight*]. This day you'll see me surely and your kindly words going along with me, you'll see me knocking a lep of wonder from the thoughts of men.

A late entry in Notebook 34 again suggests that Christy must prove himself:
'End of Pegeen's scene
My heart is back and forward round you young fellow but let ⟨you⟩ do wonders in the sports and races and you'd have a right to hope for all.'
And an entry elsewhere in the same notebook reads 'Lay stress on Pegeen's *admiration* for his valour before she goes.'

On the other hand, an undated fragment makes no mention of the sports but continues to develop the 'current' between Christy and Pegeen. Christy suggests that Pegeen will soon marry:

CHRISTY. The way you'll be turning me off that time to go walking with the strangers of the world.

PEGEEN. What was I but a stranger when you turned into this house at the fall of night, and look at you now?

CHRISTY [*sits down on a stool near her*]. Them girls that came in were strangers, but you're not a stranger at all. And why that is the truth I'd be hard set to tell to a priest.

PEGEEN [*looking down on him benignly*]. You'd be a loyal lad I'm thinking to have living at my side.

CHRISTY. Oh, I would that and it's no lie, think on the way I toiled and moiled for my poor father cutting his turf and drying his hay, and no thanks at all but blows of a thorn stick maybe and swearing out upon my head.

⁶ Not until late in November 1906 does Synge bring Shawn and the Widow Quin on together to confront Christy. The back of a very early fragment has the note 'Sudden love scene to entrance of Shawn Keogh. He is dispatched, and men come in with good news for Simon ⟨the false name given by Christy in early drafts of Act I⟩. Curtain comes down as Micheal approves of his match with Pegeen.' This is the outline of the action in the earliest typescript, in which Shawn discovers Pegeen and Christy practically in each other's arms, refuses to fight Christy, and runs out as Michael James returns from the wake. This early version of the act ends with Michael James announcing Christy's appointment as Master Pigsticker of the town and Pegeen claiming she will marry Christy. (See Appendix B.)

After this Synge apparently abandoned the idea of bringing Shawn on, and concentrated instead on the Widow Quin's attempts to woo Christy away from Pegeen. As late as draft 'F' (9 January 1906) the Widow Quin acts as the transition between the scene with Pegeen and Christy and the appearance of Old Mahon.

[*Note 6 continued on p. 116.*]

[*pulling it out*]; and my new coat is woven from the blackest shearings for three miles around [*giving him the coat*];[1] I'll give you the whole of them and my blessing and the blessing of Father Reilly itself, maybe, if you'll quit from this and leave us in the peace[2] we had till last night at the fall of dark.

CHRISTY [*with a new arrogance*]. And for what is it you're wanting to get shut of me?

SHAWN [*looking to the* WIDOW *for help*]. I'm a poor scholar with middling faculties to coin a lie, so I'll tell you the truth, Christy Mahon. I'm wedding with Pegeen beyond, and I don't think well of having a clever fearless man the like of you dwelling in her house.

CHRISTY [*almost pugnaciously*]. And you'd be using bribery for to banish me?

SHAWN [*in an imploring voice*]. Let you not take it badly, mister honey, isn't beyond the best place for you where you'll have golden chains and shiny coats and you riding upon hunters with the ladies of the land. [*He makes an eager sign to the* WIDOW QUIN *to come to help him.*]

WIDOW QUIN [*coming over*]. It's true for him, and you'd best quit off and not have that poor girl setting her mind on you, for there's Shaneen thinks she wouldn't suit you though all is saying that she'll wed you now.

[CHRISTY *beams with delight.*]

SHAWN [*in terrified earnest*]. She wouldn't suit you, and she with the divil's own temper the way you'd be strangling one another in a score of days. [*He makes the movement of strangling with his hands.*] It's the like of me only that she's fit for, a quiet simple fellow wouldn't raise a hand upon her if she scratched itself.

WIDOW QUIN [*putting* SHAWN'*s hat on* CHRISTY]. Fit them clothes on you anyhow, young fellow, and he'd maybe loan them to you for the sports. [*Pushing him towards inner door.*] Fit them on and you can give your answer when you have them tried.

CHRISTY [*beaming, delighted with the clothes*]. I will then, I'd like herself to see me in them tweeds and hat. [*He goes into room and shuts the door.*]

Notes (cont.), p. 112.

With the following suggestions in Notebook 34, Synge again brought on Shawn:

Playboy II F 3

P. There's Shawn Keogh, I'm asking what he's thinking this day of the pair of us. Say I'm out on the hill [*going into room leaving door ajar*].

SHAWN. God save you Mister.

CH. God save you.

S. Is herself within?

C. She's on the hills.

S. And Michael James.

C. At the wake.

S. Well I've a word to utter to yourself alone.

C. Well?

S. I'm after thinking this'd be a poor place for your like to live and I'm willing for to loan you a half crown for your railway to a decent town. Take ⟨it⟩ and run off before herself will come.

CH. I won't, I like this place.

S. Not if I got Father to have you made a captain on the coaster boat?

CH. No.

SHAWN. Would you think well to go to New York. If you'd think well of it I'd loan you four sovereigns and you'd have a grand life in that place, and you driving round maybe in the heel of the hunt you'd ⟨be⟩ the prince of Yankees on a golden car?

[*Shawn offers him his own wedding clothes if he will go to America.*]

'? Should not Shawn Keogh come in again at end of I to show that he does not think Ch. has gone with W.
or (better) make W. say as she goes I'll walk down and tell him now.'

By the next typescript draft ('G', 28 July 1906) Synge had developed the scene between Christy and Shawn: Shawn comes in alone with the ticket to America and his clothing in a sack; Christy, pretending great disgust at this offer of a bribe, throws the hat and coat out the door; the Widow Quin then enters carrying the hat, and Shawn runs off, leaving Christy and the Widow Quin together.

This scene is revised further, with Shawn admitting the Widow Quin's help in 'contriving' the scheme and calling for the Widow Quin, who has promised to protect him. Still dissatisfied, Synge wrote in Notebook 34 on 6 November 1906, 'see scene, C and W.Q beginning curious'. Finally, by draft 'J' (revised late November 1906), Shawn and the Widow Quin arrive together, the Widow offers to save Shawn by marrying Christy herself, and Shawn's sack has become a 'cleeve' or hamper. (This cleeve first appears in draft 'F' when the Widow Quin comes in alone with a cleeve of turf and sends Pegeen out after her sheep.) See Appendix B and notes to next scene for development of the interview between Christy and the Widow Quin.

7 A remnant of draft 'J' reads *malicious* for *amused*.

---

1 The final typescript originally read 'a poor place for a man destroyed his da, I'm a modest fellow and I'll make myself. . . '

SHAWN [*in great anxiety*]. He'd like herself to see them! He'll not leave us, Widow Quin. He's a score of divils in him, the way it's well nigh certain he will wed Pegeen.

WIDOW QUIN [*jeeringly*]. It's true all girls are fond of courage and do hate the like of you.

SHAWN [*walking about in desperation*]. Oh, Widow Quin, what'll I be doing now? I'd inform again him, but he'd burst from Kilmainham and he'd be sure and certain to destroy me. If I wasn't so God-fearing, I'd near have courage to come behind him and run a pike into his side. Oh, it's a hard case to be an orphan and not to have your father that you're used to, and you'd easy kill and make yourself a hero in the sight of all. [*Coming up to her.*] Oh, Widow Quin, will you find me some contrivance when I've promised you a ewe?

WIDOW QUIN. A ewe's a small thing, but what would you give me if I did wed him and did save you so?

SHAWN [*with astonishment*]. You!

WIDOW QUIN. Aye. Would you give me the red cow you have and the mountainy ram, and the right of way across your rye path, and a load of dung at Michaelmas, and turbary upon the western hill?

SHAWN [*radiant with hope*]. I would surely, and I'd give you the wedding-ring I have, and the loan of the new suit, the way you'd have him decent on the wedding-day. I'd give you two kids for your dinner and a gallon of poteen, and I'd call the piper on the long car to your wedding from Crossmolina or from Ballina. I'd give you. . .

WIDOW QUIN. That'll do, so, and let you whisht, for he's coming now again.

[CHRISTY *comes in very natty in the new clothes.* WIDOW QUIN *goes to him admiringly.*]

WIDOW QUIN. If you seen yourself now, I'm thinking you'd be too proud to speak to us at all, and it'd be a pity surely to have your like sailing from Mayo to the Western World.

CHRISTY [*as proud as a peacock*]. I'm not going. If this is a poor place itself, I'll make myself[1] contented to be lodging here.

[WIDOW QUIN *makes a sign to* SHAWN *to leave them.*]

¹ A fragment of draft 'H' (10 August 1906) includes the following passage:

SHAWN [*thunder-struck*]. Wed with you is it? Sure who would wed a middling aged woman is the like of you.

WIDOW QUIN [*angrily standing up*]. Aged is it? I won't be thirty till next April day and it's that age I'm telling ⟨you⟩ is the best and ripest for the body and the mind. I'm too old maybe to aid you at all so that God may save you and attend you now—[*goes towards door*].

SHAWN [*catching her*]. Don't desert me Widow for the love and friendship of the saints of peace. You know well I'm a foolish fellow and let you not heed what I say and I three-quarters of an idiot born. You're a lovely handsome woman I do know it well, and if you'll wed him I will give you what you ask at all.

This version of the pact continues through draft 'J', with the Widow 'relenting for her private ends'. However, a fairly late remnant considers another version of this scene, beginning with the Widow's reaction to Shawn's idea of running a pike into Christy:

WIDOW QUIN [*laughing*]. If you did that you'd have the lot of us all contending whether we would marry with himself or you.

SHAWN [*struck by an idea*]. Would you think to wed him yourself maybe? If you'd do that I'd give you the red cow and the mountainy ram, and the right of way across my rye patch, and seed potatoes and what more you'd ask.

WIDOW QUIN. If I did wed him he'd be Pegeen's next neighbour and I'm thinking you'd be jealous so.

SHAWN. Who am I that I'd be jealous of the likes of him, and I'm thinking with yourself he'd be in order, and not so skittish as you'd fancy now. [*There is a noise in the room.*] I'm thinking he is coming now, and I'd do right maybe for to quit from this, and if he will not seek the distant countries let you wed him and I'll make you rich and easy till the judgment day.

WIDOW QUIN. Stop and hear will he leave the land.

SHAWN. I will not Widow Quin. I get a kind of cramping from the fury of his eye. [*He runs off as* CHRISTY *comes in very natty.*]

CHRISTY. Where is he?

WIDOW QUIN. Gone off. You're to leave your answer with myself. Are you thinking to go sailing to the western world?

CHRISTY. I am not. Did he leave his clothes unto myself on loan?

WIDOW QUIN. It was I did talk him over for to leave them here. It's a joy to see a nice lad and he nicely dressed. Sit down now. . . .

² Originally Synge intended to work up the tension between Christy and the Widow Quin here, but finally decided to make it a brief transition only and develop the Widow's characterization after Old Mahon has left. (See Appendix B.)

³ Draft 'F' adds the direction *or crouches behind her petticoats*. Until draft 'E' Christy's father was called 'Old Flaherty'; he does not appear in this act until draft 'C'.

⁴ Draft 'I' originally read 'blackguard' for 'streeler'.

SHAWN. Well, I'm going measuring the race-course while the tide is low, so I'll leave you the garments and my blessing for the sports to-day. God bless you! [*He wriggles out.*][1]

WIDOW QUIN [*admiring* CHRISTY]. Well you're mighty spruce, young fellow. Sit down now while you're quiet till you talk with me.

CHRISTY [*swaggering*]. I'm going abroad on the hillside for to seek Pegeen.

WIDOW QUIN. You'll have time and plenty for to seek Pegeen, and you heard me saying at the fall of night the two of us should be great company.

CHRISTY. From this out I'll have no want of company when all sorts is bringing me their food and clothing [*he swaggers to the door, tightening his belt*], the way they'd set their eyes upon a gallant orphan cleft his father with one blow to the breeches belt. [*He opens door, then staggers back.*] Saints of glory! Holy angels from the throne of light![2]

WIDOW QUIN [*going over*]. What ails you?

CHRISTY. It's the walking spirit of my murdered da!

WIDOW QUIN [*looking out*]. Is it that tramper?

CHRISTY [*wildly*]. Where'll I hide my poor body from that ghost of hell?

[*The door is pushed open, and* OLD MAHON *appears on threshold.* CHRISTY *darts in behind door*[3].]

WIDOW QUIN [*in great amusement*]. God save you, my poor man.

MAHON [*gruffly*]. Did you see a young lad passing this way in the early morning or the fall of night?

WIDOW QUIN. You're a queer kind to walk in not saluting at all.

MAHON. Did you see the young lad?

WIDOW QUIN [*stiffly*]. What kind was he?

MAHON. An ugly young streeler[4] with a murderous gob on him and a little switch in his hand. I met a tramper seen him coming this way at the fall of night.

¹ Draft 'I' originally read 'lousy, stuttering lout'.

² A remnant of draft 'K' reads:

MAHON [*loudly*]. It's ⟨little⟩ I care if I'm mortified in the heart and soul and kidneys and I a martyred saint with nothing but destruction on me driven out in my old age with none to aid me.

WIDOW QUIN. And what is it has you destroyed? I'm thinking it's small sniffs of sanctity the Lord will find on you the way I'm thinking it's yourself has wrought your ruin if the whole was told.

³ Draft 'C' expands on Old Mahon's troubles:

. . . [*he takes out a penny*]. Let you give me a sup of something while I'll be taking my breath.

WIDOW QUIN [*moving hastily*]. Herself is out and I can't serve you with porter. There's a cup of tea will do you as well. It's a poor thing to see a man of your age walking the world with a great gash in his skull.

OLD F. [*mollified*]. I was a fine strong farmer, and fine health I had the way I thought I'd never die, and there's my farm gone from me, and there's nothing but destruction on me; I'm telling you I'm a done man.

WIDOW QUIN. That's a poor thing; what has you ruined?

OLD F. It was the misfortunate poor ass of a son I had put everything wrong the way there came a decree for debt from the shop and I was driven out in my old age with no one to aid me.

As late as draft 'E' the decree for debt is still mentioned. In one of the earliest drafts Synge has jotted down 'When he asks for a drink let Sally pretend to look for pot-boy.'

⁴ Although the first edition reads 'liar', the majority of the drafts read 'lier on walls', accepted here as more appropriate to Christy's lazy and lonely nature, despite the unreliability of Synge's spelling. Notebook 29 first records the line 'the bloody rogue does be stretched out with his belly to the sun'.

WIDOW QUIN. There's harvest hundreds do be passing these days for the Sligo boat. For what is it you're wanting him, my poor man?

MAHON. I want to destroy him for breaking the head on me with the clout of a loy. [*He takes off a big hat, and shows his head in a mass of bandages and plaster, with some pride.*] It was he did that, and amn't I a great wonder to think I've traced him ten days with that rent in my crown?

WIDOW QUIN [*taking his head in both hands and examining it with extreme delight*]. That was a great blow. And who hit you? A robber maybe?

MAHON. It was my own son hit me, and he the divil a robber or anything else but a dirty, stuttering lout.[1]

WIDOW QUIN [*letting go his skull and wiping her hands in her apron*]. You'd best be wary of a mortified scalp, I think they call it, lepping around with that wound in the splendour of the sun. It was a bad blow surely, and you should have vexed him fearful to make him strike that gash in his da.

MAHON. Is it me?[2]

WIDOW QUIN [*amusing herself*]. Aye. And isn't it a great shame when the old and hardened do torment the young?

MAHON [*raging*]. Torment him is it? And I after holding out with the patience of a martyred saint, till there's nothing but destruction on me and I'm driven out in my old age with none to aid me?[3]

WIDOW QUIN [*greatly amused*]. It's a sacred wonder the way that wickedness will spoil a man.

MAHON. My wickedness, is it? Amn't I after saying it is himself has me destroyed, and he a lier on walls, a talker of folly, a man you'd see stretched the half of the day in the brown ferns with his belly to the sun.[4]

WIDOW QUIN. Not working at all?

MAHON. The divil a work, or if he did itself, you'd see him raising up a haystack like the stalk of a rush or driving our last cow till he broke her leg at the hip, and when he wasn't at that he'd be fooling over

¹ Earlier drafts give more details of Christy's past:

OLD F. . . . broke her hinder leg close by the hip.

SALLY. And you lost her then?

FLAHERTY. We had ⟨the⟩ bone set, and herself tied up into a cart, and there she was roaring out three days till she found death, and then what did he do before we had her skinned, but hoke the ass cart and bury her below in the field and when I was going to raise my hand on him after 'I've reared her from a calf' says he 'and I wouldn't like her cut up into bits.'

SALLY. That should have been a soft lad surely.

FLAHERTY. It's true for you, and he had little birds in cages within, finches and felts and the like of them, and there he'd be fooling and fussing the length of the sacred sabbath, and when he wasn't at that he'd be making ugly mugs at his own self in the glass we had hung on the wall.

² Originally the direction read [*standing with her back against door drumming on it at times*].

³ Notebook 29 records the line 'you'll see his ears poking over a bush like a hare'.

⁴ The final drafts originally read 'throwing up and throwing up' for 'taken with contortions'; earlier drafts read 'dispensary doctor' for 'the females' nurse'.

⁵ Draft 'C' alters 'the fool of the Flahertys' to 'the looney MacMahon'.

little birds he had—finches and felts—or making mugs at his own self in the bit of a glass we had hung on the wall.[1]

WIDOW QUIN [*looking at* CHRISTY].[2] What way was he so foolish? It was running wild after the girls maybe?

MAHON [*with a shout of derision*]. Running wild, is it? If he seen a red petticoat coming swinging over the hill, he'd be off to hide in the sticks, and you'd see him shooting out his sheep's eyes between the little twigs and leaves, and his two ears rising like a hare looking out through a gap.[3] Girls indeed!

WIDOW QUIN. It was drink maybe?

MAHON. And he a poor fellow would get drunk on the smell of a pint! He'd a queer rotten stomach, I'm telling you, and when I gave him three pulls from my pipe a while since, he was taken with contortions till I had to send him in the ass cart to the females' nurse.[4]

WIDOW QUIN [*clasping her hands*]. Well, I never till this day heard tell of a man the like of that.

MAHON. I'd take a mighty oath you didn't surely, and wasn't he the laughing joke of every female woman where four baronies meet, the way the girls would stop their weeding if they seen him coming the road to let a roar at him, and call him the looncy of Mahon's.[5]

WIDOW QUIN. I'd give the world and all to see the like of him. What kind was he?

MAHON. A small low fellow.

WIDOW QUIN. And dark?

MAHON. Dark and dirty.

WIDOW QUIN [*considering*]. I'm thinking I seen him.

MAHON [*eagerly*]. An ugly young blackguard?

WIDOW QUIN. A hideous, fearful villain, and the spit of you.

MAHON. What way is he fled?

WIDOW QUIN. Gone over the hills to catch a coasting steamer to the north or south.

MAHON. Could I pull up on him now?

¹ In a revised draft of 'C' Old Flaherty is given a final speech: 'Well God bless you, and I'll see ⟨you⟩ again maybe when I'll be turning back again to the place where I was reared. [*He goes. The* WIDOW *watches him for a moment then comes back to fire and meditates.*]

The final revision of draft 'C' alters his exit to the final version.

² An early version (possibly 'B') expands this scene:

SALLY [*laughing wildly*]. There should be great doctors in that country to stitch up a poor man was splitted down to his middle. And wasn't a fine story he told of your foolishness, and I getting my death making efforts to keep the laughter from my face. Well you're the walking playboy of the western world, with your knob of his gullet and splitting him to his navel!

   [CHRISTY *has first listened attentively to* FLAHERTY's *steps retreating, then looked furtively from window, now runs to* SALLY.]

CHRISTY [*grim as death with a horrified whisper*]. What'll Pegeen say if she hears that story

Later drafts alter the direction to *grim as hell*.

³ Draft 'K' originally read 'that the scourge of God may knock a sweat out of his carcass on the brimstone tracks of hell'.

⁴ An earlier draft reads, 'that the bloody waves of Pharaoh might wash him from the world'.

WIDOW QUIN. If you'll cross the sands below where the tide is out, you'll be in it as soon as himself, for he had to go round ten miles by the top of the bay. [*She points from the door.*] Strike down by the head beyond and then follow on the roadway to the north and east.

[MAHON *goes abruptly.*][1]

WIDOW QUIN [*shouting after him*]. Let you give him a good vengeance when you come up with him, but don't put yourself in the power of the law, for it'd be a poor thing to see a judge in his black cap reading out his sentence on a civil warrior the like of you. [*She swings the door to and looks at* CHRISTY, *who is cowering in terror, for a moment, then she bursts into a laugh.*] Well, you're the walking playboy of the western world, and that's the poor man you had divided to his breeches belt.

CHRISTY [*looking out; then, to her*]. What'll Pegeen say when she hears that story? What'll she be saying to me now?[2]

WIDOW QUIN. She'll knock the head of you, I'm thinking, and drive you from the door. God help her to be taking you for a wonder, and you a little schemer making up a story you destroyed your da.

CHRISTY [*turning to the door, nearly speechless with rage, half to himself*]. To be letting on he was dead, and coming back to his life, and following me like an old weazel tracing a rat, and coming in here laying desolation between my own self and the fine women of Ireland, and he a kind of carcase that you'd fling upon the sea. . . .[3]

WIDOW QUIN [*more soberly*]. There's talking for a man's one only son.

CHRISTY [*breaking out*]. His one son, is it? May I meet him with one tooth and it aching, and one eye to be seeing seven and seventy divils in the twists of the road, and one old timber leg on him to limp into the scalding grave. [*Looking out.*] There he is now crossing the strands, and that the Lord God would send a high wave to wash him from the world.[4]

WIDOW QUIN [*scandalized*]. Have you no shame? [*Putting her hand on his shoulder and turning him round.*] What ails you? Near crying, is it?

CHRISTY [*in despair and grief*]. Amn't I after seeing the love-light of the star of knowledge shining from her brow, and hearing words would

¹ A late draft reads, 'on the holy Virgin speaking soft and sleepy to the infant Lord'.

² Late drafts add the words, 'turning the like of the whole world and speaking. . . .'

³ Late drafts add the direction [*with bitterness now in her derision*].

⁴ At one time Synge contemplated making Christy plan to leave before Pegeen's return. An early draft in Notebook 28 develops this situation:

WIDOW QUIN. God in glory save us what is this. You're a man to talk. What⟨'s⟩ to hinder you wedding some poor woman beyond and earning your bread like another.

CHRISTY. How would a man who is three weeks walking around saying over I've killed my pa go living like another and earning his bread and be then like the madmen I'm thinking who spend a while in some grand madhouse of Ireland and are never happy after in their own poor places where they live?

WIDOW QUIN. If you're set on killing you'd do well to turn a hangman of Kilmainham Jail?

CHRISTY. I'm grand at knotting but who'd be bothered hanging if they couldn't be hanging himself?

Another draft in the same notebook retains the suggestion of his retreat, but with prospects of a brighter future:

⟨CHRISTY.⟩ Oh Widow Quin have pity on me this day for the love of God. Was there ever a poor fellow had torment and long anguish the like of myself to say I did a mighty deed and was raised up a long space on the flighted track of glory is reaching to God and there I am now starting away with no hope or joy in me and a haunting evil father hounding me on my track.

WIDOW QUIN. If you got your glory in this place with telling a lie, I'm thinking you'll easy make up new glories with telling it again.

CHRISTY. What good is a lie, God help me, when you're seeing clear through it ⟨in⟩ an hour?

WIDOW QUIN. There's talking. Didn't you know rightly since the noon of day that he was⟨n't⟩ murdered at all—⟨we⟩ seen him passing the road and all the while since that you've ⟨been⟩ weaving gaudy borders to your lies and talk, and it's easy you'd be doing it away.

CHRISTY. . . . How would I say he was dead and he following me on?

WIDOW QUIN. He'll soon die I'm thinking he's the look of a man won't be long raising his toes.

Apparently not until draft 'C' did Synge think of using this scene to develop the Widow's characterization and restricting their earlier scene (before Old Mahon's appearance) to Christy's 'jubilant note' (see further extracts from Notebook 28 in Appendix B).

⁵ On the back of a revised draft of TS. 'C' Synge scribbled his first attempt to convey the Widow's amused detachment from the villagers' world below; in succeeding drafts the cynicism is toned down and the sympathy developed as Synge once more restricts the impact of her personality:

CHRISTY. You've no children.

W.Q. Two buried.

W.Q. And I do be thinking it's well for me to be sitting out there in the sun stitching a shift maybe or darning a sock, and I looking down on the glen and I saying to myself what big fools they are crawling round like vermin in a bag—all the people reaping, thatching courting, sporting, dying itself—the people in this place is fearful for dying—and making great sporting on a Sunday the ⟨way⟩ you'd think they were fiery patriots and you knowing the whole while there isn't one of them wouldn't sell the whole of Ireland for 2 shillings.

[*Notes continued on pp. 128–9.*]

put you thinking on the holy Brigid speaking to the infant saints,[1] and now she'll be turning again,[2] and speaking hard words to me, like an old woman with a spavindy ass she'd have, urging on a hill.

WIDOW QUIN.[3] There's poetry talk for a girl you'd see itching and scratching, and she with a stale stink of poteen on her from selling in the shop.

CHRISTY [*impatiently*]. It's her like is fitted to be handling merchandise in the heavens above, and what'll I be doing now, I ask you, and I a kind of wonder was jilted by the heavens when a day was by.

[*There is a distant noise of girls' voices.* WIDOW QUIN *looks from window and comes to him, hurriedly.*[4]]

WIDOW QUIN. You'll be doing like myself, I'm thinking, when I did destroy my man, for I'm above many's the day, odd times in great spirits, abroad in the sunshine, darning a stocking or stitching a shift, and odd times again looking out on the schooners, hookers, trawlers is sailing the sea, and I thinking on the gallant hairy fellows are drifting beyond, and myself long years living alone.[5]

CHRISTY [*interested*]. You're like me, so.

WIDOW QUIN. I am your like, and it's for that I'm taking a fancy to you, and I with my little houseen above where there'd be myself to tend you, and none to ask were you a murderer or what at all.[6]

CHRISTY.[7] And what would I be doing if I left Pegeen?

WIDOW QUIN. I've nice jobs you could be doing, gathering shells to make a whitewash for our hut within, building up a little goose-house, or stretching a new skin on an old curagh I have, and if my hut is far from all sides, it's there you'll meet the wisest old men, I tell you, at the corner of my wheel, and it's there yourself and me will have great times whispering and hugging . . .[8]

VOICES [*outside, calling far away*]. Christy! Christy Mahon! Christy!

CHRISTY. Is it Pegeen Mike?

WIDOW QUIN. It's the young girls, I'm thinking, coming to bring you to the sports below, and what is it you'll have me to tell them now?[9]

CHRISTY. Aid me for to win Pegeen. It's herself only that I'm seeking now. [WIDOW QUIN *gets up and goes to window.*][10] Aid me for to win

[*Text of play continued on p. 131.*]

Notes (*cont.*), p. *127.*

⁶ Late drafts continue to stress the Widow's compassion, as in these two remnants from draft 'I':

WIDOW QUIN. Didn't you see I had a kind of pity for ⟨you⟩ sitting so simple at the fall of night, and knowing your whole story I do like you more.

CHRISTY. I'm thinking that you're foolish so.

WIDOW QUIN. It's the fools and young I'm saying do be seeking wonders all time for to make their joy, but there's others would think more of a three-legged cur dog than the king of England or the prince of Spain.

WIDOW QUIN [*coaxingly, half bashful, half amused*]. If I am the Lord God's made it fitting maybe that we two should join. Rise up now till I show you. . . .

Not until his final drafts did Synge omit her concluding words: 'and myself to tend you all times, a kindly grown woman does be pitying the world'.

⁷ Conflicting directions for Christy in the late drafts indicate Synge's difficulty in maintaining a balance between Christy and the Widow: *hardly understanding her*; *beginning to understand her*. A remnant from draft 'J' gives the additional speeches,

CHRISTY. And you yourself would wed me though my da's alive?

WIDOW QUIN. I would then. What is it I cared for your romancing tale and I doing little at all but pitying the world?

⁸ Not until the final drafts does Synge cut down the Widow's reply which he originally planned for their earlier scene together. A late draft includes here the version of her speech which Synge struck out of draft 'F' of Act I (1 January 1906):

WIDOW QUIN [*brightening again*]. Wait till you see the grassy plots I have with an outlet on the mountains for my goats and geese, and the nice jobs I'll have you doing [*her voice softens gradually*]—gathering shells to make a whitewash for our hut within, or building up a little goose-house, or stretching a new skin on the old curagh I have or twisting sally burdogues for the Swinford fair, and it's there you'll have great times I'm telling you for if my hut is far from all sides it's there you'll meet the wisest old men sitting at the corner of my wheel, and windy holidays you'll see the little children sitting round the fire I have till you'd think I was the like of Columcille learning Latin to the saints of God. [*Putting her hand on his shoulder.*] Wouldn't you think well to wed me and live the like of that?

Many drafts add the final words, 'and laying lengthy curses on the foolery of men'.

⁹ Suggestions scribbled on the back of draft 'B' indicate Synge's first plan for ending this act; the character of the Widow Quin was not yet developed: 'Put in intense scene between Widow O'Flinn and Christy in the end of which she swears—for her pity's sake not to tell on Christy—motif her sympathy with his desolation—'

'When Old Flaherty goes try rapid scene of Christy rushing at Sally and imploring her not to tell Pegeen. She agrees then speech off and the news of Shawn Keogh—'

SALLY. You're thinking a sight of Pegeen?

CHRISTY. Wouldn't any young fellow do that?

SALLY. Well let you not be breaking your heart for her for here's Shawn coming up the path and it's him she's wedding in two weeks or three.

CHRISTY. Is that the truth?

Notes (cont.) p. 127.

SALLY. Bible truth. Here he is now and I'll leave you to be talking to him now.

[*She goes out.* CHRISTY *sits down at the fire as before.*]

SHAWN [*comes in*]. That's a grand day Mister.

CHRISTY. It is I'm thinking.

SHAWN. Where's Pegeen?

CHRISTY. Coming above.

[PEGEEN *enters, followed by men from wake.*]

10 See Appendix B for earlier drafts of this scene between the Widow and Christy.

Notes, p. 131.

1 In draft 'G' Christy kneels. Notebook 29 records the phrases 'that God may stretch out a holy hand to you' and 'that the immaculate holy mother may intercede for you'.

2 Late drafts give instead the direction [*coldly*].

3 Late drafts read 'by the elements and cross of Christ'.

4 The earliest drafts including Old Flaherty (up to the first draft of 'C') bring Pegeen back onstage here, Sally leaves, Michael James returns from the wake with news of the projected match between Shawn and Pegeen, and the act ends on the ousting of Shawn and betrothal of Christy and Pegeen (see Appendix B). The first unrevised version of draft 'C' reads as follows after Sally Quin has promised not to tell Pegeen of Christy's deception:

CHRISTY. Ah, . . . Ah, . . . Well, I'll be saying prayers for you this day till my tongue's stiff with the drought. . . . I'll be asking the Almighty God to stretch out his holy hand to you, and lead you by short cuts through the Meadows of Ease and up the sainted floors of Heaven to the blessed footstool of the Virgin's son . . . for you've stopped me from going off through the world the like of a strayed dog would have a broken cord hanging from its jaw, and kept me in this place where there'll be a lovely woman looking on me now.

PEGEEN [*comes in*]. I see Shawn and Micheal James and the whole set coming now. [*Going to the fire.*] Who was the old fellow coming the path as I went out?

SALLY. A kind of a pedlar.

PEGEEN. You'd have a right to keep him for me. What was he selling

SALLY. Sticking plaster. [*She goes out.*]

In the margin of this draft Synge suggests, 'Let Sally bring news of matchmaking between fathers of P and Sh? Sally Shawn's sister????' But in the next revision of draft 'C' Sally has become the Widow Quin and Synge postpones Michael James's return until the next act, where the news of the matchmaking, Shawn's ousting, and the engagement between Christy and Pegeen takes up the entire act (a four-act scheme which lasted only one revision, see Appendix B). Having decided to postpone the engagement until the next act, Synge jotted down the following suggestion on the back of yet another revision of draft 'C': 'Widow Q. tells him to wed Pegeen and then if the old fellow comes back self he'll be safe (then work this motif in 3rd act).' This advice is included until after draft 'E' (24 May 1905) which reads:

Notes, p. 131, begin on p. 129. Note 4 (cont.).

WIDOW QUIN. Stop your talk I'm saying and listen to me. If you want that girl you'd do well to have her wed you while you're new, for Shawn Keogh's a rich man and if you seen himself slipping between you, you'll be making a fine hullabaloo that day I'm thinking. ⟨. . .⟩ [PEGEEN *calls.*]

CHRISTY. Well God reward you for you've left me with a courage in me to destroy the world. [*He runs out.*]

However, on the back of this draft (TS. 'E') Synge jotted down a further suggestion: 'Make Widow Quin explain and face difficulty of his play-acting the part of father slayer when he knows that his father is really alive—.'

5 The idea of the jockey suit seems to have occurred to Synge after consultation with Jack Yeats, who sent him sketches of Christy's costume in a letter of 11 January 1907.

6 Not until a very late draft does Synge think of bringing the girls back to carry off Christy. A note on the back of a remnant from draft 'I' (24 November 1906) reads 'End of act. Girls return and take off Christy to the sports. Widow Quin looks out and sees Old M. turning back towards the place where they are *or* she asks come on did you meet an old man and they say he's asleep in the gripe of the ditch.'

7 Originally Synge considered a different comment for the curtain of Act II; Notebook 28 includes the suggestion: 'arrival of piper playing black rogue ends scene (or is that a too obvious irony).'

A tag ending for the Widow Quin apparently did not occur to him until he was revising draft 'C': 'Christy and Widow swear silence. Pegeen calls off and he goes to her. Widow puts her shawl over her head and follows. Tag on folly of Y?' Presumably this is the version he developed by draft 'E' (24 May 1905), although no early drafts emphasize youth:

WIDOW QUIN [*going to door slowly, sighing sadly*]. Well if there was any to hear me I'd say it was great game to be looking on the madmen is left running about, and they making love-talk for the laughter of the world, and there should be great sport this night I'm thinking for it's like enough Micheal James will promise that girl in Cassidy's wake. *Curtain.*

Synge kept on sharpening this ending. Draft 'F' (9 January 1906) reads simply, 'Well if there was any to hear me I'd say it was great sport to be looking on the madmen do be making game and love-talk for the laughter of the world.' Remnants of October–November 1906 reflect Synge's decision to emphasize the Widow's self-interest: 'Well I'll likely turn a trifle out of this day's play and if there was any to hear me . . .'; 'Well I've lost my bargain so I'll aid him now, and if there was any to hear me . . .'. Still dissatisfied, however, Synge in the next drafts has the Widow looking out the window: 'Faith there's the old man turning back on the sands. There'll be doing now, and if there was any to hear me . . .'. Under this version Synge wrote the directions, 'Change tag. Revise and shorten second half of P & C scene. Revise end of W.Q. and C. Polish Old Mahon and W.Q.' And out of this general overhauling he produced the first form of the final version:

WIDOW QUIN [*getting a jar for poteen and putting her shawl over her head*]. Well it's a queer case that if the worst comes there'll be none to pity him but a woman that destroyed her man. [*Goes.*]

However, at the last moment Synge apparently once more had reservations about this tag ending, which is not included in the 'final draft' sent to John Quinn, nor in the typescript sent to the printers, nor does it appear in the copyright edition of Act II printed by Quinn in New York in 1907. Presumably it was restored to the galley proofs after rehearsals had begun, as it does appear in the Maunsel first edition and the galley proofs.

her, and I'll be asking God to stretch a hand to you in the hour of death, and lead you short cuts through the Meadows of Ease, and up the floor of Heaven to the Footstool of the Virgin's Son.[1]

WIDOW QUIN. There's praying!

VOICES [*nearer*]. Christy! Christy Mahon!

CHRISTY [*with agitation*]. They're coming. Will you swear to aid and save me for the love of Christ?

WIDOW QUIN [*looks at him for a moment*].[2] If I aid you, will you swear to give me a right of way I want, and a mountainy ram, and a load of dung at Michaelmas, the time that you'll be master here?

CHRISTY. I will, by the elements and stars of night.[3]

WIDOW QUIN. Then we'll not say a word of the old fellow, the way Pegeen won't know your story till the end of time.

CHRISTY. And if he chances to return again?

WIDOW QUIN. We'll swear he's a maniac and not your da. I could take an oath I seen him raving on the sands to-day.

[GIRLS *run in.*][4]

SUSAN. Come on to the sports below. Pegeen says you're to come.

SARA TANSEY. The lepping's beginning, and we've a jockey's suit to fit upon you for the mule race on the sands below.[5]

HONOR. Come on, will you.

CHRISTY. I will then if Pegeen's beyond.

SARA. She's in the boreen making game of Shaneen Keogh.

CHRISTY. Then I'll be going to her now.[6] [*He runs out, followed by the* GIRLS.]

WIDOW QUIN. Well, if the worst comes in the end of all, it'll be great game to see there's none to pity him but a widow woman, the like of me, has buried her children and destroyed her man.[7] [*She goes out.*]

CURTAIN

[1] See Appendix B for the earliest drafts of this act. Originally Synge planned to open the act outside the chapel on Christy and Pegeen's wedding day, several months having passed, the love scene and engagement being included in the preceding act. After draft 'C', however, he decided to make the scene follow three hours later on the same day; a marginal note to this draft, which opens on Christy's entrance with Pegeen alone, reads 'Fair scene. Roulette player, piper, Town-crier etc. Christy winner.' Drafts 'D' and 'E' begin with a song by the roulette man and finally, in the first 'F' draft (24 January 1906), the act opens as in the text. With one exception, the remaining drafts are variations on this opening scene; draft 'G' omits Philly and Jimmy altogether, however, opening as follows:

> [*Same scene.* OLD MAHON *comes in and looks round then goes to window and looks out. Great cheering is heard far away.*]

OLD MAHON. There's yelling sports they have on the green below! [*He knocks on the table.*] If there's nobody in I'd best go down maybe and beg halfpence on the green. [*He goes towards door.*]

> [WIDOW QUIN *passes window rapidly and meets him as she comes into the door.*]

WIDOW QUIN [*coming in with a jar in her hand, starting as she sees him*]. You're living yet?

OLD MAHON. Living?

WIDOW QUIN. We heard you were drowned in the tide of Belmullet and you crossing the sands.

OLD MAHON [*speaking wearily*]. It was an old lousy tramper that was drownded there, and not myself at all. [*He sits down.*]

WIDOW QUIN. And we making sure it was you. [*Putting away the jar.*] There'll be doings coming on this day or I'm mistaken now.

The suggestion of hearing that Old Mahon was drowned appears to have entered in Note-book 34; Philly and Jimmy enter and Jimmy says, 'I hear them saying there was an old fellow drownded this morning beyond in Belmullet.'

[2] Draft 'F' describes Jimmy's attitude: [*as sporting man, at window*]. Until a revision of draft 'E' Jimmy was Timmy Farrel(l).

[3] The idea of Christy's luck and success at the sports first enters in draft 'B' when Philly (outside the chapel) says 'I'm told Micheal James is taking great sums since he's had that lad in it talking to the old and young, and that there isn't the like of him either for plough-ing and digging and going all sorts in field or shop or fair or town buying selling ⟨gam-ing⟩ tasting. He's a nice boy surely. . . .' The 'trick o' the loop man' was originally a 'thimble and pea man', then a 'needle and loop man', all games Synge observed on his visit to the Dingle circus (see Appendix B, Section III).

[4] A revision of draft 'H' reads: '[*with a bottle of stout*]. There's a bottle will soothe us and let you not be heeding that young lad for he'll be getting rightly hobbled yet. . . .' Beside this speech in the second draft of TS. 'F' Synge suggested, 'Give to Shawn at betrothal scene'.

[5] Earlier drafts expand this: 'which would be self-destruction and contrary to Scriptures'.

[6] Draft 'F' adds the direction *looking in*.

[7] Draft 'D' adds 'You're a simple man.' Until draft 'H' Philly was given the speeches describing the skulls in Dublin, to which Jimmy replies, 'If that's the truth the Dublin peopl⟨e⟩ should be a low mad lot and it's no lie. [*Contemptuously.*] Looking on skulls.'

ACT III

Scene, as before. Later in the day. JIMMY *comes in, slightly drunk.*

JIMMY [*calls*]. Pegeen! [*Crosses to inner door.*] Pegeen Mike! [*Comes back again into the room.*] Pegeen! [PHILLY *comes in in the same state.*] [*To* PHILLY.] Did you see herself?

PHILLY. I did not; but I sent Shawn Keogh with the ass cart for to bear him home. [*Trying cupboards which are locked.*] Well, isn't he a nasty man to get into such staggers at a morning wake, and isn't herself the divil's daughter for locking, and she so fussy after that young gaffer, you might take your death with drought and none to heed you.[1]

JIMMY.[2] It's little wonder she'd be fussy, and he after bringing bankrupt ruin on the roulette man, and the trick-o'-the-loop man, and breaking the nose of the cockshot-man, and winning all in the sports below, racing, lepping, dancing, and the Lord knows what! He's right luck, I'm telling you.[3]

PHILLY.[4] If he has he'll be rightly hobbled yet, and he not able to say ten words without making a brag of the way he killed his father and the great blow he hit with the loy.

JIMMY. A man can't hang by his own informing,[5] and his father should be rotten by now.

[OLD MAHON *passes window slowly.*[6]]

PHILLY. Supposing a man's digging spuds in that field with a long spade, and supposing he flings up the two halves of that skull, what'll be said then in the papers and the courts of law?

JIMMY. They'd say it was an old Dane, maybe, was drowned in the flood. [OLD MAHON *comes in and sits down near door listening.*] Did you never hear tell of the skulls they have in the city of Dublin, ranged out like blue jugs in a cabin of Connaught?

PHILLY. And you believe that?[7]

JIMMY [*pugnaciously*]. Didn't a lad see them and he after coming from harvesting in the Liverpool boat? 'They have them there,' says he,

¹ Draft 'D' adds the following speech before Philly's reply:

OLD MAHON [*coming forward*]. In the old times there were fine skulls and they have them above there I'm thinking making a show, for there's few young people have decent stubborn bones in them at all.

² Draft 'K' originally read 'through the armies of the land', which Synge altered to 'in a peeler or a priest itself', then struck that out and wrote 'in the cities of the world'.

³ Draft 'B' added the direction, *taking off his hat and shows his head with a black strip of plaster down the middle.*

⁴ Draft 'D' gives Old Mahon a different speech: 'If he was fine itself I'll lay a wagered bet there's no dead man or living man with finer bones than me. [*Taking off his hat.*] Look at that. Would you see another skull in Ireland would heal up the like of that after getting a great clout with a loy?'

⁵ Synge had difficulty with this transition. At first he had the men carrying off Old Mahon before the crowd entered, omitting the race and the Widow Quin, as in draft 'D':

OLD MAHON. Would you have me tell you a long story and my tongue crackling with drouth?

TIMMY. Come beyond and have a sup, there's a place beyond none knows of at all.

OLD MAHON. I will and welcome. And I'll tell you the finest story you've heard in this place I'm thinking this long many a day.

[*They go out as tumult begins L. In a moment crowd comes in half pulling and carrying* CHRISTY, *everyone shaking him by the hand.*]

Draft 'E' expands on the delight in a new story to rival Christy's:

JIMMY. Well there's great doings this time in Ireland, and come along now to ⟨a⟩ place below where we'll give you a sup, and let you tell us your whole history from the start to end.

OLD MAHON. I'll go and thank you kindly. And oh it's a great queer story I'll be telling, a great wonder I'm saying of a dark villainous deed and the treacherous idiot was my youngest son.

PHILLY and JIMMY. Let you make haste now till you tell us. That'll be a fine story to hear and Michael James and the other lad thinking they have the one wonder-story is left within the world. [*They bundle him out R.*]

The next draft, 'F' (24 January 1906), develops the characterization and introduces the race:

PHILLY [*contemptuously*]. And you're hoping maybe to sell your old corpse in the city of Dublin. And you're hoping maybe to raise a mortgage on your skull top in the Dublin show?

OLD MAHON [*taking off his hat*]. Is it making game of me you'd be? Look at that head and tell me where you'd see another man in gay spirits voyaging the world with them rags wrapping his head?

PHILLY [*with curiosity*]. Who done that?

OLD MAHON [*with impatience*]. You'd like to make more game maybe of my talking now? Go on and don't mind me at all. [*Puts on his hat.*]

JIMMY [*excited*]. You should have a great story if you tell us now.

OLD MAHON [*going to fire*]. I'll have none of your game so don't heed me at all.

PHILLY. It's little we're likely to heed you. What do the likes of us care for the old trampers is running the world.

OLD MAHON [*turning on him*]. If I wasn't wearied and disabled with that blow and I after

[*Note continued on p. 136.*]

'making a show of the great people there was one time walking the world. White skulls and black skulls and yellow skulls, and some with full teeth and some haven't only but one.'[1]

PHILLY. It was no lie, maybe, for when I was a young lad, there was a graveyard beyond the house with the remnants of a man who had thighs as long as your arm. He was a horrid man, I'm telling you, and there was many a fine Sunday I'd put him together for fun, and he with shiny bones you wouldn't meet the like of these days in the cities of the world.[2]

MAHON [*getting up*[3]]. You wouldn't is it? Lay your eyes on that skull, and tell me where and when there was another the like of it, is splintered only from the blow of a loy.[4]

PHILLY. Glory be to God! And who hit you at all?

MAHON [*triumphantly*]. It was my own son hit me. Would you believe that?

JIMMY. Well there's wonders hidden in the heart of man!

PHILLY [*suspiciously*]. And what way was it done?

MAHON [*wandering about the room*]. I'm after walking hundreds and long scores of miles, winning clean beds and the fill of my belly four times in the day, and I doing nothing but telling stories of that naked truth. [*He comes to them a little aggressively*.] Give me a supeen and I'll tell you now.

[WIDOW QUIN *comes in and stands aghast behind him. He is facing* JIMMY *and* PHILLY, *who are on the left*.]

JIMMY. Ask herself beyond. She's the stuff hidden in her shawl.[5]

WIDOW QUIN [*coming to* MAHON *quickly*]. You here, is it? You didn't go far at all?

MAHON. I seen the coasting steamer passing, and I got a drought upon me and a cramping leg, so I said, 'The divil go along with him,' and turned again. [*Looking under her shawl*.] And let you give me a supeen, for I'm destroyed travelling since Tuesday was a week.

WIDOW QUIN [*getting a glass, in a cajoling tone*]. Sit down then by the fire and take your ease for a space. You've a right to be destroyed indeed, with your walking, and fighting, and facing the sun [*giving

Note 5 (cont.), p. 135.

running the tide, I'd leave you so that every dirty daughter you have would ⟨be⟩ making her dowry selling your thigh bones to the English at Recess Hotel beyond at Ballycroy.

PHILLY [*taking off his coat*]. Old and dirty as you are I'll not take that talk of you at all.

JIMMY [*who has looked out of window*]. Don't strike him Philly. There's the young daddy-slaying lad after mounting for the mule race on the sands below. Come and there'll ⟨be⟩ more diversion in the lake. Look on the mule kicking beneath oh, the playboy, come along with me now. [*They go.*]

Next, Synge decided to leave Old Mahon on stage while Philly and Jimmy leave for the races, before the Widow Quin arrives. He struck out the quarrel in draft 'F' and had Old Mahon refusing to leave with the men, stretching out behind the counter, and startling the Widow Quin after she enters. A marginal note to this draft of TS. 'F' reads: 'Make W.Q. eject Philly and Jimmy. How?' The same draft includes an alternative entry:

WIDOW QUIN [*runs in with a jar of poteen*]. Oh, you put the fear of death in me. I didn't know any was here. What brought you back at all?

OLD MAHON. I was stuck in the tide beyond. I'm thinking he's escaped me now.

PEGEEN [*comes in with another jar*]. There was a run I thought I seen a peeler looking up from the hill. [*They hide the jars. To* WIDOW QUIN.] Who's that fellow?

WIDOW QUIN. A poor man has had trouble I met passing this morning. I was saying to him you⟨'d⟩ let him stretch a while in the room beyond. He's destroyed travelling with an injured head.

PEGEEN. He may go where he likes. They're running the mule race I⟨'m⟩ going to them now. [*She goes.*]

OLD MAHON [*going to window*]. Over who is it they're making their almighty fuss?

WIDOW QUIN. A young man is back from harvesting of the name of Christy Flin.

The next draft, a revised TS. 'F', again carries a marginal note: 'Make exit of men prior to W.Q.'s entrance. She comes in expressly to interview Old Mahon as she has seen him passing (she is bothered). Make them in hurry to get back to races.' This same draft includes references to 'an old man's after being drowned in the sand', and Synge included an alternative scene in which the Widow Quin ejected Philly and Jimmy by sending Christy the message that his father had drowned. (See Appendix B for scenario in Note-book 34.)

By draft 'H' the scene had taken its final form, although in this draft Old Mahon is given his own story of the fight: 'I was destroyed with his fooling till one day I went down on my two knees to pray for his chastisement from the Lord of Grace and himself did come behind me and hit upon me with a weighty loy and then off fleeing through the world, and myself trampling on his shadow for a mile or more.' In this same draft Old Mahon is asked his name and replies 'Christopher Mahon'.

---

¹ Struck out of draft 'J' is Philly's comment, 'Do you know what I'm thinking that man is Christy's father and he's not killed at all.'

² Draft 'J' at one time included extra dialogue here:

MAHON [*swaying himself, they all listen*]. Well that's a great alleviation from the terrors of the world. [WIDOW QUIN *goes to his side.*] Ah it's a bad case for to have his like turn upon me with the blow of a loy.

PHILLY [*in a whisper*]. The blow of a loy.

MAHON [*continuing*]. And I the one did tend him from his hour of birth, . . .

him poteen from a stone jar she has brought in]. There now is a drink for you, and may it be to your happiness and length of life.

MAHON [*taking glass greedily, and sitting down by fire*]. God increase you!

WIDOW QUIN [*taking* MEN *to the right stealthily*]. Do you know what? That man's raving from his wound to-day, for I met him a while since telling a rambling tale of a tinker had him destroyed. Then he heard of Christy's deed, and he up and says it was his son had cracked his skull. Oh, isn't madness a fright, for he'll go killing someone yet and he thinking it's the man has struck him so![1]

JIMMY [*entirely convinced*]. It's a fright surely. I knew a party was kicked in the head by a red mare, and he went killing horses a great while, till he eat the insides of a clock and died after.

PHILLY [*with suspicion*]. Did he see Christy?

WIDOW QUIN. He didn't. [*With a warning gesture.*] Let you not be putting him in mind of him, or you'll be likely summoned if there's murder done. [*Looking round at* MAHON.] Whisht! He's listening. Wait now till you hear me taking him easy and unravelling all. [*She goes to* MAHON.] And what way are you feeling, Mister? Are you in contentment now?

MAHON [*slightly emotional from his drink*]. I'm poorly only, for it's a hard story the way I'm left to-day, when it was I did tend him from his hour of birth,[2] and he a dunce never reached his second book, the way he'd come from school, many's the day, with his legs lamed under him, and he blackened with his beatings like a tinker's ass. It's a hard story, I'm saying, the way some do have their next and nighest raising up a hand of murder on them, and some is lonesome getting their death with lamentation in the dead of night.

WIDOW QUIN [*not knowing what to say*]. To hear you talking so quiet, who'd know you were the same fellow we seen pass to-day?

MAHON. I'm the same surely. The wrack and ruin of three score years; and it's a terror to live that length, I tell you, and to have your sons going to the dogs against you, and you wore out scolding them, and skelping them, and God knows what.

PHILLY [*to* JIMMY]. He's not raving. [*To* WIDOW QUIN.] Will you ask him what kind was his son?

¹ A late draft adds the direction *that makes Jimmy nod wisely at Philly.*

² A note to draft 'H' reads 'Work up Mahon's lamentation over Christy's fate which is broken in on by the cheering.'

³ A letter to his fiancée Molly Allgood on 3 September 1906 from Kerry describes the races at Rossbeigh which Synge attended with Philly Harris: 'They—the races—were run on a flat strand when the tide was out. It was a brilliant day and the jockeys and crowd looked very gay against the blue sea. . . .'

⁴ Additional stage directions from final typescripts.

WIDOW QUIN [*to* MAHON, *with a peculiar look*]. Was your son that hit you a lad of one year and a score maybe, a great hand at racing and lepping and licking the world?

MAHON [*turning on her with a roar of rage*[1]]. Didn't you hear me say he was the fool of men, the way from this out he'll know the orphan's lot with old and young making game of him and they swearing, raging, kicking at him like a mangy cur.[2]

[*A great burst of cheering outside, some way off.*]

MAHON [*putting his hands to his ears*]. What in the name of God do they want roaring below?

WIDOW QUIN [*with the shade of a smile*]. They're cheering a young lad, the champion playboy of the western world.

[*More cheering.*]

MAHON [*going to window*]. It'd split my heart to hear them, and I with pulses in my brain-pan for a week gone by. Is it racing they are?

JIMMY [*looking from door*]. It is then. They are mounting him for the mule race will be run upon the sands.[3] That's the playboy on the winkered mule.

MAHON [*puzzled*]. That lad, is it? If you said it was a fool he was, I'd have laid a mighty oath he was the likeness of my wandering son. [PHILLY *nods at* JIMMY.[4] MAHON, *uneasily, putting his hand to his head.*] Faith, I'm thinking I'll go walking for to view the race.

WIDOW QUIN [*stopping him, sharply*]. You will not. You'd best take the road to Belmullet, and not be dilly-dallying in this place where there isn't a spot you could sleep.

PHILLY [*coming forward*]. Don't mind her. Mount there on the bench and you'll have a view of the whole. They're hurrying before the tide will rise, and it'd be near over if you went down the pathway through the crags below.

MAHON [*mounts on bench*, WIDOW QUIN *beside him*]. That's a right view again the edge of the sea. They're coming now from the point. He's leading. Who is he at all?

WIDOW QUIN. He's the champion of the world I tell you, and there isn't a hap'orth isn't falling lucky to his hands to-day.

¹ The early 'F' draft, in which the Widow Quin and Old Mahon watch the race alone reads:

WIDOW [*in great excitement*]. Watch him taking the gate! More power to you Chr—
[*Claps her hand to her mouth, she is behind* MAHON.]

² The phrase 'mule kicking the stars' was originally recorded in Notebook 44.

³ Not until draft 'H' do all four watch the race together. A marginal note to draft 'G' reads 'test speed'; a later fragment still includes the instruction 'sharpen'.

⁴ A marginal note to draft 'F', the first draft with the race, reads 'This would make good exposing scene for III???????' All the typescript drafts read 'by the hairs of God' for 'the stars of God', which must have been altered at the proof stage.

PHILLY [*looking out, interested in the race*]. Look at that. They're pressing him now.

JIMMY. He'll win it yet.

PHILLY. Take your time, Jimmy Farrell. It's too soon to say.

WIDOW QUIN [*shouting*]. Watch him taking the gate. There's riding.[1]

JIMMY [*cheering*]. More power to the young lad!

MAHON. He's passing the third.

JIMMY. He'll lick them yet.

WIDOW QUIN. He'd lick them if he was running races with a score itself.

MAHON. Look at the mule he has kicking the stars.[2]

WIDOW QUIN. There was a lep! [*Catching hold of* MAHON *in her excitement.*] He's fallen! He's mounted again! Faith, he's passing them all!

JIMMY. Look at him skelping her!

PHILLY. And the mountain girls hooshing him on!

JIMMY. It's the last turn! The post's cleared for them now!

MAHON. Look at the narrow place. He'll be into the bogs! [*With a yell.*] Good rider! He's through it again!

JIMMY. He's neck and neck!

MAHON. Good boy to him! Flames, but he's in![3]

[*Great cheering, in which all join.*]

MAHON [*with hesitation*]. What's that? They're raising him up. They're coming this way. [*With a roar of rage and astonishment.*] It's Christy! by the stars of God! I'd know his way of spitting and he astride the moon.[4] [*He jumps down and makes a run for the door, but* WIDOW QUIN *catches him and pulls him back.*]

WIDOW QUIN. Stay quiet, will you. That's not your son. [*To* JIMMY.] Stop him, or you'll get a month for the abetting of manslaughter and be fined as well.

JIMMY. I'll hold him.

[1] The final typescript originally read, 'till I make a jelly of his bones and flesh to-day'.

[2] A note to the revised draft 'F' reads 'Give Old Mahon superlative Rabelaisian astonishment at what W.Q. ⟨is⟩ telling him of Christy's doings—.'

[3] The final typescript adds the words, 'and the curse of Cromwell and Judas on my crown today'.

MAHON [*struggling*]. Let me out! Let me out the lot of you! till I have my vengeance on his head to-day.[1]

WIDOW QUIN [*shaking him, vehemently*]. That's not your son. That's a man is going to make a marriage with the daughter of this house, a place with fine trade, with a licence, and with poteen too.

MAHON [*amazed*]. That man marrying a decent and a moneyed girl! Is it mad yous are? Is it in a crazy-house for females that I'm landed now?[2]

WIDOW QUIN. It's mad yourself is with the blow upon your head. That lad is the wonder of the western world.

MAHON. I seen it's my son.

WIDOW QUIN. You seen that you're mad. [*Cheering outside.*] Do you hear them cheering him in the zig-zags of the road? Aren't you after saying that your son's a fool, and how would they be cheering a true idiot born?

MAHON [*getting distressed*]. It's maybe out of reason that man's himself. [*Cheering again.*] There's none surely will go cheering him. Oh, I'm raving with a madness that would fright the world.[3] [*He sits down with his hand to his head.*] There was one time I seen ten scarlet divils letting on they'd cork my spirit in a gallon can; and one time I seen rats as big as badgers sucking the life blood from the butt of my lug; but I never till this day confused that dribbling idiot with a likely man. I'm destroyed surely.

WIDOW QUIN. And who'd wonder when it's your brain-pan that is gaping now?

MAHON. Then the blight of the sacred drought upon myself and him, for I never went mad to this day, and I not three weeks with the Limerick girls drinking myself silly and parlatic from the dusk to dawn. [*To* WIDOW QUIN, *suddenly*.] Is my visage astray?

WIDOW QUIN. It is then. You're a sniggering maniac, a child could see.

MAHON [*getting up more cheerfully*]. Then I'd best be going to the Union beyond, and there'll be a welcome before me, I tell you [*with great pride*], and I a terrible and fearful case, the way that there I was one

[1] Synge had considerable difficulty with this scene. Originally he made the Widow Quin inveigle Old Mahon off before the crowd came in with Christy, avoiding a recognition scene (see Appendix B). He then decided to make Old Mahon recognize Christy (see note 4, page 140 above), with Old Mahon innocently deciding to stay and offer the pair his blessing, as in draft 'H':

WIDOW QUIN. God help you they're making a petted angel of him this place because of his great story of the way he had you splitted to the navel with a single clout.

MAHON. Well you're bloody divils this place there's no lie at all.

WIDOW QUIN. We're the like of other mortals I'm thinking thirsting for the wonders or the deeds of men.

Mahon is then persuaded to go to the Widow's house and be made more presentable. Still undecided, however, Synge added the marginal note 'reorganize dialogue' and wrote on the back of draft 'H':

'Find good exit for quartet just after chase of Widow

Possible motive $\left\{ \begin{array}{l} \text{She gets him off to give Christy time by pretext of cleaning him} \\ \text{He goes off to get clean} \\ \text{They all go into inner room to watch the fun'.} \end{array} \right.$

Synge returned to this problem several times in his entries in Notebook 34:
'Widow tries to get him on to Castlebar as before. He recognizes Christy at last turn of the race. He wants to run down at him. Widow Quin stops him. She tells the story rubbing in jest of play and telling how she has told Christy he was dead. Old Mahon does not believe her. She puts ⟨him⟩ up into loft—or behind counter to assure himself—then she goes and other things go on as before. . . .'

'Widow Quin's object in making him hide?
    Old Mahon.   You're a liar
                 You're a liar
                 I'm saying you're a liar
                 You've as many lies as ten widows in Cork.
    Widow Q. Well if you don't believe me . . .'
'When he recognizes Christy
    Be Jasus it's him. Oh Lord let me at. Wait till I tear the pudding from him. (Widow Quin pushes him back roughly).'
Finally, in draft 'J', the exit of Old Mahon took its final form.

[2] In draft 'H' Jimmy and Philly decide not to tell Pegeen and the others of the Widow's and Christy's duplicity until they see what happens. On the back of this draft, however Synge suggests another plan:

'Make men and Widow and Old Mahon *all* into secret and all combine to push on Christy's marriage for different ends. She for pity, he for greed and the men for spite against Mike James.

Work thus—he tells men his story. W.Q. runs in with poteen and news of the mule race—tries to get men out but fails, shouting 'mule race'. Mahon recognizes Christy Widow Quin and men find out each other's knowledge. Old Mahon finds out, indignant, they combine with him and exeunt to work up his entry.'

No draft of this version has been discovered, however, and draft 'K' emphasizes Philly' suspicious nature. '"Tuesday was a week," says he, and "the blow of ⟨a⟩ loy".'

[3] Draft 'D', which omits the recognition scene altogether, still places this scene on the fairgrounds:

PEGEEN [*trying to keep next* CHRISTY]. Don't destroy him now and he pouring with sweat. Leave him place to breathe will yous.

[*Note continued on p. 146.*

time screeching in a straitened waistcoat with seven doctors writing out my sayings in a printed book. Would you believe that?

WIDOW QUIN. If you're a wonder itself, you'd best be hasty, for them lads caught a maniac one time and pelted the poor creature till he ran out raving and foaming and was drowned in the sea.

MAHON [*with philosophy*]. It's true mankind is the divil when your head's astray. Let me out now and I'll slip down the boreen and not see them so.

WIDOW QUIN [*showing him out*]. That's it. Run to the right, and not a one will see.

[*He runs off.*]¹

PHILLY [*wisely*]. You're at some gaming, Widow Quin; but I'll walk after him and give him his dinner and a time to rest, and I'll see then if he's raving or as sane as you.

WIDOW QUIN [*annoyed*]. If you go near that lad, let you be wary of your head, I'm saying. Didn't you hear him telling he was crazed at times?

PHILLY. I heard him telling a power; and I'm thinking we'll have right sport, before night will fall. [*He goes out.*]

JIMMY. Well, Philly's a conceited and foolish man. How could that madman have his senses and his brain-pan slit? I'll go after them and see him turn on Philly now.²

[*He goes;* WIDOW QUIN *hides poteen behind counter. Then hubbub outside.*]

VOICES. There you are! Good jumper! Grand lepper! Darlint boy! He's the racer! Bear him on, will you!

[CHRISTY *comes in, in Jockey's dress, with* PEGEEN MIKE, SARA, *and other* GIRLS, *and* MEN.]

PEGEEN [*to* CROWD]. Go on now and don't destroy him and he drenching with sweat. Go along, I'm saying, and have your tug-of-warring till he's dried his skin.

CROWD. Here's his prizes! A bagpipes! A fiddle was played by a poet in the years gone by! A flat and three-thorned blackthorn would lick the scholars out of Dublin town!³

Notes (cont.), p. 145.

CROWD. He's the supple lad. He's ⟨a⟩ gamey talker. He's a wonder all places with the grace of God.

The prizes first occur to Synge in draft 'E', where a marginal note reads: '(prizes?) (carvers? ivory mirror, silver cork screw)'. Prizes are then included in draft 'F', but none are brought on stage until after draft 'G'. The final typescripts include an additional prize, 'a new loy', which is struck out in galley proof.

---

¹ Drafts 'E' and 'F' have the Crowd replying, 'We'll get a scabby sheep some day and let you split her with a spade.'

² In his notes on Kerry and Mayo in Notebook 34 Synge commented, 'The town-crier is still a prominent person in these smaller towns.'

³ The first version of draft 'F' suggests an additional scene:

WIDOW QUIN [*runs in with another jar. To* PEGEEN]. There's your poteen and let you hide it now.

[PEGEEN *takes jar into inner room.*]

WIDOW QUIN [*whispers to* CHRISTY]. Your daddy is above drinking poteen in the ditch. Make her swear to wed you for fear he'd turn back in spite of me and meet you now. [*Exit.*]

⁴ Originally Act III (draft 'C') began with this scene between Christy and Pegeen, with Pegeen forcing a proposal out of Christy by telling him of the proposed meeting between Shawn's father and Michael James (see Appendix B). In draft 'D' she is more subtle:

[CHRISTY *sits down on stick or stones and she sits near with attention and admiration.*]

PEGEEN [*wiping his forehead with her shawl*]. Well you're a fine lad surely. To win the prize at lepping and the prize at pitching and the prize at racing and you the worth of two dogs for chasing sheep or turning bullocks from a hill.

CHRISTY [*looking at her with delight*]. You'll find there's few things surely where I won't lick the common lot is walking the world.

PEGEEN. That's the truth I'm thinking, and it's great times you'll have in this place poaching fish and running hares, and you sporting drinking dancing when the nights are long

CHRISTY. I never knew till this day there was this sort of a joyous place on the face of the earth, where you've civil girls and kind land and no soul to trouble you at all.

PEGEEN [*with tenderness*]. You've taken a fancy to this place is it?

CHRISTY [*with intensity*]. If I wasn't a good Christian wouldn't I go down on my two knees and saying prayers and paters to every jackstraw you have above roofing your head and every stony pebble is paving up the laneway to your door.

PEGEEN [*with delight*]. Wasn't I saying at the fall of night it was the like of a poet you were surely.

CHRISTY. Who wouldn't be a poet and he after walking the little cnuceens at your side and going again through the rush of a crowd where he'd see you the whole while he'd be lepping or running itself the like of the white clouds maybe do be turning shiny at the eve of dawn.

PEGEEN [*laying her hand on his*]. Well isn't it a great blessing from God I wasn't wedded before you came up tramping from the south. There's a great hand of Providence guarding our souls.

CHRISTY. And you'll wed with myself surely?

PEGEEN. I'm thinking I will and welcome too, for you'll be great company and if you're hanged itself it'll be a fine sight to see my own name printed out in the big papers is read by the quality and the lord bishops of Ireland.

[*Notes continued on p. 148.*

CHRISTY [*taking prizes from the* MEN]. Thank you kindly, the lot of you. But you'd say it was little only I did this day if you'd seen me a while since striking my one single blow.[1]

TOWN CRIER [*outside, ringing a bell*]. Take notice, last event of this day! Tug-of-warring on the green below! Come on, the lot of you! Great achievements for all Mayo men![2]

PEGEEN. Go on, and leave him for to rest and dry. Go on, I tell you, for he'll do no more. [*She hustles* CROWD *out;* WIDOW QUIN *following them.*][3]

MEN [*going*]. Come on then. Good luck for the while!

PEGEEN [*radiantly, wiping his face with her shawl*]. Well you're the lad, and you'll have great times from this out when you could win that wealth of prizes, and you sweating in the heat of noon!

CHRISTY [*looking at her with delight*]. I'll have great times if I win the crowning prize I'm seeking now, and that's your promise that you'll wed me in a fortnight, when our banns is called.[4]

PEGEEN [*backing away from him*].[5] You've right daring to go ask me that, when all knows you'll be starting to some girl in your own townland, when your father's rotten in four months, or five.

CHRISTY [*indignantly*].[6] Starting from you, is it! [*He follows her.*] I will not then, and when the airs is warming in four months or five, it's then yourself and me should be pacing Neifin in the dews of night, the times sweet smells do be rising, and you'd see a little shiny new moon maybe sinking on the hills.[7]

PEGEEN [*looking at him playfully*]. And it's that kind of a poacher's love you'd make, Christy Mahon, on the sides of Neifin, when the night is down?

CHRISTY. It's little you'll think if my love's a poacher's or an earl's itself when you'll feel my two hands stretched around you, and I squeezing kisses on your puckered lips till I'd feel a kind of pity for the Lord God is all ages sitting lonesome in his golden chair.[8]

PEGEEN. That'll be right fun, Christy Mahon, and any girl would walk her heart out before she'd meet a young man was your like for eloquence or talk at all.

Notes (cont.), p. 147.

Still dissatisfied, Synge wrote in the margin 'lengthen love scene' and in succeeding drafts and frequently throughout his notebooks he revised the speeches until they took their final form. However, even the final version did not completely satisfy him, and among the remnants of this act are several variations marked 'L', one step past the final draft 'K'.

⁵ Earlier drafts give a different direction: [*trying to assure herself of his affection*]. A rough passage in Notebook 32 and a fragment lettered 'L' indicate a suggested revision of the final draft:

PEGEEN. And there were not kindly girls beyond is it in the place where you were raised?

CHRISTY. It was them that near destroyed me when I'd see them plucking flowers through the birches in a showery time and they not heeding me at all.

PEGEEN [*jealous*]. If they had that charm to you, you'll be likely turning to them with your grand story when your father's rotten in four months or five.

⁶ Earlier drafts expand Christy's stage directions: [*with intensity but feeling her passion and consequently taking the upper hand*]. Marginal notes to draft 'G' read 'Keep in central motif somewhere in this scene' and 'Keep Christy's character'. In Notebook 34 Synge suggested, 'In Ch's interview with P. III make him sound her as to how she would take news of his father's survival.' However, the only dialogue developing this idea occurs elsewhere in Notebook 34:

in P.C. (duo)

I had a great fright this morning for ⟨I⟩ heard tell a man the like of him was seen here, but he was drownded by the mercy of the Lord God.

P. Why would ⟨that⟩ fright you. Do you think your father⟨'d⟩ rise up and he split to the belt?

CH. A villain the like of him God knows what he'd do. When a man's that wicket who'd know what he'd do—

⁷ Several speeches in Notebook 41 (August 1905) seem to apply here:

'For Ch. Mahon

The time the seas would be whitening and the hills would be darkening and the waters lifting up their voices to the Heavens above. . . .

out talking poetry on the highway J.M.S. . . .

with a scented stink arising J.M.S.'

⁸ Beside the version of this speech in draft 'G' Synge wrote 'condense'. Not until the final typescript did he alter the words 'holy father' to 'Lord God'.

---

¹ More than a dozen different versions of this speech exist in Synge's drafts and notebooks. A much-revised speech in Notebook 31 appears to be the first draft: 'There's not a moon of midnight wouldn't be proud to be facing you, and you rising southways like the pride of Greece along the heather of a furzy hill.' However, the first indication of its final form occurs in Notebook 34, dated 13 January 1906: 'Like the holy prophets looking through the gate of Heaven on the lady Helen and she walking back and forward with a nosegay in her shawl.' By draft 'J' (24 September 1906) the speech had come very close to its final form, but Synge wrote in the margin 'rhythm?': 'If the mitred bishops would see you that time they'd be the like of the holy prophets, I'm thinking, do be straining the bars of paradise to set their eyes on the Lady Helen abroad does be pacing back and forward (all roads) with a nosegay in her shawl (or golden shawl).'

² Not until after draft 'J' did Synge cut out a speech he introduced in draft 'G':

PEGEEN [*cuddling close to him*]. It's many girls in this place will have a yellow face of envy when they hear you talking that way to myself alone. [*She raises herself slightly and sighs with immeasurable satisfaction.*]

[*Notes continued on p. 150.*]

CHRISTY [*encouraged*]. Let you wait to hear me talking till we're astray in Erris when Good Friday's by, drinking a sup from a well, and making mighty kisses with our wetted mouths, or gaming in a gap of sunshine with yourself stretched back unto your necklace in the flowers of the earth.

PEGEEN [*in a lower voice, moved by his tone*]. I'd be nice so, is it?

CHRISTY [*with rapture*]. If the mitred bishops seen you that time, they'd be the like of the holy prophets, I'm thinking, do be straining the bars of Paradise to lay eyes on the Lady Helen of Troy, and she abroad pacing back and forward with a nosegay in her golden shawl.[1]

PEGEEN [*with real tenderness*]. And what is it I have, Christy Mahon, to make me fitting entertainment for the like of you that has such poet's talking, and such bravery of heart?[2]

CHRISTY [*in a low voice*]. Isn't there the light of seven heavens in your heart alone, the way you'll be an angel's lamp to me from this out, and I abroad in the darkness spearing salmons in the Owen or the Carrowmore.[3]

PEGEEN. If I was your wife, I'd be along with you those nights, Christy Mahon, the way you'd see I was a great hand at coaxing bailiffs, or coining funny nicknames for the stars of night.

CHRISTY. You, is it! Taking your death in the hailstones or the fogs of dawn.[4]

PEGEEN. Yourself and me would shelter easy in a narrow bush, [*with a qualm of dread*] but we're only talking maybe, for this would be a poor thatched place to hold a fine lad is the like of you.[5]

CHRISTY [*putting his arm round her*]. If I wasn't a good Christian, it's on my naked knees I'd be saying my prayers and paters to every jack-straw you have roofing your head, and every stony pebble is paving the laneway to your door.[6]

PEGEEN [*radiantly*]. If that's the truth, I'll be burning candles from this out to the miracles of God have brought you[7] from the south to-day, and I with my gowns bought ready the way that I can wed you, and not wait at all.[8]

Notes (cont.), p. 149.

³ A remnant lettered 'L' finally strikes out a speech first suggested in Notebook 32:

CHRISTY. Haven't you the glory of the Heavens in your steps alone, and you with a voice the way that when you wed me, I'll have your voice all times filling my ears, and when I'd be abroad spearing salmons in the dark night, and I thinking the whole while on yourself waiting below with a clean bed for me with two sheets upon it or your quilt of braid.

PEGEEN. My quilt is darned and blackened only Christy Mahon, the way it's likely a richer place than this old shanty you'll be seeking when the spring will come.

⁴ Although the Maunsel edition reads 'in the fogs of dawn', none of the drafts does, and it appears unnecessary to the rhythm or meaning.

⁵ Draft 'G' expanded Pegeen's fears: 'It's a poor place we have only Christy Mahon for the like of you, a place of famine and of idiots and of holy brotherhoods won't drink at all, the way it's another townland you'll be likely seeking maybe when the spring will come.'

⁶ Christy's prayer first appears in draft 'H' with the marginal note 'expand prayer': 'God be praised for leading me to this day, and I a lost man straying in the wildness of the world.' A remnant struck from draft 'L' indicates that he felt he had embroidered too much:

PEGEEN [*slyly*]. Yourself and me would shelter easy in a narrow bush the way I'd see you making a Jacob's ladder of a whiff of hail the way you're making a queen's bower of my shanty here.

CHRISTY [*putting his arm round her*]. A queen's bower is it or the yardway to the throne of God for if I wasn't a good Christian you know rightly it's on my naked knees I'd be saying my prayers and paters to every jack-straw you have roofing your head and every stony pebble is paving the laneway to your door.

PEGEEN [*playfully but tenderly*]. Well I'm thinking a lad the like of you would win the queen princess of the Eastern world, but keep your reverence with your talking Christy Mahon for it's my prayers have kept me from temptation at a later day, and I'll be burning candles from this out to the miracles of God have led you to me and I with my gowns all bought or ordered the way that I can wed you and not wait at all.

CHRISTY [*eagerly*]. You'll wed me so?

PEGEEN. I will surely.

CHRISTY [*radiantly*]. Well it's the miracles. . . .

A marginal note to this speech in draft 'K' reads 'mark moment when she gives in', and a comment following the original draft of this expanded speech in Notebook 33 may also have relevance: 'The opening of the Mer. of Venice is outside the play. Atmosphere should *be in the essence.*'

⁷ The Maunsel edition reads 'that have brought you', but none of the drafts adds the word which seems unnecessary to rhythm or meaning.

⁸ When Synge revised draft 'F' he considered giving Pegeen more business during this scene. First she brushes his clothes, then throughout the dialogue interjects comments:

. . . Wait till I get you a basin to wash. [*She takes the doughpan, wipes dough out.*]

. . . There's my comb.

. . . Look the nails you have on you come here to me. [*She gets scissors.*]

. . . Stand up till I look at you. Your head's needing clipping I'm thinking. Sit down there. [*She throws an oilskin coat round him and is going to cut his hair.*]

---

¹ Pegeen's speech in this form does not appear until draft 'J'. Earlier drafts read:

CHRISTY. There is then Pegeen Mike. And isn't it a great joy was in store for me the whole while I was walking the world, and I coming on unbeknownsted, and coming on unbeknownsted, drawing all times nearer to the golden glory of this passing day.

[*Notes continued on p. 152.*]

CHRISTY. It's miracles and that's the truth. Me there toiling a long while, and walking a long while, not knowing at all I was drawing all times nearer to this holy day.

PEGEEN. And myself a girl was tempted often to go sailing the seas till I'd marry a Jew-man with ten kegs of gold, and I not knowing at all there was the like of you drawing nearer like the stars of God.[1]

CHRISTY. And to think I'm long years hearing women talking that talk to all bloody fools, and this the first time I've heard the like of your voice talking sweetly for my own delight.[2]

PEGEEN. And to think it's me is talking sweetly, Christy Mahon, and I the fright of seven townlands for my biting tongue. Well the heart's a wonder, and I'm thinking there won't be our like in Mayo for gallant lovers from this hour to-day.[3] [*Drunken singing is heard outside.*] There's my father coming from the wake, and when he's had his sleep we'll tell him, for he's peaceful then. [*They separate.*][4]

MICHAEL [*singing outside*]—

> The jailor and the turnkey
>   They quickly ran us down,
> And brought us back as prisoners
>   Once more to Cavan town.

[*He comes in supported by* SHAWN.]

> There we lay bewailing
>   All in a prison bound. . . .

[*He sees* CHRISTY. *Goes and shakes him drunkenly by the hand, while* PEGEEN *and* SHAWN *talk on the left.*]

MICHAEL [*to* CHRISTY]. The blessing of God and the holy angels on your head, young fellow. I hear tell you're after winning all in the sports below; and wasn't it a shame I didn't bear you along with me to Kate Cassidy's wake, a fine, stout lad, the like of you, for you'd never see the match of it for flows of drink, the way when we sunk her bones at noonday in her narrow grave, there were five men, aye, and six men, stretched out retching speechless on the holy stones.[5]

CHRISTY [*uneasily, watching* PEGEEN]. Is that the truth?

Notes (cont.), p. 151.

PEGEEN. I'm thinking it's the miracles and work of God, me there sitting above like a fettered kid you'd leave tethered in the west of a yard, and I not knowing at all that the while I was waking and the while I was sleeping there was the like of you walking or coming ever forward like the stars of night.

² Apparently Synge decided not to use a speech he jotted down in Notebook 32: 'Won't it ⟨be⟩ grand setting out so early to rear a long family a dozen maybe or a score itself. Won't it be grand straying round a Sunday evening to hear the larks linnets.' A note on the back of draft 'H' also applies to the love scene: 'Work in the splendour of the day which follows the dark wet night.'

³ An early draft adds the direction [*with a touch of slyness*]. Earlier drafts read 'If it's long you were waiting itself you'll get good love and living in the end of time, for there won't be many in Ireland will have a girl will tend him the like of myself on you.' By draft 'H' Synge contemplated expanding this even more: 'I've a nice gallon of poteen I'll give to Father Reilly at the dawn of day the way that he will wed us and not wait at all. So our torments will be ended that time Christy Mahon for there's none will have a girl to tend him like myself on you.' This speech was questioned, then struck out of draft 'J'.

⁴ At one time Synge contemplated a brief scene only between Pegeen and Christy, the central emphasis on this scene with Michael James (see Appendix B). By draft 'F' he considered having Old Mahon hiding in the inner room:

[OLD MAHON *looks out of door, but at same moment drunken singing begins outside L.*]

PEGEEN. It's my father coming from the wake. Don't let on the while he's drunk.

[OLD MAHON *pulls back hastily;* MICHAEL'*s head outside.*]

⁵ The final typescript was altered considerably, perhaps as a result of the cuts made at rehearsal; draft 'K' originally read 'a bloody shame', 'pitched her bloody bones, God rest them, at the turn of noonday to her narrow grave', and 'retching, spewing speechless on the holy stones'.

---

¹ Draft 'K' originally read 'stinking' for 'rotting'.

² Struck out of draft 'D' is Christy's interjection '[*struck by the idea*]. You're thinking that?' Not until after draft 'E' is Shawn's father eliminated from the proceedings; the dispensation enters with draft 'F' (24 January 1906). Again the final typescript has been altered, originally reading 'sniffing out a bloody and a female wife' and adding the words 'and it all in comely writing from the seven sacred fingers of the holy Father in the Courts of Rome'.

³ Draft 'D' gives the direction [*with consternation*]; draft 'F' reads [*dumbfounded*].

⁴ Draft 'D' gives Michael the direction [*slyly*].

⁵ Drafts 'H' and 'K' originally added the words, 'in gallous Latin, with your two names in it the way you wouldn't know them at all'. Draft 'F' gives a different reason for the hurry: 'He'll wed you he says fearing that lad at break of day, for himself is going retreat at the fall of night.'

⁶ This form of Michael's speech did not appear until draft 'H'. Draft 'F' reads:

PEGEEN. I'd liefer wed with Mr. Mahon by your kindly leave.

MICHAEL [*thunderstruck*]. With him?

PEGEEN. Aye. Wouldn't it be a bitter thing for a girl to go marrying the like of Shaneen and he a middling kind of a scarecrow with no savagery or fine words in him at all?

MICHAEL. There's a dangerous story and I without a decent cartridge for to ram into my gun. [*He sits down centre.*]

CHRISTY. You'd do well to let her wed me or to mind her deeds.

PEGEEN. Faith I know now the way a girl should manage with a crusty da.

MICHAEL. It is then, and aren't you a louty schemer to go burying your poor father unbeknownst when you'd a right to throw him on the crupper of a Kerry mule and drive him westwards, like holy Joseph in the days gone by, the way we could have given him a decent burial and not have him rotting[1] beyond and not a Christian drinking a smart drop to the glory of his soul.

CHRISTY [*gruffly*]. It's well enough he's lying for the likes of him.

MICHAEL [*slapping him on the back*]. Well, aren't you a hardened slayer? It'll be a poor thing for the household man where you go sniffing for a female wife; and [*pointing to* SHAWN] look beyond at that shy and decent Christian I have chosen for my daughter's hand, and I after getting the gilded dispensation this day for to wed them now.[2]

CHRISTY.[3] And you'll be wedding them this day, is it?

MICHAEL [*drawing himself up*].[4] Aye. Are you thinking, if I'm drunk itself I'd leave my daughter living single with a little frisky rascal is the like of you?

PEGEEN [*breaking away from* SHAWN]. Is it the truth the dispensation's come?

MICHAEL [*triumphantly*]. Father Reilly's after reading it in gallous Latin, and 'It's come in the nick of time,' says he; 'so I'll wed them in a hurry, dreading that young gaffer who'd capsize the stars.'[5]

PEGEEN [*fiercely*]. He's missed his nick of time, for it's that lad, Christy Mahon, that I'm wedding now.

MICHAEL [*loudly, with horror*]. You'd be making him a son to me and he wet and crusted with his father's blood?

PEGEEN. Aye. Wouldn't it be a bitter thing for a girl to go marrying the like of Shaneen, and he a middling kind of a scarecrow with no savagery or fine words in him at all?

MICHAEL [*gasping and sinking on a chair*]. Oh, aren't you a heathen daughter to go shaking the fat of my heart, and I swamped and drownded with the weight of drink? Would you have them turning on me the way that I'd be roaring to the dawn of day with the wind upon my heart? Have you not a word to aid me, Shaneen? Are you not jealous at all?[6]

¹ Draft 'F' gives Pegeen a lengthier complaint:

Well it'd be a bitter thing for a poor girl to go marrying a heartless villain the like of you. Seeing a young lad carrying on beneath your eyes with your dispensed girl and not minding at all. Oh, you're the divil's villain, Shaneen Keogh, Oh wasn't it a blessing from God I didn't wed you before himself did come. Oh, isn't it a dangerous world for a poor orphaned girl the like of me?

SHAWN [*at his wit's end*]. Well aren't you a contrary female girl to be edging me on and edging me on to vex a man that killed his father the way you'll be left a kind of a widow woman maybe and you not wedded at all.

PEGEEN [*putting her handkerchief to her eyes*]. Oh, it's a heartless world, and I am seeing now you were thinking of little but the barrels of porter beyond and the bottles in the shop. Who is there to blame me this day, if I turn against you and wed the little tramper has a loyal heart.

Originally draft 'K' read: '[*turning on him with a scornful smile*]. I'll not let him touch you Shaneen let you not be quaking at all if you rise up and walk from this.'

² Beside this speech in his revised draft 'F' Synge wrote 'use perhaps elsewhere'.

³ Draft 'C' describes Shawn's gifts as 'a drift of ewes, and a little filly has the blood in her of a grand horse is after losing races the crater in all the counties of the east'. Pegeen replies in a speech not struck out until after draft 'F', 'You know rightly your heifer's a cough and your ewes have the scab.'

⁴ Originally this reply was given to Christy, who says in draft 'E', 'If he'd promised ~~the sea serpents of old Jonah's whale~~ the golden crowns and jewels of the last pharaoh I'd make her quit them this day for the choice of me, and I a man is after licking the world below, and destroying his pa, the way there'll not be a girl in the barony but'll be turning yellow green and they thinking on her luck.' The next drafts have Pegeen replying, 'Don't be blubbing Shaneen Keogh for I wouldn't wed you if I seen you driving me a million cattle from the pastures of Kildare, and you bedizened maybe in the golden diamant jewelleries of Pharaoh's ma.'

⁵ Draft 'K' adds the final direction *with a slight curtsey to him*. Synge tried various combinations in this scene. After draft 'D' he considered making Michael James exit alone, in search of a drink. This idea was developed in a revised draft of 'E', in which Michael James drags Christy off with him:

PEGEEN [*to* MICHAEL]. Is it the truth he's saying, you've promised me this day for his hand

MICHAEL [*triumphantly*]. Ay, surely, and a fine bargained match I made too, and I near roaring itself. Let you tell her, Shawn Keogh, the power I'm making you give, and let you lead me below Christy daddy-man till I quench my scalding stomach with a gallon draft of hops. [*He goes towards R. dragging* CHRISTY.]

CHRISTY. Leave me here till I talk with him. I'd liefer stay.

MICHAEL [*dragging him out*]. Come on with myself. There's foolish dribbling love talk will be coming now from them.

CHRISTY [*repeating at the same time*]. I'd liefer stay with Pegeen. I'd liefer stay I'm saying

MICHAEL. Come on for a sup. You're a decent lad. Come on now I'm saying and don't have your stomach twisted with their lisping jaw. [*He drags him out leaving* PEGEEN *and* SHAWN. *Pause while they look at each other.*] Leave them a short while to make their kisses and embraces now. [*Exeunt.*]

PEGEEN. Isn't that young fellow a great wonder. Did you ever see anyplace the like of him for a lovely young fellow, and if you'd heard him a while since making high sprightly talk of me like a Mayo song, with fine courting words in it and great guff and praises of my looks and shape.

SHAWN [*awkward and miserable*]. Is that the truth?

[*Notes continued on p. 156.*]

SHAWN [*in great misery*]. I'd be afeard to be jealous of a man did slay his da.

PEGEEN. Well, it'd be a poor thing to go marrying your like. I'm seeing there's a world of peril for an orphan girl, and isn't it a great blessing I didn't wed you, before himself came walking from the west or south.[1]

SHAWN. It's a queer story you'd go picking a dirty tramp up from the highways of the world.

PEGEEN [*playfully*]. And you think you're a likely beau to go straying along with, the shiny Sundays of the opening year, when it's sooner on a bullock's liver you'd put a poor girl thinking than on the lily or the rose.[2]

SHAWN. And have you no mind of my weight of passion, and the holy dispensation, and the drift of heifers I am giving, and the golden ring?[3]

PEGEEN. I'm thinking you're too fine for the like of me, Shawn Keogh of Killakeen, and let you go off till you'd find a radiant lady with droves of bullocks on the plains of Meath, and herself bedizened in the diamond jewelleries of Pharaoh's ma.[4] That'd be your match, Shaneen. So God save you now! [*She retreats behind* CHRISTY[5].]

SHAWN. Won't you hear me telling you. . . .

CHRISTY [*with ferocity*]. Take yourself from this, young fellow, or I'll maybe add a murder to my deeds to-day.[6]

MICHAEL [*springing up with a shriek*]. Murder is it? Is it mad yous are? Would you go making murder in this place, and it piled with poteen for our drink to-night?[7] Go on to the foreshore if it's fighting you want, where the rising tide will wash all traces[8] from the memory of man. [*Pushing* SHAWN *towards* CHRISTY.][9]

SHAWN [*shaking himself free, and getting behind* MICHAEL]. I'll not fight him, Michael James. I'd liefer live a bachelor simmering in passions to the end of time, than face a lepping savage the like of him has descended from the Lord knows where. Strike him yourself, Michael James, or you'll lose my drift of heifers and my blue bull from Sneem.

MICHAEL. Is it me fight him, when it's father-slaying he's bred to now? [*Pushing* SHAWN.] Go on you fool and fight him now.[10]

Notes (cont.), p. 155.

PEGEEN. Holy gospel truth I'm saying. You should have seen him when he was stripped below racing on the green the lovely white neck he had, and the turned leg. There's many girls in Killamuck will have sore hearts this day thinking upon him.

SHAWN [*indignantly*]. I'm thinking my own neck's as white as his is, when I've washed it clean.

PEGEEN. Your neck is it? It's more on a bullock's liver your neck'd put a young girl thinking than on the lily or the rose. [*Looking up at him with supreme contempt.*] He'd soon have me learned to talk like the poets if I was living long with him.

SHAWN. I've heard Father Reilly to say it's little but big lies and wicketness is in their rhymes at all.

PEGEEN. I'm thinking this day Shawn Keogh you'd have a right to up into the learned colleges and make yourself, it's that you do have all times running in your mind, and don't be thinking it's me would hinder you at all. I'd wed the young lad. He'd do me fine

Draft 'F' again keeps Christy and Michael James onstage throughout the scene.

⁶ A marginal note in draft 'D' reads 'Pegeen and Christy in concert set to work to terrify Shawn.' This is then developed in the next draft:

CHRISTY [*bridling up to* SHAWN]. You were in great haste young fellow to go seeking her hand and I above living in the house. You don't know at all I'm thinking that you're dealing with the likes of me.

SHAWN [*apologetically*]. It was my father did it Mister. I'd no word in it at all.

PEGEEN. There's queer talking Shawn Keogh. Is it that you're saying on your plighted day

SHAWN [*tremulously*]. And what kind of talking are you heeding now?

PEGEEN. You should have heard that lad a while since and the high talk he was makin like a Mayo song, with fine courting words in it, and great praises of my looks and shape

CHRISTY. And if I talked out high to her a while since I'll talk out this time to yourself and tell you the kind of fool you are if you're laying weight upon the spoken promise of a drunken pa will pass forgotten maybe at the dawn of day.

⁷ Earlier drafts read 'Are you going to commit murder in this house young fellow and have it written down on my licence that there was homicide made in my bar?'

Draft 'G' adds the stage direction [*getting up and balancing himself*].

⁸ Draft 'K' originally read 'wash the blood pool for all times. . . .'

⁹ Draft 'C' reads [MICHAEL *gets his hand on* SHAWN'*s neck and drags him round in front him.*]

¹⁰ Draft 'I' gives Michael the direction at the beginning of his speech [*in an hysteric falsetto*] and reads, 'Go on you fool and make your own plans with himself.'

---

¹ Earlier drafts include a mock battle between Shawn and Christy, as in draft 'D':

SHAWN. Will I strike him with my hand?

PEGEEN [*in delighted excitement*]. Take a spade to him there's a spade again the wall.

SHAWN. I'd hurt him maybe and where'd I hide me from the peelers then? Oh, wasn' a big fool to go meddling with girls, and I a rich farmer going this day to me death.

CHRISTY [*taking a spade*]. Come on now young fellow or swear again the face of G you'll leave that woman to myself.

SHAWN [*with a spade*]. Let you not strike inhuman, young fellow. Don't slay me at a
　　　　　[*They fence warily with the spades; crowd rushes in at back.*]

CROWD [*in delighted excitement*]. Good Christy. Now Shawn strike for Mayo. He's your father. . . . Slice his skull. . . .

MICHAEL [*makes a rush in between them*]. Would you commit murder in this place you fellow and the peelers not two perches down below?

[Notes continued on pp. 158 and 15]

SHAWN [*coming forward a little*]. Will I strike him with my hand?

MICHAEL. Take the loy is on your western side.

SHAWN. I'd be afeard of the gallows if I struck with that.

CHRISTY [*taking up the loy*]. Then I'll make you face the gallows or quit off from this. [SHAWN *flies out of the door*.][1]

CHRISTY.[2] Well, fine weather be after him, [*going to* MICHAEL, *coaxingly*] and I'm thinking you wouldn't wish to have that quaking blackguard in your house at all. Let you give us your blessing and hear her swear her faith to me, for I'm mounted on the spring-tide of the stars of luck the way it'll be good for any to have me in the house.[3]

PEGEEN [*at the other side of* MICHAEL]. Bless us now, for I swear to God I'll wed him, and I'll not renege.

MICHAEL [*standing up in the centre, holding on to both of them*]. It's the will of God, I'm thinking, that all should win an easy or a cruel end, and it's the will of God that all should rear up lengthy families for the nurture of the earth. What's a single man, I ask you, eating a bit in one house and drinking a sup in another, and he with no place of his own,[4] like an old braying jackass strayed upon the rocks? [*To* CHRISTY.] It's many would be in dread to bring your like into their house for to end them maybe with a sudden end; but I'm a decent man of Ireland, and I'd liefer face the grave untimely and I seeing a score of grandsons growing up little gallant swearers by the name of God, than go peopling my bedside with puny weeds the like of what you'd breed, I'm thinking, out of Shaneen Keogh. [*He joins their hands.*] A daring fellow is the jewel of the world, and a man did split his father's middle with a single clout should have the bravery of ten, so may God and Mary and St. Patrick bless you, and increase you from this mortal day.[5]

CHRISTY and PEGEEN. Amen, O Lord!

[*Hubbub outside.* OLD MAHON *rushes in, followed by all the* CROWD *and* WIDOW QUIN.[6] *He makes a rush at* CHRISTY, *knocks him down, and begins to beat him.*]

PEGEEN [*dragging back his arm*]. Stop that, will you. Who are you at all?

MAHON. His father, God forgive me![7]

Notes (cont.), p. *157.*

CHRISTY. What is it I care for the peelers? I'll murder any man this day will come between myself and that girl I've sworn by the earth and hell to wed before the face of God.

Draft 'E' has Pegeen proudly explaining to the crowd as they rush in, 'They've had a little differ on the score of me, and let you not disturb them till they fight it out.'

In Draft 'C' the crowd is told of the battle by Susan Brady, who looked in for a moment then ran out. By draft 'F' the crowd is called to his support by Shawn, and it is the Widow Quin who stirs Christy to action:

> [WIDOW QUIN *speaks at rear for a moment with* CHRISTY, *he comes over excited.*]

CHRISTY. What will the lot of us gain by making blather till the fall of night. You've said you'd wed me Pegeen Mike and let you raise and swear it in the face of God.

SHAWN. She will not.

CHRISTY [*taking up the loy*]. Then may the might of endless mercy have pity on you all.

SHAWN [*at window*]. Stop they're coming. [*At window.*] Come up the lot of you and stop my murder by the loafing man. Come on I'm saying. [CROWD *comes in.*]

By the next revision of draft 'F' the duel had been eliminated, and Synge suggested in a note, 'At match-making climax crowd comes in to say that Ch. has won a pound by his bet on the boat-race.'

² Draft 'E' adds the direction [*elated almost into a different being*].

³ Directions to draft 'C' read: [CHRISTY *puts the fear of death into the whole rout of them. Then when he is standing triumphant with* PEGEEN *and a spade in his hand* OLD FLAHERTY *enters—.*] The next two drafts develop this idea:

CHRISTY [*coming over*]. And will you promise me herself?

> [MICHAEL *struggles and both he and* SHAWN *come to the ground,* CHRISTY *stands over them with the lifted spade.*]

CHRISTY. Will you promise her this day I'm saying, or have me do you as I did my father, the devil splice him in the weeks gone by.

MICHAEL. Don't destroy me Mister and you may have her when you will. [*On his knees.*]

The same draft ('C') reads:

SHAWN [*crying from the corner*]. Have you no shame Pegeen to be turning round on me?

PEGEEN. What else would you have me do, isn't himself master in this place by the power of his arm, and the great deed he did a while since in the north or south.

⁴ The final typescript includes the words, 'and no woman at all, like an old braying jackass . . .'.

⁵ The first form of this speech read simply, 'Take her and welcome for all I care at all for there's born men I'm thinking are contrived to rule the world, and if you're a God-sent master it's not my right or duty to withstand you now.' However, while revising Old Mahon's entry (see Appendix B), Synge found it necessary to enhance the immediately preceding scene as well. Several entries in Notebook 34 first suggest his reasons for this elaboration:

'Michael James makes pseudo superfine speech and joins their hands. . .'.

'Make Michael give a lecture on matrimony III centre, interrupted by Mahon's Amen Christy kneels down and begins to pray—'

This last note is followed by what appear to be the first drafts of Michael James's speech in its expanded form:

If the will of the Lord God is written on the wall of Heaven that my head is to be ripped in two, isn't ⟨it⟩ as well to have it ripped by a handy son-in-law the like of him than by another. Isn't it all natural brother of fathers of Mayo isn't the son to take the place

[*Notes continued on p. 159.*]

Notes (cont.), p. 157.

of the father and the grandson the place of the great grandfather for ever and ever, and if he is to take ⟨it⟩ what do I care if he takes it with shovel spade or loy or billhook or with the help maybe of typhus or typhoid or of the old hen or the cholera morbus? Let him marry her I say if that is the will of God and let him take the shop and all in it and the stocking of gold if it is the will of God [*putting their hands together*]. You'll be a strong stout fell⟨ow⟩. . . .

But if the course of the world raises your hand on my poor head let you swear to God young fellow you won't ⟨put⟩ me down into the earth with⟨out⟩ decent prayers over me and a wake with them. Say the ass kicked me and I say⟨ing⟩ my prayers or any simple truth that would take in a doctor out of Trinity College in the City of Dublin. And then when your family is growing up—you'll likely have family a dozen maybe or a score itself—have them brought up little Christians with boots and shoes and white decent frilled drawers with frills on them upon the little girls and make one son a bishop of our Lady mother and one son a doctor of the Latin laws of God and God bless you so—

OLD MAHON. Amen oh Lord!

CHRISTY. In Heaven he is? Would the world believe it. [*Kneels.*] Well if it's an angel you are give me the blessing of quietness and joy. [*To* PEGEEN.] Kneel down will you. [PEGEEN *kneels.*] Have you no manners for an angel of the Lord?

[OLD MAHON *comes in behind.*] Well this is a fine house. [*Patting* CHRISTY.] Get up you schemer. . . .

The next page of Notebook 34 introduces the speech transposed from *The Aran Islands* (see Appendix D).

It is the will of God that all should get their death and it ⟨is⟩ the will of God and man that all should take wives and rear long families, for what good is a man that isn't married? He'll eat a bit in one place and a bit in another place, but he has no house of his own like an old jackass straying on the rocks. I'm thinking in a quiet failing place the like of this it's maybe the wisdom of God a fierce terror of ⟨a⟩ man should walk in to give courage to the parish to set them to fight for Ireland the foes of Ireland and to explode the law—If there'd be a great dread on many bringing the like of him in to divide my grey hairs maybe with a bloody end yet who am I that I'd be overwary of a daring man? For I'm thinking I'd liefer ⟨live⟩ in dread my own self and see a score of little grandsons standing up with flaring courage in the eye of day, than live in safety with the like of him ⟨Shawn Keogh⟩ and see me grandsons hiding in their mother's coats if a cur did lift his lip behind their heels. [*He takes and joins their hands.*] A gallant daring fellow is the jewel of the earth and world so I give your hand to him Pegeen and may the Lord God until death increase his pride of valour and his rule of men. . . .

Wasn't my grandfather transported and my father hanged, and haven't ⟨I⟩ three-quarters of the devil in myself today? Haven't I done enough to earn the gallows?

CROWD. You have Michael James. You have surely.

MICHAEL. Drunk or sober when have I been wary of curse or king or priest or prison and let him come I'm saying let him come
Haven't I given my poteen to poets. . . .

The speech, when finally included in the next typescript, draft 'G', differed little from the final text.

[6] This transition scene varied considerably throughout the drafts, as once again the Widow Quin's characterization threatened to alter the action of the play. (See Appendix B for different versions of Old Mahon's entrance.)

[7] Draft 'K' originally added the words, 'and I'll knock him into glory now'. Not until after draft 'G' did Synge change his mind about Old Mahon's entry and return to his original plan.

¹ Draft 'E' reads, 'Do you think I look so easy quenched with the touch of a loy that two ha'penny sticking plasters did make whole anew.' In the margin of draft 'C' Synge had suggested, 'Make Old Flaherty attack Christy and Michael James stops him so that throughout scene are struggles—a drunken struggle.'

² Earlier drafts give the direction [*nearly in tears*].

³ Early drafts keep Shawn on stage throughout, as in draft 'D':

PEGEEN. And to think of the fuss and welcome we're after giving him in this place, and he after doing nothing at all, but running off like a scared pup with its tail tripping its feet.

SHAWN [*with dawning triumph*]. Well aren't you a girl is easy fooled, Pegeen Mike. Was there ever the like of you for setting great store upon a fool?

PEGEEN [*with rage and bitterness*]. If it's easy fooled I was he'll pay me. Come here to me young fellow till I get my nails into your gob. Oh isn't ⟨it⟩ a pitiful country where the mighty murderers are scheming liars.

In draft 'C' Pegeen says 'If I lay a hand on you I'll make my garters of your hair' and in draft 'E' Pegeen is still threatening violence in this scene: 'Oh Lord God put some stick into my hand till I raise a ruddy welt across his scheming jaw.' In draft 'F' Synge contemplated making her turn away to Shawn:

SHAWN [*coming forward proudly*]. Now it's little gaining you had reneging me.

PEGEEN. I'll take you Shawn and bad cess to him.

⁴ Struck out of a draft 'K' remnant is an expansion of Christy's plea:

PEGEEN. . . . Oh, there's bitter hell in store for her that trusts the passions and the flights of love.

CHRISTY [*turning to her on his knees*]. For the sake of the Lord God let you not be speaking that way and driving me out lonesome through the countries of the world. Give me a fragment of the Heavens in your courtship till the day of March for why would you be in such a scorch of haste to spur me to destruction now?

⁵ Drafts 'C' and 'D' give Christy a further complaint: 'And that's the end of my fine hope and my fine house and my fine wife I was getting all lost on me [*putting out his hand towards* OLD FLAHERTY] by the flinty brazen firmness of that aging skull and it with nothing in it, but swearing out, and all the wicket wisdom of the lost in hell.'

And a lengthy exchange in draft 'G' develops most fully the 'playboy' motif, emphasizing both the 'gaming' and 'play-acting' aspects:

CHRISTY. For the love of God don't drive me lonesome through the world today. For the love of God give me a short space to the spring-time or to June itself to taste the fooleries of loving and the joys and blessing of this mortal earth. Why would you be in such a scorch of haste I'm saying to lead me this day to the threshold of the gulf of Hell.

PEGEEN. There's no decent girl would wed a man who is a liar! There's no decent girl would take a little sweaty play-boy has played fool upon the world. Oh isn't love a mighty madness and I'm hard set to think it's the same man you are that I'm after kissing half an hour gone by.

CHRISTY. That's the truth you're saying maybe I'm not left this moment the same man at all! and I seeing the stars and splendour of our life today dropping down to dusty ashes at my feet today. [*He goes up to her again.*] Oh Pegeen Mike have pity on me for I'm half thinking I'm a wonder still doing them deeds in fear and terror till herself did bring me tidings he was drownded on the sands today.

PEGEEN. Is he raving now.

WIDOW QUIN. He seen the old lad passing this way in the morning and you above on the hill. He's a queer lad to carry all before him with that dread upon his heart.

[*Notes continued on p. 162.*]

PEGEEN [*drawing back*]. Is it rose from the dead?

MAHON. Do you think I look so easy quenched with the tap of a loy? [*Beats* CHRISTY *again.*][1]

PEGEEN [*glaring at* CHRISTY]. And it's lies you told, letting on you had him slitted, and you nothing at all.

CHRISTY [*catching* MAHON'*s stick*]. He's not my father. He's a raving maniac would scare the world. [*Pointing to* WIDOW QUIN.] Herself knows it is true.

CROWD. You're fooling Pegeen! The Widow Quin seen him this day and you likely knew! You're a liar!

CHRISTY [*dumbfounded*].[2] It's himself was a liar, lying stretched out with an open head on him, letting on he was dead.

MAHON. Weren't you off racing the hills before I got my breath with the start I had seeing you turn on me at all?

PEGEEN. And to think of the coaxing glory we had given him, and he after doing nothing but hitting a soft blow and chasing northward in a sweat of fear. Quit off from this.[3]

CHRISTY [*piteously*]. You've seen my doings this day, and let you save me from the old man; for why would you be in such a scorch of haste to spur me to destruction now?[4]

PEGEEN. It's there your treachery is spurring me, till I'm hard set to think you're the one I'm after lacing in my heart-strings half-an-hour gone by. [*To* MAHON.] Take him on from this, for I think bad the world should see me raging for a Munster liar and the fool of men.[5]

MAHON. Rise up now to retribution, and come on with me.

CROWD [*jeeringly*]. There's the playboy! There's the lad thought he'd rule the roost in Mayo. Slate him now, Mister.[6]

CHRISTY [*getting up in shy terror*]. What is it drives you to torment me here, when I'd ask[7] the thunders of the might of God to blast me if I ever did hurt to any saving only that one single blow.

MAHON [*loudly*]. If you didn't, you're a poor good-for-nothing, and isn't it by the like of you the sins of the whole world are committed?[8]

Notes (cont.), p. 161.

PEGEEN [*to* CHRISTY]. And you went letting on you were a mighty man, and snaring my soul, and you knowing the whole while you were a mouthy Munster liar and the fool of me⟨n⟩?

CHRISTY [*nearly in tears*]. If ⟨it⟩ was play-acting what is it you were at and you sighing out your sighs of passion in my arms today?

PEGEEN [*threatening him*]. Go on from this or maybe I will do with you what you'd lied today.

Gradually this scene was shortened, the reference to 'play-acting' finally struck out of draft 'J' with the marginal note 'strengthen'.

⁶ Draft 'H' has the Crowd say 'Let you skelp him Mister Mahon for the glory of us all.' Earlier drafts added further interjections. In draft 'B' Timmy says, shaking his head, 'Didn't I say the day he walked in he was a wicket looking yo̸ ̸ ̸g fellow. I'm not easy fooled. That lad's fat under his eye.'

⁷ The Maunsel edition reads 'asked', which seems unnecessary as all the drafts read 'ask'.

⁸ In draft 'C' it is the Crowd that condemns Christy:

CROWD. You're a poor good for nothing. Isn't it by the like of you the sins of the whole world is committed.

MAHON. That's the truth they're saying and I'm thinking the divil himself laid his mark on you the day you were born the way yourself or me would lay a black mark on the thighs of a lamb.

Old Mahon's remark is still in draft 'J' with the direction [*laughs and curses*], and draft 'D' gives the 'retribution' motif to Mahon also: 'The day of quitment has come down from God. [*To* PEGEEN.] Let you leave him to myself young woman, I'll take him with me this day and let him earn his torment with complaining brow.'

---

¹ Draft 'B' reads:

OLD FLAHERTY. Let you not be tormenting the Lord God. Would you have him sending down droughts and big winds, and the blight on the spuds and typhus and typhoid, and the 'ould hin', and the Cholera Morbus?

CHRISTY. What'll I do at all from this day if I can't say my prayers out itself without bringing torment on me head?

² See Appendix B for the first version of the Widow Quin's reply. Drafts 'B' and 'C' are similar, with Christy's plea to the Widow, 'Will you take me to your house I'm saying I'm thinking you wouldn't ever turn again me the like of that gamey flightish young one winking me beyond.'

The first draft of 'F' reads:

PEGEEN [*derisively*]. Take him surely, Widow Quin, you'd be a fine mock-murdering pair and it's no lie.

CHRISTY. You'd have me there toiling moiling for your kindly sake, cutting reaping sowing by the stars of Heaven's light, or cleaning your floor or combing your hair if it's a middling aging woman that you are itself.

WIDOW QUIN. There's a change in your tune since the talk I heard yo making above a while since of the glories of Pegeen, and all your blathering song-bosh of her sleepy drawl.

CHRISTY [*looking at* PEGEEN, *with horror*]. Oh there's great concealed torture. . . .

Not until the revised draft 'F' does the Widow reject him: 'And a while since you'd hardly look upon my face. I'm destroyed with my efforts for you and I'm wearied now, for when all's said I'm seeing you've no heart in you at all.'

[*Notes continued on p. 164.*]

CHRISTY [*raising his hands*]. In the name of the Almighty God . . . .

MAHON. Leave troubling the Lord God. Would you have him sending down droughts, and fevers, and the old hen and the cholera morbus?[1]

CHRISTY [*to* WIDOW QUIN]. Will you come between us and protect me now?

WIDOW QUIN. I've tried a lot, God help me! and my share is done.[2]

CHRISTY [*looking round in desperation*]. And I must go back into my torment is it, or run off like a vagabond straying through the Unions with the dusts of August making mudstains in the gullet of my throat, or the winds of March blowing on me till I'd take an oath I felt them making whistles of my ribs within.

SARA. Ask Pegeen to aid you. Her like does often change.

CHRISTY. I will not then, for there's torment in the splendour of her like and she a girl any moon of midnight would take pride to meet, facing southwards on the heaths of Keel. But what did I want crawling forward to scorch my understanding at her flaming brow?[3]

PEGEEN [*to* MAHON, *vehemently, fearing she will break into tears*]. Take him on from this or I'll set the young lads to destroy him here.

MAHON [*going to him, shaking his stick*]. Come on now if you wouldn't have the company to see you skelped.[4]

PEGEEN [*half laughing, through her tears*]. That's it, now the world will see him pandied, and he an ugly liar was playing off the hero and the fright of men!

CHRISTY [*to* MAHON, *very sharply*].[5] Leave me go!

CROWD. That's it. Now Christy. If them two set fighting, it will lick the world.

MAHON [*making a grab at* CHRISTY]. Come here to me.

CHRISTY [*more threateningly*]. Leave me go, I'm saying.

MAHON. I will maybe when your legs is limping, and your back is blue.

CROWD. Keep it up, the two of you. I'll back the old one. Now the playboy.[6]

Notes (cont.), p. 163.

³ Omitted in the final draft is the direction [*looking at her intently*].
Draft 'F' expands Christy's speech:

CHRISTY [*looking at* PEGEEN, *with horror*]. Oh there's great concealed torture in the splendour of her like, and she a girl no moon of midnight wouldn't be proud to meet facing the south or the heaths of Keel like the Lady Helen in a silver light on the heaths of Knock-na-dreen. And what at all did I want I'm asking myself now going up to scorch my understanding at her flaming brow?

MICHAEL. Spit out on him Pegeen to cool his talk. That's no fit speaking for a Christian lad.

In the next draft it is the crowd that urges Pegeen to spit on Christy. Draft 'J' adds the marginal direction 'Work up Romantic note in Christy's speeches in this scene broken speech by speech of the others. Vivify crowd.'
Much of this speech was cut during the first production.

⁴ A late remnant gives Mahon the reply, 'And what indeed did you want so raising your eyes unto the like of her, and you a lad the devil laid his mark on in the hour of birth? Come on now to hide your folly in our townland or I'll skelp you here.' In earlier drafts Pegeen does not appear so upset.

⁵ A late fragment includes the directions [*Mahon makes a grab at Christy. Christy excited by Pegeen's words shakes him off.*]
A marginal note to draft 'G' reads 'Expand making P. jeer at him for not having killed his father and Old Mahon aggravate him.'

⁶ Apparently until the final draft Synge contemplated 'vivifying' the crowd by giving additional interjections as well as the chorus; various drafts read:

SARA. It'll be great luck if one or other do be slaughtered here. . . .

WIDOW QUIN. Fight him young fellow for the love of God. . . .

SARA TANSEY. Please God the old man will be vanquished the way we'll have the young lad for the dance tonight. . . .

WIDOW QUIN. I'll bet a keg of poteen that the lepper'll win.

---

¹ Draft 'J' elaborates Christy's retort:

CHRISTY. You're the mighty mortal strong men of a Mayo bog. What ails you at all? I'm saying. You're after making a mighty man of me from the word of my mouth, and turning on me like a drift of curs when you seen me staining my soul and life. I'm thinking this day if it's a bitter thing to be lonesome, it's worser maybe to come mixing with the fools of men, and if herself put up the light of glory to my eyes today, and it was herself did show me when the hour was come that the braying bitter folly of her like and kind, that did regard me only for the swinging gallows that was near me then.

PEGEEN [*mockingly*]. Wouldn't it have been a grand sight to see my own name printed out in the big papers is read by the high quality and Lord Bishops of Ireland, and hadn't I a right to turn again you, and you nothing at all but a little lying beggar with great lying in your jaw.

² A late remnant adds the direction [*working himself up with a subdued delirium*].

³ Originally the play ended here, without the 'second murder' and with the Widow Quin winning Christy (see Appendix B for earliest drafts). In draft 'C' the Widow Quin holds Old Flaherty captive so that Christy can escape; in draft 'E' Christy rejects the Widow Quin and goes out with Old Mahon. Finally in draft 'F' Synge introduced the second battle, with a corresponding role for the Widow Quin, rescuing Christy from the crowd rather than from Old Mahon. The first draft of 'F' reads: [*With a yell of rage he rushes at*

[*Notes continued on p. 166.*]

CHRISTY [*in low and intense voice*]. Shut your yelling, for if you're after making a mighty man of me this day by the power of a lie, you're setting me now to think if it's a poor thing to be lonesome, it's worse maybe go mixing with the fools of earth.[1]

[MAHON *makes a movement towards him.*]

CHRISTY [*almost shouting*]. Keep off . . . lest I do show a blow unto the lot of you would set the guardian angels winking in the clouds above. [*He swings round with a sudden rapid movement and picks up a loy.*]

CROWD [*half frightened, half amused*]. He's going mad! Mind yourselves! Run from the idiot!

CHRISTY.[2] If I am an idiot, I'm after hearing my voice this day saying words would raise the topknot on a poet in a merchant's town. I've won your racing and your lepping and . . . .

MAHON. Shut your gullet and come on with me.

CHRISTY. I'm going but I'll stretch you first.

[*He runs at* OLD MAHON *with the loy, chases him out of the door, followed by* CROWD *and* WIDOW QUIN.[3] *There is a great noise outside, then a yell, and dead silence for a moment.* CHRISTY *comes in, half dazed, and goes to fire.*]

WIDOW QUIN [*coming in, hurriedly, and going to him*]. They're turning again you. Come on or you'll be hanged indeed.[4]

CHRISTY.[5] I'm thinking from this out, Pegeen'll be giving me praises the same as in the hours gone by.

WIDOW QUIN [*impatiently*]. Come by the back-door. I'd think bad to have you stifled on the gallows tree.

CHRISTY [*indignantly*]. I will not then. What good'd be my life-time if I left Pegeen?[6]

WIDOW QUIN. Come on and you'll be no worse than you were last night; and you with a double murder this time to be telling to the girls.

CHRISTY. I'll not leave Pegeen Mike.

WIDOW QUIN [*impatiently*]. Isn't there the match of her in every parish public, from Binghamstown unto the plain of Meath? Come on, I tell you, and I'll find you finer sweethearts at each waning moon.

Notes (cont.), p. 165.

MAHON *and takes him by the throat. There is a momentary struggle; then he flings* OLD MAHON *on the ground and turns triumphant to centre.* WIDOW QUIN *comes to his side others crying against him.*]

In the revised draft 'F' Christy commits the deed outside:

[*He makes a rush at* OLD MAHON *who flies out of the door just escaping a blow of the loy, followed by* CHRISTY. CROWD *rush after them and there are shouts outside, then* CHRISTY *comes in dejectedly and sits down by the fire. The people come in and make group at door whispering together.*]

But, still dissatisfied, Synge suggested in the margin: 'alternative make Christy knock the old man into the corner stunned. The crowd re-enters as before and ties Christy up when old man revives.'

In the next draft he had once more decided to have the battle offstage, but a marginal note to draft 'H' makes one further suggestion which apparently was never developed: 'keep M. James drunk on stage as link'.

⁴ A late remnant reads 'Come on now or you'll be hanged indeed. They'll turn again you with that corpse in the yard.' This scene with the Widow Quin is first suggested on the back of draft 'J' (24 September 1906):

'After Christy's return give him short tender scene with the Widow Quin???

a) to finish her off
b) to break length of storm

Work by giving W.Q. one quick eager speech?'

⁵ A late remnant adds the direction [*looking up at her with his simple smile*].
⁶ Draft 'K' contemplated the alternative reply, 'I'd be stifled with my sighing if I quit Pegeen.'

———

¹ Originally the final typescript read 'stripped itself' in place of the offending 'shifts'.
² Sara Tansey is not included until a very late draft. A remnant of 'J' reads:

CHRISTY. I'm not going at all. I'll leave my chances to my one choice Pegeen Mike.

WIDOW QUIN. Then I'll not stop to see you sailing with your fool's romancing to your end today but I'll be going above to ask the Lord to pity all romancers in a heartless world. [*She goes out quickly.* CHRISTY *subsides in a dream.*]

This is then struck out and Sara enters.

³ The final typescripts have Christy struggling to untie the knot in the petticoat as he sits by the fire and the men crowd in the doorway: '[*in desperation, struggling with knot*]. It's to make a show of folly of me they wanted tying me in this rag before Pegeen would come.'
⁴ Draft 'F' reads:

PHILLY. Would we fetch him the peelers?

MICHAEL. And the place stinking with poteen? Fetch you the rope Jimmy.

SHAWN. You go Pegeen. He'd never raise his hand upon your like.

⁵ In a late remnant they steal forward with the rope held on a pitchfork and drop it over his head.

CHRISTY. It's Pegeen I'm seeking only, and what'd I care if you brought me a drift of chosen females, standing in their shifts[1] itself maybe, from this place to the Eastern World.

SARA [*runs in, pulling off one of her petticoats*]. They're going to hang him. [*Holding out petticoat and shawl.*] Fit these upon him and let him run off to the east.

WIDOW QUIN. He's raving now; but we'll fit them on him and I'll take him in the ferry to the Achill boat.

CHRISTY [*struggling feebly*]. Leave me go, will you, when I'm thinking of my luck to-day, for she will wed me surely and I a proven hero in the end of all. [*They try to fasten petticoat round him.*]

WIDOW QUIN. Take his left hand and we'll pull him now. Come on, young fellow.

CHRISTY [*suddenly starting up*]. You'll be taking me from her? You're jealous, is it, of her wedding me? Go on from this. [*He snatches up a stool, and threatens them with it.*]

WIDOW QUIN [*going*]. It's in the mad-house they should put him not in jail at all. We'll go by the back-door to call the doctor and we'll save him so.

[*She goes out, with SARA, through inner room.[2] MEN crowd in the doorway. CHRISTY sits down again by the fire.*][3]

MICHAEL [*in a terrified whisper*]. Is the old lad killed surely?

PHILLY. I'm after feeling the last gasps quitting his heart. [*They peer in at CHRISTY.*]

MICHAEL [*with a rope*]. Look at the way he is. Twist a hangman's knot on it and slip it over his head while he's not minding at all.

PHILLY. Let you take it, Shanecn. You're the soberest of all that's here.

SHAWN. Is it me to go near him, and he the wickedest and worst with me? Let you take it, Pegeen Mike.[4]

PEGEEN. Come on, so. [*She goes forward with the others, and they drop the double hitch over his head.*][5]

CHRISTY. What ails you?

¹ Draft 'H' reads, 'A strange man is a grand thing and he walking in with novelty and wondrous talk, but what at all is it to see a little quarrel in your back-yard and a sneaky blow of a loy.' The next draft reads, 'I'll say it was an ugly villain's murder the way I've no heart for you at all. There's a mighty gap between a gallous story and a dirty deed the way I'm thinking this day you're a saucy liar and the whole that's bad.'

² Draft 'F' reads 'like the Kerry madmen'; draft 'H' reads 'like the madmen of Camp Keel'.

³ Synge questioned, then struck out of a late remnant a reply here by Christy: 'You're the devil's lot and I'd think well of any did pass his time in this place killing girls or women, or young boys and men.'

SHAWN [*triumphantly, as they pull the rope tight on his arms*]. Come on to the peelers till they stretch you now.

CHRISTY. Me!

MICHAEL. If we took pity on you, the Lord God would maybe bring us ruin from the law to-day, so you'd best come easy, for hanging is an easy and a speedy end.

CHRISTY. I'll not stir. [*To* PEGEEN.] And what is it you'll say to me and I after doing it this time in the face of all?

PEGEEN. I'll say a strange man is a marvel with his mighty talk; but what's a squabble in your back-yard and the blow of a loy, have taught me that there's a great gap between a gallous story and a dirty deed.[1] [*To* MEN.] Take him on from this, or the lot of us will be likely put on trial for his deed to-day.

CHRISTY [*with horror in his voice*]. And it's yourself will send me off to have a horny-fingered hangman hitching his bloody slip-knots at the butt of my car?

MEN [*pulling rope*]. Come on, will you?

[*He is pulled down on the floor.*]

CHRISTY [*twisting his legs round the table*]. Cut the rope, Pegeen, and I'll quit the lot of you and live from this out like the madmen of Keel,[2] eating muck and green weeds on the faces of the cliffs.

PEGEEN. And leave us to hang, is it, for a saucy liar, the like of you? [*To* MEN.] Take him on out from this.

SHAWN. Pull a twist on his neck, and squeeze him so.

PHILLY. Twist yourself. Sure he cannot hurt you, if you keep your distance from his teeth alone.[3]

SHAWN. I'm afeard of him. [*To* PEGEEN.] Lift a lighted sod will you and scorch his leg.

PEGEEN [*blowing the fire with a bellows*]. Leave go now young fellow or I'll scorch your shins.

CHRISTY. You're blowing for to torture me? [*His voice rising and growing stronger*.] That's your kind, is it? Then let the lot of you be

¹ Earlier drafts read 'suck' for 'shed'.

² Until the final typescript this read 'hanging by your own guts', perhaps another cut in rehearsal.

³ Evidently Synge intended at one time to emphasize the role of Shawn Keogh. Notebook 34 includes the comment:

In desperation scene FIII

CROWD. Now he is jealous of Shaneen Keogh.

CHRISTY. Jealous? How would I be jealous of his like at all. I'd be jealous of a worthy man but what would make you jealous of the like of him when you'd have disgust would turn your stomach of a woman that would touch his hand.

⁴ On the back of draft 'H' Synge wrote 'give Christy an outburst that has majesty and poetry' and 'Give Christy big speeches while he is on the ground', both directions evidently intended for this final scene.

⁵ Late drafts read '. . . killed one father two times and been swearing love and falsehoods for one autumn day.'

⁶ Not until the late drafts does Pegeen burn Christy with the sod. In draft 'F' Pegeen gets the sod but as she comes towards Christy the Widow Quin enters. In a fragment of a later draft she is still hesitant:

PEGEEN. Maybe we'd do right to let him go his way. He's a gay one and it's not a lie.

MEN [*fiercely*]. Burn him will you. Don't be afraid. . . .

wary, for if I've to face the gallows I'll have a gay march down, I tell you, and shed[1] the blood of some of you before I die.

SHAWN [*in terror*]. Keep a good hold, Philly. Be wary for the love of God, for I'm thinking he would liefest wreak his pains on me.

CHRISTY [*almost gaily*]. If I do lay my hands on you, it's the way you'll be at the fall of night hanging[2] as a scarecrow for the fowls of hell. Ah, you'll have a gallous jaunt I'm saying, coaching out through Limbo with my father's ghost.[3]

SHAWN [*to PEGEEN*]. Make haste, will you. Oh, isn't he a holy terror, and isn't it true for Father Reilly that all drink's a curse that has the lot of you so shaky and uncertain now.

CHRISTY. If I can wring a neck among you, I'll have a royal judgment looking on the trembling jury in the courts of law. And won't there be crying out in Mayo the day I'm stretched upon the rope with ladies in their silks and satins snivelling in their lacy kerchiefs, and they rhyming songs and ballads on the terror of my fate?[4] [*He squirms round on the floor and bites* SHAWN's *leg*.]

SHAWN [*shrieking*]. My leg's bit on me! He's the like of a mad dog, I'm thinking, the way that I will surely die.

CHRISTY [*delighted with himself*]. You will then, the way you can shake out hell's flags of welcome for my coming in two weeks or three, for I'm thinking Satan hasn't many have killed their da in Kerry and in Mayo too.[5]

[OLD MAHON *comes in behind on all fours and looks on unnoticed*.]

MEN [*to PEGEEN*]. Bring the sod, will you.

PEGEEN [*coming over*]. God help him so. [*Burns his leg*.][6]

CHRISTY [*kicking and screaming*]. Oh, glory be to God!

[*He kicks loose from the table, and they all drag him towards the door*.]

JIMMY [*seeing* OLD MAHON]. Will you look what's come in?

[*They all drop* CHRISTY *and run left*.]

CHRISTY [*scrambling on his knees face to face with* OLD MAHON]. Are you coming to be killed a third time or what ails you now?

¹ A late remnant reads, 'For what are you martingaled and fettered now?' In draft 'F' the Widow still rescues Christy:

WIDOW QUIN [*comes in as they get to door*]. What in glory are yous doing here?

CHRISTY. They're taking me to the police for to hang me now. Oh, have mercy on me for the love of Heaven's light.

WIDOW QUIN [*to* MEN]. Leave him go the lot of you. His father's after rising up again and there ⟨he⟩ is now stepping out the road to Castlebar, and he as sound as a salmon swimming from the sea.

CROWD [*falling back*]. Well aren't they a deceitful couple. You couldn't trust ⟨them⟩ at all.

In this draft Pegeen and Michael James loosen Christy and he leaves with the Widow Quin. Marginal notes to the revised draft 'F' read, however: 'Make Old Mahon come in at door on his hands and knees.' In draft 'H' Old Mahon comes in on his hands and knees with a bit of sacking held up to his face, and in this draft both Mahons leave with the Widow Quin:

CHRISTY. You're living?

MAHON. You did hardly flatten out my plasters with the flat of the spade.

CHRISTY. I'm rescued so. [WIDOW QUIN *comes in.*]

MAHON. For what are you tied?

CHRISTY. Taking me off they were to the peelers to be hanged and quartered maybe for my slaying you.

MAHON. And it's informers and spies they are is it, men would sell a decent poor boy for a copper halfpenny or a taste of drink.

CHRISTY. Loose me will you? Loose me and let me get on from this for I'm destroyed with my adventures since the fall of night.

MAHON [*looses him with* WIDOW QUIN]. Where at all will ⟨we⟩ go now Christy for you're all in shakes and trembles and my head is smashed to putty with your skelping blow.

WIDOW QUIN [*coming down to them*]. Come on with me. [*To* CHRISTY.] I'm thinking now with your connivings since the dawn of day you'll likely feel the quiet of my houseen where I tell you I am lonesome too, and the day herself weds Shaneen Keogh I'll wed the one or other of you and you'll have a house and settlement and quiet so.

However, instructions in Notebook 34, dated 6 November 1906, read 'In III condens (W.Q. exit) revise Curtain', evidently carried out in draft 'H'. By draft 'J' Christy reject both Old Mahon and the Widow Quin and becomes The Playboy.

² Struck out of the final draft is the direction [*a little querulously*].

³ Draft 'J' originally read, 'That's a set of filthy swine you are, to sell a decent Christia to the English courts.'

⁴ Apparently Synge did not think of making Christy turn the tables on his father until the last drafts. A rough draft in Notebook 34 contemplates giving Old Mahon a surpris triumph, while still giving the Widow Quin the right to Christy:

O.M. Touch me would you?

CH. If I missed you one time I'll not miss you again. [*Scuffle. He flings* OLD MAHON *ha behind counter, then goes across half-dazed and sits by the fire.*] . . .

MICHAEL JAMES. Lift a coal of fire Pegeen and scorch his leg.

[*Notes continued on pp. 174 and 175*]

MAHON. For what is it they have you tied?[1]

CHRISTY.[2] They're taking me to the peelers to have me hanged for slaying you.

MICHAEL [*apologetically*]. It is the will of God that all should guard their little cabins from the treachery of law and what would my daughter be doing if I was ruined or was hanged itself?

MAHON [*grimly, loosening* CHRISTY]. It's little I care if you put a bag on her back and went picking cockles till the hour of death; but my son and myself will be going our own way and we'll have great times from this out telling stories of the villainy of Mayo and the fools is here. [*To* CHRISTY, *who is freed.*] Come on now.[3]

CHRISTY. Go with you, is it! I will then, like a gallant captain with his heathen slave. Go on now and I'll see you from this day stewing my oatmeal and washing my spuds, for I'm master of all fights from now. [*Pushing* MAHON.] Go on, I'm saying.

MAHON. Is it me?

CHRISTY. Not a word out of you. Go on from this.

MAHON [*walking out and looking back at* CHRISTY *over his shoulder*]. Glory be to God! [*With a broad smile.*] I am crazy again! [*Goes.*]

CHRISTY. Ten thousand blessings upon all that's here, for you've turned me a likely gaffer in the end of all, the way I'll go romancing through a romping lifetime from this hour to the dawning of the judgment day. [*He goes out.*][4]

MICHAEL. By the will of God, we'll have peace now for our drinks. Will you draw the porter, Pegeen?

SHAWN [*going up to her*]. It's a miracle Father Reilly can wed us in the end of all, and we'll have none to trouble us when his vicious bite is healed.

PEGEEN [*hitting him a box on the ear*]. Quit my sight. [*Putting her shawl over her head and breaking out into wild lamentations.*] Oh my grief, I've lost him surely. I've lost the only playboy of the western world.[5]

CURTAIN

Notes (cont.), p. 173.

CH. Will yous not torment me. Isn't the world a wicket place to be bringing anguish on the like of me. Leave me go. Wouldn't any squelch the like of him for an old and crawling vermin weighed with loads of infamy would crush the jennets of the plain of Hell.

OLD MAHON [*comes forward on his hands and knees*]. Hold him steady till I reach him now!

CROWD [*flies off in terror*]. He's risen again. He isn't right. Didn't I say he'd never die.

   [CHRISTY *gets up in awkward position bound with the rope.* OLD MAHON *face to face with him on three legs.*]

OLD MAHON. Is it certain sure you are he won't slip from the rope.

WIDOW QUIN. Mind out, I'll loose him now.

MAHON. Wait will you.

WIDOW [*catches hold of him*]. You won't touch him while he's fettered. Lie down or I'll twist your neck.

MICHAEL JAMES [*centre*] [*tag*]. Stop your sporting now aren't we all wearied and destroyed with drought. What do the two of you want destroying the trade of an honest poor fellow the like of me. Go on the two of you from this house and do what murder you think fitting on the sands below. The two aren't the worth of watching on a droughty day.

CROWD. Fire them out Michael. Aren't we tormented with their jaw.

CHRISTY. I'll not quit Pegeen Mike this day at all.

WIDOW QUIN. Come here to me Michael James. Take this old warrior beyond the door and fire him adrift upon the world of pain and give me Christy for I'll take him I'm thinking for to wed with me.

CROWD. And what at all will we do with the old pauper?

MAHON. Pauper?

MICHAEL. What is it else you are.

   [*Hide his fortune in his bandage which comes off.*]

However, no typescript draft examined corresponds to this version and Synge's next idea was the triumph of Christy. Draft 'J' reads:

MAHON. And it's the will of God maybe that the lot of you should be a pack of spies. [*To* CHRISTY.] Come on now we'll quit the lot of them and have our own ways in the world.

CHRISTY. I'll follow my own traces from this day out, I've seen this day the tide of girls romancing and a widow's mighty wisdom turning round upon me at the turn of luck. Faith I'll have great times now I'm thinking and I knowing the true ways as well as any to go fool all fools that would go fooling me. [*He goes out.*]

MICHAEL [*to* MAHON]. Let you go on with him. We don't need you here.

WIDOW QUIN. Come with me Mister, if I fooled you it was all I could. [*They go out.*]

A later version of draft 'J' (?) develops Old Mahon's part:

CHRISTY [*shaking himself free*]. I'll follow my own traces from this out, Mister, and I'll have great times I'm thinking and I learned this day in girls' romancing and the laughter of the world. Faith I'll have great times I'm saying and I a likely man I'm thinking to make a fool of all fools would go fooling me. [*He goes out.*]

[*Notes continued on p. 175.*]

Note 4 (cont.), p. 173.

MAHON. Well I'm proud to think I've skelped him to his sense in the end of time. It's not many fathers I'm thinking would risk their two gaps upon their brainpans for an only son itself. I'll be going now to tell my story north and southwards and have plenty so. [*He goes out.*]

On the back of this draft is scribbled the final version of Christy's and Old Mahon's exit.

5 Gradually Synge developed the brief curtain scene, each version strengthening Pegeen's lamentations.

Draft 'F' reads:

SHAWN. Isn't it a blessing this morning he didn't take the four sovereigns I'd have loaned him then.

PEGEEN. I'll wed ⟨you⟩ after all Shawn with the help of God. [*Tag and curtain.*]

Draft 'G' gives Shawn no final speech:

PEGEEN [*sitting down on a chair centre and putting her apron over her eyes*]. I've lost him. I've lost the play-boy of the western world. Oh wasn't I a mad one to go turn against him when he struck his da.

The next version appears to be this note scribbled on the back of a fragment (draft 'I'?):
'For tag III Pegeen "Isn't mighty love the like of his love the flower of the world and now that he is banished I am dropped to Hell."'

Draft 'J' includes her rejection of Shawn:

SHAWN. Now we'll get wedded on our Dispensation and have no more to trouble us when I get my bite healed.

PEGEEN [*hitting him a sounding box on the ear*]. Go off from this for I won't look on you now I've seen a decent man [*breaking out into lamentations*]. Oh, my grief that I have lost him in my hurry and my rage today. I've lost the only playboy of the western world.

A later draft of 'J' combines several of these lines:

Let you quit my sight, I tell you till the judgment day. [*Breaking out in lamentations.*] Oh, love the like of his love is the flower of the world. Oh my grief I've lost him surely. I've lost the only playboy of the western world.

[*Quick Curtain.*]

Finally, by draft 'K', Synge arrived at the final form of Pegeen's lament. However, this draft has an additional piece of business which was evidently cut after rehearsals had begun:

[*She makes a rush out of the door upsetting two chairs.*]

CROWD [*loudly all together*]. Well now.

[*Quick Curtain*]

See Appendix B for various scenario drafts of the curtain scene in Notebook 34.

DEIRDRE OF THE SORROWS

A PLAY IN THREE ACTS

PREFACE TO *DEIRDRE OF THE SORROWS*
by W. B. YEATS

It was Synge's practice to write many complete versions of a play, distinguishing them with letters, and running half through the alphabet before he finished. He read me a version of this play the year before his death,[1] and would have made several more always altering and enriching. He felt that the story, as he had told it, required a grotesque element mixed into its lyrical melancholy to give contrast and create an impression of solidity, and had begun this mixing with the character of Owen, who would have had some part in the first act also, where he was to have entered Lavarcham's cottage with Conchubor. Conchubor would have taken a knife from his belt to cut himself free from threads of silk that caught in brooch or pin as he leant over Deirdre's embroidery frame, and forgotten this knife behind him. Owen was to have found it and stolen it. Synge asked that either I or Lady Gregory should write some few words to make this possible, but after writing in a passage we were little satisfied and thought it better to have the play performed, as it is printed here, with no word of ours. When Owen killed himself in the second act, he was to have done it with Conchubor's knife.[2] He did not speak to me of any other alteration, but it is probable that he would have altered till the structure had become as strong and varied as in his other plays; and had he lived to do that,

[1] 'Synge has taken charge of the Theatre in my place and is rehearsing the people now, and so on. It has probably interrupted his *Deirdre*, which is going to be very fine. He has written it in slight dialect so far as the king and queen are concerned, a little more dialect than there is in Lady Gregory's books, but he has given the minor characters a great deal of peasant idiom. The result is that the play, while seeming perfectly natural, has much the same atmosphere so far as the speech goes as his other plays. There is, however, nothing grotesque in it, and an astonishing amount of sheer lyrical beauty. It is much more beautiful than, though not at its present stage anything like so dramatic as, his other work. I think it would be impossible to any company except ours. I can't imagine anybody getting his peculiar rhythm without being personally instructed in it.' (Letter to John Quinn, 27 April 1908, *The Letters of W. B. Yeats*, ed. Allan Wade, p. 510.)

[2] 'I saw Synge to-day and asked how much of his *Deirdre* was done. He said the third act was right, that he had put a grotesque character, a new character, into the second act and intended to weave him into Act One. He was to come in with Conchubar, carrying some of his belongings, and afterwards at the end of the act to return for a forgotten knife—just enough to make it possible to use him in Act Two. He spoke of his work this winter doubtfully, thought it not very good, seemed only certain of the third act.' (W. B. Yeats, *Estrangement: Extracts from a Diary kept in 1909* (1926), in *Autobiographies* (Macmillan, 1961), p. 487.)

'Deirdre of the Sorrows' would have been his masterwork, so much beauty is there in its course, and such wild nobleness in its end, and so poignant is an emotion and wisdom that were his own preparation for death.

W. B. Yeats. April, 1910

PERSONS[1]

LAVARCHAM, a wise woman and servant of Conchubor, about fifty

OLD WOMAN, cook and Deirdre's foster-mother

CONCHUBOR, High King of Ulster, about sixty

FERGUS, Conchubor's friend and warrior of the Red
Branch of Ulster

DEIRDRE

NAISI, son of Usna, Deirdre's lover

AINNLE ⎱ brothers to Naisi, with him heroes of
ARDAN ⎰   the Red Branch

OWEN, Conchubor's spy

TWO SOLDIERS

SCENE

*The first Act takes place in Lavarcham's house on Slieve
Fuadh; the second Act in a wood outside the tent of Deirdre
and Naisi in Alban; the third Act in a tent below Emain
Macha.*

---

[1] Synge originally planned to call the play *The Sons of Usnach*, but had altered the title
to *Deirdre of the Sorrows* by April 1908. No cast list or scene exist in manuscript for this
play. The Cuala edition lists persons in order of appearance as above except for Owen,
who is placed before Conchubor, presumably in deference to Synge's wish to include
him in Act I. The descriptions above are taken from the various typescript drafts.
Whenever possible the text itself follows Synge's final typescript, with variations from
the posthumous Cuala and Maunsel editions noted. See Appendix C.

¹ The need for this furniture becomes apparent later in the act, although Synge omit it in his description.

² The Cuala and Maunsel editions read 'wasn't'.

ACT I

LAVARCHAM's *house on Slieve Fuadh. There is a door to the inner room on the left, and a door to the open air on the right. Window at back and a frame with a half-finished piece of tapestry; a high chair of state centre stage with a stool near it.*[1] *There are also a large press and heavy oak chest near the back wall. The place is neat and clean but bare.* LAVARCHAM, *a woman of fifty, is working at tapestry frame.* OLD WOMAN *comes in from left.*

OLD WOMAN. She hasn't come yet is it, and it falling to the night?

LAVARCHAM. She has not. [*Concealing her anxiety.*] It's dark with the clouds are coming from the west and south, but it isn't later than the common.

OLD WOMAN. It's later surely, and I hear tell the Sons of Usna, Naisi and his brothers, are above chasing hares for two days or three, and the same a while since when the moon was full.

LAVARCHAM [*more anxiously*]. The gods send they don't set eyes on her [*with a sign of helplessness*] . . . yet if they do, itself, it wasn't *my* wish brought them or could send them away.

OLD WOMAN [*reprovingly*]. If it was not,[2] you'd do well to keep a check on her, and she turning a woman that was meant to be a queen.

LAVARCHAM. Who'd check her like was made to have her pleasure only, the way if there were no warnings told about her you'd see troubles coming when an old king is taking her, and she without a thought but for her beauty and to be straying the hills.

OLD WOMAN. The gods help the lot of us. . . . Shouldn't she be well pleased getting the like of Conchubor, and he middling settled in his years itself? I don't know what he wanted putting her this wild place to be breaking her in, or putting myself to be roasting her suppers, and she with no patience for her food at all. [*She looks out.*]

LAVARCHAM. Is she coming from the glen?

¹ Notebook 28, in use in Kerry in September 1903, records the phrase 'to be abroad — to be outside'.

² The Abbey Theatre TS. 'B' of Act I (1 November 1907) includes the clause,' and then he'd be figuring out stories and tricks in his mind, and he. . . .

OLD WOMAN. She is not. But whisht . . . there's two men leaving the furze. . . . [*Crying out.*] It's Conchubor and Fergus along with him! Conchubor'll be in a blue stew this night and herself abroad.[1]

LAVARCHAM [*settling room hastily*]. Are they close by?

OLD WOMAN. Crossing the stream, and there's herself on the hillside with a load of twigs. Will I run out and put her in order before they'll set eyes on her at all?

LAVARCHAM. You will not. Would you have him see you,[2] and he a man would be jealous of a hawk would fly between her and the rising sun. [*She looks out.*] Go up to the hearth and be as busy as if you hadn't seen them at all.

OLD WOMAN [*sitting down to polish vessels*]. There'll be trouble this night, for he should be in his tempers from the way he's stepping out, and he swinging his hands.

LAVARCHAM [*wearied with the whole matter*]. It'd be best of all maybe if he got in tempers with herself, and made an end quickly, for I'm in a poor way between the pair of them. [*Going back to tapestry frame.*] There they are now at the door.

[CONCHUBOR *and* FERGUS *come in.*]

CONCHUBOR and FERGUS. The gods save you.

LAVARCHAM [*getting up and curtseying*]. The gods save and keep you kindly, and stand between you and all harm forever.

CONCHUBOR [*looking around*]. Where is Deirdre?

LAVARCHAM [*trying to speak with indifference*]. Abroad upon Slieve Fuadh. She does be all times straying around picking flowers or nuts, or sticks itself, but so long as she's gathering new life I've a right not to heed her, I'm thinking, and she taking her will.

[FERGUS *talks to* OLD WOMAN.]

CONCHUBOR [*stiffly*]. A night with thunder coming is no night to be abroad.

LAVARCHAM [*more uneasily*]. She's used to every track and pathway and the lightning itself wouldn't let down its flame to singe the beauty of her like.

¹ An alternative speech, qualified by a question mark in the Texas TS., reads, 'She's right Conchubor, and let you not be uneasy. Sit down and take. . . .'

² See note 1, p. 190.

³ The typescript here is considerably crossed out and written over, and Lavarcham' first sentence as given here is scrawled in pencil on the back of the preceding page. The stage directions as given are taken from different typescript drafts.

In the margin of TS. 'I' (7 March 1908) Synge suggests: 'Make C. annoy Lav. to motiv her frankness.' However, the origin of Lavarcham's reply can be traced to a manuscrip emendation of TS. 'H' (15 February 1908):

c. It's good work but it's not ⟨that⟩ I'm seeking only. . . . You'd best speak out this nigh Lavarcham and tell me out the lot you know. Is she growing wiser in her thoughts a all?

LAV. What's wise or foolish when the whole is said? You'll get little pleasure hearing m speak out C., for I do be thinking odd times she's growing. . . .

FERGUS [*cheerfully*]. She's right Conchubor, and let you sit down[1] and take your ease [*he takes a wallet from under his cloak*] . . . and I'll count out what we've brought, and put it in the presses within.

[*He goes into the inner room with* OLD WOMAN.]

CONCHUBOR [*sitting down and looking about*]. Where are the mats and hangings and the silver skillets I sent up for Deirdre?

LAVARCHAM. The mats and hangings are in this press, Conchubor. She wouldn't wish to be soiling them, she said, running out and in with mud and grasses on her feet, and it raining since the night of Samhain. The silver skillets and the golden cups, we have beyond locked in the chest.

CONCHUBOR. Bring them out and use them from this day.

LAVARCHAM. We'll do it, Conchubor.

CONCHUBOR [*getting up and going to frame*]. Is this hers?[2]

LAVARCHAM [*pleased to speak of it*]. It is, Conchubor. All say there isn't her match at fancying figures and throwing purple upon crimson, and she edging them all times with her greens and gold.

CONCHUBOR [*a little uneasily*]. Is she keeping wise and busy since I passed before, and growing ready for her life in Emain?

LAVARCHAM [*drily*]. That's questions will give small pleasure to yourself or me. . . . [*She sits on a stool and faces him, making up her mind to speak out.*] If it's the truth I'll tell you, she's growing too wise to marry a big king and she a score only.[3] Let you not be taking it bad, Conchubor, but you'll get little good seeing her this night, for with all my talking it's wilfuller she's growing these two months or three.

CONCHUBOR [*severely, but relieved things are no worse*]. Isn't it a poor thing that you're doing so little to school her to meet what is to come?

LAVARCHAM. I'm after serving you two score of years, and I'll tell you this night, Conchubor, she's little call to mind an old woman when she has the birds to school her, and the pools in the rivers where she goes bathing in the sun. I'll tell you if you seen her that time, with her white skin, and her red lips, and the blue water and

¹ In his typescript Synge questions an alternative speech:

CONCHUBOR. And you're thinking I'll live this way all times seeing Fergus pleased and happy and he plotting for Ireland, and Naisi merry with his dogs on the sides of the hills, and I lonesome in the Duns of Emain. . . . It's little I heed. . . .

the ferns about her, you'd know maybe, and you greedy itself, it wasn't for your like she was born at all.

CONCHUBOR. It's little I heed for what she was born; she'll be my comrade surely. [*He examines her workbox.*]¹

LAVARCHAM [*sinking into sadness again*]. I'm in dread, so, they were right saying she'd bring destruction on the world, for it's a poor thing when you see a settled man putting the love he has for a young child, and the love he has for a full woman, on a girl the like of her, and it's a poor thing, Conchubor, to see a High King the way you are this day, prying after her needles and numbering her lines of thread.

CONCHUBOR [*getting up*]. Let you not be talking too far and you old itself. [*Walks across the room and back.*] . . . Does she know the troubles are foretold?

LAVARCHAM [*in the tone of the earlier talk*]. I'm after telling her one time and another but I'd do as well speaking to a lamb of ten weeks and it racing the hills. . . . It's not the dread of death or troubles that would tame her like.

CONCHUBOR [*looking out*]. She's coming now, and let you walk in and keep Fergus, till I speak with her a while.

LAVARCHAM [*going left*]. If I'm after vexing you, itself, it'd be best you weren't taking her hasty or scolding her at all.

CONCHUBOR [*very stiffly*]. I've no call to. I'm well pleased she's light and airy.

LAVARCHAM [*offended at his tone*]. Well pleased is it? [*With a snort of irony.*] It's a queer thing the way the likes of me do be telling the truth and the wise are lying all times!

[*She goes into room left.* CONCHUBOR *arranges himself before a mirror for a moment, then goes a little to the left and waits.* DEIRDRE *comes in poorly dressed with a little bag and a bundle of twigs in her arms. She is astonished for a moment when she sees* CONCHUBOR; *then she makes a curtsey to him, and goes to the hearth without any embarrassment.*]

CONCHUBOR. The gods save you, Deirdre. I have come up bringing you rings and jewels from Emain Macha.

¹ The use made of Deirdre's embroidery changes considerably through the variou
drafts of Act I. The earliest versions of the scene have Conchubor inquiring closely into
her 'stitching' as evidence of her training to be Queen of Emain Macha, and he look
diligently through the press. The next drafts, belonging to late November and Decembe
1907, use the fancywork as a motive for sending Conchubor out of the room; the Ol
Woman takes Conchubor in to see the silver embroidery Deirdre has hanging over he
bed. On the back of a page from TS. 'B' (1 November 1907), Synge explores the pos
sibilities of this situation: 'Lavarcham tells Fergus that Old W. is an ally of N's and i
trying to have Deirdre taken away. Motive for L & F scene.'

By draft 'F' (10 January 1908), Synge has decided to keep Conchubor on stage, sendin
Fergus out to examine the gold cups and skillets. In a letter to Molly dated 6 January 190
he writes: 'I am working at Deirdre—I can't keep away from her till I get her right. I hav
changed the first half of the first Act a good deal, by making Fergus go into the inne
room instead of Conchubor, and giving C. an important scene with Lav. Then D. come
in and Lav. goes out and D and C have an important scene together. That—when it i
done—will make the whole thing drama instead of narrative and there will be a goo
contrast between the scenes of Deirdre and Conchubor and Deirdre & Naisi. It is quit
useless trying to rush it. I must take my time and let them all grow by degrees.'

Gradually the embroidery takes on further significance in the scene between Deirdr
and Conchubor until it provides the stimulus for Deirdre's references to the Sons of Usn
as in the final TS. 'I'.

Throughout all drafts Synge retains the reference to Conchubor's plight as half-love
half-father, 'prying after her needles and numbering her lines of thread', although in th
early drafts the line was given to Fergus rather than to Lavarcham.

² This speech in draft 'H' (15 February 1908) reads as follows: 'It's soon you'll have dog
and hawks your own self Deirdre, to be chasing in the woods of Emain Macha, for I hav
white hounds rearing up for you, and grey horses, and high seats where you'll be drivin
things I've chosen from what is finest in Ulster and Britain and Gaul.'

After various ink revisions on his final typescript Synge left the speech as printed in th
text, but indicated his dissatisfaction by a question mark in the margin.

DEIRDRE. The gods save you.

CONCHUBOR. What have you brought from the hills?

DEIRDRE [*quite self-possessed*]. A bag of nuts, and twigs for our fires at the dawn of day.

CONCHUBOR [*showing annoyance in spite of himself*]. And it's that way you're picking up the manners will fit you to be Queen of Ulster?

DEIRDRE [*made a little defiant by his tone*]. I have no wish to be a queen.

CONCHUBOR [*almost sneeringly*]. You'd wish to be dressing in your duns and grey, and you herding your geese or driving your calves to their shed . . . like the common lot scattered in the glens?

DEIRDRE [*very defiant*]. I would not, Conchubor. [*She goes to tapestry and begins to work.*] A girl born, the way I'm born, is more likely to wish for a mate who'd be her likeness . . . a man with his hair like the raven maybe and his skin like the snow and his lips like blood spilt on it.

CONCHUBOR [*sees his mistake and after a moment takes a flattering tone, looking at her work*]. Whatever you wish there's no queen but would be well pleased to have your skill at choosing colours and making pictures on the cloth. [*Looking closely.*] What is it you're figuring?

DEIRDRE [*deliberately*]. Three young men, and they chasing in the green gap of a wood.[1]

CONCHUBOR [*now almost pleading*]. It's soon you'll have dogs with silver chains to be chasing in the woods of Emain, for I have white hounds rearing up for you, and grey horses, that I've chosen from the finest in Ulster and Britain and Gaul.[2]

DEIRDRE [*unmoved, as before*]. I've heard tell in Ulster and Britain and Gaul, Naisi and his brothers have no match and they chasing in the woods.

CONCHUBOR [*very gravely*]. Isn't ⟨it⟩ a strange thing you'd be talking of Naisi and his brothers or figuring them either, when you know the things that are foretold about themselves and you! Yet you've little knowledge and I'd do wrong taking it bad when it'll be my share from this out to keep you the way you'll have little call to trouble for knowledge or its want either.

¹ This sentence, added to the typescript in Synge's hand, is omitted in the Cuala edition. The Maunsel edition includes it, however.

² The illegibility of Synge's emendations to this page of the typescript has led to a different interpretation in the Cuala and Maunsel editions:

DEIRDRE. What is it has you that way ever coming this place, when you'd hear the old woman saying a good child's as happy as a king?

³ The Cuala and Maunsel editions omit the second 'I' from this speech: '. . . and wil stand between you . . .'.

DEIRDRE. Yourself should be wise surely.

CONCHUBOR. The like of me have a store of knowledge that's a weight and terror; it's for that we do choose out the like of yourself that are young and glad only. I'm thinking you're gay and lively each day in the year?

DEIRDRE. I don't know if that's true, Conchubor.[1] There are lonesome days and bad nights in this place like another.

CONCHUBOR. You should have as few sad days I'm thinking as I have glad and good ones.

DEIRDRE. What is it has you that way, Conchubor? Ever this place you hear the old women saying a good child's as happy as a king.[2]

CONCHUBOR. How would I be happy seeing age come on me each year when the dry leaves are blowing back and forward at the gate of Emain, and yet this last while I⟨'m⟩ saying out when I'd see the furze breaking and the daws sitting two and two on ash-trees by the Duns of Emain, 'Deirdre's a year nearer her full age when she'll be my mate and comrade,' and then I'm glad surely.

DEIRDRE [*almost to herself*]. I will not be your mate in Emain.

CONCHUBOR [*not heeding her*]. It's there you'll be proud and happy and you'll learn that if young men are great hunters yet it's with the like of myself you'll find a knowledge of what is priceless in your own like. What we all need is a place is safe and splendid, and it's that you'll get in Emain in two days or three.

DEIRDRE [*aghast*]. Two days?

CONCHUBOR. I've the rooms ready, and in a little while you'll be brought down there, to be my queen, and queen of the five parts of Ireland.

DEIRDRE [*standing up frightened and pleading*]. I'd liefer stay this place, Conchubor. . . . Leave me this place where I'm well used to the tracks and pathways and the people of the glens. . . . It's for this life I'm born surely.

CONCHUBOR. You'll be happier and greater with myself in Emain. It is I will be your comrade, and I will stand between you and the great troubles are foretold.[3]

¹ The Cuala and Maunsel editions read: 'I'm a long while. . . .'

DEIRDRE. I will not be your queen in Emain when it's my pleasure to be having my freedom on the edges of the hills.

CONCHUBOR. It's my wish to have you quickly, and I'm sick and weary thinking of the day you'll be brought down to me and seeing you walking into my big empty halls. I've made all sure to have you —and yet all said there's a fear in the back of my mind I'd miss you and have great troubles in the end. It's for that, Deirdre, I'm praying that you'll come quickly. And you may take the word of a man has no lies you'll not find with any other the like of what I'm bringing you in wildness and confusion in my own mind.

DEIRDRE. I cannot go, Conchubor.

CONCHUBOR [*taking a triumphant tone*]. It is my pleasure to have you and I a man is waiting a long while on the throne of Ulster. Wouldn't you liefer be my comrade growing up the like of Emer and Maeve, than to be in this place and you a child always?

DEIRDRE. You don't know me, and you'd have little joy taking me, Conchubor. . . . I'm too long[1] watching the days getting a great speed passing me by, I'm too long taking my will and it's that way I'll be living always.

CONCHUBOR [*drily*]. Call Fergus to come with me. This is your last night upon Slieve Fuadh.

DEIRDRE [*now pleadingly*]. Leave me a short space longer, Conchubor. Isn't it a poor thing I should be hastened away when all these troubles are foretold? Leave me a year Conchubor, it isn't much I'm asking.

CONCHUBOR. It's much to have me two score and two weeks waiting for your voice in Emain, and you in this place growing lonesome and shy. I'm a ripe man and I've great love and yet, Deirdre, I'm the King of Ulster. [*He gets up.*] I'll call Fergus and we'll make Emain ready in the morning. [*He goes towards door on left.*]

DEIRDRE [*clinging to him*]. Do not call him, Conchubor. . . . Promise me a year of quiet. . . . It's one year I'm asking only.

CONCHUBOR. You'd be asking a year next year, and the years that follow. [*Calling.*] Fergus. . . Fergus. . . . [*To* DEIRDRE.] Young girls are slow always; it is their lovers that must say the word. [*Calling.*] Fergus!

[DEIRDRE *springs away from him as* FERGUS *comes in with* LAVARCHAM *and* OLD WOMAN.]

<hr />

¹ The Cuala edition inverts the last two words: 'like her'. The Maunsel edition, how-ever, reads as printed here.

<hr />

² The Abbey Theatre TS. 'B' adds the interjection:

LAVARCHAM [*sharply*]. What is it you know of the Sons of Usnach?

DEIRDRE. The goat-boy has told me about them. [*More decidedly.*] Would those three stand out against Conor?

CONCHUBOR [*to* FERGUS]. There is a storm coming and we'd best be going to our people when the night is young.

FERGUS [*cheerfully*]. The gods shield you, Deirdre. [*To* CONCHUBOR.] We're late already, and it's no work the High King to be slipping on stepping stones, and hilly pathways when the floods are rising with the rain. [*He helps* CONCHUBOR *into his cloak.*]

CONCHUBOR [*glad that he has made his decision, to* LAVARCHAM]. Keep your rules a few days longer and you'll be brought down to Emain, you and Deirdre with you.

LAVARCHAM [*obediently*]. Your rules are kept always.

CONCHUBOR. The gods shield you.

[*He goes out with* FERGUS. OLD WOMAN *bolts the door.* DEIRDRE *covers her face.*]

LAVARCHAM [*looking at* DEIRDRE]. Wasn't I saying you'd do it? . . . You've brought your marriage a sight nearer not heeding those are wiser than yourself.

DEIRDRE [*with agitation*]. It wasn't I did it. Will you take me from this place, Lavarcham, and keep me safe in the hills?

LAVARCHAM. He'd have us tracked in the half of a day, and then you'd be his queen in spite of you, and I and mine would be destroyed forever.

DEIRDRE [*terrified with the reality that is before her*]. Are there none can go against Conchubor?

LAVARCHAM. Maeve of Connaught only, and those that are her like.[1]

DEIRDRE. Would Fergus go against him?

LAVARCHAM. He would maybe and his temper roused.

DEIRDRE [*in a lower voice, with sudden excitement*]. Would Naisi and his brothers?

LAVARCHAM [*impatiently*]. Let you not be dwelling on Naisi and his brothers.[2] . . . In the end of all there is none can go against Conchubor, and it's folly that we're talking, for if any went against

¹ The Abbey Theatre TS. 'B' does not include Deirdre's long speech, but does add the following speech for Lavarcham:

LAVARCHAM [*getting mats out of presses and laying them out*]. She will have her will. It's for that I'm thinking there is a blood cloud hanging upon Emain since the day she was born.

² In the Texas TS. Synge strikes out in ink the words included in the Cuala and Maunse editions: 'I will not be a child or plaything, I'll put on my robes. . . .'

Conchubor it's sorrows he'd earn and the shortening of his day of life.

[*She turns away, and* DEIRDRE *stands up stiff with excitement, then goes to the window and looks out.*]

DEIRDRE. Are the stepping stones flooding, Lavarcham? Will the night be stormy in the hills?

LAVARCHAM [*looking at her curiously*]. The stepping stones are flooding surely, and the night will be the worst I'm thinking we've seen these years gone by.

DEIRDRE [*tearing open the press and pulling out clothes and tapestries*]. Lay these mats and hangings by the windows, and at the tables for our feet, and take out the skillets of silver, and the golden cups we have, and our two flasks of wine.

LAVARCHAM. What ails you?

DEIRDRE [*gathering up a dress*]. Lay them out quickly Lavarcham, we've no call dawdling this night. Lay them out quickly; I'm going into the room to put on the rich dresses and jewels have been sent from Emain.

LAVARCHAM. Putting on dresses at this hour and it dark and drenching with the weight of rain! Are you away in your head?[1]

DEIRDRE [*gathering her things together with an outburst of excitement*]. I will dress like Emer in Dundealgan or Maeve in her house in Connaught. If Conchubor'll make me a queen I'll have the right of a queen who is a master, taking her own choice and making a stir to the edges of the seas. . . . Lay out your mats and hangings where I can stand this night and look about me. Lay out the skins of the rams of Connaught and of the goats of the west.[2] I'll put on my robes that are the richest for I will not be brought down to Emain as Cuchulain brings his horse to its yoke, or Conall Cearneach puts his shield upon his arm. And maybe from this day I will turn the men of Ireland like a wind blowing on the heath.

[*She goes into inner room.* LAVARCHAM *and* OLD WOMAN *look at each other; then* OLD WOMAN *goes over, looks in at* DEIRDRE *through chink of the door, and then closes it carefully.*]

¹ The Cuala and Maunsel editions read: '. . . in her skin; she's putting her hair . . .'.

² As late as draft 'H' (15 February 1908) Lavarcham's speech includes a reference to the supernatural:

LAVARCHAM. It isn't for nothing there's a blood cloud hanging upon Emain since the hour she was born, and it's more than Conchubor'll be sick and sorry, I'm thinking before this story is told to the end.

³ References to Deirdre's encounter with the Sons of Usna in the hills occur in the earliest extant draft of this scene, but in earlier drafts Synge included another motive for their arrival also, curiosity. In TS. 'B' (1 November 1907) the Sons confess that they were led here by Conchubor's 'striving to lay bonds on all not to come this place'. By draft 'E' (30 December 1907) and 'F' (10 January 1908), Ainnle simply answers: 'There was talk of strange things in these places it was that has brought us to them.'

OLD WOMAN [*in a frightened whisper*]. She's thrown off the rags she had about her, and there she is in her skin putting her hair in shiny twists.[1] Is she raving Lavarcham, or has she a good right turning to a queen like Maeve?

LAVARCHAM [*putting up hangings, very anxiously*]. It's more than raving's in her mind, or I'm the more astray, and yet she's as good a right as another, maybe, having her pleasure though she'd spoil the world.

OLD WOMAN [*helping her*]. Be quick before she'll come back. . . . Who'd have thought we'd run before her and she so quiet till tonight. Will the High King get the better of her, Lavarcham? If I was Conchubor I wouldn't marry with her like at all.

LAVARCHAM. Hang that by the window. That should please her surely. . . . When all's said it's her like will be the master till the ends of time.

OLD WOMAN [*at the window*]. There's a mountain of blackness in the sky, and the greatest rain falling has been these long years on the earth. The gods help Conchubor, he'll be a sorry man this night reaching his Dun, and he with all his spirits, thinking to himself he'll be putting his arms around her in two days or three.

LAVARCHAM. It's more than Conchubor'll be sick and sorry, I'm thinking, before this story is told to the end.[2]

[*Loud knocking on door at right.*]

LAVARCHAM [*startled*]. Who is that?

NAISI [*outside*]. Naisi and his brothers.

LAVARCHAM. We are lonely women. What is it you're wanting in the blackness of the night?

NAISI. We met a young girl in the woods who told us we might shelter this place if the rivers rose on the pathways and the floods gathered from the butt of the hills.[3]

[OLD WOMAN *clasps her hands in horror.*]

LAVARCHAM [*with great alarm*]. You cannot come in. . . . There is no one let in here, and no young girl with us.

¹ The manuscript emendations to the typescript are incomplete here; this conjecture follows the Cuala and Maunsel editions. The original line in TS. 'I' reads: 'Come in so, and your bloods be on your heads forever.'

² The Cuala and Maunsel editions read: 'and you'd best be going quickly.'

NAISI. Let us in from the great storm. Let us in and we will go further when the cloud will rise.

LAVARCHAM. Go round east to the shed and you'll have shelter. You cannot come in.

NAISI [*knocking loudly*]. Open the door, or we will burst it.

[*The door is shaken.*]

OLD WOMAN [*in a timid whisper*]. Let them in, and keep Deirdre in her room tonight.

AINNLE AND ARDAN [*outside*]. Open. . . . Open. . . .

LAVARCHAM [*to* OLD WOMAN]. Go in and keep her.

OLD WOMAN. I couldn't keep her. I've no hold on her. . . . Go in yourself and I will free the door.

LAVARCHAM. I must stay and turn them out. [*She pulls her hair and cloak over her face.*] Go in and keep her.

OLD WOMAN. The gods help us. [*She runs into inner room.*]

VOICES. Open!

LAVARCHAM [*opening the door*]. Come in then, and ill luck if you'll have ⟨it⟩ so.[1]

[NAISI *and* AINNLE *and* ARDAN *come in, and look around with astonishment.*]

NAISI. It's a rich man has this place and no herd at all.

LAVARCHAM [*sitting down with her head half-covered*]. It is not, and you'd do best going quickly.[2]

NAISI [*hilariously, shaking rain from his clothes*]. When we've the pick of luck finding princely comfort in the darkness of the night? Some rich man of Ulster should come here and he chasing in the woods. May we drink? [*He takes up flask.*] Whose wine is this that we may drink his health?

LAVARCHAM. It's no one's that you've call to know.

NAISI [*pouring out wine for the three*]. Your own health then and length of life. [*They drink.*]

[1] The Cuala edition takes an earlier manuscript reading: 'we're wanting only.' The Maunsel edition reads as in text.

[2] Although it appears in neither of the two last typescript drafts, the Cuala and Maunsel editions add the word 'then' before 'you'll hear'.

[3] This reply is scribbled on the back of the preceding page. The Maunsel edition reads as in text, but the Cuala edition interprets it as follows:

NAISI [*idly*]. Here's health to herself and you.

LAVARCHAM [*very crossly*]. You're great boys taking a welcome where it isn't given, and asking questions where you've no call to. . . . If you'd a quiet place settled up to be playing yourself maybe with a gentle queen, what'd you think of young men prying around and carrying tales? When I was a bit of a girl, the big men of Ulster had better manners and they the like of your three selves in the top folly of youth. That'll be a great story to tell out in Tara that Naisi is a tippler and stealer, and Ainnle the drawer of a stranger's cork.

NAISI [*quite cheerfully, sitting down beside her*]. At your age you should know there are nights when a king like Conchubor would spit upon his arm ring and queens will stick their tongues out at the rising moon. We're that way this night, and it's not wine we're asking[1] only. . . . Where is the young girl told us we might shelter here?

LAVARCHAM. Asking me you'd be? . . . We're decent people, and I wouldn't put you tracking a young girl, not if you gave me the gold clasp you have, hanging on your coat.

NAISI [*giving it to her*]. Where is she?

LAVARCHAM [*in a confidential whisper, putting her hand on his arm*]. Let you walk back into the hills, and turn up by the second cnuceen where there are three together. You'll see a path running on the rocks and[2] you'll hear the dogs barking in the houses and their noise will guide you till you come to a bit of cabin at the foot of an ash-tree. It's there there is a young and flighty girl that I'm thinking is the one you've seen.

NAISI [*hilariously*]. Here's health then to herself and you![3]

ARDAN. Here's to the years when you were young as she!

AINNLE [*in a frightened whisper*]. Naisi. . . .

[NAISI *looks up and* AINNLE *beckons to him. He goes over and* AINNLE *points to something on the golden mug he holds in his hand.*]

NAISI [*looking at it in astonishment*]. This is the High King's. . . . I see his mark on the rim. Does Conchubor come lodging here?

LAVARCHAM [*jumping up with extreme annoyance*]. Who says it's Conchubor's? How dare young fools the like of you [*speaking with vehement insolence*] come prying around, running the world into troubles for some slip of a girl? What brings you this place straying

¹ This stage direction is omitted in the Cuala edition but is included in the Maunsel edition. Earlier typescript drafts refer even more directly to Lavarcham's manner.

TS. 'B' (1 November 1907):

NAISI [*coming over to the fire, sitting with his back to the left*]. This is a hut of Conor's. And you should be his servant for there are none like the women he has known for rudeness and a saucy tongue.

LAVARCHAM. If I am I have as much joy in making princes run from me with a word alone, as you have striking down your fifties in battle.

NAISI [*to* ARDAN]. Is the rain easing. It wasn't for a scolding woman we came knocking here.

² A stage direction in TS. 'H' (15 February 1908) indicates the action Synge had in mind here and explains Naisi's words:

NAISI [*sharply to* ARDAN *who is fumbling with door*]. Lift the bolt and pull it.

³ Synge has scribbled beside Deirdre's entrance in TS. 'H' the following description: 'her excitement turned into a sort of dignity which is new and surprising to herself'.

⁴ The Cuala and Maunsel editions add the final word 'singing' which, although not struck out when Synge revised the speech, seems to destroy the rhythm. It belongs to an earlier version:

NAISI [*transfixed with amazement*]. And it is you who go around in the woods, making the hares bear a grudge against the Heavens for your lightness, and the thrushes for your voice singing?

⁵ The Cuala and Maunsel editions break the rhythm by placing 'I have fooled them here' as a separate sentence, which seems to be unnecessary for clarity.

Synge later thought better of a stage direction included in TS. 'B' (1 November 1907):

DEIRDRE. It is I surely you have met with. [*She strikes the silver rod of authority.* OLD WOMAN *and* LAVARCHAM *come to her bearing themselves as servants who have found their master.*] Take Ainnle and Ardan. . . .

⁶ The words 'for the first time' have been added from TS. 'H'.

An early draft (possibly TS. 'A') has Deirdre and Naisi at the embroidery centre stage as above, but adds the following directions for the others: [AINNLE *and* ARDAN *inquire anxiously from the women who she is, but keep far away at the fire.*]

from Emain? [*Very bitterly.*][1] Though you think maybe young men can do their fill of foolery and there is none to blame them.

NAISI [*very soberly*]. Is the rain easing?

ARDAN. The clouds are breaking. . . . I can see Orion in the gap of the glen.

NAISI [*still cheerfully*]. Open the door and we'll go forward to the little cabin between the ash-tree and the rocks. Lift the bolt and pull it.[2]

[DEIRDRE *comes in on left royally dressed and very beautiful. She stands for a moment, and then as the door opens she calls softly.*]

DEIRDRE. Naisi. . . . Do not leave me, Naisi, I am Deirdre of the Sorrows.[3]

NAISI [*transfixed with amazement*]. And it is you who go around in the woods, making the thrushes bear a grudge against the heavens for the sweetness of your voice?[4]

DEIRDRE. It is with me you've spoken surely. [*To* LAVARCHAM *and* OLD WOMAN.] Take Ainnle and Ardan, these two princes, into the little hut where we eat, and serve them with what is best and sweetest. I have many things for Naisi only.

LAVARCHAM [*overawed by her tone*]. I will do it, and I ask their pardon I have fooled them here.[5]

DEIRDRE [*to* AINNLE *and* ARDAN]. Do not take it badly, that I am asking you to walk into our hut for a little. You will have a supper that is cooked by the cook of Conchubor, and Lavarcham will tell you stories of Maeve and Nessa and Rogh.

AINNLE. We'll ask Lavarcham to tell us stories of yourself, and with that we'll be well pleased to be doing your wish.

[*They all go out except* DEIRDRE *and* NAISI.]

DEIRDRE [*sitting in the high chair in the centre for the first time*[6]]. Come to this stool, Naisi. [*Pointing to the stool.*] If it's low itself the High King would sooner be on it this night, than on the throne of Emain Macha.

NAISI [*sitting down*]. You are Fedlimid's daughter that Conchubor has walled up from all the men of Ulster?

[1] Although the manuscript emendations are difficult to follow in this passage, this is the wording Synge seems to have intended. The Cuala and Maunsel editions read, 'It's a long while men have been talking of Deirdre the child who had all gifts, and the beauty that has no equal, there are many know it; and there are kings would give a great price. . . .'

On a loose sheet of paper preserved among the early drafts of Act III there are two rough drafts in Synge's hand of a different reply to Deirdre's question:

NAISI. I've not been like the other young men that ⟨go⟩ in crowds in Emain, for I heard my teacher telling the story of all that is foretold about ourselves and you, the way that since that day when I am catching trout or salmon, and it a delicate evening with swifts crying high up, I do be saying over wouldn't ⟨it⟩ be better work to be taking Deirdre's two hands. And when my dogs are killing a stag maybe I am saying it's that colour will be on my blood and yours when we are killed on grass in fresh. . . .

The passage on the other half of the page gives even more details: 'I climbed up into an apple-tree behind the gable when there was a white moon on the wheat beyond the trees, then my ears came up to the window of the loft and I heard my teachers talking, and they were telling the story of what was foretold.'

[2] The stage directions for Naisi and Deirdre are taken from TS. 'H' (15 February 1908)

[3] The Abbey Theatre TS. 'B' gives Naisi a lengthier reply: 'It would be well that you were in Emain Macha with Emer the wife of Cuchulain, and Lendabair the wife of Conal Cearneach, and with Fedelm of the fresh heart, hearing of the great deeds of the men of Ulster. It is a lonesome thing. . . .'

[4] The Cuala and Maunsel editions retain an earlier version: 'It is I who have the best company. . . .'

[5] Stage direction from TS. 'H'.

[6] In an undated passage, probably very early, Synge considered making Naisi fight more strongly against his fate:

NAISI. I'd be proud to lead you with me for an hour only, but what would we gain, going forward to face destruction and the ending of our lives. There isn't many'd have the heart to say this to your like maybe but I and my two brothers aren't lives that any'd do well to be casting away. Isn't it a short space only Deirdre ⟨we⟩ have to be young and triumphant and brave? [*He goes to the door.*]

DEIRDRE [*getting up*]. When it is a short space it's a small thing maybe if it's seven days or seven years or seven times of either. You must not go Naisi and leave me to the High King an old man with his duns and silver and gold. I will not live to be shut up in Emain when you are out racing the woods. Do you dread the ruin is foretold about me and the sons of Usna?

DEIRDRE. Do many know what is foretold, that Deirdre will be the ruin of the Sons of Usna, and have a little grave by herself, and a story will be told forever?

NAISI. It's a long while men have been talking of Deirdre the child who had all gifts, and the beauty that has no equal. Many know it, and there are kings would give a great price to be in my place this night, and you grown to a queen.[1]

DEIRDRE. It isn't many I'd call, Naisi. . . . I was in the woods at the full moon and I heard a voice singing. Then I gathered up my skirts, and I ran on a little path I have to the verge of a rock, and I saw you pass by underneath, in your crimson cloak, singing a song, and you standing out beyond your brothers are called the flower of Ireland.

NAISI [*in a low voice*]. It's for that you called us in the dusk?

DEIRDRE [*in a low voice also*].[2] Since that, Naisi, I have been one time the like of a ewe looking for a lamb that had been taken away from her, and one time seeing new gold on the stars and a new face on the moon, and all times dreading Emain.

NAISI [*pulling himself together and beginning to draw back a little*]. Yet it should be a lonesome thing to be in this place and you born for great company.[3]

DEIRDRE [*softly*]. This night I have the best company in the whole world.

NAISI [*still a little formally*]. It's yourself is your best company,[4] for when you're queen in Emain you will have none to be your match or fellow.

DEIRDRE. I will not be queen in Emain.

NAISI. Conchubor has made an oath you will surely.

DEIRDRE. It's for that maybe I'm called Deirdre, the girl of many sorrows [*she looks up at him*][5] . . . for it's a sweet life you and I could have Naisi. . . . It should be a sweet thing to have what is best and richest if it's for a short space only.

NAISI [*very distressed*]. And we've a short space only to be triumphant and brave.[6]

¹ Even after much revision, Synge's marginal question mark indicates his dissatisfaction with the form of this speech. TS. 'H' (15 February 1908) begins with the reply: 'There's no long space but will pass quickly. You must not go Naisi. . . .'

² Synge's handwriting is particularly difficult to read in his emendation of this passage. The Cuala and Maunsel editions interpret the last phrase as 'the sides of the hills'. When one considers the topography of County Wicklow, either reading makes sense.

³ Although this speech is struck out in the typescript after several emendations, it appears necessary to the exchange between Naisi and Deirdre which follows and which Synge added on the back of the preceding page of his last typescript. However, the Cuala and Maunsel editions read:

DEIRDRE [*despondently*]. His messengers are coming.

The origin of this stage direction is unknown, nor does there appear to be any foundation for this abbreviated form of Deirdre's speech; rather, the information contained in the form printed in the text seems essential to Naisi's understanding of the situation.

⁴ Although Synge's emendations to his text are clear, the Cuala and Maunsel editions retain the former version of Naisi's words: 'Then we'll go away. It isn't I will give your like. . . .'

⁵ This stage direction is taken from TS. 'H'.

⁶ It is difficult to ascertain where Synge intended the words 'on the hillside' to go in the sentence. The Cuala and Maunsel editions omit the phrase. TS. 'H' gives Naisi the line 'From this out your troubles are mine Deirdre and your joys also and we'll have a life and death will bring jealousy to kings forever.'

DEIRDRE. You must not go Naisi, and leave me to the High King, a man is ageing in his Dun, with his crowds round him and his silver and gold. [*More quickly.*] I will not live to be shut up in Emain, and wouldn't we do well paying, Naisi, with silence, and a near death? [*She stands up and walks away from him.*] I'm a long while in the woods with my own self, and I'm in little dread of death, and it earned with richness would make the sun red with envy and he going up the heavens, and the moon pale and lonesome and she wasting away. [*She comes to him and puts her hands on his shoulders.*] Isn't it a small thing is foretold about the ruin of ourselves, Naisi, when all men have age coming and great ruin in the end?[1]

NAISI. Yet it's a poor thing it's I should bring you to a tale of blood, and broken bodies and the filth of the grave. . . . Wouldn't we do well to wait, Deirdre, and I each twilight meeting you on the side of the hills?[2]

DEIRDRE. Messengers are coming tomorrow morning or the next morning to bring me down to Conchubor to be his mate in Emain.[3]

NAISI. Messengers are coming?

DEIRDRE. Tomorrow morning or the next surely.

NAISI. Then it isn't I[4] will give your like to Conchubor, not if the grave was dug to be my lodging when a week was by. [*He looks out.*] The stars are out Deirdre, and let you come with me quickly, for it is the stars will be our lamps many nights and we abroad in Alban, and taking our journeys among the little islands in the sea. There has never been the like of the joy we'll have Deirdre, you and I having our fill of love at the evening and the morning till the sun is high.

DEIRDRE [*sinking on his shoulder,[5] a little shaken by what has passed*]. And yet I'm in dread leaving this place where I have lived always. Won't I be lonesome and I thinking on the little hill beyond and the apple trees do be budding in the springtime by the post of the door? . . . Won't I be in great dread to bring you to destruction, Naisi, and you so happy and young?

NAISI. Are you thinking I'd go on living after this night, Deirdre, and you with Conchubor in Emain? Are you thinking I'd go out after hares on the hillside when I've had your lips in my sight?[6]

[LAVARCHAM *comes in as they cling to each other.*]

[1] The second part of the stage direction is taken from TS. 'H'.

LAVARCHAM. Are you raving, Deirdre? . . . Are you choosing this night to destroy the world?

DEIRDRE [*very deliberately, letting go of* NAISI *slowly*[1]]. It's Conchubor has chosen this night, calling me to Emain. [*To* NAISI.] Bring in Ainnle and Ardan, and take me from this place where I'm in dread from this out of the footstep of a hare passing.

[NAISI *goes.*]

DEIRDRE [*clinging to* LAVARCHAM]. Do not take it bad I'm going, Lavarcham. It's you have been a good friend and given me great freedom and joy, and I living on Slieve Fuadh, and maybe you'll be well pleased one day, saying you have nursed Deirdre.

LAVARCHAM [*moved*]. It isn't I'll be well pleased and I far away from you. Isn't ⟨it⟩ a hard thing you're doing, but who can help it? Birds go mating in the spring of the year, and ewes at the leaves falling, but a young girl must have her lover in all the courses of the sun and moon.

DEIRDRE. Will you go to Emain in the morning?

LAVARCHAM. I will not, I'll go to Brandon in the south, and in the course of a piece maybe I'll be sailing back and forward on the seas to be looking on your face, and the little ways you have that none can equal.

[NAISI *comes back with* AINNLE *and* ARDAN *and* OLD WOMAN.]

DEIRDRE [*taking* NAISI'*s hand*]. My two brothers, I am going with Naisi to Alban and the north, to face the troubles are foretold. Will you take word to Conchubor in Emain?

AINNLE. We will go with you.

ARDAN. We will be your servants and your huntsmen, Deirdre.

DEIRDRE. It isn't one brother only of you three, is brave and courteous. . . . Will you wed us Lavarcham, you have the words and customs?

LAVARCHAM. I will not then. . . . What would I want meddling in the ruin you will earn?

¹ The last page of TS. 'I' contains Ainnle's final speech only. It is the only unnumbered page, and the type differs from the preceding twenty-five pages. It may be a copy made by the estate or the first editors from earlier drafts in order to make up a complete version of Act I. Among the remnants preserved in Box File F is a version typed on the back of page 17 of TS. 'C'; it reads as follows:

AINNLE [*joining their hands*]. By the sun and moon and the whole earth, I wed Deirdre to Naisi [*he steps back and holds up his hands*]. May the air bless you and water and the wind on the sea, and all the hours of the sun and moon.

Originally Synge closed the Act without bringing Ainnle and Ardan back on stage:

NAISI. I went out hunting this morning and I have won yourself Deirdre the crown of conquest of the world. [*They go out.*]

NAISI. Let Ainnle wed us. . . . He has been with wise men and he knows their ways.

AINNLE [*joining their hands*]. By the sun and moon and the whole earth, I wed Deirdre to Naisi. [*He steps back and holds up his hands.*] May the air bless you, and water and the wind, the sea, and all the hours of the sun and moon.[1]

CURTAIN

¹ Earlier drafts add the detail *with bright sun*.

² This last descriptive phrase is taken from TS. 'K', and is the last remnant of a speech by Lavarcham to Naisi (TS. 'F'):

LAVARCHAM. I see Deirdre coming the little path from the well [*looking out without rising*]. Isn't it a great wonder the way her beauty is growing richer, and the way she is passing herself each year and she in the wild air of the woods. . . .

NAISI [*still lightly*]. Deirdre is well surely . . . she has nothing to fret her in this place but odd dreams, and fancyings do rise up in her sleep from the warnings that were laid upon her.

³ The sentences set off in angular brackets are not included in what may be the final draft of this scene, in Notebook 48. Throughout the fifteen typescript drafts of Act II, this scene is the one most heavily revised. Originally Synge planned to make Naisi greet Lavarcham, to assure her of their happiness in the woods before Lavarcham brings her bad tidings to Deirdre. It is not until draft 'L' (21 November 1908) that the act opens as in the text, although for a short time in November 1907 (one draft only, TS. 'G') Synge had considered strengthening Ainnle's part by giving him the opening scene with Deirdre. (See Appendix C.)

In addition to the fifteen typescript drafts of this scene, there are at least five drafts in the two notebooks, 47 and 48, which were in use the last six months of Synge's life. A scenario in Notebook 47 gives a motive for Deirdre's packing during her scene with Owen by opening the scene with Naisi's telling her to pack for their move that evening to Glen da Ruadh. (See Appendix C.)

⁴ It was not until TS. 'L' (21 November 1908) that Synge omitted the following narrative in this scene between Lavarcham and Deirdre (TS. 'J', 10 March 1908, is the most complete version):

DEIRDRE. What had Conchubor in his mind sending Fergus for ourselves?

LAVARCHAM. It's that many are asking. . . . There was a great dinner in Emain Macha and the musicians were playing their music, and the story-tellers telling tales. Then Conchubor hit on his silver bar. 'Is there a better house than Emain Macha this night in the whole world?' says Conchubor. 'There is not' says the people. 'Do any know of a great trouble and want, that is upon us?' says Conchubor. 'We do not' says the people 'It is this,' says Conchubor, 'that the three best men in the whole world, the three sons of Usna, should be put away from us, for the sake of any woman that is living.' 'We would have said that if we had dared,' says the people, 'for they are three wonders for hardness and bravery.' Then it was made up that Fergus should be sent to bring you and that he should be your surety with Conchubor.

DEIRDRE [*thoughtfully after a moment*]. What way is Conchubor living?

LAVARCHAM. Stiff and lonesome on his throne, and he raging out at all who go against him. And when he hears any person saying a word of the woods of Alban, and the life in them you'll see his eyes growing wicked and drawing back into his head.

At one time Synge also contemplated introducing the story of the banquet into Act III TS. 'B' of Act III (before November 1907) gives this narrative to Conchubor himself when he invites the Sons of Usna to a banquet.

⁵ Notebook 48 reads:

D. There's little power in oaths to stop what's coming, and little power in what I'd do Lavarcham to turn a bad end from the face of Emain.

The oath gradually loses significance through the various drafts. In TS. 'B' (6 November 1907) and a passage in Notebook 42, Lavarcham herself makes Naisi swear an oath he will not return to Emain, and in later drafts Deirdre persuades him to swear, which he does by her beauty. In both cases Naisi uses the oath as his reason to Fergus for not returning with him. It is not until TS. 'J' (10 March 1908) that the oath is deleted, apparently at the same time that Owen is introduced into Act II and Naisi first confesses his fears of the future.

ACT II

Alban, early morning in the beginning of winter.[1] *A wood, outside the tent of* DEIRDRE *and* NAISI. LAVARCHAM *comes in, muffled in a cloak.*

LAVARCHAM [*calling*]. Deirdre. . . Deirdre. . . .

DEIRDRE [*coming from tent, radiant and mature*[2]]. My welcome, Lavarcham. . . . Whose curagh is rowing from Ulster? ⟨I saw the oars through the tops of the trees, and I thought it was you were coming towards us.

LAVARCHAM. I came in the shower was before the dawn.

DEIRDRE. And who is coming?⟩[3]

LAVARCHAM [*mournfully*]. Let you not be startled or taking it bad, Deirdre. It's Fergus bringing messages of peace from Conchubor to take Naisi and his brothers back to Emain. [*Sitting down.*]

DEIRDRE [*lightly*]. Naisi and his brothers are well pleased this place and what would take them back to Conchubor in Ulster?[4]

LAVARCHAM. Their like would go any place where they'd see death standing. [*With more agitation.*] I'm in dread Conchubor wants to have yourself, and to kill Naisi, and that that'll be the ruin of the Sons of Usna. I'm silly maybe to be dreading the like, but those have a great love for yourself have a right to be in dread always.

DEIRDRE [*more anxiously*]. Emain should be no safe place for myself and Naisi, and isn't it a hard thing, they'll leave us no peace Lavarcham, and we so quiet in the woods?

LAVARCHAM [*impressively*]. It's a hard thing surely, but let you take my word and swear Naisi by the earth, and the sun over it, and the four quarters of the moon he'll not go back to Emain for good faith, or bad faith, the time Conchubor's keeping the high throne of Ireland. . . . It's that would save you surely.

DEIRDRE [*without hope*]. There's little power in oaths to stop what's coming, and little power in what I'd do Lavarcham, to change the story of Conchubor and Naisi and the things old men foretold.[5]

¹ The word 'great' is omitted from TS. 'O' and the Cuala and Maunsel editions, but occurs in all earlier versions.

² TS. 'M' (30 November 1908) adds the stage direction *with reproaches that she does not mean.*

³ The Cuala and Maunsel editions read: 'Let you end; such talking is a fool's only . . .', but the additional punctuation destroys a sentence pattern frequently used in the play.

⁴ This stage direction from TS. 'M' seems more specific than the words [*with emotion*] from TS. 'O'.

⁵ The Cuala and Maunsel editions omit the second article: 'a happy and sleepy queen'

⁶ In the margin of an undated draft, (? late November 1908) Synge has marked this speech 'climax Deirdre' and added the stage direction *almost overcome.*

⁷ In an undated draft in Notebook 47 (probably October–November 1908), Synge contemplated giving Lavarcham a motif later expressed by Owen:

D. I've dread going and dread staying—it's lonesome Lavarcham to be living this place thinking when a person has no call to think, and I watching the leaves coming like raindrops from the trees are growing naked in the morning fog.

L. And what things is it ail you now [*she pauses and looks at her inquiringly, then with a sort of insinuation*]. Seven years is a long time with one man. Maybe there'll be better men in Emain Macha. I was great that way and I the age of you!

D. [*with sad amusement*]. If anything harmed Naisi it isn't I would live after him.

⁸ The stage direction is added from TS. 'M'.

LAVARCHAM [*aggressively*]. Was there little power in what you did the night you dressed in your finery and ran Naisi off along with you, in spite of Conchubor, and the big nobles did dread the blackness of your luck? It was power enough you had that night to bring distress and anguish, and now I'm pointing you a way to save Naisi, you'll not stir stick or straw to aid me.

DEIRDRE [*a little haughtily*]. Let you not raise your voice against me Lavarcham, if you have great[1] will itself to guard Naisi.

LAVARCHAM [*breaking out in anger*]. Naisi is it? I didn't care if the crows were stripping his thigh-bones at the dawn of day. It's to stop your own despair and wailing, and you waking up in a cold bed, without the man you have your heart on, I am raging now. [*Starting up with temper.*[2]] Yet there's more men than Naisi in it, and maybe I was a big fool thinking his dangers, and this day, would fill you up with dread.

DEIRDRE [*sharply*]. Let you end such talking is a fool's only,[3] when it's well you know if a thing harmed Naisi it isn't I would live after him. [*With distress.*] It's well you know it's this day I'm dreading seven years, and I, fine nights, watching the heifers walking to the haggard with long shadows on the grass [*with a thickening in her voice*],[4] or the time I've been stretched in the sunshine when I've heard Ainnle and Ardan stepping lightly, and they saying, 'Was there ever the like of Deirdre for a happy and a sleepy queen?'[5]

LAVARCHAM [*not fully pacified*]. And yet you'll go and welcome is it, if Naisi chooses?

DEIRDRE. I've dread going or staying, Lavarcham. It's lonesome this place having happiness like ours till I'm asking each day, will this day match yesterday, and will tomorrow take a good place beside the same day in the year that's gone, and wondering all times is it a game worth playing, living on until you're dried and old, and our joy is gone forever.[6]

LAVARCHAM. If it's that ails you, I tell you there's little hurt getting old, though young girls and poets do be storming at the shapes of age.[7] [*Passionately.*] There's little hurt getting old, saving when you're looking back, the way I'm looking this day, and seeing the young you have a love for breaking up their hearts with folly. [*Going to* DEIRDRE, *making a last attempt.*][8] Take my word and stop Naisi, and

¹ After several emendations, Synge's marginal question mark indicates his dissatisfaction with this speech.

² The stage direction is added from TS. 'M'.

³ In the margin of an undated draft (probably late November 1908) Synge has written 'climax Lavarcham' opposite this speech.

On the back of a page of TS. 'F' (23 November 1907) Synge has scribbled 'Lavarcham's exit = plain women are foolish but when they have beauty they have great knowledge and are wise always.'

⁴ See Appendix C for alternative versions of Owen's entrance.

⁵ The stage direction is taken from TS. 'M'.

⁶ TS. 'O' adds the words *cutting it with Conchubor's knife.* At this time, January 1909 Synge was apparently planning to include Owen in Act I, as Yeats mentions in his Preface. The Cuala and Maunsel editions modify the direction slightly: *cutting it with a large knife.*

the day'll come you'll have more joy having the senses of an old woman and you with your little grandsons shrieking round you, than I'd have this night putting on the red mouth, and the white arms you have, to go walking lonesome byeways with a gamey king.

DEIRDRE. It's little joy of a young woman or an old woman I'll have from this day surely. But what use is in our talking when there's Naisi on the foreshore, and Fergus with him.[1]

LAVARCHAM [*getting up despairingly*].[2] I'm late so with my warnings, for Fergus'd talk the moon over to take a new path in the sky. [*With reproach.*] You'll not stop him this day, and isn't it a strange story you were a plague and torment since you were that height to those did hang their life-times on your voice. . . . [*Overcome with trouble, gathering her cloak about her.*] Don't think bad of my crying. I'm not the like of many and I'd see a score of naked corpses and not heed them at all, but I'm destroyed seeing yourself in your hour of joy, when the end is coming surely.[3]

[OWEN *comes in quickly, rather ragged, bows to* DEIRDRE.][4]

OWEN [*to* LAVARCHAM]. Fergus's men are calling you. You were seen on the path and he and Naisi want you for their talk below.

LAVARCHAM [*looking at him with dislike*]. Yourself's an ill-lucky thing to meet a morning is the like of this. Yet if you are a spy itself I'll go and give my word that's wanting surely. [*She goes out slowly.*][5]

OWEN [*to* DEIRDRE]. So I've found you alone, and I after waiting three weeks getting ague and asthma in the chill of the bogs, till I saw Naisi caught with Fergus.

DEIRDRE. I've heard news of Fergus, what brought you from Ulster?

OWEN [*who has been searching, finds a loaf and sits down eating greedily*[6]]. The full moon I'm thinking and it squeezing the crack in my skull. Was there ever a man crossed nine waves after a fool's wife and he not away in his head?

DEIRDRE [*absently*]. It should be a long time since you left Emain, where there's civility in speech with queens.

OWEN. It's a long while surely. It's three weeks I am losing my manners beside the Saxon bull-frogs at the head of the bog. Three weeks

¹ The exchange set off by angular brackets has been struck out in TS. 'O' with the marginal note 'Fill up from MS.' The manuscript referred to might be a scene in Notebook 47 which includes several important variations and additional details. (See Appendix C, pp. 383–92.)

² Notebook 47 elsewhere contains an alternative speech which happily Synge discarded: 'Would you be well pleased living seven years on chops from the left of a hog?'

³ The stage direction is from TS. 'M'.

⁴ This speech is taken from Synge's ink emendations of TS. 'O'. The Cuala edition is similar to the printed text, but the Maunsel edition retains a phrase struck out by Synge and differs considerably in punctuation:

OWEN [*sharply*]. Well, go, take your choice. Stay here and rot with Naisi or go to Conchubor in Emain. Conchubor's a wrinkled fool with a swelling belly on him, and eye. falling downward from his shining crown; Naisi should be stale and weary. Yet there are many roads, Deirdre, and I tell you. . . .

The additional stage direction included in the text here printed is taken from TS. 'M' is a long space, and yet you're seven years spancelled with Naisi and the pair!

〈DEIRDRE [*beginning to fold up her jewels*]. Three weeks of your days might be long surely; yet seven years are a short space for the like of Naisi and myself.

OWEN [*derisively*]. If they're a short space there aren't many the like of you. Wasn't there a queen in Tara had to walk out every morning till she'd meet a stranger and see the flame of courtship leaping up within his eye?〉[1] Tell me now [*leaning towards her*], . . . are you well pleased that length with the same man snorting next you at the dawn of day?[2]

DEIRDRE [*very quietly*]. Am I well pleased seven years seeing the same sun throwing light across the branches at the dawn of day? [*With abstracted feeling.*][3] It's a heart-break to the wise that it's for a short space we have the same things only. [*With contempt.*] Yet the earth itself is a silly place maybe, when a man's a fool and talker.

OWEN [*sharply*]. Well go take your choice. Stay here and rot with Naisi, or go to Conchubor in Emain. Conchubor's a swelling belly, and eyes falling down from his shining crown, Naisi should be stale and weary; yet there are many roads, Deirdre [*he goes towards her*],[4] and I tell you I'd liefer be bleaching in a bog-hole than living on without a touch of kindness from your eyes and voice. It's a poor thing to be so lonesome you'd squeeze kisses on a cur dog's nose.

DEIRDRE. Are there no women like yourself could be your friends in Emain?

OWEN [*vehemently*]. There are none like you, Deirdre. It's for that I'm asking are you going back this night with Fergus?

DEIRDRE. I will go where Naisi chooses.

OWEN [*with a burst of rage*]. It's Naisi, Naisi is it? Then I tell you you'll have great sport one day seeing Naisi getting a harshness in his two sheep's eyes and he looking on yourself. Would you credit it, my father used to be in the broom and heather kissing Lavarcham, with a little bird chirping out above their heads, and now she'd scare a raven from a carcass on a hill. [*With a sad cry that brings dignity into his voice.*] Queens get old Deirdre, with their white and long arms

¹ Synge's question marks in the margin indicate his dissatisfaction with Owen's speeches here. Other variations on this passage suggest that Synge considered this Owen's most important scene. (See Appendix C.)

² The Cuala and Maunsel editions read Synge's handwriting as 'I'm doing'.

³ During his last months of work on this act, Synge evidently contemplated several different versions of Owen's exit also. Notebook 47 brings Lavarcham on stage as messenger and again draws an interesting parallel between Lavarcham and Owen; elsewhere in the same notebook Synge considered making Naisi and Owen confront each other. (See Appendix C.)

Fergus's two sons, Iollan and Buinne, remain in the text until Synge revised TS. 'I' (late December 1907/early 1908), but do not seem to have been fully developed as characters.

⁴ This stage direction is omitted in the Cuala and Maunsel editions. Synge has clearly written *to net* and later *netting*, and this seems more in keeping for Deirdre than *knitting*, although in view of Synge's cavalier attitude towards spelling the latter reading is possible.

⁵ The Cuala and Maunsel editions read, 'There are your sureties and . . .'.

going from them, and their backs hooping. I tell you it's a poor thing
to see a queen's nose reaching down to scrape her chin.[1]

DEIRDRE [*looking out, a little uneasy at his tone*]. Naisi and Fergus are
coming on the path.

OWEN. I'll go so . . . for if I had you seven years I'd be jealous of the
midges and the dust is in the air. [*With a sort of warning in his voice,
muffling himself in his cloak.*] I'll give you a riddle, Deirdre. Why isn't
my father as ugly and as old as Conchubor? You've no answer? . . .
It's because Naisi killed him. [*With a curious expression.*] Think of
that and you awake at night hearing Naisi snoring, or the night
you'll hear strange stories of the things I've done[2] in Alban or in
Ulster either.

[*He goes out, and in a moment* NAISI *and* FERGUS *come in on the other
side.*][3]

NAISI [*gaily*]. Fergus has brought messages of peace from Conchubor!

DEIRDRE [*greeting* FERGUS]. He is welcome. Let you rest Fergus, you
should be hot and thirsty after mounting the rocks.

FERGUS. It's a sunny nook you've found in Alban, yet any man would
be well pleased mounting higher rocks, to fetch yourself and Naisi
back to Emain.

DEIRDRE [*with keenness*]. They've answered? They would go?

FERGUS [*benignly*]. They have not [DEIRDRE *begins to net*[4]], but when
I was a young man we'd have given a lifetime to be in Ireland a
score of weeks, and to this day the old men have nothing so heavy
as knowing it's in a short while they'll lose the high skies are over
Ireland, and the lonesome mornings with birds crying on the bogs.
Let you come this day for there's no place but Ireland where the Gael
can have peace always.

NAISI [*gruffly*]. It's true surely. Yet we're better this place while Conchubor's in Emain Macha.

FERGUS [*giving him parchments*]. These are your sureties with[5] Conchubor's seal. [*To* DEIRDRE, *who stops netting during his speech.*] You'll
not be young always, and it's time you were making yourselves
ready for the years will come, building up a homely Dun beside the
seas of Ireland, and getting in your children from the princes'

¹ In TS. 'E' (14 November 1907) and TS. 'F' (23 November 1907) Naisi tells Lavarcham, 'We have put our children where they are well fostered, and we are leading the life of the woods that has no worry.'

² Synge's customary marginal question mark indicates his doubt over this speech. The Abbey Theatre TS. 'F' includes the following exchange at this point:

DEIRDRE. What is one's own country Fergus but the place where we have peace and great possessions?

FERGUS [*shocked*]. I know no country in the whole world but Ireland that has the sweet skies in Autumn, and lonesome mornings with birds crying and great stillness in the woods. I know no country but Ireland where the great kings are poets and players on the harp and the poets are kings and princes; and where it is women like yourself Deirdre who rule the poets and the kings with them.

DEIRDRE [*rising and going up the stage*]. No one is ruler in Ireland but Conchubor only.

³ The Cuala and Maunsel editions print a stage direction struck out in TS. 'O': [*He gets parchments from his cloak and gives them to Naisi.*] The duplication of action seems unnecessary here, since Conchubor's seal would be affixed to all the parchments as indication of royal pleasure.

⁴ It is not until Synge revises draft 'L' (end of November 1908) that he removes all mention of the supernatural in Deirdre's conversation with Fergus, although gradually there is less urgency. The earlier drafts include two interruptions of the discussion between Fergus and Naisi, as in the following from TS. 'J' (10 March 1908):

DEIRDRE [*crying out suddenly*]. It isn't pleasure they'd have but great sorrow, for I have seen Naisi without his strength, and Conchubor asking for blood, and myself Deirdre with tears crying.

. . . .

DEIRDRE [*crying out with more agitation*]. I have seen three birds coming from Ireland with drops of honey in their mouths, and it was drops of our own blood they took away with them. I have seen a son of Fergus wanting his head, and a son of Fergus in the way of troubles, and Ainnle and Ardan going to a grave where there was none to keep them.

By draft 'L' Deirdre's vision has become 'a story' she has heard 'of three birds coming from Ireland with drops of honey . . .'.

⁵ In an earlier typescript (November–December 1908) Synge wrote 'Expand' in the margin beside Naisi's speech, but evidently the final typescript version did not satisfy him either, for the usual question mark is accompanied by the word 'sickly'.

wives.[1] It's little joy wandering till age is on you and your youth is gone away, so you'd best come this night, for you'd have great pleasure putting out your foot and saying 'I am in Ireland surely'.[2]

DEIRDRE. It isn't pleasure I'd have while Conchubor is king in Emain.

FERGUS [*almost annoyed*]. Would you doubt the seals of Conall Cearneach and the kings of Meath?[3] [*More gently.*] It's easy being fearful and you alone in the woods yet it would be a poor thing if a timid woman [*taunting her a little*] could turn away the Sons of Usna from the life of kings. Let you be thinking on the years to come, Deirdre, and the way you'd have a right to see Naisi a high and white-haired Justice beside some king of Emain. Wouldn't it be a poor story if a queen the like of you should have no thought but to be scraping up her hours dallying in the sunshine with the sons of kings?

DEIRDRE [*turning away a little haughtily*]. I leave the choice to Naisi. [*Turning back towards* FERGUS.] Yet you'd do well Fergus to go on your own way, for the sake of your own years, so you'll not be saying till your hour of death, maybe it was yourself brought Naisi and his brothers to a grave was scooped by treachery. [*She goes into tent.*][4]

FERGUS. It's a poor thing to see a queen so lonesome and afraid. [*He watches till he is sure* DEIRDRE *cannot hear him.*] Listen now to what I'm saying. You'd do well to come back to men and women are your match and comrades, and not be lingering until the day that you'll grow weary, and hurt Deirdre showing her the hardness in your eyes. . . . You've been here years and plenty to know it's truth I'm saying.

[DEIRDRE *comes out of tent with a horn of wine. She catches the beginning of* NAISI's *speech and stops with stony wonder.*]

NAISI [*very thoughtfully*]. I'll not tell you a lie. There have been days a while past when I've been throwing a line for salmon, or watching for the run of hares, that I've had a dread upon me a day'd come I'd weary of her voice [*very slowly*] . . . and Deirdre'd see I'd wearied.[5]

FERGUS [*sympathetic but triumphant*]. I knew it, Naisi. . . . And take my word Deirdre's seen your dread and she'll have no peace from this out in the woods.

¹ An earlier typescript (probably late November 1908) carries the marginal note 'climax' beside this speech.

² In a heavily revised draft of November–December 1908, Synge thought of making Naisi realize that Deirdre had overheard his speech to Fergus: 'She's heard me Fergus. There was terror that time in her eyes. [*He throws ⟨down⟩ the parchments.*] I'll not go Fergus. . . . [*He speaks close to* DEIRDRE'*s tent to make sure she hears him.*]'

In this exchange between Naisi and Fergus, the Maunsel edition corresponds to the text printed here, but the Cuala edition appears to combine two drafts. It omits Naisi's statement 'I will not' yet takes the remainder of his speech of refusal from the final manuscript draft scribbled on the back of the preceding page of Synge's typescript. However, in place of Fergus's question as printed here, it prints the earlier superseded version, 'It's that you mean surely?'

³ A late draft in Notebook 47 adds another speech by Naisi: '[*confidentially*]. Another thing Fergus. You and I aren't certain of the thing C. has in his mind, and there is no day I'd choose a risk of leaving Deirdre desolate, for she and I are as close as daylight and the sun.'

⁴ The Abbey Theatre TS. 'F' (23 November 1907) emphasizes the final bitterness between Fergus and Naisi here, omitting Naisi's preceding confidences:

FERGUS [*more bitterly*]. It is a poor thing when any woman can turn away the sons of Usnach from the life of Emain. [*Beginning to speechify.*] Where Conchubor and Cathladh are two counsellors that have no equal, and Cuchulain and Conall Cearneach do great deeds and battles. It is a poor thing to come from Emain [*he turns away from* NAISI *and looks round*] to spear salmon in the streams of Alban, or set snares for hares or foxes the way it will be said from this out, that Naisi was a hunter only.

NAISI [*with vehemence*]. It will not be said that I sat quiet to hear you scolding the Sons of Usnach, who have hunted nations when it pleased them.

FERGUS [*coldly*]. I have not come from Emain to quarrel with you, who are my friend for ever . . . where are Ainnle and Ardan my message is to them also?

NAISI [*still angry*]. Go up the little path by the quickens, and then you will see Ainnle and Ardan by the stream, and you can give them your message. They have not sworn an oath.

[FERGUS *goes out.*]

⁵ The Cuala and Maunsel editions give this stage direction to Naisi, but TS. 'O' and earlier drafts have Deirdre crossing the stage and sitting down.

NAISI [*with confidence*]. She's not seen it. . . . Deirdre's no thought of getting old or wearied, it's that puts wonder in her ways, and she with spirits would keep bravery and laughter in a town with plague.

[DEIRDRE *drops the horn of wine and crouches down where she is.*]

FERGUS. That humour'll leave her. But we've no call going too far, with one word borrowing another. Will you come this night to Emain Macha?

NAISI. I'll not go, Fergus. I've had dreams of getting old and weary, and losing my delight in Deirdre, but my dreams were dreams only. What are Conchubor's seal and all your talk of Emain and the fools of Meath beside one evening in Glen Masain? We'll stay this place till our lives and time are worn out. It's that word you may take in your curagh to Conchubor in Emain.[1]

FERGUS [*gathering up his parchments*]. And you won't go surely?

NAISI [*gaily*]. I will not. . . .[2] I've had dread, I tell you, dread winter and summer, and the autumn and the spring-time, even when there's a bird in every bush making his own stir till the fall of night. But this talk's brought me ease, and I see we're as happy as the leaves on the young trees and we'll be so ever and always though we'd live the age of the eagle and the salmon and the crow of Britain.[3]

FERGUS [*very much annoyed*]. Where are your brothers? My message is for them also.

NAISI. You'll see them above chasing otters by the stream.

FERGUS [*bitterly*]. It isn't much I was mistaken, thinking you were hunters only.[4]

[*He goes.* NAISI *turns towards tent, and sees* DEIRDRE *crouching down with her cloak round her face.* DEIRDRE *comes out.*]

NAISI. You've heard my words to Fergus? [*She does not answer. A pause. He puts his arm round her.*] Leave troubling, and we'll go this night to Glen da Ruadh where the salmon will be running with the tide.

[DEIRDRE *crosses and sits down.*][5]

DEIRDRE [*in a very low voice*]. With the tide in a little while we will be journeying again, or it is our own blood maybe will be running

¹ In early drafts of this scene Deirdre adds further details of the vision she mentions to Fergus. A passage from TS. 'I' (11 December 1907) reads:

DEIRDRE. I see a cloud in the Heaven, Naisi, a cloud of red blood that is over the greenness of Ireland.

NAISI. Leave troubling, Deirdre, tomorrow we will go to Glen da Ruadh [*with a sort of irony*]—Where the salmon will be running with the tide.

DEIRDRE [*still with a visionary intonation*]. With the tide in a little while we will be going to Ireland, for I have seen the end of peace and the closing of a quiet year. And again in a little while it is your blood will be running away.

Further, in draft 'H' (23 November 1907) Deirdre tells Naisi she has been 'dreaming strange dreams and seeing strange sights' since the night of Samhain. And on the back of an early draft (about March 1908) Synge has scribbled the following exchange:

D [*testing him*]. Some say in seven years the most lovers do be weary.

N [*gaily*]. That's the talk of messengers and horseboys, and Lavarcham's company, but if we'd the age of the salmon—⟨I⟩ and my two brothers—

D [*pleased but pleadingly*]. Let you swear to send back Fergus—For I'm in dread this last while and I dreaming strange dreams—

It is not until Naisi voices his own fears for the future (after March 1908) that direct reference to the supernatural is omitted from this scene between Deirdre and Naisi, but it is retained in the scene with Fergus until December 1908.

A draft of 'Scene III Deirdre and Naisi' in Notebook 47 combines all of these references in one speech:

D. You've seen Fergus?

N. I have surely, and I said that it's ⟨no⟩ call we had travelling and we with great joy in this place.

D [*suddenly*]. I'm in dread Naisi. I've seen a cloud of red blood over the greenness of Ireland. I've seen three birds coming over with drops of honey in their mouths, and it was drops of our own blood they took away with them. I have seen a son of Fergus wanting his head and a son of Fergus in the way of troubles, and Ainnle and Ardan going to a grave where there was none to keen them—[*She covers her head.*]

NAISI. Let you not be troubling when Fergus has his answer and tomorrow we'll go to Glen da Ruadh. . . .

But even in the final typescript the supernatural is not completely eradicated, as can be seen in Deirdre's later speech: 'And it's in the quiet woods I've seen them digging our grave. . . .'

² Although the Cuala and Maunsel editions omit it, it is evident from the typescript that Synge wished the question mark to be printed at the end of Naisi's speech.

³ In the final TS. 'O' Synge struck out, then questioned, this beginning to Naisi's reply: 'Is it my talk has moved you of the dread is hidden in a joy's too wild? [DEIRDRE *shakes her head*.]'

⁴ The Abbey Theatre TS. 'F' inserts the following stage direction here: [*she turns and puts her arms on his shoulder*].

⁵ Stage direction from earlier drafts.

away.[1] [*She turns and clings to him.*] The dawn and evening are a little while, the winter and the summer pass quickly, and what way would you and I Naisi, have joy forever?

NAISI. We'll have the joy is highest till our age is come, for it isn't Fergus's talk of great deeds could take us back to Emain.

DEIRDRE. It isn't to great deeds you're going but to near troubles, and the shortening of your days the time that they are bright and sunny and isn't it a poor thing that I, Deirdre, could not hold you away?

NAISI. I've said we'd stay in Alban always?[2]

DEIRDRE. There's no place to stay always. . . . It's a long time we've had, pressing the lips together, going up and down, resting in our arms, Naisi, waking with the smell of June in the tops of the grasses, and listening to the birds in the branches that are highest. . . . It's a long time we've had, but the end has come surely.

NAISI. Would you have us go to Emain, though if any ask the reason we do not know it, and we journeying as the thrushes come from the north, or young birds fly out on a dark sea?[3]

DEIRDRE. There's reason all times for an end that's come. . . . And I'm well pleased, Naisi, we're going forward in the winter the time the sun has a low place, and the moon has her mastery in a dark sky,[4] for it's you and I are well lodged our last day, where there is a light behind the clear trees, and the berries on the thorns are a red wall.

NAISI [*with a new rush of love, eagerly*].[5] If our time this place is ended, come away without Ainnle and Ardan to the woods of the East, for it's right to be away from all people when two lovers have their love only. Come away and we'll be safe always.

DEIRDRE [*broken-hearted*]. There's no safe place, Naisi, on the ridge of the world. . . . And it's in the quiet woods I've seen them digging our grave, throwing out the clay on leaves are bright and withered.

NAISI [*still more eagerly*]. Come away, Deirdre, and it's little we'll think of safety or the grave beyond it, and we resting in a little corner between the daytime and the long night.

DEIRDRE [*clearly and gravely*]. It's this hour we're between the daytime and a night where there is sleep forever, and isn't it a better thing to be following on to a near death, than to be bending the head down,

¹ The Abbey Theatre TS. 'F' (23 November 1907) varies considerably here in both subject and phrasing:

NAISI. Come away, Deirdre, from Conchubor and Fergus and all kings for ever, and what will we think of graves when I have your voice speaking [*growing excited*] and your cheek that is like a white moon to my lips, and we resting in a little corner, and between the day-time and the long night?

DEIRDRE. It is this hour we are between the day-time and a night where there is sleep for ever, and it is a better thing Naisi to meet death quickly than to be bending the head down and dragging with the feet, till there is a blight showing on love where it is sweet and tender.

NAISI [*slowly*]. It is a hard thing for a beggar to lose his raggedness or a king to lose his kingdom and bright crown, but what will be my sorrow, if I lose the earth with its company of the stars and you Deirdre who are their flower and their crown for ever. Come away Deirdre, where there is no one to speak the name of Conchubor but rocks only.

DEIRDRE. Where would we go Naisi? There are as many ways to put ruin upon life and love as there are stars in a night of Samhain, but there is no way, Naisi, to keep life or love with it a short space only . . . it's for that there is nothing lonesome like a love is watching out when most lovers do be sleeping. It's for that the two of us are going back to Ulster when the tide turns in the bay.

NAISI. It's for that surely. [*There is a short pause, while they cling to each other. Then* NAISI *moves.*] I see Fergus coming and Lavarcham with him and my two brothers.

² At one time (possibly late November 1908) Synge contemplated ending the scene here: [*the Curtain falls stealthily?*] Presumably this was before he realized the possibilities of Owen. (See Appendix C.)

³ On the reverse side of the page in TS. 'O' Synge has considerably altered the action of this scene, without bothering to cross out the superseded passage in the typescript itself. The Cuala and Maunsel editions differ in several places from the text given here:

(*a*) They retain a final sentence in Naisi's speech to Deirdre, 'There are Fergus and Lavarcham and my two brothers. [DEIRDRE *goes.* NAISI *sits with his head bowed.* . . .]'

(*b*) They give to Naisi the announcement of Fergus's arrival, 'There he is.' However, this version from the Cuala and Maunsel editions seems to duplicate the action and deprive Owen's sudden appearance of its full impact. Further, it is Owen who has been above watching Fergus, and it seems more logical that he should herald Fergus's appearance. Naisi then has more opportunity to prepare his announcement to the company.

The additional stage directions are taken from the final typescript and a version in Notebook 48 which can be dated the last week of November 1908.

and dragging with the feet, and seeing one day, a blight showing upon love where it is sweet and tender?

NAISI [*his voice broken with distraction*]. If a near death is coming what will be my trouble losing the earth and the stars over it, and you Deirdre are their flame and bright crown? Come away into the safety of the woods.

DEIRDRE [*shaking her head slowly*]. There are as many ways to wither love as there are stars in a night of Samhain, but there is no way to keep life or love with it a short space only. . . . It's for that there's nothing lonesome like a love is watching out the time most lovers do be sleeping. . . . It's for that we're setting out for Emain Macha when the tide turns on the sand.

NAISI [*giving in*]. You're right maybe. . . . It should be a poor thing to see great lovers and they sleepy and old.

DEIRDRE [*with a more tender intensity*]. We're seven years without roughness or growing weary, seven years so sweet and shining, the gods would be hard set to give us seven days the like of them. . . . It's for that we're going to Emain where there'll be a rest forever, or a place for forgetting, in great crowds and they making a stir.

NAISI [*very softly*]. We'll go surely,[1] in place of keeping a watch on a love had no match and it wasting away.

[*They cling to each other for a moment, then* DEIRDRE *stands up slowly, and goes into the tent with her head bowed down without looking at* NAISI. NAISI *sits with his head bowed.*[2] OWEN *runs in stealthily, comes behind* NAISI *and seizes him round the arms;* NAISI *shakes him off and whips out his sword.*]

OWEN [*screaming with derisive laughter and showing his empty hands*]. Ah Naisi, wasn't it well I didn't kill you that time! There was a fright you got. I've been watching Fergus above—don't be frightened— and I've come down to see him getting the cold shoulder and going off alone. . . . There he is.

[*Voices are heard on the right, and* AINNLE, ARDAN, FERGUS *and* LAVARCHAM *come in. They are all subdued like men at a queen's wake.*][3]

NAISI [*goes to* FERGUS, *putting up his sword*]. We are going back when the tide turns, I and Deirdre with yourself.

¹ The Cuala and Maunsel editions retain the following speeches which are very lightly struck out by Synge in TS. 'O':

AINNLE. And you'll end our life with Deirdre, though she has no match for keeping spirits in a little company is far away by itself?

ARDAN. It's seven years myself and Ainnle have been servants and bachelors for yourself and Deirdre. Why will you take her back to Conchubor?

NAISI. I have done what Deirdre wishes and has chosen.

However, comparing this passage with the versions in Notebook 48, one must conclude that it belongs to a slightly earlier period when Synge was still considering strengthening Ainnle's part. (See Appendix C.)

The Abbey Theatre TS. 'F' emphasizes the motif an early scenario outlines for Ainnle here (see Appendix C):

AINNLE. They say good fortune makes fools of the whole world, and it is likely you've forgotten Naisi, you have the choice of the whole world for your comrade only.

LAVARCHAM. Fergus said you were after swearing an oath you would not go.

AINNLE [*to* NAISI]. Are you coming to look out for kingdoms, and their like in place of this life where we have peace and happiness?

NAISI. I have done what Deirdre asked me.

AINNLE. If she asked folly, you had no call to.

NAISI. Who will tell me if her choice is folly?

AINNLE. The choice of leaving this life that has no worry, and the quiet air of the woods is a fool's choice surely.

NAISI. You lead me on to quarrelling, that is a fool's business only.

AINNLE. There is no foolishness would not fit you this day Naisi.

² Again in TS. 'O' Synge has lightly struck out the following verse to be chanted by Owen as he scatters the gold pieces; it is conceivable that he might have retained it if he had had time to develop Owen's part as he wished (see Appendix C):

> That's for your journey out, and that is for your journey home.
> That's for your smile
> That's for guile,
> That's for your wile
> And that's for the bile
> You'll sweat in a while.

³ In a draft in Notebook 48, written the last week of November 1908 or later, Synge considered making Lavarcham remain behind to pick up the gold scattered by Owen. The version given here, from TS. 'O', apparently still did not satisfy him, for he has written in the margin '? send Lav. out?'

⁴ In TS. 'O' Synge has struck out the following speech which obviously belongs to his alternative plan for Owen (see Appendix C):

NAISI [*giving* DEIRDRE *her ring*]. He was always a thief and rogue, and he'd stolen your ring. [DEIRDRE *takes it quietly.*]

ALL. Going back?[1]

FERGUS. You've made a choice wise men will be glad of in the five ends of Ireland.

OWEN. Wise men is it and they going back to Conchubor? I could stop them only Naisi put in his sword among my father's ribs and when a man's done that he'll not credit your oath. Going to Conchubor! I could tell of plots and tricks and spies were well paid for their play. [*He throws up a bag of gold.*] Are you paid, Fergus? [*He scatters gold pieces over* FERGUS.][2]

FERGUS. He is raving. . . . Seize him. . . .

OWEN [*flying between them*]. You won't. Let the lot of you be off to Emain but I'll be off before you. . . . Dead men, dead men, men who'll die for Deirdre's beauty, I'll be before you in the grave!

[OWEN *runs out with his knife in his hand. They all run after him except* LAVARCHAM, *who looks out and then clasps her hands.* DEIRDRE *comes out to her in a dark cloak.*][3]

DEIRDRE. What has happened?

LAVARCHAM. It's Owen gone raging mad and he's after splitting his gullet beyond at the butt of the stone. There was ill luck this day in his eye. And he knew a power if he'd said it all.

[NAISI *comes back followed by the others.*][4]

AINNLE [*coming in very excited*]. That man knew plots of Conchubor's. . . . We'll not go to Emain where Conchubor may love her and has hatred for yourself.

FERGUS. Would you mind a fool and raver?

AINNLE. It's many times there's more sense in madmen than the wise. We will not obey Conchubor.

NAISI. I and Deirdre have chosen, we will go back with Fergus.

ARDAN. We will not go back. . . . We will burn your curaghs by the sea.

FERGUS. My sons and I will guard them.

AINNLE. We will blow the horn of Usna and our friends will come to aid us.

¹ The stage direction is taken from an earlier undated typescript draft.

² The passage from Fergus's speech 'My sons and I will guard them' down to the end of this speech by Deirdre is taken from a page included in this final typescript compilation, but is numbered only (c). It evidently belongs to the stage in which Synge contemplated an alternative plan for Owen, for struck out after Deirdre's first speech is the following exchange:

OWEN. Myself and Fergus have called out for peace.

DEIRDRE [*to* AINNLE]. What has brought you and Ardan to this rage I heard?

In this alternative plan, this page evidently followed the page preserved among the drafts in Box File F and quoted in Appendix C, p. 383.

³ The Cuala and Maunsel editions place this stage direction before Deirdre's reply to Ainnle, but it occurs in TS. 'O' as in the text.

NAISI. It is my friends will come.

AINNLE. Your friends will bind your hands and you out of your wits.

[DEIRDRE *comes forward quickly and comes between* AINNLE *and* NAISI.]

DEIRDRE [*in a low voice*]. For seven years the Sons of Usna have not raised their voices in a quarrel.

AINNLE. We will not take you to Emain.

ARDAN. It is Conchubor has broken our peace.

AINNLE. Stop Naisi going. What way would we live if Conchubor should take you from us?

DEIRDRE [*winningly putting her hands on his shoulders*].[1] There is no one could take me from you. . . . I have chosen to go back with Fergus. Will you quarrel with me Ainnle, though I have been your queen these seven years in Alban?[2]

AINNLE [*subsiding suddenly*]. Naisi has no call to take you.

ARDAN. Why are you going?

DEIRDRE [*to both of them and the others*]. It is my wish. . . . It may be I will not have Naisi growing an old man in Alban with an old woman at his side, and young girls pointing out and saying 'that is Deirdre and Naisi, had great beauty in their youth'. . . . It may be we do well putting a sharp end to the day is brave and glorious, as our fathers put a sharp end to the days of the kings of Ireland, . . . or that I'm wishing to set my foot on Slieve Fuadh where I was running one time and leaping the streams [*to* LAVARCHAM], and that I'd be well pleased to see our little apple-trees Lavarcham, behind our cabin on the hill, or that I've learned Fergus, it's a lonesome thing to be away from Ireland always.

AINNLE [*giving in*]. There is no place but will be lonesome to us from this out and we thinking on our seven years in Alban.

DEIRDRE. It's in this place we'd be lonesome in the end. . . . [*To* NAISI.][3] Take down Fergus to the sea. . . . He has been a guest had a hard welcome and he bringing messages of peace.

FERGUS. We will make your curagh ready and it fitted for the voyage of a king. [*He goes with* NAISI.]

¹ It is not clear whether Synge intended to have horse-boys on stage. In the earlier drafts they are included, and as late as draft 'K' he has them objecting to the departure from Alban: 'We'll stay with Deirdre always. . . .'

² There are two important differences in the version of this last speech as printed in the Cuala and Maunsel editions:

(*a*) The second stage direction is omitted, thereby depriving this final moment of the dramatic impact of Owen's death and its effect on Deirdre.

(*b*) The phrase 'dear country of the East', which is struck out in the final typescript, is added after 'woods of Cuan'.

The final version of this speech, as printed in the text, is scribbled on the back of the last page of typescript, superseding the following farewell speech:

DEIRDRE [*clasping her hands*]. Woods of Cuan it is in yourselves our time would pass quickly and I with Naisi always. It is in Glen Laid I would sleep under soft covering. It is in Glen Masain where there was high garlic we were rocked with quietness. It was in Glen Arcan with the pleasant sides I made our first house where the voice of the cuckoo was in the tops of the trees.

NAISI [*behind*]. Deirdre. . . . Deirdre. . . .

DEIRDRE. Dear country of the East I would not leave you if it was not with Naisi I was going. [*She goes out slowly.*]

CURTAIN

DEIRDRE. Take your spears Ainnle and Ardan, and go down before me, and take your horse-boys to be carrying my cloaks are on the threshold.[1]

AINNLE [*obeying*]. It's with a poor heart we'll carry your things this day, we have carried merrily so often and we hungry and cold.

[*They gather up things and go out.*]

DEIRDRE [*to* LAVARCHAM]. Go you too, Lavarcham. You are old and I will follow quickly.

LAVARCHAM. I'm old surely, and the hopes I had my pride in, are broken and torn. [*She goes out, with a look of awe at* DEIRDRE.]

DEIRDRE [*clasping her hands*]. Woods of Cuan, woods of Cuan. . . . It's seven years we've had a life was joy only and this day we're going west, this day we're facing death maybe, and [*goes and looks towards* OWEN] death should be a poor untidy thing, though it's a queen that dies. [*She goes out slowly.*][2]

CURTAIN

¹ Synge's earliest drafts set this act in Conchubor's palace with the High King receiving the various entrants from his high throne. TS. 'C' (5 November 1907) sets the scene in a camping place in the meadows before Emain Macha. TS. 'D' (10 November 1907) removes it to the setting in the text, adding *At the back there is a long sea.*

² In TS. 'G' (29 November 1907) Conchubor asks if Eoghan has come with news. Conchubor's attendants also vary in the different drafts of this opening scene. In what appears to be TS. 'A' Lavarcham and Treundorn are called in to Conchubor's presence to give their conflicting reports of Deirdre's appearance; in TS. 'B' the Old Woman brings in Lavarcham, confiding that Conchubor has been drinking heavily with Gelban, 'the man ⟨who⟩ has ill-will to Naisi'; in TS. 'C' Gelban brings in Eoghan's description of Deirdre; later typescripts do away with Gelban and bring in Eoghan (or Owen) himself; by TS. 'H' (17 March 1908) Eoghan has been reduced to the anonymity of 'A Soldier'. Apparently Treundorn, Gelban, Eoghan, and the Captain/Soldier are all earlier prototypes of Owen. (See Appendix C.)

³ An earlier undated draft here adds the stage direction [CONCHUBOR *looking involuntarily at back cloth.*]

ACT III

Tent below Emain, with shabby skins and benches. There is an opening at each side and at back, the latter closed. OLD WOMAN *comes in with food and fruits and arranges them on table.* CONCHUBOR *comes in on right.*[1]

CONCHUBOR [*sharply*]. Has no one come with news for me?[2]

OLD WOMAN. I've seen no one at all, Conchubor.

CONCHUBOR [*watches her working for a moment, then makes sure opening at back is closed*]. Go up then to Emain, you're not wanting here. [*A noise is heard left.*] Who is that?

OLD WOMAN [*going left*]. It's Lavarcham coming again. . . . She's a great wonder for jogging back and forward through the world and I made certain she'd be off to meet them, but she's coming alone, Conchubor, my dear child Deirdre isn't with her at all.

CONCHUBOR. Go up so and leave us.

OLD WOMAN [*pleadingly*]. I'd be well pleased to set my eyes on Deirdre if she's coming this night, as we're told.

CONCHUBOR [*impatiently*]. It's not long till you'll see her. But I've matters with Lavarcham and let you go on now I'm saying.

[*He shows her out right, as* LAVARCHAM *comes in on the left.*]

LAVARCHAM [*looking round her, with suspicion*]. This is a queer place to find you, and it's a queer place to be lodging Naisi and his brothers, and Deirdre with them, and the lot of us tired out with the long way we have been walking.

CONCHUBOR. You've come along with them the whole journey?

LAVARCHAM. I have then, though I've no call now to be wandering that length to a wedding or a burial or the two together.[3] [*She sits down wearily.*] . . . It's a poor thing the way me and you is getting old, Conchubor, and I'm thinking you yourself have no call to be loitering this place getting your death, maybe, in the cold of night.

¹ A question mark in the margin again signifies Synge's dissatisfaction with this speec⸝ as it occurs in the final draft. An earlier version of Lavarcham's reply in Notebook 4⸝ and similar to TS. 'G' (29 November 1907), reads: 'It's a poor way she's coming t Emain. Beauty goes quickly in the woods and Deirdre's years are mounting up thoug that's a hard thing to say to you and yourself a big boy the time her father was born.'

Another rough draft from Notebook 48, written some time after the last week ⸝ November 1908, indicates Synge's last-minute attempt to emphasize the role of Ower

LAV. It's that Owen the man saying I'm told is beyond in Alban.

CONCHUBOR. It's being lonesome uses many ⟨madmen⟩ and fools, are matched surel Will she make a gay right comrade if I have her for myself.

LAV. She'll make no right comrade for your like. Isn't ⟨it⟩ 7 years I've said the like ⸝ that.

² The Cuala edition reads 'for it's I did rear her from a child. I should have . . Although the manuscript emendations in the typescript make this alternative readir possible, it seems unnecessary to break the rhythm.

The Abbey Theatre TS. 'D' (10 November 1907) gives Conchubor the reply '[*with cynical smile*]. Was it for a woman who is seamed and ugly that the Sons of Usnach we driven many places by kings of Alban.'

³ Stage direction from TS. 'I'.

⁴ Notebook 48 adds the direction [*driving her with vehemence*].

⁵ This word is underlined in TS. 'K'.

⁶ Second stage direction from TS. 'I'.

⁷ Stage direction from TS. 'I'.

CONCHUBOR. I'm waiting only to know is Fergus stopped in the north.

LAVARCHAM [*more sharply*]. He's stopped surely, and that's a trick has me thinking you have it in mind to bring trouble this night on Emain and Ireland and the big world's east beyond them. [*She goes to him.*] . . . And yet you'd do well to be going to your Dun, and not putting shame on her meeting the High King, and she seamed and sweaty, and in great disorder from the dust of many roads. [*Laughing derisively.*] Ah, Conchubor, my lad, beauty goes quickly in the woods, and you'd let a great gasp, I tell you, if you set your eyes this night on Deirdre.[1]

CONCHUBOR [*fiercely*]. It's little I care if she's white and worn, for it's I did rear her from a child should have a good right to meet and see her always.[2]

LAVARCHAM [*put back*].[3] A good right is it? Haven't the blind a good right to be seeing and the lame to be dancing, and the dummies singing tunes? It's that right you have to be looking for gaiety on Deirdre's lips. [*Coaxingly.*] Come on to your Dun, I'm saying, and leave her quiet for one night itself.

CONCHUBOR [*with sudden anger*]. I'll not go, when it's long enough I am above in my Dun[4] stretching east and west without a comrade, and I more needy maybe than the thieves of Meath. . . . You think I'm old and wise, but I tell you the wise know the old must die, and they'll leave no chance for a thing slipping from them, they've set their blood to win.

LAVARCHAM [*nodding her head*]. If you're old and wise, it's I'm the same, Conchubor, and I'm telling you, you'll *not*[5] have her though you're ready to destroy mankind, and skin the gods to win her. . . . There's things a king can't have, Conchubor, and if you go rampaging this night you'll be apt to win nothing but death for many, and a sloppy face of trouble on your own self before the day will come.

CONCHUBOR. It's too much talk you have. [*Goes right, anxiously.*[6]] Where is Owen, did you see him no place and you coming the road?

LAVARCHAM [*stiffly*].[7] I seen him surely. . . . He went spying on Naisi, and now the worms is spying on his own inside.

¹ Stage direction from TS. 'I'. Also in TS. 'I', Synge has written 'climax' in the margin beside this speech.

² TS. 'I' has the stage direction [*sits down defeated*].

³ Synge's marginal question mark suggests that as late as January 1909 he was still undecided as to whether he should bring on Ainnle and Ardan with Deirdre and Naisi. His early drafts of the scene demand the presence on stage of all three Sons of Usna and as late as TS. 'G' (29 November 1907) their speeches are significant in this scene. (See Appendix C.)

⁴ Stage direction from TS. 'I'.
In an undated earlier draft (probably late November 1907) Conchubor adds the following words: 'You'll get the truth odd times from those have great hate, but lovers and the faithful will tell lies forever.'

⁵ In TS. 'B' Lavarcham sends the Old Woman to the sons of Fergus for help.

CONCHUBOR [*exultingly*]. Naisi killed him?

LAVARCHAM. He did not then. . . . It was Owen destroyed himself, running mad because of Deirdre. . . . Fools and kings and scholars are all one in a story with her like, and Owen thought he'd be a great man, being the first corpse in the game you'll play this night in Emain.

CONCHUBOR [*turning to her with excitement*].[1] It's yourself should be the first corpse, but my other messengers are coming, men from the clans that hated Usna.

LAVARCHAM [*drawing back hopelessly*].[2] Then the gods have pity on us all.

[MEN *come in with weapons.*]

CONCHUBOR. Are Ainnle and Ardan separate from Naisi?[3]

MEN. They are, Conchubor. We've got them off, saying they were needed to make ready Deirdre's house.

CONCHUBOR. And Naisi and Deirdre are coming?

SOLDIER. Naisi's coming surely, and a woman with him is putting out the glory of the moon is rising, and the sun is going down.

CONCHUBOR [*triumphant, to* LAVARCHAM]. That's your story that she's seamed and ugly?[4]

SOLDIER. I have more news. When that woman heard you were bringing Naisi this place, she sent a horse-boy to call Fergus from the north.[5]

CONCHUBOR [*to* LAVARCHAM]. It's for that you've been playing your tricks, but what you've won is a nearer death for Naisi. [*To* SOLDIERS.] Go up and call my fighters, and take that woman up to Emain.

LAVARCHAM. I'd liefer stay this place. I've done my best but if a bad end is coming surely, it would be a good thing maybe I was here to tend her.

CONCHUBOR [*fiercely*]. Take her to Emain; it's too many tricks she's tried this day already.

[*A* SOLDIER *goes to her.*]

¹ The Cuala and Maunsel editions give this stage direction to Lavarcham and omit Conchubor's order, adding the words CONCHUBOR *makes a sign to* SOLDIERS as an explanation of Lavarcham's words, 'I'm going surely . . .'. Although the final TS. 'K' has some confusion at this point, it seems evident that Synge's final version is that printed here in the text.

An earlier draft gives the following speech to Conchubor: 'Go up then and keep your satire for a day when it is wanted.'

² The passage in angular brackets is emended in TS. 'K' almost to the point of confusion, finally with a pencil line drawn diagonally across it. In the margin in W. B. Yeats's hand is the following: 'In spite of the pencil line this seems to be intended to remain. Mr. Stephens ⟨Synge's brother-in-law⟩ I hear made some pencil lines where he thought things were taken out. This line may be his. W. B. Y.' The remainder of this page is not crossed out in the typescript but an emended version of its lines (as printed here in the text) appears alone on a page numbered 7(b) with the words in Synge's hand at the top 'Act III K (revised)'. As emended, this page appears to be Synge's final version, after he deleted Ainnle and Ardan from the scene.

LAVARCHAM. Don't touch me. [*She puts her cloak round her and catches* CONCHUBOR's *arm.*] . . . I thought to stay your hand with my stories till Fergus would come to be beside them, the way I'd save yourself, Conchubor, and Naisi and Emain Macha, but I'll walk up now into your halls and I'll say [*with a gesture*]. . . it's here nettles will be growing, and beyond thistles and docks. I'll go into your High Chambers, where you've been figuring yourself stretching out your neck for the kisses of a queen of women, and I'll say it's here there'll be deer stirring, and goats scratching, and sheep, waking and coughing when there is a great wind from the north.

CONCHUBOR [*shaking himself loose*]. Take her away.[1]

⟨LAVARCHAM. I'm going surely, and in a short space I'll be sitting up with many listening to the flames crackling, and the beams breaking, and I looking on the great blaze will be the end of Emain. [*She goes out.*]

CONCHUBOR [*looking out left*]. I see two people in the trees. It should be Naisi and Deirdre. [*To* SOLDIER.] Let you tell them they'll lodge here tonight.

[*He goes off right.* NAISI *and* DEIRDRE *come in on left, very weary.*]

NAISI. Is it this place he's made ready for myself and Deirdre?

SOLDIER. The Red Branch House is being aired and swept and you'll be called there when a space is by. Till then you'll find fruits and drink on this table, and so the gods be with you. [*Goes right.*]⟩[2]

NAISI [*looking round*]. It's a strange place he's put us camping and we come back as his friends.

DEIRDRE. He's likely making up a welcome for us, having curtains shaken out and rich rooms put in order; and it's right he'd have great state to meet us, and you his sister's sons.

NAISI [*gloomy*]. It's little we want with state or rich rooms or curtains, when we're used to the ferns only, and cold streams and they making a stir.

DEIRDRE [*roaming round room*]. We want what is our right in Emain [*looking at hangings*] . . . and though he's riches in store for us it's a shabby ragged place he's put us waiting, with frayed rugs and skins are eaten by the moths.

¹ Preserved among the remnants of this act are two manuscript pages headed 'D and Naisi last scene together'. They correspond to the earlier drafts of the scene in bringing Ainnle and Ardan on stage (although Synge may have intended to reinclude them); the following exchange takes place after the brothers' exit:

DEIRDRE [*playing with the earth beneath her*]. This is fresh earth, with the mark of the spade.

NAISI. It is the burrow of a rabbit that is behind us in the trees.

DEIRDRE [*looks into the bushes and starts back*]. There is a deep grave hidden away among the trees!

Evidently this action takes place in the drafts before TS. 'D' (10 November 1907) when Synge removed the setting to a tent.

On another undated fragment Synge has written in the margin beside Deirdre's speech the words 'make important'.

² Stage direction from TS. 'J'. The same draft adds the following:

DEIRDRE. Take me to Cuchulain until Fergus comes.

NAISI [*gloomily*]. Cuchulain is all times straying the hills.

³ A question mark in the margin again indicates Synge's doubts about this speech. TS. 'J' includes the following:

. . . [*wildly*]. It's not like truth it should be I am this place trapped by Conchubor for death.

DEIRDRE [*very quietly*]. It's not like truth we've been most happy of all breathing things, in those days, Naisi, that went by so quick in Alban.

Earlier drafts vary Naisi's speech: 'We are shut in with a thicket of swords and I have not Ainnle to stand on my left side, nor Ardan to stand behind me. [*They go back to centre of stage.*]'

⁴ Although rewritten many times, this speech also bears Synge's question mark. On the back of the page of TS. 'J' he considered the following:

DEIRDRE. We have had no match in life will have no ⟨match⟩ in getting death, but what do I want talking out when all I'd say is Naisi. . . .

NAISI. There⟨'s⟩ no one knows a death the like of mine, for there's ⟨no⟩ one lost his own life and you with it.

NAISI [*a little impatiently*]. There are few would worry over skins and moths on this first night that we've come back to Emain.

DEIRDRE [*brightly*]. You should be well-pleased it's for that I'd worry all times, when it's I have kept your tent these seven years, as tidy as a bee-hive or a linnet's nest. If Conchubor'd a queen like me in Emain he'd not have stretched these rags to meet us. [*She pulls hanging, and it opens.*] . . . There's new earth on the ground and a trench dug. . . . It's a grave Naisi, that is wide and deep.[1]

NAISI [*goes over and pulls back curtain showing grave*]. And that'll be our home in Emain. . . . He's dug it wisely at the butt of a hill with fallen trees to hide it. . . . He'll want to have us killed and buried before Fergus comes.

DEIRDRE [*in a faint voice*]. Take me away. . . . Take me to hide in the rocks, for the night is coming quickly.[2]

NAISI [*pulling himself together*]. I will not leave my brothers.

DEIRDRE [*vehemently*]. It's of us two he's jealous. Come away to the places where we're used to have our company. . . . Wouldn't it be a good thing to lie hid in the high ferns together? [*She pulls him left.*] I hear strange words in the trees.

NAISI. It should be the strange fighters of Conchubor, . . . I saw them passing as we came.

DEIRDRE [*pulling him towards the right*]. Come to this side; listen, Naisi!

NAISI. There are more of them. . . . We are shut in and I have not Ainnle and Ardan to stand near me. Isn't it a hard thing that we three who have conquered many may not die together?[3]

DEIRDRE [*sinking down*]. And isn't it a hard thing that you and I are this place by our opened grave, though none have lived had happiness like ours those days in Alban that went by so quick.

NAISI. It's a hard thing surely we've lost those days forever, and yet it's a good thing maybe that all goes quick, for when I'm in that grave it's soon a day'll come you'll be too wearied to be crying out, and that day'll bring you ease.[4]

DEIRDRE. I'll not be here to know if that is true.

¹ The first stage direction is from TS. 'I' and occurs also in a late draft in Notebook 4

² One of the many drafts of this scene in Notebook 48 reads: 'I'll not live not her
[*She takes his knife.*] Look Naisi.' In the Abbey Theatre TS. 'D' (10 November 190
Deirdre says 'Give me your knife Naisi, with the sharp point, for the strange fighters w
not tether me like a ewe and lead me to Conchubor. [NAISI *gives her a knife.*] That is
good gift Naisi, for I would not know that there is a world left like a handful of ash
and the fire quenched from them. That I may never hear of your loss Naisi is the who
that I am thinking.'

³ This final emendation is scribbled on the back of the preceding page of TS. 'K'. T
Cuala and Maunsel editions differ slightly: 'If there isn't, it's that grave when it's clos
will make us one for ever, and we two lovers have had great space without weariness
growing old or any sadness of the mind.'

⁴ A late draft in Notebook 48 adds the direction [*his voice shaken with emotion*].

NAISI. It's our three selves he'll kill tonight, and then in two months, or three, you'll see him walking down for courtship with yourself.

DEIRDRE. I'll not be here.

NAISI [*hard*]. You'd best keep him off maybe, and then, when the time comes, make your way to some place west in Donegal, and it's there you'll get used to stretching out lonesome at the fall of night, and waking lonesome for the day.

DEIRDRE. Let you not be saying things are worse than death.

NAISI [*a little recklessly*]. I've one word left. . . . If a day comes in the west that the larks are cocking their crests on the edge of the clouds, and the cuckoos making a stir, and there's a man you'd fancy, let you not be thinking that day, I'd be well pleased you'd go on keening always.

DEIRDRE [*half-surprised,*[1] *turning to look at him*]. And if it was I that died, Naisi, would you take another woman to fill up my place?

NAISI [*very mournfully*]. It's little I know. . . . Saving only that it's a hard and bitter thing leaving the earth, and a worse and harder thing leaving yourself alone and desolate to be making lamentation on its face always.

DEIRDRE. I'll die when you do, Naisi.[2] I'd not have come from Alban but I knew I'd be along with you in Emain, and you living or dead. . . . Yet this night it's strange and distant talk you're making only.

NAISI. There's nothing surely the like of a new grave of open earth for putting a great space between two friends that love.

DEIRDRE. If there isn't maybe it's that grave when it's closed will make us one forever, and we two lovers have had a great space without weariness or growing old or any sadness of the mind.[3]

[CONCHUBOR *comes in on right*.]

CONCHUBOR. I'd bid you welcome, Naisi.[4]

NAISI [*standing up, watching himself*]. You're welcome, Conchubor. . . . I'm well pleased you've come.

CONCHUBOR [*blandly*]. Let you not think bad of this place where I've put you, till other rooms are readied.

1 Until quite late in the development of this act, apparently until his first draft omitting Ainnle and Ardan from the previous scene (TS. 'I', 10 December 1908), Synge planned two separate entrances for Conchubor. He gradually condensed his material, but many versions exist in both typescript and notebook form of an earlier scene between Conchubor, Naisi, and Deirdre. The following examples illustrate the manner in which he compressed his material.

(*a*) Undated typescript similar to a draft in Notebook 47, labelled only '(middle) D & N'

D. It's this night is our last. It seems a silly common night, with common food before us and wind along the path, and yet this night will have no match for sadness in all years

[*Enter* CON.]

CON. I have come to look on Deirdre.

NAISI. You can see her if your sight's not dim.

CON. There are big crowds this night in the Red Branch. I thought you'd be more homely here.

DEI. We've seen the home you've readied. Ah, Conchubor you've got a home in store for us where there's no king.

NAISI [*more keenly*]. You've little manners showing us this trench ⟨so⟩ plainly. There were days I tell you I'd have laid my hands upon ⟨those⟩ did that.

CON. Do what you will. I've brought no weapon. Hide me in that grave and run for Fergus.

(*b*) Typescript perhaps as early as 'F' (25 November 1907):

CON. enters. 'I have come' etc. the same as in text to 'more homely here'.

D. We've seen the house you've readied. Ah, Conchubor this seems a common night with common earth before us, and yet the night will be no match for sadness in years.

CON. leaves.

N. It would be a good thing if all was done.

D. It would Naisi. . . . I went and looked on Owen in the trees, Death should be a trouble nasty thing no matter who may die.

(*c*) Manuscript version written on the back of a letter dated 28 August 1908 from the Abbey Theatre secretary, W. A. Henderson:

Deirdre's and Conchubor's first speeches as in example (*a*), then

N. Look at her!

C. You are grown manly Naisi

N. That's easy said

C. [*uncomfortable*]. Have you all you need?

N. All, even our grave . . . stop fetch us some chess men and we'll play while they leave us here.

(*d*) Manuscript in Notebook 48, fairly late, headed 'C.N.D.':

N. It's no ⟨?truth⟩ to be in a trap before. There were days I've pitied old men yet this night I'm thinking it is a good lucky chance to have lived on like you to be near the full of kings.

C. Have ⟨you⟩ everything needful for a while to come?

N. Send us a bag of chessmen till we (shorten the evening) pass the evening putting check mate on a king—

C. I've other men than chessmen to shorten this your night [*goes*].

[*Notes continued on p. 2.*

NAISI [*breaking out*]. We know the room you've readied. We know what stirred you to send your seals, and Fergus into Alban, and to stop him in the north [*opening curtain, and pointing to the grave*] . . . and dig that grave before us. Now I ask what brought you here?

CONCHUBOR. I've come to look on Deirdre.

NAISI. Look on her. You're a knacky fancier and it's well you chose the one you'd lure from Alban. Look on her, I tell you, and when you've looked I've got ten fingers will squeeze your mottled goose neck though you're king itself.[1]

DEIRDRE [*coming between them*]. Hush Naisi, maybe Conchubor'll make peace. . . . Do not mind him Conchubor, he has cause to rage.

CONCHUBOR. It's little I heed his raging, when a call would bring my fighters from the trees. . . . But what do you say, Deirdre?

DEIRDRE. I'll say so near that grave we seem three lonesome people, and by a new made grave there's no man will keep brooding on a woman's lips, or on the man he hates. It's not long till your own grave will be dug in Emain and you'd go down to it more easy if you'd let call Ainnle and Ardan, the way we'd have a supper all together, and fill that grave, and you'll be well pleased from this out having four new friends the like of us in Emain.

CONCHUBOR [*looking at her for a moment*]. That's the first friendly word I've heard you speaking, Deirdre. A game the like of yours should be the proper thing for softening the heart and putting sweetness in the tongue, and yet this night when I hear you, I've small blame left for Naisi that he stole you off from Ulster.[2]

DEIRDRE [*to NAISI*]. Now, Naisi, answer gently and we'll be friends tonight.

NAISI [*doggedly*]. I have no call but to be friendly, I'll answer what you will.

DEIRDRE [*taking NAISI's hand*]. Then you'll call Conchubor your friend and king, the man who reared me up upon Slieve Fuadh.

[*As CONCHUBOR is going to clasp NAISI's hand, cries are heard behind.*]

CONCHUBOR. What noise is that?

Notes (cont.), p. 253.

² A slightly earlier version of this speech, found in an undated typescript and more fully in Notebook 48, makes use of the following ritual:

DEIR. [*takes* NAISI's *wrist in her left hand*]. Then let us make peace this night Conchubor. So near that grave we're but three lonesome people in a night that's cold. We'll forget the stories of the old priests in Emain, and my long growing up upon Slieve Fuadh. We'll do well forgetting the way Naisi and myself went off that windy night and we'll forget we've not always been friends. There's ⟨no⟩ peace-maker I've heard old men to say beside the like of a new grave that's empty still. [*She gets a loaf and breaks it giving half to* NAISI *and half to* CONCHUBOR.] There. Eat up these broken crusts and all the spite and grudges of these years. Send off your soldiers Conchubor and call for Ainnle and Ardan and we'll light a fire and fill up that grave and then we'll tell old stories what this man's done and that—as if you were our guest in some dark wood in Alban. We'll have a merry supper in these trees and you'll find a new heart Conchubor having the like of us for four new friends in Emain.

CON. That's the first friendly welcome you've put before me Deirdre, and hearing your voice so kindly I've small blame left that Naisi stole you off that night from Ulster.

---

¹ The draft in Notebook 48 is more specific here:

AINNLE [*behind*]. Naisi run from death.

² The usual question mark in the margin indicates Synge's dissatisfaction with this speech.

³ Stage direction from Notebook 48.

⁴ The Abbey Theatre TS. 'D' (10 November 1907) gives a brief version of this exchange:

DEIRDRE [*drawing back*]. That is the first roughness of our whole life; for seven years you have been kindly.

NAISI [*angry with himself, and her*]. I will not be held back by any.

DEIRDRE [*pointing to the door*]. Go up to the battle. The unseemliness of death has come between us. Go up or we will put a stain on our brightness to the end of life and time

AINNLE [*behind*]. Naisi . . . Naisi. . . . Come to us, we are betrayed and broken.

NAISI. It's Ainnle crying out in a battle!

CONCHUBOR. I was near won this night, but death's between us now. [*He goes out.*]

DEIRDRE [*clinging to* NAISI]. There is no battle. . . . Do not leave me, Naisi.

NAISI. I must go to them.

DEIRDRE [*beseechingly*]. Do not leave me, Naisi. Let us creep up in the darkness behind the grave. . . . If there's a battle, maybe the strange fighters will be destroyed, when Ainnle and Ardan are against them.

[*Cries are heard.*][1]

NAISI [*wildly*]. I hear Ardan crying out. Do not hold me from my brothers.[2]

DEIRDRE [*broken after the strain*].[3] Do not leave me, Naisi. Do not leave me broken and alone.

NAISI. I cannot leave my brothers when it is I who have defied the king.

DEIRDRE. I will go with you.

NAISI. You cannot come. . . . Do not hold me from the fight. [*He throws her aside almost roughly.*]

DEIRDRE [*with restraint.*] Go to your brothers. . . . For seven years you have been kindly, but the hardness of death has come between us.

NAISI [*looking at her aghast*]. And you'll have me meet death with a hard word from your lips in my ear?

DEIRDRE. We've had a dream, but this night has waked us surely. In a little while we've lived too long, Naisi, and isn't it a poor thing we should miss the safety of the grave, and we trampling its edge?[4]

AINNLE [*behind*]. Naisi, Naisi, we are attacked and ruined.

DEIRDRE. Let you go where they are calling! [*She looks at him for an instant coldly.*] Have you no shame loitering and talking and a cruel death facing Ainnle and Ardan in the woods?

¹ After much emendation, Synge was still doubtful of this speech.

² The Cuala and Maunsel editions read 'in this place'.

³ This last stage direction is taken from TS. 'I', as it seems necessary to explain the presence of Naisi's cloak on stage. The origin of the action can be found in an earlier draft in which the following speech is struck out and marked 'change':

NAISI [*taking off his sword and cloak*]. There are my sword and knife Deirdre, I will go to Ainnle and Ardan but I have no thought from this out to lift a hand in battle. [*He slips out stealthily.*]

⁴ The final stage direction about the tent is taken from TS. 'I'.

Preserved among the fragments of earlier drafts are four pages in manuscript of the final scene between Deirdre and Naisi which were apparently written some time in November 1907. They include two different sketches for this next scene.

(*a*) The first outline has Lavarcham on stage during Deirdre's and Naisi's last speeches: '(When Naisi goes out Conor is heard off crying "It is Naisi strike him," then there is a fierce cry. Lav. leaves D. for an instant then comes in with Conor. Conor and Lav. speak while the bodies are carried past in the darkness and buried in the grave. Then there is a cry. Fergus has come back and is setting flame to Emain. Deirdre rises and goes to grave then?'

(*b*) The second outline omits Lavarcham and bears a striking resemblance to *Riders to the Sea*. It may correspond in time to the scenario in which Synge describes the ending as 'Rider-like' (see Appendix C): '(He tears himself free and runs out, Deirdre falls senseless on the stage which grows dark. There is a cry behind. Then in dim light a procession bringing the three bodies of the Sons of Usnach and putting them into the grave to a sustained keen of many. Then Deirdre drags herself to the head of the grave.)'

⁵ TS. 'D' reads, 'Three malefactors have met their death . . . they will be buried as it is right beyond the rim of Emain Macha.' Deirdre replies '[*with cold wonder and terror*]. From this day I will be a beggar that is tired out with begging and what call had you Conchubor to blot out three lives when they were sweetest?'

⁶ TS. 'G' has the stage direction [*beginning to plead with her for his forlorn hope of life*].

NAISI [*frantic*]. They'll not get a death that's cruel and they with men alone. It's women that have loved are cruel only, and if I went on living from this day I'd be putting a curse on the lot of them I'd meet walking in the east or west, putting a curse on the sun that gave them beauty, and on the madder and the stone-crop put red upon their cloaks.[1]

DEIRDRE [*bitterly*]. I'm well pleased there's no one this place[2] to make a story that Naisi was a laughing-stock the night he died.

NAISI. There'd not be many'd make a story, for that mockery is in your eyes this night will spot the face of Emain with a plague of pitted graves. [*He draws out his sword, throws down belt and cloak,[3] and goes out.*]

CONCHUBOR [*outside*]. That is Naisi. Strike him.

[*Tumult.* DEIRDRE *crouches down on* NAISI's *cloak.* CONCHUBOR *comes in hurriedly, and closes tent so that the grave is not seen any more.*][4]

CONCHUBOR. They've met their death, the three that stole you Deirdre, and from this out you'll be my queen in Emain.[5]

[*A keen of men's voices is heard behind.*]

DEIRDRE [*bewildered and terrified*]. It is not I will be a queen.

CONCHUBOR. Make your lamentation a short while if you will, but it isn't long till a day'll come when you'll begin pitying a man is old and desolate and High King also. . . . Let you not fear me for it's I'm well pleased you have a store of pity for the three that were your friends in Alban.[6]

DEIRDRE. I have pity surely. . . . It's the way pity has me this night, when I think of Naisi, that I could set my teeth into the heart of a king.

CONCHUBOR. I know well pity's cruel, when it was my pity for my own self destroyed Naisi.

DEIRDRE [*more wildly*]. It was my words without pity gave Naisi a death will have no match until the ends of life and time. [*Breaking out into a keen.*] But who'll pity Deirdre has lost the lips of Naisi from her neck, and from her cheek forever: who'll pity Deirdre has

¹ This direction from TS. 'I' is more accurate than the one in the final typescript quoted by the Cuala and Maunsel editions: [*A keen is heard.*] Presumably the keen is heard in the background throughout the scene, from the time the Sons of Usna are killed.

² Struck out of the final typescript is the stage direction [*a sort of panic coming over him*]. Earlier drafts such as the Abbey Theatre TS. 'D' (10 September 1907) offer a different exchange here:

CONCHUBOR. I'd think it a good bargain if it was I was in the grave this night and you keening over me, and it was Naisi who was old and desolate. It's for that I've set a stake upon you till I'd think little of burning the earth like a dry thatch and putting out the sun as you quench a torch and it flaring, in a dark pool.

DEIRDRE. What is your age Conchubor but the time of desolation? . . .

³ The word 'your' is underlined in TS. 'I'.

⁴ Stage direction from TS. 'I'.

⁵ In earlier drafts Synge evidently envisaged some kind of folding doors at the back of the stage, for in TS. 'G' (29 November 1907) *Eoghan opens the three doors and shows grav* and in TS. 'H' (17 March 1908) 'the wide doors' are open behind with moonlight shining on the grave.

lost the twilight in the woods with Naisi, when beech-trees were silver and copper, and ash-trees were fine gold?

CONCHUBOR [*bewildered*]. It's I'll know the way to pity and care you, and I with a share of troubles has me thinking this night, it would be a good bargain if it was I was in the grave, and Deirdre crying over me, and it was Naisi who was old and desolate.

[*A keen rises loudly over the grave.*][1]

DEIRDRE [*wild with sorrow*]. It is I who am desolate, I, Deirdre, that will not live till I am old.

CONCHUBOR. It's not long you'll be desolate,[2] and I seven years saying, 'It's a bright day for Deirdre in the woods of Alban,' or saying again, 'what way will Deirdre be sleeping this night, and wet leaves and branches driving from the north?' Let you not break the thing I've set my life on, and you giving yourself up to your sorrow when it's joy and sorrow do burn out like straw blazing in an east wind.

DEIRDRE [*turning on him*]. Was it that way with *your*[3] sorrow, when I and Naisi went northward from Slieve Fuadh and let raise our sails for Alban?

CONCHUBOR [*after a moment*][4]. There's one sorrow has no end surely, that's being old and lonesome. [*With extraordinary pleading.*] But you and I will have a little peace in Emain, with harps playing, and old men telling stories at the fall of night. . . . I've let build rooms for our two selves Deirdre, with red gold upon the walls, and ceilings that are set with bronze. There was never a queen in the east had a house the like of your house, that's waiting for yourself in Emain.

SOLDIER [*running in*]. Emain is in flames. Fergus has come back and is setting fire to the world. Come up Conchubor, or your state will be destroyed.

CONCHUBOR [*angry and regal again*]. Are the Sons of Usna buried?

SOLDIER. They are in their grave, but no earth is thrown.

CONCHUBOR. Let me see them. Open the tent. [SOLDIER *opens back of tent and shows grave.*][5] . . . Where are my fighters?

SOLDIER. They are gone to Emain.

¹ In a letter to Molly Allgood dated 9 November 1907 Synge writes, 'Since yesterday I have pulled two acts into one, so that, if I can work it, the play will have three acts instead of four, and that has of course given me many problems to think out. As it is, I am not sure that the plan I have is a good one.' Only remnants of the opening scene of Act IV exist, but apparently Synge wished it to open with Deirdre by the grave, discovered by Lavarcham and the Old Woman. Pages 1 to 4 of what is probably TS. 'A' have a young man digging quietly in the grave at the back and then Deirdre with the help of the women lifting Naisi's body into the finished grave. Only the first page of TS. 'B' exists; it is dated 5 November 1907 but is then emended to III 'C', 12 November 1907.

² Earlier drafts of this speech begin, 'It is you who were the white stags upon the mountain; it is you three that were company to me when the lights on the hilltops were put out. . . .'

³ Earlier drafts give the stage directions [*going to her softly*] to Lavarcham and [*not heeding her*] to Deirdre.

⁴ The Cuala and Maunsel editions begin this speech with 'If it is that way you'd be . . .' but the form given here in the text is taken from an emendation of the final typescript. The Abbey Theatre TS. 'D' (10 November 1907) gives the earlier form for this reply '[*more eagerly*] I have set up a little beehive in the shade of Brandon, where you can show off your beauty to the sun and moon and stretch for great resting in the sunshine when the summer comes.'

CONCHUBOR [*to* DEIRDRE]. There are none to harm you. Stay here until I come again. [*Goes out with* SOLDIER.]

[DEIRDRE *looks round for a moment, then goes up slowly and looks into grave. She crouches down and begins swaying herself backwards and forwards keening softly. At first her words are not heard, then they become clear.*][1]

DEIRDRE. It's you three will not see age or death coming, you that were my company when the fires on the hill-tops were put out and the stars were our friends only.[2] I'll turn my thoughts back from this night—that's pitiful for want of pity—to the time it was your rods and cloaks made a little tent for me where there'd be a birch tree making shelter, and a dry stone: though from this day my own fingers will be making a tent for me, spreading out my hairs and they knotted with the rain.

[LAVARCHAM *and* OLD WOMAN *come in stealthily on right.*]

DEIRDRE [*not seeing them*]. It is I Deirdre will be crouching in a dark place, I Deirdre that was young with Naisi, and brought sorrow to his grave in Emain.

OLD WOMAN. Is that Deirdre broken down that was so light and airy?

LAVARCHAM. It is, surely, crying out over their grave. [*She goes to* DEIRDRE.]

DEIRDRE. It will be my share from this out to be making lamentation on his stone always, and I crying for a love will be the like of a star shining on a little harbour by the sea.

LAVARCHAM [*coming forward*]. Let you rise up Deirdre, and come off while there are none to heed us the way I'll find you shelter, and some friend to guard you.

DEIRDRE.[3] To what place would I go away from Naisi? What are the woods without Naisi, or the seashore?

LAVARCHAM [*very coaxingly*]. If it's keening you'd be come till I find you a sunny place where you'll be a great wonder they'll call the queen of sorrows, and you'll begin taking a pride to be sitting up pausing and dreaming when the summer comes.[4]

¹ Stage direction from TS. 'I'.

² A question mark in the margin beside this final cadence indicates Synge's struggles to achieve satisfaction. TS. 'K' reads:

~~going~~ to rest

the moon ~~herself~~ / ~~among the edges of the hills.~~

her

Finally on the back of the preceding page Synge scribbled the version printed here in the text. The Cuala and Maunsel editions combine the two: 'pausing to rest her'.

³ Earlier drafts read 'his concubine' for 'the High King's slave'.

⁴ The Abbey Theatre TS. 'D' gives Lavarcham the additional speech, 'There is a time when joy and sorrow are the one thing only, and if you come with me you'll have great pride one day saying over "It is I Deirdre that was the Queen of Sorrows".'

DEIRDRE. It was the voice of Naisi that was strong in summer, the voice of Naisi that was sweeter than pipes playing, but from this day will be dumb always.

LAVARCHAM [*to* OLD WOMAN, *also sobbing*].[1] She doesn't heed us at all. We'll be hard set to rouse her.

OLD WOMAN. If we don't the High King will rouse her coming down beside her with the rage of battle in his blood, for how could Fergus stand against him.

LAVARCHAM [*touching* DEIRDRE *with her hand*]. There's a score of woman's years in store for you, and you'd best choose will you start living them beside the man you hate, or being your own mistress in the west or south.

DEIRDRE. It is not I will go on living after Ainnle and after Ardan. After Naisi I will not have a lifetime in the world.

OLD WOMAN [*with excitement*]. Look, Lavarcham! There's a light leaving the Red Branch. Conchubor and his lot will be coming quickly with a torch of bog-deal for her marriage throwing a light on her three comrades.

DEIRDRE [*startled*]. Let us throw down clay on my three comrades. Let us cover up Naisi along with Ainnle and Ardan, they that were the pride of Emain. [*Throwing in clay.*] There is Naisi was the best of three, the choicest of the choice of many. It was a clean death was your share Naisi, and it is not I will quit your head when it's many a dark night among the snipe and plover that you and I were whispering together. It is not I will quit your head Naisi, when it's many a night we saw the stars among the clear trees of Glen da Ruadh, or the moon pausing on the edges of the hills.[2]

OLD WOMAN. Conchubor is coming surely. I see the glare of flames throwing a light upon his cloak.

LAVARCHAM [*eagerly*]. Rise up Deirdre and come to Fergus, or be the High King's slave[3] forever.

DEIRDRE [*imperiously*]. I will not leave Naisi who has left the whole world scorched and desolate, I will not go away when there is no light in the heavens, and no flower in the earth under them, but is saying to me, that it is Naisi who is gone forever.[4]

¹ There is a question mark in the margin beside the beginning of this speech. It may indicate Synge's doubts about striking out a phrase in the typescript, 'It's yourself, the high King, has made . . .', or his doubts might have extended to the entire speech.

.

² Stage direction from TS. 'G'.

The Abbey Theatre TS. 'D' (10 November 1907) extends Deirdre's keen instead: '[*keening as before*]. I will not live lonesome, I that had the choice of company, I will not set eyes any more on the rushes do have dew on them when the sun goes up, or the frost on the stones in autumn. I will not wait to see the foxgloves rising up when Naisi is laid down for ever.'

CONCHUBOR [*behind*]. She is here. . . . Stay a little back.

[LAVARCHAM *and* OLD WOMAN *go into the shadow on left as* CONCHUBOR *comes in.*]

CONCHUBOR [*with excitement, to* DEIRDRE]. Come forward and leave Naisi the way I've left charred timber and a smell of burning in Emain Macha, and a heap of rubbish in the storehouse of many crowns.

DEIRDRE [*more awake to what is round her*]. What are crowns and Emain Macha when the head that gave them glory is this place Conchubor, and it stretched upon the gravel will be my bed tonight?

CONCHUBOR. Make an end with talk of Naisi, for I've come to bring you to Dundealgan since Emain is destroyed. [*Makes a movement towards her.*]

DEIRDRE [*with a tone that stops him*]. Draw a little back from Naisi who is young forever. Draw a little back from the white bodies I am putting under a mound of clay and grasses that are withered—a mound will have a nook for my own self when the end is come.

CONCHUBOR [*roughly*]. Let you rise up and come along with me in place of growing crazy with your wailings here.

DEIRDRE. It's yourself has made a crazy story, and let you go back to your arms, Conchubor, and to councils where your name is great, for in this place you are an old man and a fool only.[1]

CONCHUBOR. If I've folly I've sense left not to lose the thing I've bought with sorrow and the deaths of many. [*He moves towards her.*]

DEIRDRE. Do not raise a hand to touch me.

CONCHUBOR. There are other hands to touch you. My fighters are set round in among the trees.

DEIRDRE [*almost mockingly*].[2] Who'll fight the grave, Conchubor, and it opened on a dark night?

LAVARCHAM [*eagerly*]. There are steps in the wood. . . . I hear the call of Fergus and his men.

CONCHUBOR [*furiously*]. Fergus cannot stop me. . . . I am more powerful than he is though I am defeated and old.

[*A red glow is seen behind the grave.*]

¹ Again a question mark in the margin indicates Synge's dissatisfaction with Conchubor's speech.

An early typescript ('C'?, 5 November 1907) had Lavarcham leaving the stage for a moment, then returning with the following news:

LAVARCHAM. Fergus your men have left you for Conchubor's gold. We are ruined and she's his forever.

FERGUS. What are my men or armies when I have my sword to meet him and in a little while the north will come to join me.

² A question mark in the margin again indicates Synge's attitude towards this speech. The original typescript before emended in manuscript to the above version reads as follows: 'It's your death you'll get this night if my strength is left.'

Fergus's reply in TS. 'I' is 'It's little if a fool should rot.'

³ Stage direction from TS. 'G'.

FERGUS [*comes in to* DEIRDRE]. I have destroyed Emain, and now I'll guard you all times, Deirdre, though it was I, without knowledge, brought Naisi to his grave.

CONCHUBOR. It's not you will guard her, for my whole armies are gathering. Rise up, Deirdre, for you are mine surely.

FERGUS [*coming between them*]. I am come between you.

CONCHUBOR [*wildly*]. When I've killed Naisi and his brothers is there any man that I will spare? . . . And is it you will stand against me, Fergus, when it's seven years you've seen me getting my death with rage in Emain?[1]

FERGUS. It's I surely will stand against a thief and traitor.[2]

DEIRDRE [*stands up and sees the light from Emain*]. Draw a little back with the squabbling of fools when I am broken up with misery. [*She turns round.*] . . . I see the flames of Emain starting upward in the dark night, and because of me there will be weasels and wild cats crying on a lonely wall where there were queens and armies, and red gold, the way there will be a story told of a ruined city and a raving king and a woman will be young forever. [*A pause.*[3] *She looks round.*] . . . I see the trees naked and bare, and the moon shining. Little moon, little moon of Alban, it's lonesome you'll be this night, and to-morrow night, and long nights after, and you pacing the woods beyond Glen Laid, looking every place for Deirdre and Naisi, the two lovers who slept so sweetly with each other.

FERGUS [*going to* CONCHUBOR's *right and whispering*]. Keep back or you will have the shame of pushing a bolt on a queen who is out of her wits.

CONCHUBOR. It is I am out of my wits, with Emain in flames, and Deirdre raving, and my own heart gone within me.

DEIRDRE [*in a high and quiet tone*]. I have put away sorrow like a shoe that is worn out and muddy, for it is I have had a life that will be envied by great companies. It was not by a low birth I made kings uneasy, and they sitting in the halls of Emain. It was not a low thing to be chosen by Conchubor, who was wise, and Naisi had no match for bravery. . . . It is not a small thing to be rid of grey hairs and the loosening of the teeth. [*With a sort of triumph.*] . . . It was the choice

¹ In TS. 'F' Deirdre's tone is described as *high and prophetic*.

Three important emendations were made to this speech in the final typescript draft: 'shoe' for 'cloak', 'by a low birth I made kings uneasy' for 'a low birth made kings uneasy', and 'is not a small thing' for 'was not a small thing'. In all cases the emendations do not appear in any other draft examined, although the speech in other ways has retained its form since the very early drafts; further, the pencil alterations could conceivably be in some hand other than Synge's. It is possible that they were dictated by him to Molly Allgood.

² Earlier drafts add the direction [*He makes a movement towards her.*]

³ The final typescript reads, 'I have a little key to unlock the prison of Naisi, to open the door is shut on Ainnle and on Ardan. Keep back Conchubor. . . .' Although these additional words are not struck out in the typescript, Synge does indicate by a series of dashes enclosed by parentheses the emendation which is scribbled on the back of the preceding page. Under these circumstances, it is difficult to tell whether Synge intended to add to the speech or to replace a portion of it. The version printed here follows the Cuala and Maunsel editions as presenting least difficulty with rhythm.

⁴ The Abbey Theatre TS. 'D' reads in place of these words: 'A child crying, a girl singing, a deep sorrow, and a rest for ever, that is the story of Deirdre who was chosen by the princes of Ulster and the story of all who have life for ever. [*Stepping down into the grave.*] It is a cold place. . . .'

⁵ Above this final stage direction Synge has written in blue pencil the word 'query', indicating a possible doubt as to the stage effect.

In his attempts to emphasize the role of Owen, Synge at one time considered placing his death scene just before Fergus's oration (see Appendix C).

⁶ The final typescript reads, 'That is the fate of the Children of Usna and for this night. . . .' Again using blue pencil, Synge has underlined the words 'Children of Usna' and scrawled above in almost illegible handwriting 'Deirdre and Naisi next the'. Although the last two words are very difficult to make out, it seems that he intended to retain emphasis on the *four* deaths. Another possible reading, although the position of his emendation does not support it, is 'Deirdre and Naisi and the rest of the Children of Usna'. The Cuala and Maunsel editions read 'Deirdre and the Children of Usna', omitting the obvious 'Naisi'

⁷ The final typescript gives the following ending:

CONCHUBOR [*with the voice of an old man*]. Take me with you I'm hard set to see the way before me.

LAVARCHAM [*to* OLD WOMAN]. Let you watch the grave. This way Conchubor. [*They go out as* OLD WOMAN *kneels by the grave.*]

Curtain

However, this ending is superseded by the manuscript version written on the reverse side of the final page of typescript:

[LAVARCHAM *sends out* CON *with* OLD WOMAN *then speaks tag.*]

LAVARCHAM. Deirdre is dead, and Naisi is dead, and if the oaks and stars could die for sorrow it's a dark sky and a ~~bare~~ hard and naked ~~wor~~ earth we'd have ~~to~~ this night in Emain.

Curtain

The Old Woman's speech is taken from a late draft in Notebook 47:

End of play

OLD W. This way Conchubor

LAV. Naisi and his brothers are dead they're dead the lot of them—and Deirdre's dead for love. It'd be a dark and naked earth we'd have this night if the trees and stars she had love for knew a way to get their own death upon her grave.

of lives we had in the clear woods, and in the grave we're safe
surely. . . .[1]

CONCHUBOR. She will do herself harm.[2]

DEIRDRE [*showing* NAISI's *knife*]. I have a little key to unlock the
prison of Naisi,[3] you'd shut upon his youth forever. Keep back
Conchubor, for the High King who is your master has put his hands
between us. [*She half turns to the grave.*] . . . It was sorrows were foretold, but great joys were my share always,[4] yet it is a cold place I
must go to be with you, Naisi, and it's cold your arms will be this
night that were warm about my neck so often. . . . It's a pitiful thing
to be talking out when your ears are shut to me. It's a pitiful thing,
Conchubor, you have done this night in Emain, yet a thing will be
a joy and triumph to ⟨the⟩ ends of life and time.

[*She presses knife to her heart and sinks into the grave.* CONCHUBOR
and FERGUS *go forward; the red glow fades leaving the stage very dark.*[5]]

FERGUS. Four white bodies are laid down together, four clear lights
are quenched in Ireland. [*He throws his sword into the grave.*] . . There
is my sword that could not shield you, my four friends that were the
dearest always. The flames of Emain have gone out: Deirdre is dead
and there is none to keen her. That is the fate of Deirdre and Naisi
next the Children of Usna[6] and for this night Conchubor, our war is
ended. [*He goes out.*]

LAVARCHAM. I have a little hut where you can rest Conchubor, there
is a great dew falling.

CONCHUBOR [*with the voice of an old man*]. Take me with you, I'm
hard set to see the way before me.

OLD WOMAN. This way, Conchubor.

LAVARCHAM. Deirdre is dead, and Naisi is dead, and if the oaks and
stars could die for sorrow it's a dark sky and a hard and naked earth
we'd have this night in Emain.[7] ·

CURTAIN

APPENDIX A

THE TINKER'S WEDDING:
WORKSHEETS AND COMMENTARY

I. DESCRIPTION OF TEXTUAL SOURCES

(Unless otherwise stated, unpublished material is in the possession of the Synge Estate.)

A. STANDARD EDITION

The Tinker's Wedding: A Comedy in Two Acts (*Dublin, Maunsel, 1907*).

Synge copyrighted the play at the Abbey Theatre on 23 December 1907; in a letter now in the Library of Trinity College, Dublin, to Leon Brodzky of 28(?) December 1907 he writes, 'We will send you the Tinkers at once. It was to be out today.'

B. *There was no other edition of the play during Synge's lifetime.*

C. EXTANT MANUSCRIPTS/TYPESCRIPTS

1. *In Notebook H, sixteen pages in ink interspersed with dialogue for* Riders to the Sea *and* The Shadow of the Glen. *Summer 1902.*

2. *In Notebook 30, draft scenario of Act I. Spring 1903 ?*

3. *In Notebook 31, one page in ink. Summer 1903.*

4. *In Box File D, over two hundred typescript pages and fragments, most of them heavily emended. October 1903–December 1907. (It is possible that these drafts were arranged and ordered after Synge's death, although the order of drafts seems very clear. Lettering has been added for easier identification.)*

a. *TS. 'A': thirteen pages and a title-page, apparently made up from at least two earlier discarded typescript drafts and italicized for the printer. Persons include Mary Byrne, Micheal Byrne, Nora Casey, the Priest, two nameless tinker children, and a village woman, who buys the tin can from the tinkers. Autumn 1903.*

b. *TS. 'B': two-act version with alternative title* Movements of May; *Act I 21 pages, Act II 19 pages, heavily emended and italicized for printer. Tinker children are named Micky and Nanny, their mother still Nora Casey; little girls from the village, dressed in white for their confirmation by the awaited bishop, are added. Ending as in TS. 'A' with village children behind priest. Spring 1904.*

c. *TS. 'C': two-act version; Act I 24 pages, Act II 20 pages, heavily emended and italicized for printer. Village woman is omitted, Nora becomes Sarah Casey, and Mary Byrne steals the can. Title-page has MS. annotation,* 'Open scene with children seeking priest, and seeing hen. Put more current into Duos (cut* out girls in white in 2)'. *Ending as in TSS. 'A' and 'B'. September 1905–March 1906.*

d. *TS. 'D': carbon of TS. 'F'; two-act version; Act I 15 pages, Act II 15 pages, pagination added in ink, comparatively few emendations, not prepared for printer. Tinker children are struck out of title-page and text; village children are omitted altogether; spelling of Michael as in final text; ending includes priest tied in sacking. Spring 1906.*

e. *TS. 'E': carbon of TS. 'F' but emended differently from either TS. 'D' or TS. 'F'. No pagination added to Act II and the last ten pages are clean copy with no emendations. Possibly the copy sent to Max Meyerfeld early April 1906. Spring 1906.*

f. *TS. 'F': sixth and final version as prepared for printing with printer's and compositors' annotations. No title-page, but additional slips are included giving final version of the ending with the Priest's Latin malediction. Summer–Autumn 1907*

5. *In Box File D, the corrected galley proofs for the entire play and Preface, excluding the title-page and list of characters. November 1907. (Preface dated 20 November 1907.*

6. *In Envelope 52, two typescript drafts of the Preface with many emendations and manuscript additions, both undated, and one page of manuscript notes, also undated November 1907 ?*

II. DRAFT MANUSCRIPTS

A. *The earliest draft of* The Tinker's Wedding *appears to be the following sixteen pages of a notebook in use the summer of 1902 and now preserved in Envelope H of Box File E. This large notebook, its covers gone, also contains early drafts of* Riders to the Sea *and* The Shadow of the Glen; *apparently Synge was working on all three plays at the same time. The first two pages of* The Tinker's Wedding *begin at the 'wrong' end of the notebook; the remaining fourteen pages follow consecutively from the other end after the draft of* The Shadow of the Glen, *with one intervening page of dialogue for* Riders to the Sea.

[NORA CASEY *is washing her⟨self⟩ briskly and doing her hair with piece of blank tin as a mirror.* MARY BYRNE *moves and wakes up.*]–

MARY. It's a grand morning for the fair, by the grace of God,—[*she looks inquisitively at* NORA]—You're making a great stir with your washing Nora Casey, I'm that used to the hammer it wouldn't move me at all but washing is a rare sound and you're after waking me up and I dreaming a fine dream of the priest.

NORA. He's after passing.

MARY BYRNE. You were talking with him?

NORA. A short while—[*arranging her hair*]––What was it you dream

MARY. Himself was out on a big field and he with two wild geese yoked to a plough, but the devil a bit would they plough for him and he blessing them and cursing them again till they flew up into a river on the far ⟨end?⟩ of Glen Macanass.

MICHEAL [*to* NORA]. Herself does be hearing when it's asleep she is.

MARY [*suspiciously though with⟨out⟩ malice*]. And what was it I heard?

MICH. Herself talking with the priest.

MARY. Is ⟨it⟩ at marrying you she's fooling again? I was thinking the like of it when I seen her making a mess with water.

NORA. It's married I'll be now surely in a short while and there'll be no one now will have a right to be calling me a dirty name and I selling your cans to the men.

MARY. Have you a ring itself.

NORA. I have surely I got one with the money I had after selling songs in Aughrim.

MARY. It's a power of money you have to spend and what is it you're giving himself.

MICH. The half of a sovereign herself has in her purse and this can I'm finishing. 'You're a thieving lot,' says he 'and I'ld do right to make you give a pound surely but maybe if I left the like of that bit of money with you you'ld be drinking it below in the fair.'

NORA. Would you have them calling me bad name⟨s⟩ below in the fair and I selling the cans to the young men do be walking round in it. Why wouldn't a woman does be sleeping under a cart have as good ⟨or⟩ the same right to a decent marriage as a woman does be sleeping in a bit of a sty the like of the house beyond?—[*The house door opens and a woman comes with a can, she goes over to the well and fills it and comes back on the road.* MIKE *is finishing his can.*]—

WOMAN [*to* MIKE]. My head's ~~murdered~~ destroyed with your clattering there since the sun went up. You have a right to take your rest like the rest of us and not be waking us all up as if it was geese and ducks or the like of them dumb creatures we were.

MIKE. When would you see the like of that can, woman of the house, I'm thinking if you were able to make the like of that it's not when the cocks crowed you'd be beginning to work but night and morning every day of the week.

WOMAN [*puts down her own can and takes the other in her hand*]. It's a fine can surely. Is it this morning you're after doing the whole of that Micheal Byrne?

MIKE. The whole surely but a bit I was doing when the sun went down.

WOMAN. You're a great worker, God help you.

NORA [*angrily*]. Take up your old can, woman of the house and don't be making a puddle on us against the fire itself.

WOMAN [*taking it up it leaks*]. Glory be to God there is the bottom coming out of it again and it with two holes in were soldered by Dan Connor a while ago.

MARY BYRNE. Maybe himself would do it for you again.

WOMAN [*throws the water out of it and shows it to him*]. Would you mend this tinker?

MIKE. Faith I wouldn't woman of the house. The divil himself couldn't mend that, the tin's destroyed with the rust in it and it's a new can you'll be wanting.

WOMAN. Is it a great deal you're asking for the one you're after making, Micheal Byrne?

NORA. His reverence is after that.

WOMAN. Is it his reverence? and he with a power of the finest zinc buckets were sent him from the city of Dublin?

MARY BYRNE. We do be selling them cans for ⟨size?⟩ & when they're that size for shilling and sixpence.

WOMAN. Is it rob me you would? I'll give a shilling and it's dear at that but what way would I carry up water if I have no can in it at all?

MIKE. It's one and six I'm telling you.

NORA. And it⟨'s⟩ a lie you're telling for his reverence has the can.

MIKE [*under his breath*]. Hold your mouth Nora Casey. Isn't ⟨ten⟩ shillings a heap of money for a rich man the like of him. We'll tel him the ass is after putting his foot through it and then we'll have enough for a drink and we passing Bally & Clash.

MARY BYRNE [*to* WOMAN]. Give us one and three, it⟨'s⟩ a fine can and the blessing of God be on you.

WOMAN. Well it's a big price surely but himself will be having my life if he comes down from the hills and I have no water in it to give him his tea.—[*She gives them the money fills the can again and goes back to her house*]—

NORAH. You're the devil's own son Micheal Byrne and I'm thinking he'll not marry ⟨us⟩ at all after him letting on to take the can and he not wanting it at all.

MIKE [*getting up and smoothing his hair in a sheet of tin for a mirror*]. Don't let on we've sold it at all and maybe he'll not ask to see it and he'll marry us first. I'm thinking if it's once married we are the devil himself would⟨n't⟩ be able to break it open again.

NORA. He could not surely—[*she arranges her shawl*]—We'll let on we're after leaving it round in the kitchen with Mrs. Brady the cook.

MICH. Is she in it? I did⟨n't⟩ set eyes on her this time.

NORA. Isn't it always in it she is?

PRIEST [*opens the chapel door in his surplice*]. Is it the whole day you're going to keep me standing here saying me prayers?

MICH. We're coming now your reverence.

[MARY BYRNE *puts in the donkey.*]

PRIEST. Have you the money itself.

NORA. It's here your reverence.

PRIEST. And the can?

NORA. We're after leaving it round.

P⟨RIEST⟩. Round where?

NORA. With Mrs. Brady, your reverence.

PRIEST. And what did she say?

NORA. She said—she said she'd never seen the like of it for a long time.

PRIEST. Go along now like two of the divil's sinners that you are. Mrs. Brady's away miles in Kilgrade marrying her own daughter. And you thought you'ld do with the can, did you, and I marrying you for a little sum special, a little sum wouldn't marry a child.

NORA. Marry us, your reverence, isn't a half a sovereign a great price surely for people as poor as the like of us.

PRIEST. Is it I marry ⟨you?⟩ Get along now quickly or I'll be putting a big curse God forgive me—would carry you down into hell.

MIKE. Marry us your reverence and I⟨'ll⟩ make the loveliest can with a fine handle on it when I come from the fair. What was that for a can to carry the water ⟨of⟩ a holy man of God. ,

PRIEST [*threatening them and pushing them down the path*]. Go along I'm telling and let you not come back to me sight.

MARY BYRNE [*laughing*]. There's a fine blessing on a young pair surely.

PRIEST [*slamming the gate*]. If I catch you again in this village you bawdy thief I⟨'ll⟩ tell the peelers who it was stole the grey ass was belonging to Paddy O'Hea and I'll tell them what hay it is that ass does be eating and it lying down to its sleep.

NORA [*and M picking up stones*]. Go along you old miser.

PRIEST. There are the peelers above on the road and if you don't get along you⟨'ll⟩ have a queer dry lodging tonight, instead of lying in a stinking ditch with the dumb beasts.

MARY BYRNE. How is it the like of you would know where it is we'll be lodging tonight. It's rich we are now with two shillings in silver and ten shillings in gold. Would you think it was a fine thing if you had that money away from us and what was ⟨it⟩ you'ld give us instead? You and your marriage! Isn't generations and generations we are walking round under the Heavens and what is it we ever wanted with ⟨your like?⟩ Let you not be talking. We have the hot suns and the cold night and our bits to eat and sups to drink and a power of children and what more is it we want. Is it rings we want when the frost does catch on our fingers. Let you listen to this. When a man parts with copper to put rings in a pig's nose and you'ld like us to pay you with the time you'ld put an old ring on ourselves. You would surely. Herself is a young woman and the young never know the things they want. I've had one husband and another husband and a power of children God help them and it's little they or myself even with your old rings to help us on in the world. Good day now your reverence and let you be putting rings on your own pigs and not minding ourselves it's ten generations I was saying we've been walking round on the roads and never a marriage in the family.

MIKE. The peelers are coming let you hold your gab and come with us. Gee up. [*He drives off the donkey. They go out.*]

CURTAIN

An alternative speech is given to Mary Byrne when the Priest asks for the can: 'We're after selling it to a woman beyond for two silver shillings your reverence, I'm thinking that's a sight better for the like of us than all marriages itself.'

B. TS. '*A*', *the first complete version extant in typescript, appears to have been made up from several intervening typescript drafts. It is in one act and includes a title page; apparently it was prepared for the printer:*

Persons:—

MICHEAL BYRNE (a tinker)
NORA CASEY
MARY BYRNE (old woman, mother of Micheal)
A PRIEST
A VILLAGE WOMAN
TINKER CHILDREN

The scene is in a Wicklow village far away from the sea.

Scene: a roadside at the end of a village; chapel door to the right, with low railings to it, and gate; Cottages on the other side of the stage with blinds down and the doors shut. There is a spring well coming out of the ditch near the middle of the scene with an unyoked donkey cart near it and a fire. MICHEAL BYRNE *is finishing a tin-can.* NORA CASEY *is washing her face eagerly in an old bucket and arranging her hair.* MARY BYRNE *is asleep under the ditch. Two children are playing about. The priest is seen for a moment at the chapel door, then he goes in again.—*

—[MARY BYRNE *is beginning to waken up, one of the children comes over to* MICHEAL.]—

CHILD [*to* MICHEAL]. Will you get us a hapworth of sweets this day in the fair?

MICH. [*looking round to see that* MARY *does not hear him*]. We'll not have a penny at all going down this day, but you'd do right to beg a halfpenny off his reverence and he passing up along the road.—[*Child goes down into the ditch.*]—

MARY [*yawning and looking at* NORA *inquisitively*]. You're making a great stir with your washing, Nora Casey, I'm that used to the hammer I wouldn't hear it at all, but washing is a rare thing, and you're after waking me up and I having a grand dream of his reverence. . . .

NORA [*hardly minding her*]. He's after passing. . . .

MARY. Was he talking with you, itself?

NORA. A short while. . . .—[*She goes on arranging her hair.*]—

MICHEAL [*to* MARY]. What is it you're after dreaming for it's queer dreams you have?

MARY. Himself was out in the bit of a thrifling field he has, and he with two wild geese yoked into a plough, and there he was blessing them and cursing them, and making great persuasion, but not a bit would they stir. . . .

MICH. [*considering, to* NORA]. Didn't I tell you herself could hear the time she was sleeping?

MARY [*suspiciously*]. What was it I heard?

MICHEAL. You heard herself I'm thinking talking with the priest. . .

MARY [*sitting up eagerly*]. Is it at being married she's fooling again? was thinking as much when I seen her making a mess there on the road. . . .

NORA [*triumphantly*]. It's married I'll be now in a short while and let the like of you say what you will. . . . From this day there will no one have a right to call me a dirty name, and I selling cans in Wicklow, or Wexford, or the Carlow plain.

MARY. And what is it he's making you give?

MICHEAL. The ten shillings in gold herself has in the purse and this tin can will be done in a minute. 'You're a thieving lot', says he, 'and I'd do right to make you pay me a pound surely, but maybe if I let the like of that money with you, you'ld be drinking it below in the fair, so I'll marry you for the bit of gold and the tin can.'

MARY [*shaking her head*]. Isn't it a great wonder you'ld be paying a man for putting a kind of a chain on you, and you free and happy to this day?

MICH. I said the like of that to himself, and 'For what would you pay more,' says he, 'than keeping yourselves safe from the Almighty God?'

MARY. What is it the Almighty God would care of the like of us? You'ld never see the Almighty doing a thing to the larks or to the swallows or to the swift birds do be crying out when the sun is set, or to the hares do be racing above in the fine spring, and what way would he be following us in the dark nights, when it's quiet and easy we are, and we never asking him a thing at all?

—[*The first cottage door opens and a woman is seen on the step.*]—

NORA [*contemptuously*]. It isn't of the Almighty I'm thinking, God help you, but why wouldn't a woman does be sleeping under a cart have as good a right to decent marriage as a woman does be sleeping in a bit of a black sty like the house beyond?

—[*The woman comes out of the cottage door with an old can in her hand and goes down towards the spring well.*]—

WOMAN. It's a grand day for the fair. The summer's coming this time and there's no lie in it.

MICH. It's a grand day surely, thank God, and no cloud passing since the sun went up.

WOMAN. My head's destroyed with your clattering since the sun went up. You'ld have a right to be taking your rest like a Christian, and not be waking us up as if it was the like of the ducks, or geese, or the dumb beasts you were.

MARY [*derisively*]. It's grand Christians they'll be in a short while . . . . Grand Christians surely.

—[*Woman fills her can and comes back from the ditch.*]—

MICH. [*holding up his can which is finished*]. Where would you see the like of that can, woman of the house, that I'm after making the better part of this day the time you were taking your rest?

WOMAN [*laying down her can and taking the new one*]. You're a fine man at the trade, God bless you, a fine worker surely.

NORA [*crying out angrily*]. Take up your old can out of that woman of the house, and don't be making a mess here close to the tea, and running down a stream into the fire.

WOMAN [*crying out*]. Glory be to God, is it leaking it is?

NORA. Leaking? Was the Lough Nahanagan leaking when the flood burst from it that washed ten ricks from the glen?

WOMAN [*looking at her can*]. The bottom's tumbling out of it again God help me, and it only two weeks or three since I paid them to fix it.

MARY. Maybe himself would fix it and make it hold for a year.

MICH. [*looking at the can*]. How would anyone hold water in a thing like it and the bit of tin as rotten as an old rag you'ld find hung on a bush?

WOMAN [*looking doubtfully at the two cans*]. What is it you're asking for the can you're after making?

NORA [*impatiently*]. It's nothing at all we're asking. . . . His reverence is after taking that, and let you be going up now into your house, for it's a great power of things we have to do before the turn of the day

WOMAN [*contemptuously*]. It's mighty huffy you are, woman of the roads, is it the like of that old can his reverence would take and he with the finest zinc buckets were sent him from the city of Dublin.

MICH. [*with surprise*]. Is that the truth?

WOMAN. It is surely.

MARY [*taking up the new can*]. We do give the like of that can for shilling and sixpence, woman of the house. It's a grand can with nothing in it but the best of tin.

WOMAN. Maybe I'ld give a shilling for it, but it's a big price itself.

NORA [*anxiously, to* MICH. *in a low voice*]. How would she give any price, and his reverence after taking the can?

MICH. [*in a low voice*]. Hold your tongue, Nora Casey. If he has zinc buckets—the devil split them—from the city of Dublin, it's only humbugging us he was, and he'll marry us for the ten shillings in gold.... We'll let on the ass is after putting out her foot through the head of the can and then we'll have a bit of money to drink in Killacree.

MARY [*to the woman*]. Give us one and three, and we'll put a blessing on every sup you drink from the rim of it.

WOMAN. You're a thieving lot, surely, but it's a good can—[*taking money from her pocket*]—There's six pence and another six pence, and three pence—[*She pours the water from the old can into the new one.*]—

WOMAN. God bless you now, and I'm hoping it's long it will stand.

MARY. God bless you.—[*Woman goes back to her cottage.*]—

NORA [*in a disappointed voice*]. I'm thinking now he'll not marry us at all.

MICHEAL [*smoothing his hair, with a piece of tin for a glass*]. Maybe he'll not ask to see it till he'll have married us first.

NORA [*arranging her shawl*]. If he asks to see it we'll let on we're after leaving it round with Mary Brady the cook.

MICHEAL. Is she in it itself?

NORA. Where else would she be?

—[*She goes to the cart and gets a bright handkerchief which she puts round her head.* MICHEAL *settles his boots. The children take up the old can left by the woman.*]—

1ST CHILD. We'll make a drum from this bit of a can the way we'll be like the green man we seen in the fair.

2ND CHILD. How would we be like the green man, and not a green rag on us at all?

1ST CHILD. We'll put a bit of rushes round our heads, and then we'll be like the green man surely, and it's a power of money we'll get for sweets beating that thing through the fair.—[*He begins tying a string to the old can to make it hang like a drum.*]—

NORA [*to* MICHEAL]. Are you ready now I hear himself at the door?

—[*Priest, fat man, comes down from the chapel.*]—

PRIEST [*calling out impatiently*]. Is it the whole day you'ld keep me here saying my prayers, and I getting my death with not a bit in my stomach, and my breakfast going to ruin beyond in the house?

MICH. We're coming now, father.

PRIEST [*coming to the chapel railing*]. Give me the bit of money now into my hand.

NORA [*taking out an old purse*]. It's here father. . . .

PRIEST [*looking round suspiciously*]. And where is the can?

NORA. We're after leaving it round, your reverence, and it's fine prayers I'll be saying now for your reverence. It's . . .

PRIEST [*interrupting her*]. Round where?

NORA. With Mrs. Brady, your reverence, and I was saying she'ld do right to put the first sup of water into it out of the blessed well beyond on the hill.

PRIEST [*with a queer look*]. And what was it she said?

NORA. She said the blessing of God was upon your reverence morning and night but she'ld do it surely, and she said it wasn't since the old times she'd seen the like of that can.

PRIEST [*breaking out*]. Let you go along now, Nora Casey, let you go along now I'm telling you, like the devil's daughter you are, for Mary Brady is this two days below in Kilquade, and isn't it a black shame that it's deceiving me you'ld be, and I marrying you for a little sum wouldn't marry a child?

—[*Woman comes out of her cottage door with the can in her hand and fills a kettle from it.*]—

PRIEST. Glory be to God, and there's the can surely. . . .

NORA [*with a whining voice*]. Marry us, your reverence, isn't the half sovereign I'm stretching out in my hand to you a great price for the

like of us, and we'll be making you a can in the morning after the
fair, a can fit for your reverence. Sure the like of that can wouldn't
do for you, at all, and it only a can you'ld be carrying muck in the
time you'ld be feeding a pig.

PRIEST. Get out of my sight I'm telling you, or I'll be putting a black
curse on you, God forgive me, would make the tin burn in your
hand.

NORA [*whining as before*]. Marry us your reverence, and we'll make you
a can with a fine handle on it—we're getting the stuff in Arklow
tomorrow,—a can would be fit to carry water for the Holy Man of
God. . . .

PRIEST [*shouting at her*]. Would you have me curse you I'm saying. . . .

MARY BYRNE [*derisively, yoking the ass and cart*]. He's a grand man to
talk, God spare him, and there's a fine blessing surely for a young
pair would be making themselves Christians at the dawn of day.

NORA [*as before, putting her apron to her eyes*]. If we gave you the little
sixpence we had for the can, your reverence, it was a sixpence we
had only and it a thin one at that.

PRIEST. Go out of this parish I'm telling you and if ever I set an eye on
you again you'll hear me telling the peelers who it was stole the grey
ass from Paddy O'Hea, and whose hay it is the black ass does be
eating.

NORA [*putting down her apron and looking at him in wonder*]. You'ld do
that?

PRIEST. I would surely.

NORA. Then it'll be all the tinkers of Wicklow and Wexford and the
Carlow plain you'll be getting together to put up block tin in the
place of glass in your windows. . . .

—[*The PRIEST shades his eyes with his hands and looks up the road.*]—

NORA [*continuing*]. It'll be a fine time then for the tinkers and they
taking a big price of you for climbing up on the chapel with tin
nails in their hands. . . .

PRIEST. There are the peelers above now on the road, and if you don't
go along with you, it's a dry lodging you'll have this night instead

of the stinking ditch where you do be lying down with the dumb beasts.

—[NORA *looks up the road hastily, then she and* MICHEAL *begin bundling their things into the cart.*]—

MARY [*to the priest*]. How is it the like of you knows where it is we'll be lodging tonight, for it's rich we are now with three pennies, and a shilling in silver, and ten shillings in gold. If you'd got that money off us wouldn't it have been a fine thing for the like of you, but what is it you'd give in the place of it? It's a long time we are now going round on the roads, father and son and his son after him, or maybe mother and daughter and her daughter again, and what is it we wanted any time with going up into the church, and swearing—I'm told there's swearing in it—a word no man would believe? Or what is it we wanted with putting dirty rings on our fingers would be cutting our skin maybe in the cold nights when we'd be taking the ass from the shafts, and pulling the straps the time they'ld be slippy with going round under the heavens in the rain falling?

PRIEST. What is it I care if the like of you are married or not? It's herself is after talking me round with the long tongue she has.

MARY. Herself is young, God help her, and the young don't be knowing any time the thing they want. But I've had one man and another man, and a power of children, and it's little need we had of your swearing, or your rings with it, to get us our bit to eat, and our bit to drink, and our time of love when we were young men or women, and were fine to look at.

MICHEAL [*to* MARY]. Come along now and don't be minding him at all. The peelers are above on the road, and maybe they'ld be fining us if they knew it was eleven good shillings we had. Come along now I'm telling you, and it's a grand time we'll have spending a bit of gold below in the fair.—[*He hits the ass a great smack with stick and they go out, the children with rushes round their heads walking behind the cart and beating loudly on the old tin-can.*]—

2ND CHILD [*as they go by, in a shrill voice*]. Give us a half-penny, your reverence, give us a half-penny. . . .

PRIEST [*crossing himself*]. The Lord protect us, there's heathen surely. . . .

CURTAIN

C. *Notebook 30 (spring 1903?) contains the following scenario for Act I. It is immediately followed by a two-act scenario for* When the Moon Has Set, *and appears to be Synge's first plan for a two-act play:*

Act I. Mick. making ring out of tin with Nora's help. Children come in. Mary comes in with a jug of porter in a humorous-psychic mood. Mick and Nora go—when others are asleep to make their bargain with the priest—(Curtain).

D. *TS. 'B' is the first typescript version in two acts and includes much additional material contrasting the tinker children with little girls from the village:*

1. *TS. 'B', Act I, pp. 6-8 (after the introductory scene between Nora and Micheal):*

—[*The two children,* MICKY & NANNY, *come in.*]—

NORA [*to the children*]. Is his reverence above in the house?

MICKY. There wasn't a light at all in the big window & we were there a long while looking around, and we afraid to go in on the grass fearing there'ld be a dog in it the like of the dog in Killacree.

NORA. Did you not see a person at all?

MICKY. A kind of a girl came of the gate the time we were standing round, and 'Is his reverence in it?' says I. 'He is not,' says she, 'but what at all is that to the like of you?'—[*He sits down by the fire.*]— Give us a bit to eat now, for we're destroyed with the hunger.

NORA [*giving them food out of the pot*]. When you have that down it's away off you'll go again to find out what place he is surely.

NANNY. I'm not going off again this night for I've a thorn in my foot.

NORA [*looking at her foot*]. Where, God help you?

NANNY. Below by my big toe. . . a long cruel thorn with no butt on it at all.

NORA [*trying to take out the thorn*]. How was it you got the like of that thorn, Nanny? Didn't you ever hear me saying to you, you don't be minding at all the place where you'ld be laying your feet?

MICKY. She got that thorn running up the field and we after making a fine job for himself in the morning.

MICHEAL. Is it a job for myself?

MICKY. A fine job and it's no lie.—[*He stops suddenly.*] Whisht—whisht now till herself will be gone. . . .

> —[*A woman comes down the road and goes into the cottage where the light was seen. She shuts the door after her.*]—

MICKY [*whispering*]. We were going across the field to his reverence and herself from that house beyond was above feeding her calf. Then she went down to be speaking with someone—with a man I'm thinking—in the dark lane, and Nanny took the can.

NANNY. It's not lies he's telling this time. . . . There isn't a lie in it at all.

MICKY. There was the bottom on the old can, and it after being by someone wasn't half a tinker I'm thinking, and what did I do but put down my stick into it, and 'Now Nanny,' says I, 'let you hit a little soft crack on my stick and the bottom will be sprung.'

NANNY. Then I hit a little weechy crack, and we heard herself coming and we run and we run. . . . It was that time I got the thorn.

NORA [*to* MICHEAL, *in a friendly voice*]. They're a great pair, God bless them, Micheal Byrne, a great pair surely. [*To* NANNY.]—There's the thorn out of you now Nanny. It was a bad thorn and it's no lie.

MICHEAL [*to the children*]. Did you set your eye, on a hen or a chicken, or a thing at all a man could eat?

MICKY. We seen two fine hens of Tim O'Flaherty's out rousting in the ash tree above the well, and they bending down the branch with the fat on them as if it was myself was climbing.

MICHEAL [*to* NORA, *who stands up*]. If herself was come now with the porter we'ld have a right to pass round there for the hen this night, Nora Casey, for it'ld be a fine night to be out walking round with the Beauty of Ballinacree, and it's a long while since it was a good hen we had to eat.

NORA. I'ld go with you and welcome, Micheal Byrne, if we had his reverence seen, now I've the ring done in my hand.

MICHEAL [*looking down to the left*]. There's someone coming forward now & he talking to himself above on the road.

NORA [*comes forward and listens*]. It's someone coming forward from the doctor's door, Micheal Byrne.

MICHEAL. It's often his reverence does be in there, and they playing cards, or drinking a sup till the dawn of day.

NORA. It's a big boast of a man with drink taken, & a trumpeting voice—[*crying out*] It's his reverence surely.—[*She comes back to the fire speaking hurriedly to the children.*] Let you go in now under the cart, and be going to sleep, for there isn't anything more you'll need to do this night at all. [*The children go in under the cart.*]

2. TS. 'B', *Act II, pp. 23–24 (after Mary Byrne wakens and discovers the marriage plans):*

—[*Two little girls dressed for confirmation in white dresses pass down the road towards the chapel.*]—

1ST GIRL [*in a whisper*]. The tinkers are in it.

2ND GIRL. They'll be gone please God, before the bishop will come up. What would he think at all, if he seen the like of them heathens sitting there doing their hairs by the door of the Church?

1ST GIRL. And it's that lot is the worst lot of the whole of them, Mary Kate, for I've heard tell it was the old one below in the ditch stripped off the better part of her clothes a while ago in Ballinacree, and beat two peelers, and they big men, fifty yards through the fair.

—[*They go into the chapel railing.*]—

MARY. That's the first of the like of them I've seen this year Nora Casey, and it's as sure a sign of summer they are, God bless them, as the white tree over your head.

NORA [*looking after them*]. Wouldn't it be a grand thing to see Nanny, God help her, dressed up the like of one of them, and she walking up in the face of the Lord Bishop on a summer's day?

MARY. And wouldn't it be a fine thing to see yourself, Nora Casey, and you driving to the races in a gold coach, the like of the grand Lady Lieutenant. . . . It's a finer woman you are surely.

—[NORA *begins washing again without answering her; the two tinker children seem to see something up the road, and go and sit down near* MARY.]—

MICHEAL [*to* MARY]. There's the priest coming down now on the road, and let you not be saying queer things to him this time, when you've not been drinking at all. . . . He'ld take it bad I'm thinking in the morning of the day.

—[PRIEST *comes hurrying in buttoning his cuffs.*]—

3. TS. 'B', *Act II, pp. 32–33 (after Mary tries to dissuade Nora from marrying)*:

—[NORA *and* MICHEAL *go to the cart and begin arranging their clothes, putting coloured handkerchiefs round their necks etc. A little girl in white comes down the road and stops at the cottage door, talking to the people inside.* NANNY *and* MICKY *are left on the road, they take up the old can the woman has left behind her.*]—

MICKY. We'll make a drum now from this bit of a can, and then we'll be like the green man we seen below in the fair.

NANNY. We won't be like the green man, and not a green rag on us at all.

MICKY. We'll put a bit of rushes round our heads and then we'll be like the green man surely, and it's a power of money for sweets we'll get beating that thing through the fair.—[*He begins tying a string round the old can to make it hang like a drum. Two more little girls come down the road in white; they are joined by the girl who was at the door of the cottage and they pass together.*]—

1ST GIRL. Did you hear what the pig did last night, the pig Biddy's father was taking to the fair?

2ND GIRL. I did not.

1ST GIRL. It's after tearing the front out of her frock, and there she is now getting her death fretting, and she with nothing to put on her at all.

2ND GIRL. They bought that pig from the old minister & I'm thinking the devil was in it. Didn't you ever hear tell of the devils going down into the swine?

2ND GIRL. An old daddy goat is the devil, Barbara Neill, with the long beard on him, and the horns above. Didn't you ever hear tell of the goats and the sheep?

1ST GIRL. Let you not be talking bad talk this day, Kitty Brien. Haven't you every day to do that?

—[*They go into the chapel gate. The* PRIEST *comes down from the Chapel. He takes out his watch and speaks with them fussily.*]—

III. RELATED PASSAGES FROM NOTEBOOKS

(*Unless otherwise indicated the Oxford* Poems *and* Prose *editions will be used*)

A. *POEMS AND TRANSLATIONS*

  1. 'Danny', *pp. 56–57.*
  2. 'An Old Woman's Lamentations', *p. 80.*

B. *IN WICKLOW, WEST KERRY AND CONNEMARA*

  1. ' "That man is a great villain.... One time he and his woman went up to a priest in the hills and asked him would he wed them for half a sovereign...." ', '*At a Wicklow Fair*', *pp. 228–9.*

  2. ' "I remember one time, a while after I was married, there was a tinker down there in the glen, and two women along with him.... They're gallous lads for walking round through the world...." ', '*The Vagrants of Wicklow*', *pp. 203–4.*

  3. 'These people are nearly always at war with the police, and are often harshly treated...', '*The Vagrants of Wicklow*', *pp. 206–7.*

  4. 'The other day near Ballyduff I met one of the most delightful old women that I have yet fallen in with.... At the next turn in the road near Laragh I came on a tinkers' camp in a fragment of a wood that grows at the apex of the meeting between the Annamoe river and the waters from Glendalough and Lough Nahanagan...', '*People and Places*', *pp. 198–9.*

C. *From Notebook 33, directly following the passages describing the old woman and the two tinker children, probably written in 1907 but drawing together incidents occurring over a number of years:*

'I had to leave Bray late in the twilight to make my way to Annamoe. Near Farraroe I passed four carts full of tinkers moving towards Kilmacanogue. They had many horses with them—it was not many days after the Wicklow horse fair—tied in various ways to their carts which were filled with women and children. A few of the men were on their feet and seemed more than usually drunk. A little further on I came to another cart coming towards me in an opposite direction. One young man of this party was a little behind and I had to get down and tell him where I ⟨had⟩ seen the other cavalcade, how many carts there were and what way they were taking.

'When he was satisfied with my directions he wanted me to buy some of his tin cans, and then to give him a 'chew' of tobacco. By the time I left him his companions were lost in the darkness under the trees and he set off at a shaky run to overtake them. I had to stop for a moment at the public house in Kilmacanogue, which had the usual mournful note that is peculiar to these places in wet weather. There were some men talking slowly and heavily over their porter at the half-dusky end of the shop, a woman or two buying a few things at the counter and the rain hissing outside where a drunken tramp was staggering about the doorway.

'The rocky valley when I reached it seemed gloomier than I have ever seen ⟨it⟩ and my eyes sharpened by the darkness grew unspeakably weary of the endless rushing of water that was tumbling away by the roadside.'

IV. EARLIER DRAFTS OF THE PREFACE TO *THE TINKER'S WEDDING*

1. *The following appears to be the earliest form of the Preface; now preserved among the papers in Item 52, it is on one typed page with heavy manuscript alterations and additions that continue in ink on the back of the page. Not all the manuscript alterations are legible, nor is it possible to ascertain which are final.*

Fielding and others have made comparisons ⟨between⟩ works of literature and the dishes served up on the table where we eat. These comparisons have some value, in the drama at least, for we should go to the theatre as we go to a dinner where many are together, and where the food we live on is taken with pleasure and excitement. It was ⟨so⟩ with the Elizabethans and the stories of Chaucer ⟨?⟩. . . . However today we go to a playhouse either as we go to the drug or dram shop, that is when we go to Brieux or Ibsen or the Germans, or when on a different taste to the last musical comedy. Honey and fruit and strong meat ⟨are⟩ always useful and pleasant, and it is only diseased and foolish people who spend their time in places where there is a smell of ammonia and quinine or of absinthe and vermouth (both marks of disease).

Putting the comparison aside, it should be remembered that literature is not serious—in the French sense—when it is taken up with what are in themselves serious problems, as all disease is serious, but when it is taken up with those fresh views of what is fine and essential in manhood and the world and in the variations which give them richness.

The Tinker's Wedding is not a discussion of bad behaviour ⟨but⟩ is an attempt to catch some of the humour and freshness which is in all life, and which are the only food on which the mind can live healthily. It is a mistake altogether to say that ⟨the⟩ dramatist is to teach, his duty is to feed only. Teaching is always presumptuous, the position of the view of some fallible person, but literature is a preparation more or less unique and skilful of the everlasting fruits of the imagination and the body. In literature as in love and war—where the eminently real and personal ⟨prevail⟩—there is no division of labour, and the poet must hunt his game in many strange moods before he draws and roasts it. That is one reason, there are a few good ones only—why the poet is more thought of than the cook or poulterer.

2. *The following draft from Item 52, again on one typescript page with manuscript alterations, is less heavily emended, but the passages in parentheses were later crossed out.*

PREFACE—TO TINKERS

(We should use literature as we use fruit and honey and meat, as a thing that we cannot go without, and we should remember that it has no likeness with the black drafts that are made up by serious apothecaries.

That is to say literature is necessary—all arts are necessary—yet they have nothing to do with rules of behaviour and the problems that are connected with the details of life.

The value of good literature is measured by its uniqueness, and in works that are not purely subjective by its richness also. But when a work is rich and unique it must be taken freshly and directly from life, and it must be many-sided, so that it has a universal quality, and is therefore sane, as all insanity is due to a one-sided exaggeration of the personality.)

Certain portions of life, wild and coarse in a sense, that we can never get away from can only be looked at safely when they are seen with the humour which makes them human for no vice is humorous (bestial is opposed to the very idea of humour and as far as the person is concerned we may say also almost that) and whatever can be done gaily is not criminal. Baudelaire hated the laugh of a healthy man and calls laughter somewhere the greatest mark of the Satanic element in man, and wherever a country loses its humour as Ireland is doing, there will be morbidity of mind, as Baudelaire's mind was morbid, and many people will be ripe for the asylums.

V. FIRST PRODUCTION

The Tinker's Wedding *was not produced during Synge's lifetime. It was first produced by the Afternoon Theatre Company at His Majesty's Theatre, London, 11 November 1909, with the following cast:*

MICHAEL BYRNE	Jules Shaw
A PRIEST	Edmund Gurney
MARY BYRNE	Clare Greet
SARAH CASEY	Mona Limerick

APPENDIX B

THE PLAYBOY OF THE WESTERN WORLD: WORKSHEETS AND COMMENTARY

I. DESCRIPTION OF TEXTUAL SOURCES

(Unless otherwise stated, unpublished material is in the possession of the Synge Estate.)

A. STANDARD EDITIONS

1. The Playboy of the Western World. A Comedy in Three Acts. *Theatre Edition (Dublin, Maunsel, 1907). Being Volume X of the Abbey Theatre Series.*

When this was reprinted in June 1909 the preface from the regular edition was included.

2. The Playboy of the Western World. A Comedy in Three Acts *(Dublin, Maunsel, 1907). With a preface by Synge and a portrait of the author sketched at rehearsal by J. B. Yeats, dated 25 January 1907.*

The preface is dated 21 January 1907 and the edition was issued in February 1907; it was reprinted in April 1907. Technically, it appears to be the same edition as the Theatre Edition, and a letter to Synge from George Roberts of Maunsel & Co. implies it was to be issued simultaneously.

A limited edition of twenty-five copies on hand-made paper was issued at the same time, again technically the same edition. Two advance copies of the play are in existence also, differing from the regular edition only in the binding and the omission of the portrait.

B. OTHER EDITIONS DURING SYNGE'S LIFETIME

The Playboy of the Western World: A Comedy by John Synge. Act II *(New York, printed for John Quinn, 1907). A limited edition of twelve copies, registered for copyright on 6 March 1907.*

C. EXTANT MANUSCRIPTS/TYPESCRIPTS

1. *In Notebook 32, eighteen pages interspersed with notes on County Mayo and analyses of Racine and Molière, early sketches for all three acts. September 1904.*
2. *In Notebook 28, sixteen pages interspersed with dialogue for* When the Blind See (The Well of the Saints), National Drama, When the Moon Has Set, *and*

notes about County Kerry, slightly later dialogue for all three acts. Winter 1904–Spring 1905.

3. *In Notebook 31, nine pages of dialogue for 'The Fool of Farnham'. Spring 1905.*

4. *In Notebook 34, forty-five pages of dialogue and scenarios for Acts II and III and first draft of the preface. January and November 1906.*

5. *In Notebook 33, two pages of dialogue for Act III. Autumn 1906.*

6. *In Box Files A and B, over a thousand typescript pages and fragments, all of them heavily emended. Autumn 1904–January 1907. Not all drafts are dated, and very few are complete:*

a. *Act I—'Murder Will Out Act II'* ⟨*i.e. Act I*⟩; *'Murder Will Out Act I'; 'closing scene of Act I. Peg. and Christy'; 'Murder Will Out (A)'; revision of concluding scenes to TS. 'A'; 'Murder Will Out (B)' or 'The Fool of the Family'; 'Murder Will Out I (B) (End)'; 'Murder Will Out (C)'; TS. 'D'; 'Christy Mahon (E)' (23 May 1905); TS. 'F' (1 January 1906); revision of Widow Quin scene in TS. 'F'.*

b. *Act II—'Murder Will Out Act III'* ⟨*i.e. Act II*⟩; *'Murder Will Out Act II'; 'Murder Will Out II (B)'; 'Murder Will Out (C)'; revisions of Widow Quin scenes in TS. 'C'; TS. 'D'; TS 'E' (24 May 1905); TS. 'F' (9 January 1906); TS. 'G' (28 July 1906); TS. 'H' (10 August 1906); remnants of TS. 'I' (24 September 1906); TS. 'J' (1 November 1906); remnants of TS. 'K' (6 November 1906).*

c. *Act III—'Murder Will Out Act III'; 'Act III (A)'; 'Act III (B)'; TS. 'C'; TS. 'D'; TS. 'E' (May 1905); TS. 'F' (24 January 1906)* ⟨*first version*⟩; *TS. 'F'* ⟨*second version*⟩; *TS. 'G'; TS. 'H'; remnants of TS. 'I'; TS. 'J' (24 September 1906); remnants of TS. 'K' (4 October 1906); remnants of TS. 'L' (? December 1906).*

7. *In the Lilly Library, Indiana University, the complete typescript draft sold to John Quinn by Synge as the final draft of the play, but differing occasionally from the printed text:*

> *Act I—TS. 'G' (18 September 1906)*
> *Act II—TS. 'K' (6 November 1906)* ⟨*misdated October*⟩
> *Act III—TS. 'K' (4 October 1906).*

8. *In Box File A, all but two pages from Act II of the final typescript draft, including the preface, prepared by Synge for the printers, with printer's annotations; undated.*

9. *In Box File A, galley proofs corrected by Synge. 12–21 January 1907.*

II. DRAFT MANUSCRIPTS

A. *Many rough scenarios and outlines exist for* The Playboy, *scribbled on the available typescript draft or notebook so that they cannot always be dated accurately, and frequently representing the revision period between full drafts, so that they do not always correspond to specific typescripts. In each case an estimated date is given in parentheses and Synge's abbreviations are written out in full for the sake of clarity; relevant comments and additional notes by Synge are included in the order in which they occur in the manuscript.*

1. *Three outlines of the complete play exist, all in three acts, although some of the typescript drafts indicate that at one time Synge contemplated a four-act scheme.*

a. *In Notebook 32, what appears to be the earliest record of the play (Autumn 1904); the notebook is mutilated and an early draft of the first scene torn out:*

THE MURDERER (A FARCE)

Christy O'Flaherty—son
   Old   ,,
~~Shemus O'Flaherty~~—Father

Act I

(a potato garden) Old O'Flaherty describes his son's life and exasperates him so much that in the end he takes the loy and hits his father on the head with it then rushes across stage and out on left.

Act II

(public house bar or shebeen) Christy bossing the show. Tells his story three times of how he killed his father, police afraid to follow him and other bombast, love affairs etc. At the slightest provocation he starts off again with his story.

Act III

(he is being elected county councillor) Old man comes in first, and shows his head to everybody. He is as proud of it as his son is, as he is going round the crowd. His son comes out the elected member. He is put on a table to make a speech, he gets to the point where he is telling how he killed his father when the old man walks out—'You're a bloody liar, that's what you are'. Son attacks father and is handcuffed, then with his former dejection. He says

b. *On the back of Act I, unrevised 'C' draft of* Murder Will Out or The Fool of the Family *(Winter 1904–5?):*

A⟨ct⟩ I   Pegeen complains of her loneliness to Shawn
             Men come and Shawn goes
             He returns
             Christy comes
               long scene
             Men go
             Shawn is kicked out

~~to rewrite~~ ‖Long duo ⟍ (Ch. states former life (a)
‖Widow Quin
and conclusion

II   Monologue   (b) Ch. states hope
Crowd of girls
Pegeen comes
Duo
to rewrite   ‖Widow and Christy ⎱ hopes sprouting
‖Widow and Old F   ⎰ check   ⎱ keep co
‖Widow and Christy ⎰ forlorn hope

III   Duo ⎯⎯⎯⎯ ⎱ apparent   wild
to rewrite   Micheal and Christy ⎰ realization   joy

expand   ⎧ Pegeen Shawn and Ch.
and tighten   ⎪ Enter men and girls
conclusion   ⎪ Old Flaherty and Widow Quin   tragic
above all   ⎨   Total climax   farce
strengthen   ⎪ Old F. drives out Christy
Christy's   ⎪   followed by Widow Quin
appeal   ⎪ Pegeen and Shawn make it up
⎩ Curtain

c. *Two sides of a quarto page, undated, probably about November 1906.*

Act I	1 Pegeen and Shawn current her loneliness crescendo	comedy and locality
	2 Ditto and 3 men current keeping of Shawn climax	Molièrean climax of farce
	3 Ditto and Christy current (a) to find out his crime (b) to keep him exits climaxed by Shawn's	savoury dialogue
	4 Pegeen and Christy current (sub)—growing love interest	Poetical— to be very strong
	5 Ditto and Widow Quin current taking off of Christy	to be Rabelaisian—very strong
	6 Pegeen and Christy short finale	diminuendo ironical

II	1	solo Christy	character
	2	Christy and girls current (sub) of flattery	comedy
	3	Ditto and Pegeen short episode	comedy
	4	Pegeen Christy current his worked fear leading to second love stage	Poetical
	5	Shawn and Christy current Shawn's effort to get rid of him and Christy's pride	comedy
	6	Christy and Widow Quin current his getting away from her	comedy and character
	7	Ditto and Old Mahon current *opposition*?	stationary comedy

	8	Widow Quin and Christy
		current her effort to win him
		      her going over to him
		      his thanks etc.
			Poetical

III	1	Philly and Timmy and Old Mahon current Mahon	plot in comedy
	2	interlude Mahon and Widow current she tries to get him off	Rabelaisian
	3	Christy and Pegeen current marriage hopes?	Poetical make her play round him a little at first to get the hook into him?
	4	Ditto and Michael James current opposition	Rabelaisian
	5	Ditto and crowd current Christy swears	drama
	6	Ditto and Old Mahon	drama
	7	finale	to be an elaborate mélange

2. *Only one plan of Act I alone remains, scribbled at the bottom of a page of an early draft of the act (Winter 1904-5 ?); the number 6 corresponds to the number of scenes planned for the act:*

6 {
Shawn and Pegeen
Shawn and Pegeen and Micheal and men
Pegeen, Micheal and men
Pegeen, Micheal and men and Shawn and Christy
Shawn Christy and Pegeen
Pegeen and Christy — — —
}

Ending on admiration and kindliness of Pegeen and Christy—

3. *Three plans of Acts II and III together exist among the papers.*

a. *In Notebook 28 interspersed with dialogue for 'The Fool of Farnham I end' (early 1905 ?); the number '3' refers to the third scene of Act II, while the small letters indicate alternative plans:*

II (3) (a) Old F. comes and tells Pegeen that etc. She misdirects him. Christy's gratitude interrupted by Shawn. He is dispatched. Men come in hilarious and Christy and Pegeen are fianceed. (Pegeen is ready to wed because she can have a man who has the glory of having killed his father without the fear of having him hanged—)

Act III. Moods moving as before, Old Flaherty comes exposes Christy. Men turn on him, but as Old Flaherty is driving him off girls interpose—general row. Pegeen hesitates between Christy and Shawn. Marries Shawn, marries Old Man, or goes out with Christy.

II 3 (b) Sally Quin comes back for tobacco Christy and Pegeen go out to drive the sheep. Old man comes. Sally misdirects him. Christy comes back. Sally does, or does not, tell him. Shawn kicked out.

b. *Scribbled on the back of draft 'B' of Act III (early 1905 ?):*

Widow Quin overhears Christy and Pegeen
Then short sympathetic scene with Christy
        Scene with Old Flaherty
He goes
Christy and Pegeen come back

Christy more jubilant than ever. Widow Quin pities him and goes
as Party come in

Then matchmaking ends with Christy's alliance with Pegeen.

III Opening as before.

Widow and Christy (queer suggestive sympathetic ⟨scene⟩ and then
entry of Pegeen and preparation of marriage broken by Old
Flaherty. Pegeen scoffs Christy and the Widow Quin takes him
into her care.)

Old Flaherty begins telling cock and bull story of the way he got his
skull cracked then goes with ⟨them?⟩

*c. Scribbled on the back of the first scene with the alliance between Christy and Pegeen
taking place in Act III (probably early 1905 also):*

Keep Christy behind door in scene with Widow Quin and Old
Flaherty. When Old Flaherty goes Widow Quin and Christy
(decide) to deceive Pegeen etc. i.e. Christy talks her over or some
such thing.

Pegeen calls and exit Christy.

Michael James comes in and talks to Widow Quin (?) (tells that
Shawn is to wed Pegeen)

He sees her to gate and meanwhile enter Pegeen and Christy, as
in p. 28

(Michael James returns with Shawn big scene ending in alliance of
Pegeen and Christy)

Act III opens as before. Widow Quin.

Widow Quin Old Flaherty comes up behind Christy

Christy at first tries to attack him but when he finds that sympathy
of whole crowd has gone round against him he changes and falls
back to previous dejection—appeals to Widow Quin. Final Scene
Old Flaherty, Christy and Widow Quin ⟨two lines illegible⟩

(centre of scene Christy's sudden onslaught on Old Flaherty. He is
held back by people. Humour of it after a moment same people
are holding back Old Flaherty??)

For final curtain try Old Flaherty driving out Christy then Widow
Quin addresses crowd and follows them—curtain their consternation—

To write next begin at exit of Old Flaherty—

4. *Synge's outlines for Act II are more in the manner of notes and suggestions than the scheme for an individual act, and all existing comments are late enough to be easily dated.*

a. *On the back of the first draft 'F' of Act III (24 January 1906) the 'iron spoon' corresponds to an idea he contemplated after draft 'E' of Act II:*

> ? Ballad singer?
> Trio Widow Quin Shawn and Old Mahon
>   Widow, Pegeen and Old Man
> Men exit, old man left. Enter Widow Quin Pegeen to him.
> Widow Quin hustles him into side room by stratagem.
> Christy comes.
> Widow Quin takes out iron spoon. Old Mahon begins to abuse in
>   inner room.

b. *On a separate piece of paper fastened to the bottom of draft 'H' of Act III (summer 1906?); with the heading 'Notes':*

> Make quarrel told of arise because he is threatened with a wife (fat
>   fiery widow Rabelaisian to delight of girls)
> Make Widow Quin be present?
> Work father etc. into lonesome portion of II, get breeze into
> Elaborate Christy Shawn duo.
> Elaborate Old Mahon's account of quarrel in ⟨Act⟩ three and make
>   the Widow hear it.
> How will Widow theme work with Old Mahon's view of his future,
>   and with finale!
> Make Widow Quin take him on her knee! in II
> Elaborate Finale of II

c. *In Notebook 34, interspersed with notes about various scenes in Act II (November 1906):*

> 1 Christy solo
> 2 Christy and girls with gifts *very quick*
> 3 Christy and girls and Widow Quin speaks of sports
> 4 Christy's story?
> 5 Pegeen's entry   is jealousy big enough motive?
>   duo { frightens Christy
>   { sports he must win her

5. Again, the various rough outlines to Act III indicate Synge's problems with the action and the interweaving of both characters and plots.

a. In Notebook 28, the only extant draft showing the four-act scheme, which apparently occurred to Synge after he started expanding the earlier acts and including more Widow Quin material (late spring, 1905?); the additional material inserted before Act IV appears to have been added later:

Scenario of Act III D

Michael comes in drunk with the Widow Quin. She proposes to him in scene of grotesque futile love-making. As he is going to pledge himself to her Shawn comes in and reminds him that he (Shawn) is fianceed to Pegeen with the condition that Michael remains a bachelor—a condition due to Shawn's father—Widow and Shawn fight she threatens him to break off his marriage. Enter Pegeen and Christy Widow Quin works up Christy to terrify Shawn and in the end he retreats leaving Christy accepted suitor and widow for his mother-in-law. (Insert allusions to this affair in earlier acts)

(Old Mahon comes in after having fallen into bog-hole abuses the world then goes into inner room to rest, then entry of Christy and Pegeen as in C)

Act IV Opening as before Widow Quin sees Old Flaherty and tries to keep him till wedding is over so that she may wed old man. She fails, when Shawn reoffers for Pegeen there is a general row in the end old Michael James renounces Widow Quin so she takes Christy instead.

b. On the back of draft 'D' of Act III (probably following directly after the above outline):

3 pages of crowd
1 crowd and Christy
2 Pegeen and Christy climax
    of subjective jubilation
3 Michael Christy Pegeen Shawn
6 to entry of Mahon leading through
    climax of public triumph

   15

(a) give Pegeen big
        tirades
(b) Mahon   } 5 Row climax of pity for Christy
(c) Christy's appeal

3 Denouement—with irony worked by influence of Widow Quin and representing relationship of Pegeen and Shawn
  as seen in first act. Pegeen gives him
  her letter to post—
  and Roulette man cries 'Play me a game' etc.

c. *On the back of draft 'E' of Act III (May 1905):*

III

mid-day in Pegeen's kitchen. Timmy and Philly
come in. Tell of old man and wonder what he is   1

crowd escort home Christy in jubilation. They are
called out to see Michael coming up hill, or to run   2
the next race. Christy stays proposes to Pegeen accepted
  (strong scene)   3

broken by Michael drunk and Shawn
Michael leads out Christy   4

Pegeen and Shawn re-enter crowd   5

fiancailles interrupted by Old Mahon—climax
  Climax   Climax   6

d. *On the back of draft 'F' of Act III (24 January 1906):*

Scenario III

	Timmy and Philly	show what has happened short and humorous
	Plus Old Mahon	shows that he has returned, boasts of his bones
P. of Widow Quin	Pegeen in hurry bundles out men as Widow Quin comes.	two women's attitude Widow Quin gets Old Mahon into inner room to avoid the noisy crowd.
	enter to cheering	Widow Quin takes the iron spoon

	Christy and crowd	Widow warns Christy to swear Pegeen goes with crowd
Poetry of Christy	Pegeen and Christy Jealousy and Shawn	he makes her promise to swear
	Pegeen and Shawn	short comedy
	Christy crowd and all	oath in
	Old Mahon	pro⟨cess⟩

e. *In Notebook 34, several pages of possible curtain scenes, intermingled with rough scenario drafts (late spring, 1906 ?):*

Possible curtain ? ? ?
> Widow Quin holding Christy—
> Pegeen holding Old Mahon—
> One two three—(curtain)

Scenario
> Enter Jimmy and Philly in a hurry for a drink—to tell how Christy has carried all before him.
> Enter Old Mahon to them—to prepare for his entrance, develop his character and (?) make of drowning story.
> Exeunt Jimmy and Philly to race.
> Enter Widow Quin bothered
>> (a) she tries to get Old Mahon off
>> (b) race comes. He recognizes Christy
>> (c) she gets him away first to have on new rags and then up to climb the gable
>
> Exeunt
> Pegeen and Christy
> Plus Michael and Shawn
> Plus Crowd
> Plus Widow Quin who keeps telegraphing to Old Mahon in gable
> Plus Old Mahon
>> Climax Christy throws down Old Mahon
> He is bound

Possible curtain
> Christy ⟨is⟩ dragged away to (a) justice
>> (b) or set free by Widow Quin Old Mahon being really dead

> or (c) Old Mahon revives on stage and
> there is grotesque scene of
> the two of them on their
> knees

They shake hands on prodigiously fantastic treaty of amity and curtain on that.

Make Old Mahon come in (by Widow's advice ????????) as friendly as possible to bless the match because he sees that Christy has won the day, then to his surprise Pegeen flings him over, crowd dittos, and Old Mahon turns on him. Then as before.—

Old Mahon in gable when Michael James blesses them cries 'Amen. Oh Lord.'

Show collapse of Christy's genius in face of Old Mahon.

Widow Quin behind Christy and Pegeen behind Old Mahon throw their aprons over their heads to shut their blaspheming that would stink the nation.

Michael James (c) lifts up his hands and says—*quick curtain*

Tie them up in their aprons and run them out
Tie them together (motive)?
Michael. 'Well isn't the sports that Father Reilly and the Sergeant Brown do work upon the green little diversion at all besides looking on the gamey villains is all places walking the world.' *Curtain.*

B. FIRST DRAFTS

Synge appears to have set to work in earnest on his new play in the autumn of 1904, although none of his early typescripts are dated. He first contemplated a play in three acts, but by the time he had begun to write had moved to a plan in four acts. No draft of his original first act remains, however, and he moved back to the three-act form by draft 'B'.

ACT II MURDER WILL OUT

Scene: small country public house. Counter skew ways at right. Fire on left. Card table down right. Door centre. Benches etc.

PEGEEN, *bold big girl of about twenty-five, rural barmaid manners, is sweeping up the floor with homemade birch twig.*

SHAWN [*coming in shyly; abashed when he sees no one but herself*]. Where's himself?

PEGEEN [*bluntly*]. He's coming.

SHAWN. I didn't see him coming the road.

PEGEEN. What way would you see him, and it dark night. Have you the eyes of a cat?

SHAWN. I stood a bit outside wondering if I'd do right to pass, or walk in to see you, and there wasn't a step walking any place from this to the bridge.

PEGEEN. He's above at Tim Raftery's getting four men are going with him to the wake. [*Going up to him.*] So you're after standing outside wondering if you'd come in?

'Work up her fear of being left alone and through it marriage theme with Shawn.'

SHAWN. I am for two minutes or three.

PEGEEN. And why didn't you pass?

SHAWN. I'm after buying the wedding ring for the two of us and not paying a great sum at all.

PEGEEN. And we not getting married till after the new year? It's in a mighty hurry you are with your ring.

SHAWN. It's as well to have it. He said it wouldn't get rusty at all, I asked him that, if I keep it below in my breeches pocket.

PEGEEN. They're coming now. Sit down and don't be talking of the ring.

'Expand and link.'

[MICHEAL *and* MEN *come in.*]

MICHEAL. Sit down now for a bit and take your rest. It's early we are still.

PEGEEN. You'll be gone the whole night?

MICHEAL. Would you have me drowning myself walking home in the dark night and I after drinking a sup?

1ST MAN. The last wake we were at above we were coming home and himself saw a bog hole with the stars shining out of it, and he thought it was a house, and 'God save all here' says he, walking into it. [*The* MEN *all laugh.*]

PEGEEN. Shut your mouth, Timmy Farrell, when I'm asking what I'll do at all sitting lonesome in this place with no moon shining itself. I'll be shaking the bed trembling every time a dog runs round through the haggard.

2ND MAN. What is there to hurt you?

PEGEEN. Isn't there harvest boys with their tongues red hot for a drink? And isn't there tinkers in the east glen? And a thousand militia walking idle, bad cess to them, and they wicket lads would twist your neck as easy as I'd twisted the neck of the old moulting cock I sold last week to the priesteen, at Drumnamoe?

MICHEAL. Let Shawn stay with you, it's he has best right to be seeing after you now.

SHAWN [*covered with confusion*]. I would and welcome Micheal James, but I'm afeard of Father Reilly. What would he say at all if he heard I did the like of that?

MICHEAL. God help you! Can't you sit here in the shop with the lamp lit, and herself will be beyond in the room? You'll do that surely, for I'm minding now I seen a dark queer lad slinking and slinking beyond me in the ditch and I going for the lads.

SHAWN. Amn't I afeard of Father Reilly, I'm saying. Let you not be tempting me, and she your own daughter itself.

3RD MAN. Put a fetter of rope on him Micheal James, and tie him up to the butt of the house; he'll stay then and have no sin at all to be telling to the Priest.

MICHEAL. Throw me the bit of rope is beyond there at your hand.

[1ST MAN *flings it to him;* SHAWN *makes a comic rush out of the door and the* MEN *roar laughing.*]

2ND MAN. You'll have a fine honest man for your husband, Pegeen Mike, and you'll have no call to be spying after him, or holding him from the girls.

PEGEEN. You're an unbelieving heathen pack to be making game of poor lad for minding the priest. And it's his own the fault is [*pointing to her father*] for not paying a pot-boy to stand by me and give a hand with the work.

2ND MAN. Maybe the pot-boy'ld be fearing his reverence as well as Shawn Keogh?

PEGEEN. Sure the pot-boy'd be paid for it.

MAN. He would surely. I wasn't thinking of that.

[*The door opens a chink, and* SHAWN *puts in his head.*]

SHAWN [*in a frightened voice*]. Micheal James.

MICHEAL. What ails you?

SHAWN [*in a loud whisper*]. There's a queer black fellow beyond stretched in the ditch. He's one of the tinkers maybe is come stealing your hens.

MICHEAL. Did he see you coming back?

SHAWN [*looking over his shoulder*]. God help me he's here at my heels. [*He runs into the room, and goes over to the fire.*] And maybe he's heard what I said. Oh, glory he'll be having my life now and I walking home by myself.

[CHRISTY O'FLAHERTY *is seen in the door. Young man, very tired and frightened, and dirty, but more like a farmer than a tramp.*]

CHRISTY [*coming timidly, and looking round*]. God save all here.

MEN. God save you kindly.

CHRISTY [*taking out a penny, to* PEGEEN]. I'd trouble you for a glass of porter, woman of the house.

PEGEEN [*serving him*]. You're one of the tinkers, young fellow?

CHRISTY. I am not; but I'm destroyed travelling.

MICHEAL. Go up to the fire, you're shaking with the cold.

CHRISTY. God reward you. [*He goes over, and puts his glass near him at the fire. He looks at the* MEN, *and looks away, looks again fumbling with something in his pocket; turns his back on them and pulls out a white turnip, and begins to eat it eagerly.*]

MEN. What is it he's got?

1ST MAN [*tearing up a bit of paper and going over to the fire as if to light his pipe,* CHRISTY *wheels away from him, but* MAN *looks over his shoulder*]. God help us, he's eating a turnip.

MICHEAL [*taking a bit of bread*]. Maybe you're hungry, young fellow. It's hungry travelling.

CHRISTY. God reward you. [*He starts and looks towards the door.*] Is it often the police do be coming into this house, Mister?

MICHEAL. The polis? If you'd come in better hours you'd have seen 'licenced for the sale of beer and spirits to be consumed on the premises' above the door. What is it the polis would be wanting with me and not a house within four mile the way every living Christian is a bona fide.

CHRISTY. There's no offence, Master of the house?

MICHEAL. Why would there? [*Speaking lower.*] Is it for yourself you're fearing? You're wanting maybe?

CHRISTY [*with a certain pride*]. There's many wanting?

MICHEAL [*picking up odd stocking etc. from hearth*]. It's larceny I'm thinking.

CHRISTY [*bewildered*]. Larceny... I was thinking it was a different word, and a bigger... Larceny?

PEGEEN [*impatient with curiosity*]. Larceny's stealing, young fellow. Were you never in school, or the petty sessions itself?

CHRISTY [*with a despondent recollection*]. I'm slow at learning.

MICHEAL. If you are itself you've learned that much this day. Is it for stealing you're wanted?

CHRISTY [*with a sudden fury*]. Stealing is it? And I the son of a strong Limerick farmer [*with a sudden qualm*]—God rest his soul, could have bought up the whole of your old house from one of his pockets, and not have missed the weight of it gone.

MICHEAL [*much impressed*]. Maybe it's for something big.

CHRISTY [*encouraged at the impression he has*]. Ay, maybe it's for something big.

PEGEEN. Is it the girls you were after. You look wicket surely?

CHRISTY [*scandalized*]. Oh, the saints forbid.

2ND MAN. I'll tell you. He said his father was a farmer, and there's he now in a poor state. Maybe his farm was grabbed from him, and he did something that any decent lad would do.

MICHEAL [*making a movement as if shooting a gun*]. Was it landlords?

CHRISTY. Divil a one.

MICHEAL [*as before*]. Agents?

CHRISTY. Divil a one. . . . You'd see the like of that in any of the papers but I never heard tell of any person did the like of myself.

[MICHEAL *fills his glass and they all crowd round him with great curiosity. It must be made very plain that* CHRISTY *is continually growing in his own estimation as the interest in him increases.*]

3RD MAN. Did you marry two wives, young fellow. I'm told there's many have done that in the big world?

CHRISTY [*shyly*]. I was never married with one, let alone with two.

2ND MAN. Maybe he went fighting for the Boers the like of Colonel Lynch, God shield him, who was condemned a while back to be hanged quartered and drawn. Were you beyond in the wars, young fellow, you may tell it here, we're all safe men.

CHRISTY. I never left my own parish till yesterday was a week.

PEGEEN. He's done nothing at all. [*To* CHRISTY.] If you didn't commit murder, or a thing with women, or robbery, there isn't anything would be worth a man's while to run away from. You did nothing at all.

CHRISTY. That's not a kindly thing to be saying to a poor orphaned traveller, has a prison behind him, and hanging before, and hell's black gob yawning at his feet.

PEGEEN. You're only saying it. [*With a sign to the men.*] You did nothing at all. A poor soft lad the like of you wouldn't slit the throat on a pig.

CHRISTY. You're not speaking the truth.

PEGEEN. Not speaking the truth. . . You mouldy headed liar. . .

CHRISTY [*starting up*]. Liar? I killed my own father for saying the like of that.

MICHEAL. You killed your father?

CHRISTY. With the help of God, I did surely.

MEN [*drawing back to the door*]. He should be a dangerous fellow. Open the latch Timmy.

MICHEAL [*going behind the counter*]. That's a hanging crime, Mister. You should have had good reason?

CHRISTY. He was just turning crusty like, and he an old spare man the spit of him in the corner.

PEGEEN. And you shot him dead?

CHRISTY. I never used weapons, I've no licence, and I'm a God-fearing man.

MICHEAL. Then it was with a knife. I'm told beyond in the big world it's mostly knives they do use.

CHRISTY. Do you take me for a butcher's boy?

PEGEEN. You never hanged him the way Timmy Farrell hanged his dog a while since, and had it screeched and leaping for three hours at the tail of a string?

CHRISTY. I just riz the loy, and let fall the edge of it on the ridge of his skull, and he went down at my feet like an empty sack God spare his soul, and never let a groan or grunt from him at all.

1ST MAN. And you buried him then?

CHRISTY [*hesitates for a moment*]. I buried him then.

1ST MAN. And run from the place?

CHRISTY. I did surely.

MICHEAL. And didn't the peelers come after you the whole week that you're out?

CHRISTY. Not a one of them.

2ND MAN. Maybe they never came on the body.

CHRISTY. Maybe they didn't. It was among the spuds I buried him.

3RD MAN. If they found it itself I'm thinking they'd be afeard to come after him. Sure they never touched Lynchehaun when they knew the kind he was. It's only a common, week-day kind of a murderer them lads would lay their hands to at all.

CHRISTY [*expanding*]. It's true I seen two of them one night in Glencar, and when they seen me coming they put out their pipes and went in and hid in the ditch.

3RD MAN. Didn't I tell you?

3RD MAN [*to* MICHEAL]. Now if you had that lad in the house there isn't one of them not the sub-inspector himself, bad cess to his head, would come smelling round after the poteen you have hid in the dunghill behind the house.

MICHEAL. That's the truth maybe.

PEGEEN. We were saying a while back we were in need of a pot-boy and if you took that lad I'd never be afeard more of the harvest do come pulling my coats.

MICHEAL. Would you stay here a while and be pot-boy Mister, and we'll give you good food, and wages, and lodging and all a man could ask.

CHRISTY. And you're thinking I'd be safe from the polis?

PEGEEN. You would surely. Let you stay a short while anyhow. Sure you're destroyed walking.

CHRISTY. Well I will and thank you kindly.

1ST MAN [*jumping up*]. Well herself ⟨will be⟩ safe surely, this night thank God, with a man who killed his father minding the door. Come on now lads, or they'll have the best of the stuff drunk up at the wake.

PEGEEN. God speed ye, and see ye safe home.

MICHEAL *and* MEN. God protect you. [*They go out.*]

PEGEEN [*looking at* SHAWN KEOGH]. Are you not afeard to be sitting too late, Shawn Keogh? The Joeys will be out walking if you sit delaying like that.

SHAWN. Aren't you after saying you ⟨were⟩ wanting me to stop the whole night and keep you from harm?

PEGEEN. And didn't I hear you say you were fearing Father Reilly?

SHAWN. I've no fear to stay in it now, with himself in it too.

PEGEEN. You wouldn't stay when there was a need for you and walk now and good weather behind you.

SHAWN [*awkward and jealous*]. It's a lonesome place to leave a man the like of that with a young motherless girl.

PEGEEN. Isn't the like of him a fit man to keep a young girl safe from the militia or tinkers, or the polis itself?

SHAWN. Have you the bolt itself fixed on your door?

PEGEEN [*picking up a spade*]. I'll split your own skull with the loy, if you stand plaguing me here. [SHAWN *flies. She bolts the door.*]

CURTAIN

Succeeding drafts of this first act vary little in outline, Synge gradually lengthening it with a development of the discussion between Pegeen and Christy, and finally, with draft 'C', the introduction of the Widow Quin. (See below for the ballad-framework of draft 'E'.)

2. *The first extant draft to the second act is again altered to fit his four-act scheme. The draft ends suddenly, the last few speeches scribbled in by hand:*

a.

ACT III

Same scene. Morning. CHRISTY *behind counter cleaning glasses, clean, shaved, and bright.*

KITTY [*opens door softly*]. God save you, Mister.

CHRISTY. God save you.

KITTY. Is Pegeen within?

CHRISTY. She's after going up on the hill to search for the goats, the way she'd have a sup of goats' milk for my tea. Go up to the fire.

KITTY. I've heard the old people to say that goat's milk is the best of any milk for giving a good taste to your tea, and that any little sup of it is as good as a pint of the milk you'd get from the cow.

CHRISTY. It is maybe.

KITTY. Begging your pardon. Is it yourself is the man killed your father?

CHRISTY. I am surely.

KITTY. I'm the sister of Shawn Keogh was in here last night and it was he was telling me. He met five girls and told us all on the road and he going home last night.

CHRISTY. No, did he?

KITTY [*a little awkwardly*]. Are you fond of fresh duck eggs, Mister?

CHRISTY. I am maybe.

KITTY. I'm after bringing up two of them, thinking you'd like them maybe for your breakfast. [*Shows eggs.*] Pegeen's ducks is no good, and these should be the real rich sort for we bought the ducks of a tinker had them of a farmer who had them straight from the Department. Did ever you see eggs the size of that Mister in your own county?

CHRISTY. I'm not minding whether I did or not. I've other things than the like of that to be filling my mind.

KITTY. You have surely, God bless you. [*Looking into the teapot.*] Is she after wetting the tea?

CHRISTY. She is I'm thinking. [*He looks out of the window.*]

KITTY. Well I'll just put down the eggs in the saucepan the way they'll be handy the time the milk will come. [*She puts eggs into saucepan, and puts it by the fire.*]

[SUSAN BLAKENEY *comes in.*]

SUSAN. Is Pegeen within.

CHRISTY. She's coming now. Go up to the fire.

SUSAN [*whispering to* KITTY]. Is that himself?

[KITTY *nods.*]

SUSAN [*opening her shawl*]. My mother's after churning this morning Mister, and I was thinking maybe if Pegeen had no fresh butter for your breakfast—she⟨'s⟩ a poor hand with a house—I'd have a right to bring up a small bit for you. It'd be a bad thing to have you eating your bread dry in this parish, and you after travelling a long way since the beginning of the week.

CHRISTY. Thank you kindly.

ELLEN [*coming in*]. Is Pegeen within?

CHRISTY. She⟨'s⟩ coming; go up to the fire.

[ELLEN *going to fire, she takes something from her pocket, and shows it to the girls, they begin to giggle.*]

CHRISTY. You've great joking this day, God bless you.

KITTY. She's after bringing a book Mister.

CHRISTY. Well God bless her.

SUSAN. She says she's thinking you don't know rightly the real name for the thing you did, and Pegeen Mike's a poor innocent girl God help her, could never tell you at all.

CHRISTY. And what is the word.

ELLEN. I'm after going down this morning, and loaning the word book from the master's wife. Oh, a queer book, Mister, with all words in it, the good ones and the bad. [*Holds out the book.*] I'm after finding it, and there it is now, but it's a hard word to say.

[CHRISTY *comes over and takes the book, and sits down beside the* GIRLS.]

CHRISTY. It's a hard long word, God help me, and I'm slow at learning.

SUSAN. Glory be to God, Kitty Kinsella are you boiling the eggs into stones. Have you no shame to be destroying his stomach and he with a great weight on his mind. [*They whip out the eggs.*]

KITTY. You'd have a right to begin your breakfast with what you have, Mister, God knows but Pegeen'll be the whole ⟨day⟩ above running her goats, and leaving ⟨you⟩ near starving itself.

CHRISTY. Well I will.

[*They give him breakfast, with great eagerness.*]

ELLEN [*after the* GIRLS *have whispered together*]. The girls is very eager, Mister, that you'd tell them the way it was done.

CHRISTY. And why wouldn't they?

SUSAN. Tell us now *a gradh*, I never seen a man before who killed his father.

ELLEN. It's in the lonesomest wildest bit of country you'd see anyplace, that we do live Mister, the way it's little we hear or see at all of the wonders of the world.

KITTY. Tell us now, Mister. We're all safe girls.

CHRISTY [*with gusto*]. 'You're a liar,' says he. 'I'm not,' says I. 'I'm saying, you're a liar, Christy,' says he, 'with the oath of God'. And with that I riz the loy and hit him a blow with it on the ridge of his skull had him split to the chin. . . .

ELLEN. You're a great terror, God forgive you, and it's no lie.

KITTY. Would you do the like of that if you had a wife?

CHRISTY [*looking from one to the other with dawning admiration, and surprise at himself*]. My wife'd want to mind.

SUSAN. Maybe you've a wife already beyond in the south.

CHRISTY. If I have itself I'm thinking it's a new one I'll be needing now.

ELLEN [*pushing* KITTY *forward*]. There's a girl Mister is wanting to wed.

[CHRISTY *catches her by the shawl and pulls her into his arms just as the door opens, and* PEGEEN *comes in. She stands aghast on the door step, for a moment. The* GIRLS *huddle together covering their mouths with their shawls.*]

PEGEEN [*taking up the loy, to* KITTY]. Are you wanting anything?

KITTY [*doubtfully*]. Me father was asking an ounce of tobacco.

PEGEEN. Have you tuppence?

KITTY. I've forgotten my purse.

PEGEEN. Walk off then and get it, and don't be fooling us here.

[KITTY *goes.*]

PEGEEN [*to* SUSAN]. And what is it you're wanting.

SUSAN [*looking innocent*]. A pen'orth of starch.

PEGEEN [*breaking out*]. I'll starch you, and you without a white shift or a shirt in your whole family. Get along now the pack of you, or you'll have me splitting your skulls.

> [GIRLS *run off.* PEGEEN *busies herself about the house without speaking to* CHRISTY.]

CHRISTY [*after a moment, very uneasily picking up a loy and sharpening the edge*]. It was with a loy the like of that I killed my father. 'You're a liar,' says he,

PEGEEN [*interrupting him*]. You've told me that story six times since the dawn of day.

CHRISTY. It's a queer thing you wouldn't care to be hearing it and those poor girls after walking four miles to hear it, since the sun went up

PEGEEN [*astonished*]. Four miles? ? ?

CHRISTY [*apologetically*]. Didn't himself say there was only bona fide living in the parish?

PEGEEN [*laughing*]. Oh, glory. . . . It's bona fides by the road they are but the like of them comes over the river lepping the stones. . . . It' not five perches when you come like that.

CHRISTY. Is that the truth?

CHRISTY. And did the white lad was talking with you when I com last night go home by the stones?

PEGEEN [*bitterly*]. He does be afeard to lep when the night's down s he takes off his boots and walks through groping with his stick lik a blind man in a bog.

CHRISTY. He should be an innocent fellow. That man's father nee have no fear in him at all.

PEGEEN. He hasn't surely.

CHRISTY [*finding the ring*]. Here's a wedding ring, Pegeen Mike, is to yourself it does belong?

PEGEEN. Give it here to me.

CHRISTY [*screwing up his courage*]. I won't.

PEGEEN [*changing her tone*]. That's for my own wedding, Christy Flaherty. Are you good at all, at dancing? There'll be fine music.

CHRISTY [*crestfallen*]. And with who will you be wed?

PEGEEN [*watching him closely*]. With Shawn Keogh—the lad you seen.

CHRISTY. He has great fortune.

PEGEEN. Were there many young girls you did be thinking on, beyond where you did the deed?

CHRISTY [*with a great effort to play his part*]. I didn't ever count them. [*Then he falls back with relief to his early voice.*] I'm slow at reckoning.

PEGEEN. What'll they be saying now you're after going away from them, and you a great fellow will be the talk of the world, for if you're hanged itself we'll be seeing your name on all the big papers of the country and the city of Dublin.

CHRISTY [*with a qualm at the thought*]. Oh, if they see that Pegeen they'll be crying tears down. If I'm hanged, I'm saying, there'll be noise and a·lamentation you wouldn't pass in the pig fair of Rathmuck.

PEGEEN [*putting her apron to her eyes*]. It'd be a sad end surely for a fine handsome lad the like of you.

CHRISTY [*goes over to her, overcome by her sympathy*]. It'd be a sad day, Pegeen Mike, and it's no lie.

PEGEEN [*sobbing*]. It'd make the grey stones cry to think of you swinging east and west like a shirt on a bush. [*She pats him on the neck.*] And you with a fine strong neck, God bless you, the way it's likely it's near a half an hour you'll be in great agony getting your death.

CHRISTY [*clinging to her neck*]. Oh, wasn't my poor mother a wicket woman to bring me to the world.

[SHAWN *comes in unseen.*]

PEGEEN. If she seen you this day, she'd have great joy at the sight of you, a lovely white soft boy the like of you.

[SHAWN *drops the loy on the ground to draw their attention.* CHRISTY *and* PEGEEN *run right and left both drying their eyes.*]

SHAWN. You're taking on God help yous.

PEGEEN [*looks at him sharply*]. Did you not see me weeping in his arms, Shawn Keogh?

SHAWN. I did surely.

PEGEEN. And don't you want to strike him.

[SHAWN *makes anxious signs to her to stop.*]

PEGEEN. Will you not say a word after seeing me sobbing my soul out in the strong arms of a man?

SHAWN. I'm thinking he's strong surely.

PEGEEN [*looking at him, more and more dubiously*]. It's mighty flat a woman'd be and she married with the like of you.

SHAWN. Is that the truth?

PEGEEN [*going up to him*]. You're a heartless villain, Shawn Keogh, to see me there the like of that and not say a word. Have you no shame at all.

.SHAWN [*penitently*].

b. *The next draft of this scene develops the dialogue but does not significantly alter the action. It does, however, provide the following scene continuing the action of the preceding draft:*

SHAWN [*makes violent signs to her to be quiet*]. Would you have me killed and yourself left a kind of a widow woman and you not married at all?

PEGEEN. I⟨'m⟩ hard set to know what I want but I'm saying you've good call to be jealous. What else would make a man jealous than to see his woman crying out her soul in the strong arms of a man?

SHAWN. Let you not be raising your voice.

PEGEEN. You seen me in his arms, I'm saying, and if you don't go and hit him a lick I won't wed you at all.

SHAWN [*going over timidly to* CHRISTY]. Sure you won't strike me with the loy, Mister, I'm a quiet man.

CHRISTY [*getting round behind a chair*]. If you are you'd better keep off from me. . . . Let you bear in mind the lick I hit my father had him split to the navel.

SHAWN [*piteously to* PEGEEN]. Do you hear that, Pegeen Mike. Would you have ⟨me⟩ destroyed and you with the rings bought and your white clothes stitched in the cupboard.

PEGEEN. I'm thinking I'd be mighty flat and I married with the like of you. Let you strike him now, I'm saying or I won't wed you at all.

[SHAWN *comes forward again, and* CHRISTY *takes up the spade.* SHAWN *runs round behind* PEGEEN. PEGEEN *makes a sign to* CHRISTY *to put him out, he chases* SHAWN, SHAWN *runs out of the door colliding with* MICHEAL JAMES, *recoils into* CHRISTY *who drops* ⟨*the spade.*⟩ *They run opposite ways* SHAWN *out,* CHRISTY *in.*]

   c. *The third draft of this act, entitled 'Murder Will Out (A)', finally provides a curtain scene, apparently still an afterthought:*

(END OF ACT II)

[PEGEEN *and* CHRISTY. *To them* MICHEAL JAMES *and* MEN.]

MICHEAL. The blessing of God on you, and what way have you been?

PEGEEN. Grand.

MICHEAL. We're after getting you a grand job young fellow, and making you the bosheen of a co-operative pig-sticking business is starting in the town.

PEGEEN. What are you after doing that for when we're needing him here as pot-boy in the house.

MICHEAL. Sure the days is short and he'll only be pig-sticking below by the light of Heaven and when that work's done on him, he can walk up here and be pot-boy when the night is come, and there are men in it drinking and talking with their friends.

CHRISTY. And what ⟨way⟩ was it you got that job for the like of me?

MICHEAL. The Ryans and the Cullens were both wanting it for themselves, and Father Reilly was in dread that there'd be spilling blood this night on the highways of the land if we gave it to one or the other. Then up I get on my two feet and they shaky as they were, and so says I, 'There's a man above of great courage and he with great knowledge of the world. It's him you should have.' Then the Ryans said we'd have a right to take ⟨him⟩, and they fearing the Cullens ⟨and the Cullens⟩ said we'd have a right to take him, and they fearing the Ryans, and Father Reilly said we'd have a right to take him, and he fearing the shedding out of Christ⟨ian⟩ blood till it'd be running down red streams into the bog. So what did they ⟨do⟩ but make yourself the Master Pigsticker of this townland.

PHILLY. You see now Pegeen Mike the great wicketness of drink, for if he'd been a sober sensible man he⟨'d⟩ have maybe got the job for Shawn Keogh and then you'd have had great wages till the day of your death.

PEGEEN. Who's talking of me marrying Shawn Keogh? It's that man I'll marry at the turn of the year.

MICHEAL [*looking at him a little dubiously*]. Whisper now, young fellow, is there no fear of your doing the like with your father-in-law as you did with your father in the natural life.

CHRISTY. I will not Mister sure you're a quiet man.

MICHEAL. Then the blessing of God be on you both. . . .

CURTAIN

At least two more complete drafts retained this engagement scene in Act II, until finally with the development of the Widow Quin and the entrance of Old Mahon, sheer bulk of material forced it into the next act.

3. *After it became apparent that Michael's return and the engagement scene would have to be pushed ahead to Act III, Synge simply transposed the scene given below, striking out the page numbers (30–32 of Act II) and renumbering them (pp. 2–4), leaving the opening page to be devised later.*

a. *Untitled first draft of opening for Act III:*

PEGEEN [*looking from door*]. There's the whole of them now mounting the lane. Himself and Timmy and Philly O'Cullen, and who's that? Ay. It's Shawn with them. [*Turns to* CHRISTY.] What do you think of that lad, Christy Flaherty?

CHRISTY. What would I think?

PEGEEN. The Lord knows, but I'm thinking ⟨if⟩ you don't mind he'll be attempting to wed myself from under your nose, God help you, and I'm thinking you wouldn't be pleased at all to see him do the like of that?

CHRISTY [*troubled*]. And you'd marry the like of him, and myself this half a day living at your side?

PEGEEN. He's a strong wealthy farmer.

CHRISTY. Oh, glory. What at all will I be doing now?

PEGEEN. You'd think well to wed myself and be living all your days here with ourselves?

CHRISTY. I would surely.

PEGEEN. Well I'm thinking if you put the fear of death into that lad he'd never come near to me again. ⟨You⟩ seen last night the way he run off from the door.

CHRISTY. I did surely.

PEGEEN. We'll be hard set to gain my Pa. But if we are itself he should be soft bendy this day and he after passing his whole night at a wake.

CHRISTY. Fathers is a bad lot, God help us.

[*There is a noise at the door and crowd comes in.*]

MICHAEL [*half drunk*]. God save every one of you. [*Goes to* CHRISTY *and shakes his hand.*] The blessing of God and the holy apostles on your arm and head young fellow. Is it good sleep and rest you've had since I left you resting at the fall of night. It was a bloody shame I'm thinking I didn't lead you over to the wake—the⟨re's not⟩ a place in ⟨the⟩ whole world would you see the like of the drink—and laid out Kate Cassidy this morning in her narrow grave. There were four men and five men and six men lying speechless on the holy stones. Isn't it a bloody shame I'm saying you didn't lay your poor father over an ass and drive him into this place over land and sea the way we could have given him a Christian wake, and not have him buried beyond and he lying naked in the wormy earth like the way the polis do be burying the fevered swine.

CHRISTY [*embarrassed*]. You should have had good drinking beyond to have the whole host ⟨of⟩ peelers is walking Ireland slipped out of your mind. Wouldn't I look well driving through the walled cities with my murdered pa?

MICHAEL [*shaking him with maudlin humour*]. Come on you father slayer. Come on here you head-splitting grave-digging murder-man till I show you the fine lad I'm after getting for a husband for that lonesome girl. [*He drags* CHRISTY *over to the side of* SHAWN.] Look on that lad now young fellow. Isn't that a fine boy and he with sheeps and yearlings ⟨and⟩ a brace of bursting swine.

b. *The lettering 'A' to this draft is confusing, especially as it bears the marginal note* 'C to work with C version'. *It is possible that Synge first intended to write Act III in two scenes, the 'A' therefore referring to Scene 1, for the corresponding 'Act III (B)' continues the action from where this draft leaves off:*

ACT III (A)

Same scene. Half an hour later. PEGEEN *is heard laughing outside then she enters in high spirits followed by* CHRISTY *grinning from ear to ear.*

PEGEEN. Well you're worth two sheepdogs young fellow any hour of the year. I never seen the like of you till this day for lepping a gap. [*Ha ha ha.*] You're a wonder surely.

CHRISTY [*excited and hilarious*]. It's not the first time I've been lepping a gap. [*He sits down and watches her with delight.*] You'll find there's few things I'm telling you I'm not fit to lick all the common lot is walking the world.

PEGEEN. That's the truth I'm thinking, and it's great times you'll have here with the running of hare and the watching for wrack, and you should be grand dancing I'm thinking on a holy night.

CHRISTY. I am surely, or if I amn't itself it's not long till I will be and living in a place the like of this, with grand civil girls and flat earth and no soul troubling you at all.

PEGEEN. You're liking this place I'm thinking?

CHRISTY [*with a cry*]. Liking is it, and I ready to sink upon my bended knees, and say my prayers and paters to every jackstraw you have roofing your head, and every stony pebble is paving the laneway to your door.

PEGEEN. Wasn't I saying at the fall of night it was the like of a poet you were surely?

CHRISTY. Who is there wouldn't be the like of a poet and he after running through the heathers and green ferns at the side of yourself with the honey smells circling his feet and bees stirring all roads in your sight?

PEGEEN. Shawn Keogh never talked to me the like of that although it's him they're saying I should wed.

CHRISTY. Wouldn't you think wise to be wedding myself if you're taking kindly to my airy words, and you setting great store on a man would have the savagery to destroy his Pa.

PEGEEN. Isn't it hard set a young girl is to know what man she'd have?

CHRISTY. The sorra hard or trouble you'll have this day if you'll heed to my words, for if that lad comes walking round I'll put a fear of death in him will drive him this day from your sight.

PEGEEN. You'd be good company I'm thinking surely, and if you're hanged itself it'd be a great sight to see my own name printed out in the big papers the quality read.

CHRISTY. Well now let you give me your aid when that lot comes— I hear them mounting the lane—and before the fall of night I'll have you promised for my ward and wife.

[*Bustle outside, then* MICHAEL *comes in leaning on* SHAWN, *& followed by* MEN *as before.*]

MICHAEL [*hilariously to* CHRISTY, *while* PEGEEN *talks with* SHAWN]. The blessing of God and the holy angels on your hand and head young fellow. [*He takes* CHRISTY *by the hand and shakes it with maudlin cordiality.*] And is it good rest you're after having since I left you dozing at the fall of night?

CHRISTY. The grandest surely.

MICHAEL. I was thinking beyond it was a bloody shame I didn't lead you along with me to Kate Cassidy's wake—oh, it was a lovely wake—a wake you'd never see the like of for the flows of drink, the way when we got her into her grave there were four men and five men, and six men I'm thinking lying speechless on the holy stones.

CHRISTY. That should have been a fine sight surely.

MICHAEL [*slapping him on the back*]. And yourself's the bloody schemer to go burying your poor Pa unbeknownst, and you had a good right to lay him across an ass and drive him into this place over land and sea, the way we could have given him a Christian wake, and not have him lying naked beyond in the wormy earth and not a prayer said for his soul.

CHRISTY. I'd look well I'm thinking driving through the Saxon cities with me murdered Pa?

MICHAEL. Ah ha you hardened slayer. It'll be a bad day for the old men in the house where you'll go courting a wife. Look beyond see the quiet easy lad I've chosen this day for my daughter's man.

CHRISTY. You've fixed and promised that she'd wed the like of him?

MICHAEL. Fixed and promised in the name of God. Is it a fool you think me young fellow to leave her living single in the house with a little flighty rascal is the like of you?

PEGEEN [*coming across to them*]. Is it the truth Shawn Keogh is saying that I'm promised to the likes of him?

MICHAEL. It is surely and give thanks to God.

[CHRISTY *walks over near* SHAWN, *and* SHAWN *to avoid him walks back to others.*]

PEGEEN [*to* SHAWN]. You'd a right to come in this morning early Shawn Keogh to hear the talk I had with that lad from the dawn of day, he's ⟨a⟩ lovely lad I'm telling you to be talking to a girl.

[CHRISTY *comes over again and* SHAWN *edges away from him.*]

SHAWN. He should be God help him.

PEGEEN. It was great talk he made of love and kissing and fine courting praises of my hair and voice.

SHAWN. It wasn't lies he was telling if he praised you surely.

PEGEEN. And he rose up his strong arm that killed his father a while since and threw it round on my neck. You never in this place seen the like of him for talking love.

SHAWN. Is that the truth?

PEGEEN. Isn't it a bitter thing for a poor girl the like of me to be wed to yourself and you with no bravery, or fine words in you at all.

SHAWN [*meekly*]. It is maybe.

PEGEEN. And is that the best you have to say to me, my plighted day?

SHAWN. My father's after promising a drift of ewes.

PEGEEN. Ewes, is it? Well a woman would be mighty flat I'm thinking and she wedded with the likes of you.

CHRISTY [*coming up to them*]. Wouldn't you do better to wed with a man the like of me that sliced down his Pa to the belt, and then you'd be thinking all days on the young girls below are envying your luck.

PEGEEN. Do you hear that talking, Shawn Keogh? You'll have good call I'm thinking to be growing jealous of him soon.

SHAWN [*in a loud whisper*]. Will you be quiet Pegeen Mike. Would you have me vexing a man that killed his Pa?

PEGEEN. What do I care who you'd vex?

SHAWN. Would you have yourself left a kind of a widow woman and you not wedded at all?

CHRISTY. How would she be a widow and myself left walking the world?

PEGEEN. Now you're hearing him, Shawn Keogh, and have you no wish to rise up and strike him at all.

SHAWN. Who is there in the whole world would dare be jealous of him when he's killed his Pa?

PEGEEN. Well you're a heartless villain Shawn Keogh, and if you don't lift up and strike him a lick I'll not wed you for all the sheep and cattle you'd meet walking to the Crossmolina fair.

SHAWN. With what will I strike him?

PEGEEN. There's a spade at your west.

SHAWN. I'd hurt him maybe, and where'd I hide me from the peelers then?

CHRISTY. Well if you daren't strike me let you clear off from us now.

[*He takes up a loy or something of the kind.* MICHAEL *rouses up.*]

MICHAEL. What in glory are yous doing here? Are you going to commit murder in this house young fellow and have it written down on my licence that there was homicide made in my bar? If yous want to fight go down there on the seashore where the tide's out there⟨'s⟩ a grand hard floor for your feet, and if you bleed him itself there'll be the tide coming in a short while to wash out the red drops from the sand.

SHAWN. I'm not asking to fight.

MICHAEL. Well go along from this house, and don't be tormenting us won't we see a sight too much of you when you're wedded with herself?

[*He hustles* SHAWN *out of the door,* CHRISTY *stands doubtfully for an instant.*]

PEGEEN [*to him*]. Well young fellow aren't ⟨you going⟩ down to talk to him below and see which one of yous is going to be master in this house?

CHRISTY. I am surely. [*He runs out.*]

PEGEEN [*looking from window*]. Well I never knew till this day Shawn was that supple on his ⟨feet,⟩ look look, will you, on him lepping the ditch?

MICHAEL. Isn't the young lad a divil to run. Begob he'll be up with him now . . . . Oh, glory . . . .

PEGEEN. Whisht . . . Whisht . . . . There's Shawn giving one lep over the high wall into ⟨the⟩ green bed of the Minister's geraniums. That's a cowardly kind of a lad and I'll not wed with him at all.

MICHAEL. Who'll you wed?

PEGEEN. That young fellow I'll put on my shawl now and walk down and ask Father Reilly will he wed us in two weeks or three. . . .

MICHAEL. And he a young lad without a copper farthing at all. You're raving mad I'm thinking.

PEGEEN. He'll be a great man for a publican, and there'll be all sorts coming here to be talking to him now. And whether there is or not it's him I'll wed.

MICHAEL. You'll not surely. . . .

PEGEEN [*going out*]. Wait till you see, I'm telling you. Wait till you see. [*Goes.*]

MICHAEL. That'll be a dangerous fellow to have in the house. And it's great mastery they'll be taking upon me. God help me, and ⟨I'd⟩ do right maybe to slip out and bury the loy. [*He takes it up.*]

CURTAIN

c. *This is the first draft of the concluding scenes of the final act; it seems likely that this setting, outside the chapel, occurred to Synge when he was still contemplating a four-act (or four-scene) scheme, and is based on a rough draft in Notebook 32:*

MURDER WILL OUT. ACT III ⟨(B)⟩

Scene: outside chapel. PHILLY CULLEN, TIMMY FARRELL, SHAWN KEOGH, GIRLS *and others standing about.*

TIMMY FARRELL. He's a fine day for his marriage, and it after raining a week . . . . It's easy seen himself's a lucky man.   'John Doyle's'

PHILLY. He'll be getting rightly hobbled yet I'm thinking for he can't talk half an hour with man woman or child without making a boast of the great blow he hit with the loy.

TIMMY. Isn't it in law a man can't hang by his own informing—which would ⟨be⟩ self-destruction and contrary to scripture—and I'm thinking his father's rotten by now.

[OLD F. *seen on left.*]

TIMMY. He should be, but suppose some day there's a man digging spuds in that garden with a long spade. And supposing he flings up the two halves of that skull what'll be said then in the papers of Ireland and the courts of Law? Tell me that?

TIMMY. Wouldn't they say it was a skull of the Danes or of the old sinful heathens were drowned in the flood. Did you never hear of the big dressers they have in the city of Dublin with skulls ranged on them the same as you'd see blue jugs in any cabin of Connaught?

PHILLY. And you believe that, Timmy Farrell? You're a simple man.

TIMMY [*defiantly*]. Didn't a man in the parish of Knock-Na-Lee see them and he after coming home from harvesting in the Liverpool boat? There were white skulls says he, and black skulls, yellow skulls and some had full teeth in them, and some hadn't only but one.

OLD F. [*coming forward*]. It's in the old times there were fine skulls surely, and I'm thinking they have them there the way they have horse shows and cattle shows to let all people see what is good. And there's one thing I'm telling you there isn't any man in Ireland under fifty or three score maybe with a decent stubborn skull on him.

PHILLY. What does the like of you know about skulls? You're a sexton maybe. . . . He's telling the truth maybe. I'm minding when I was a young lad there was a graveyard beyond the house, and there was the bones in it of a big terrible man with thigh-bones as long as your arm. Oh, he was a horrid man I'm telling you, and there's many a fine Sunday I put him together for fun.

OLD F. I've as good bones myself as any man in all the countries of the world, though to look on me, you'd think maybe I was only a tramp.

TIMMY. And what else are you.

OLD F. I'm evicted for debt.

PHILLY. That should be a great misfortune on an old man.

OLD F. I've worse still than that. [*He takes off his hat and shows his cracked skull.*] Do you see that?

TIMMY. You fought with the bailiffs?

OLD F. What misfortune would that be to have a little blow from a bailiff.

PHILLY. Who was it did it?

OLD F. [*with great unction*]. My own son.

PHILLY. Is that the truth?

OLD F. You may believe that and if it wasn't that I've a grand strong skull on me I'd have been buried this long while.

TIMMY. And what became of the villain. Did you take the law of him?

OLD F. I broke every bone in his body. He's not expected, God pardon his sins.

TIMMY. Have you left him lying in the Union?

OLD F. He's after crawling away to die in the hills like a wounded cat.

PHILLY. Well there's great doings in Ireland a while back and it's no lie, what with our own man and this man, and the slaying of pigs.

[*They talk* R. CHRISTY *and* PEGEEN *dressed for a wedding come in* L. *with crowd and the girls of Act I.* MICHEAL JAMES *comes to chapel door.*]

MICHEAL. Welcome to you the priest's waiting inside.

CHRISTY. We're coming now. [*He stops.*]

SALLY. Well you've been a lucky man Christy Sheehan and it's that is the truth with your making money at pig-slaying and your marrying into a rich licensed house. You'll have a great life and I'm thinking it's only what you've a right to. You're a strong masterful man God bless you.

CHRISTY [*excited and puffed up*]. The blessing of God on you Sally Quin. And if I wasn't marrying Pegeen herself there isn't one I'd liefer marry than you. [*Laughter.*]

NELL. He's a free-spoken jolly-tongued man, and Pegeen'll have great company now.

[SHAWN *comes down* R. *and talks with* OLD FLAHERTY *in dumb show. Presently* OLD F. *takes off his hat and shows* SHAWN *his wound with the gestures as before.*]

PHILLY. Well it's few would think killing your father would on such luck upon a man.

CHRISTY. It wouldn't maybe on all. But it was a great terrible hit that split him to the navel, and it's men with great power have the luck of ⟨the⟩ world with women and the world.

OLD F. [*coming forward*]. You're a bloody liar.

CHRISTY [*aghast*]. God help us. . . .

OLD F. Ah, you lousy looking cur is ⟨it⟩ letting on you were, you had me tombed in the spuds? Is it after deceiving this parish you are with your blather and lies?

CHRISTY. And who was it mended your head?

OLD F. What mend⟨ing⟩ do I want for a little bruise the like of that [*showing his head*]. Isn't it a useless fool you are when you can't break an old man's head and you striking down with a loy.

PEGEEN [*almost speechless with rage, to* CHRISTY]. And it was lies you told us of slaying him and making his grave in the spuds?

CHRISTY. I struck the blow.

PEGEEN [*examining* F's *skull*]. I could have struck a better blow than that with one hand of my own.

CHRISTY [*trying to laugh it off*]. Well it's pleased you should be we can wed now in peace and quietness, and not have me getting red or white in ⟨the⟩ face when a man speaks of the gallows all the days of my life.

PEGEEN. Who's talking of being wed? Do you think I'll wed you now, and you after coming round with your big talk and taking in a poor motherless girl?

SHAWN [*triumphantly*]. Ah, you were easy fooled, Pegeen Mike, to be setting such store on his like.

PEGEEN. If it's easy fooled I was he'll pay for it now, I'm telling you for I'll drive him off from this parish and his luck and his pig-sticking will be turned on him from this hour till the judgement day.

SHAWN. It's the truth you're saying now, and you'd have a right to marry myself and not have them all making game of you and you going home single with your new dress on you, and the fine linen clothes I seen you stitching above.

CHRISTY. Hold your talk Shawn Keogh, if I missed one blow with the loy maybe I'll live to hit another will be stronger with the blessing of God.

SHAWN [*bridling up to him*]. Get along you impostor. Who is it will give heed to you now, and you after hitting that little blow, and then running off with your stomach turned with the fear?

CHRISTY [*looking from one to the other, with despair*]. And is that the end I'm having after three months of great doings in the world.

'Make old F. have bandaged head and show himself off by getting the people to peep under the ⟨linen⟩.'

CHRISTY. Will you have no thought of me this day Pegeen Mike, and of all ⟨the⟩ grand talking we've had above in the evening and the morning on the brow of the hill. Sure you won't turn from me this day, and drive me off wandering the world?

PEGEEN. How would I wed with a man would tell me that long story of lies? There is no decent girl I'm thinking on the face of Ireland would marry a man who is a liar. I'm a God-fearing girl I'd have you know and I wouldn't do the like of that, not if you were an angel of the Almighty God.

SALLY QUIN. You'd have a right to marry the old man who's neither done a murder nor told a lie, and then you can keep the young lad for your son.

SHAWN. It's myself she'll marry and let you not be making a noise with your talk. [*He looks up centre.*] There's Father Reilly now coming down into the church. [*He takes* PEGEEN *by the arm.*] Let you come on now and be wedded to myself.

PEGEEN [*looking at him uncertainly*]. You're not dressed for a wedding, with that old hat on you, and a raggedy coat.

SHAWN. If bad dressed I have money to buy what I'm wanting below in the fair, where they've a grand clothes stall, and two Jews selling the finest clothing of the world.

OLD F. I'll give you his coat and hat, for five shillings if you have the money in your purse.

SHAWN. I have surely. [*He goes up to* CHRISTY.] Give me your hat and your coat.

CHRISTY [*his courage oozing away*]. I won't.

OLD F. You won't is it? Strip off now or I'll get you ten years beyond hard-labouring in the English jails.

CHRISTY. Would you have me lose the fine job I have in co-operative pig-sticking?

TIMMY [*with triumphant malice*]. Divil a pig more will you stick in this parish, me boy-o, a lying frothy fool the like of you.

SUSAN. Strip off his coat Shawn Keogh, and send him off to the Soupers of Achill. We won't put up with the like of him at all.

OLD F. [*to* CHRISTY *threateningly*]. Do you hear me speaking to you. Let you give up your old coat and hat.

[CHRISTY *strips off his coat and hat while* SHAWN *gives* OLD F. *money.* SHAWN *puts on* CHRISTY's *clothes and* CHRISTY *half-dazed puts on* SHAWN's.]

MICHEAL JAMES. Come along now, and let you not keep Father Reilly waiting. He'd not ⟨be⟩ pleased if we kept him waiting in a God-fearing parish the like of Kilamuck.

PEGEEN. Let you come on Shawn Keogh. [*They turn up into the church noisily.*]

OLD F. [*watches them into the chapel then turns to* CHRISTY *who is standing bewildered C.*]. Come on now, till I pay you for your lies come on now I'm saying.

'Christy relapses into the sleepy fool of Act I and Old F. drives him out.'

d. *Synge then rewrote these final scenes outside the chapel, expanding the dialogue but not significantly altering the action. The final six pages of the draft ('Act III B') below appear to be the first plan for the exits of Christy and his father. The action continues where the draft above left off:*

[*They all go into chapel except* OLD F., CHRISTY, *and* SALLY QUIN. CHRISTY *without coat or hat.*]

OLD F. [*shaking his stick*]. Now the day of quitment has been sent from God. Now you'll get your wages for your demon doings in the north and south.

CHRISTY [*slinking round behind* SALLY]. May God help and pity me this dreadful day.

OLD F. Let you not be tormenting the Lord God. Would you have him sending down droughts and big winds, and the blight on the spuds and typhus and typhoid, and the 'ould hin', and the Cholera Morbus?

CHRISTY. What'll I do at all from this day if I can't say my prayers out itself without bringing torment on me head?

OLD F. Come along I'm saying till I work the evil from your heart.

CHRISTY. Oh, Sally Quin for the love of God protect ⟨me⟩ from his hands. What did I ever do that I should have him badgering, and badgering round as if I was an evil person or a son of hell.

OLD F. Doesn't the whole world know you're a poor good for nothing and isn't it by the likes of you that the sins of the whole world are committed. Didn't the divil himself lay his mark on you the day you were born the way yourself or me would put a black mark on the thighs of a lamb?

CHRISTY. Oh, Sally Quin for the love of Heaven won't you step out between the two of us now?

SALLY QUIN. What would you have me do for you at all?

CHRISTY. Let you not have me sent out this day to be a lonesome poor tramper on the face of the world, walking from Union to Union with the ground white and hard to my feet, and the old lad pacing behind me the way the lost spirits do be following and following the saints of God.

SALLY. How would I stop him?

CHRISTY. Couldn't you wed me maybe, and take me to live in your house the way I'd have a strong door to lock against my father's gob.

OLD F. Did ever any hear the like of that? You that'd have run a while since from the fringe of a shawl?

CHRISTY [*not minding him*]. Oh, let you wed me Widow Quin for the love and kindness of the holy Christy. And you'll have me there toiling and moiling for your kindly sake, cutting reaping sowing by the stars of Heaven's light, cleaning your floor, combing your hair— the way I combed Pegeen above—if it's an ugly woman that you are itself.

SALLY. Do you hear that talk Mr. Flaherty from the lad you said a while since had no voice in him at all?

OLD F. [*looking at him inquiringly*]. What ails him?

CHRISTY. Wasn't I three weeks thinking you dead?

SALLY. The thought of you rotting beyond put heart and soul into his limbs.

OLD F. If it did let the knowledge of my life destroy him now. [*Threatens him again.*] Come on now till I make garters of your skin, till I knock the sweat from you the way you'd see a big storm knocking smoke out of the earth.

CHRISTY [*to* SALLY]. Do you hear that talk Widow Quin? Have you no pity in you to send me off. Have you no pity to think of me rising each day from my bed to see that wicket fellow looking wicket at my face, and hearing his voice speaking sharp lies would lift out a welt upon your skin.

[BOY *runs in.*]

BOY [*to* OLD FLAHERTY]. There's two peelers beyond seeking an old fellow with ⟨a⟩ patched head on him for beating a poor woman last night when he'd drink taken at Glen Na Buigh. You'd have a good right to run if it's yourself it is.

OLD F. [*puzzled*]. I've no memory of doing the like of that.

CHRISTY. It should be you surely. Isn't it what you always did?

OLD F. It's the truth maybe. Which way will I run.

BOY. Run now across the sands. Come this way till I show you. . . .

[BOY *and* FLAHERTY *run out.*]

CHRISTY. He's off. . . . Oh glory to God. [*He is still holding* SALLY *by the arm.*]

OLD F. [*catches* CHRISTY *by the arm*]. Come along now you divil you come along I'm saying . . . .

CHRISTY. Will you save me from him Sally Quin. Will you save me for the love of God . . . .

SALLY [*catching him by the other hand*]. I'll hold to you. Pull stoutly. Don't be afeard.

[*She and* CHRISTY *pull* CHRISTY *towards* L. BOY *catches* OLD F. *and pulls* R.]

BOY. Leave him go and come along Mister or they'll have you in gaol.

FLAHERTY. To hell with their gaol. I'll bring this lad with me too.

BOY. Look beyond there's their caps passing the ditch . . . .

FLAHERTY. Well the divil save him let him go to hell. [*He lets go and he and* BOY *run out L.*]

CHRISTY [*to* SALLY]. Come down now to the steamer and come along till we'd get married in the north, and go some place where ⟨the⟩ old lad wouldn't set his eye on us at all.

SALLY. Well I'm thinking I'll go with you, young fellow, you're a funny lad, and it's a fine thing to have a fellow with you would keep you all times laughing at the heavens and earth. [*They go out R.*]

'If this finale is retained give Old Mahon a line in II to W.Q. to say that if peelers come after him she is to misdirect them as he thinks he may have beaten someone the night before.'

Gradually as Synge developed the action and dialogue of the play, he provided the necessary transition scenes with the increased characterization of Old Mahon (Flaherty) and the Widow (Sally) Quin, and Act III arrived at its final form.

4. *For a while he contemplated a ballad framework for the play, apparently after he altered the chapel setting to a fair green, but after draft 'E' discarded the idea and moved the setting indoors.*

a. *In Notebook 28, a rough sketch of the concluding scenes of Act I:*

P. You're thinking bad of women.

CH. Wasn't I telling you I never met till this day the like etc. dd. from the d. to d.

P. There's many young lads do be slaving the length of the day and having great times after with the girls.

CH. [*despondingly*]. It's little I know if they have or not.

P. I'm ⟨thinking⟩ you know as little of the young lads as you do or girls?

CH. It's true maybe, isn't ⟨it that⟩ they're the divil's drove?

P. You'd've had a right to have seen the last pot-boy we had—a kind of a fiery patriot had knocked the left eye from a peeler and got six months again for maiming yearlings not far off I'm told from Athenry, a man was a great warrant to tell stories of Holy Ireland till he'd have the old women shedding down tears about their feet.

CHRISTY [*pricking his ears, jealous*]. Talking of Ireland is it. [*He pulls out papers from his pocket.*] If he was a warrant itself to tell stories you should hear me singing songs of Holy Ireland, till you'd think that would draw tears out of the moon.

PEGEEN. Is it songs there you have?

CHRISTY [*handing them out sheet by sheet*]. The croppy boy. The night before Larry was stretched. Green upon the cape. Johnny I hardly knew you. Colleen Rue—Them is lovely songs I'm telling you and I'd be saying them over the time I'd be out by my own self on a dark night snaring rabbits on a hill for I was a divil to poach I'm telling you and I got six weeks one time for stabbing a salmon with a dung-fork and I coming from work. There's a lovely song—It's a great time I had I'm saying to be thinking over the sad stories of Ireland and I abroad with my snares looking on the fog making patches on the earth till I'd hear a rabbit starting to screech, God help it, and I'd go running in the furze.

P. Can you sing the lot of them?

CH. I can surely.

P. Sing out one to me now.

CH. Ah I won't Pegeen Mike amn't I destroyed walking. You should have heard me singing in a little soft ⟨voice⟩ the time I'd a good set of rabbits taken and I'd be coming down through the village where you'd see the ducks and the geese stretched sleeping on the highway of the road and then before I'd come to the cabin we had I'd hear himself snoring—a loud lonesome sort of a snore—you'd hear him making all times the while he was ⟨sleeping⟩ the way you'd hear him swearing all times and he sitting talking with yourself and me.

PEG. And there was none in it at all but the [*etc. as before*] dark of night.

PEGEEN [*turning songs*]. You've great songs of hanging and the like of that?

CH. I have then.

P. Your father must have been a hard lot to the lot of you curse him like that.

CH. Would the Lord God etc. woman the like of you.

P. Have you the singing song of the Colleen Rue?

CH. I have. [*He sings.*]
  As I was walking up Wexford Street
    etc.
  As I was mounting on the platform high
  My aged father was standing by
  My aged father did me deny
  And the name he gave me was the Croppy Boy.

[*Someone knocks as he is singing.*]

PEG. Who's that.

VOICE. Me.

P. Who's me.

VOICE. The Widow Quin.

PEG. Ah bad cess to her. [*Opens door.*] Stretch out now and don't be talking to her at all etc.

WIDOW QUIN. I met Shawn Keogh below and he was telling me you were lonesome and wanting someone to stop with ⟨you⟩ this night and a strange kind of man lodging with you now. I didn't think much of that but when I heard a fellow singing I thought I'd step in and see maybe if he'd got roaring drunk upon your hands.

PEG. [*stiff*]. Not he drunk and I'm needing no one to guard me this night and thank you kindly for your care.

WIDOW QUIN. I'll stop a short while to get my breath and I lonesome mounting the hill.

PEG. It's a queer thing you'd be lonesome and you out all times pacing the roads.

V.Q. [*to* CHRISTY]. You're a quiet looking young fellow. You should have had great torment to rouse your spirits to a deed of blood.

PEG. It didn't take much torment to rouse you to strike down your poor husband with a rusted pick.

W.Q. You're minding that! You're grand at minding God bless you and I near forgetting I was ever wedded at all.

P. If you are you're not forgetting you're wishing to be wedding anew.

W. Is that the truth? Maybe when all's out I'll have a husband to wed me the day you're wedding with Shawn Keogh.

PEG. Who says I'm wedding S.K.?

W.Q. Who says it? Young and old I'm thinking and them that's neither like myself.

PEG. It's mighty busy the lot of you are tattling around of what doesn't concern you at all—

WIDOW Q. [*to* CHRISTY]. Is that songs you have there young fellow?

CHRISTY. It is. I'm great for songs.

WIDOW [*taking a broad-sheet*]. There's great songs of the freedom of Ireland. But what good is the like of them when you'd be hard set to find a man singing them that wouldn't sell the whole of Ireland for two sheep.

CHRISTY. There's love songs maybe then would affect you.

W.Q. [*crosses*]. War and History, that noble victor who died—etc.

PEG. This is ⟨a⟩ queer time of the night to be expatiating on the sound of songs Widow Quin. It'd be better you went.

WIDOW. I'm thinking it's jealous she is. Well a new young lad's great treasure for a flighty girl. God give a good night young fellow and we'll have a good talk for two hours or three before you go [*Exit.*]

CH. Is it true you're wedding with Shawn Keogh the poor fellow

b. In Act III of drafts 'D' and 'E' (contemporaneous with Notebook 28) this addi-
tional framework is developed even further, bringing in other wandering characters also:

ACT III (E)

Afternoon on sporting green; sports in progress; people in groups.
Roulette man passes.

ROULETTE MAN [*singing*].
  Come play me a game of Timmon and Tup
  The more you puts down the more you takes up. etc.

Is there any sportsman here in a hat or a cap or a wig or a waistcoat
will play a go with me now. [*To* PHILLY O'CULLEN *and* TIMMY
FARRELL.] Take notice gentlemen I come here to spend a fortune
not to make one. Will you play me a turn gentlemen the luck is on
green.

TIMMY. We will not Mister.

ROULETTE MAN [*to* PHILLY]. And you Mister. You have the look of
  luck within ⟨your⟩ eye. I'm two thirds fearing you?

PHILLY. I'm lucky surely but I'm not eager for sporting this day so you
  may stroll on east with yourself and don't be troubling us at all.

ROULETTE MAN [*going left*].
  Come play me a game of Timmon and Tup
  The more you puts down the more you takes up.

PHILLY. They say Christy the daddy-man is after lifting a power off
  that fellow and they playing on the green.

TIMMY. Isn't he a lucky fellow after winning all things right and left
  lepping, racing, pitching, and the Lord knows what.

PHILLY. He's a right lad surely, but he'll be getting rightly hobbled
  yet, I'm thinking and he not talking ten words without making a
  brag of the way he killed his father and the great blow he hit with
  the loy.

TIMMY. Isn't it in law a man can't hang by his own informing which'd
  be self-destruction and contrary to scripture, and I'm thinking his
  father's rotten by now.

  [OLD MAHON *is seen behind.*]

The final scenes of draft 'E' continue the process, introducing a real Ballad Man:

CHRISTY. You'd a right to turn again me maybe as I'm turned on you, for what would any do I'm thinking but turn again and curse the multitudes of mass of men, you carcase pecking scald-crows that you'll hear screeching south and eastward on the ridges of the world.

WIDOW QUIN [*taking him by the arm*]. Say out now what you have of any kind again of me.

CHRISTY [*taken aback*]. Of you is it?

WIDOW QUIN. Ay.

CHRISTY. It's true you lied this morning when the old man came seeking me and Pegeen upon the hill. It's true you didn't raise your speaking with them howling swine. It's true surely.

WIDOW QUIN. And where is it that you're off to now?

CHRISTY [*rapidly subsiding*]. The Lord of Heaven knows it for there's nothing in me this day, but wild words and pain.

WIDOW QUIN. And what is it you were saying a while since to myself?

CHRISTY. I was asking ⟨you⟩ to step out between myself and him, and wed me maybe in the face of the world.

WIDOW QUIN. I will then if you wish I have nice little bit of a house above where we'd be great company.

CHRISTY. No no, I'd be fearing always the old fellow'd get the better of me still.

WIDOW QUIN. Will we get two bags, and go walking the world?

CHRISTY. No. What good is it walking the world.

WIDOW QUIN [*shaking him*]. Stir up there what ails you at all.

OLD MAHON. Don't mind his tantrums. It's only foxing he is. [*To* CHRISTY.] Come on now before the fall of night we've a great tract to walk. [*They go out.*]

BALLAD MAN [*singing as he comes in*].
      Young Christopher the daddy man came walking from Tralee
      And his father's bloody ghost the while did keep him company . . . .

SHAWN [*jostling him*]. Hold your jaw there his father's not murdered at all.

BALLAD MAN. Oh, God help me and I after spending the half of me day making of his deed.

SHAWN. He's not murdered I'm saying and we want none of your lies.

BALLAD MAN. But it's a lovely song. . . .

PEGEEN. What do we want with lies.

BALLAD MAN. Well I'll sing it other road⟨s⟩ where he's not known at all. It's a lovely song surely.

SHAWN. Come on now to the green. [*Pipes are heard behind.*] There's the piper and we'll have great dancing till the fall of night.

CURTAIN

C. ADDITIONAL SCENES

In striving to maintain the balance between the 'Romantic' and the 'Rabelaisian' elements, Synge seems to have had most difficulty with the Widow Quin, who frequently threatened to run away with one or the other motif. She began in the earliest drafts as Sally Quin, one of the village girls. Then Synge decided that a more colourful foil was required for Pegeen, and gradually her personality became so intriguing that she in turn became a foil to Christy and, further, a key to Old Mahon's character also.

    1. *Act II, the transitional scenes with Christy:*

    a. (1) *Originally Synge appears to have planned the first of these transition scenes (before Old Mahon's appearance) to develop sympathy for the Widow Quin, as in this early draft 'C' (the first draft in which Christy's father appears in Act II):*

WIDOW QUIN. Look at you now, and you dancing like a starving tom-cat would be smelling a fish. Listen now what I'm telling you, that⟨'s a⟩ foolish girl and flighty with it, and you'd do right not to mind her at all, and to walk down when you're lonesome and be talking with myself, for I'm no fool and you've heard them tell you maybe the way I was married a while since, and hit himself such a blow with a rusted pick, that he never overed it, God help him, and he died after.

CHRISTY [*stopping suddenly and looking at her with surprise*]. Well isn't it a grand place I've come with a power of grand kindly women walking around.

WIDOW QUIN. If you're thinking well of me, let you stay and talk with me now.

CHRISTY [*trying to get past her*]. Haven't I long years to be talking with yourself, and let ⟨me⟩ go now to Pegeen, for she wouldn't think well of me not running out to her aid, and she after lifting me up with her kind words again the doors of light.

(2) *On the back of this draft he wrote,* 'She gives sounding note, the maturity of feeling', *which is then further developed in the next revision of draft 'C', when he decided to make Christy leave before his father appears:*

CHRISTY [*going up to her with intense curiosity*]. Do they be making game of you, telling lies on you, and talking stories again you on a dry Sunday at the public-house corner?

WIDOW QUIN. It's times they do.

CHRISTY. Well isn't that a great wonder and you after striking your man for you seen this day the way they're all coming making great rejoicings at the sight of me!

WIDOW QUIN. You're setting great store on their rejoicings young fellow, but let you wait a while and you'll see them turning dry and crusty on you yet.

CHRISTY. Is it Pegeen?

WIDOW QUIN. Pegeen too, maybe.

CHRISTY. You didn't see the kind look myself seen come into her eyes. That's foolish talk you're making I'm thinking, for if you struck your man itself, you didn't hit him a blow sliced him to the belt, and it's for that maybe they're not heeding you at all.

[PEGEEN's *voice calls off*.] Christy, Christy F.

CHRISTY. I'll go to her aid, and not be lingering more—

WIDOW QUIN [*looking from window*]. Stay. There's a frisky old fellow mounting the lane, you'd have a right to stay and serve him in the shop.

CHRISTY. What is it I know of serving. Let you bid him wait till we come down from the hill. [*Goes.*]

[WIDOW QUIN *watches someone for a moment from the window then someone knocks violently on the door with a stick.*]

(3) *A fragment from another early draft, possibly TS. 'D', has the marginal note* 'Revise this scene and bring out Christy's bragging element to contrast with the story given of him in following scene. It might be worked on the greyness of her mood.' *Elsewhere the same draft has the marginal note* 'He has to explain reason of his new joy.'

(4) *However, what appear to be the next drafts, while emphasizing the Widow's* '*grey mood*', *also emphasize her strength at the expense of Christy's:*

CHRISTY. Wouldn't you easy find a husband if you're wanting one at all?

WIDOW QUIN. I'm not the kind would wed an old man with a shiny head on him, or white hairs itself, and the young men in this place are in dread I'd maybe trip them as I tripped poor Marcus Quin.

CHRISTY. And is there never decent strangers passing the way?

WIDOW QUIN. And I'm thinking if it wasn't that you've done a deed the like of me you'd be dreading yourself maybe to be talking to me now, for I won't tell you a lie, and I'm certain sure it's only letting on you are to have great courage in your heart.

CHRISTY [*sulky*]. And what call have you to say the like of that to me?

WIDOW QUIN. It's this I'm saying. In a short while the whole lot will find out the way you are, and then they'll be making game of you with their teasing and tormenting as they treated me, so you'd do best to wed myself—I've a nice plot of decent land and an outlet on the hills—and then who'd know if you are brave or scarey or what kind you are at all for I'm a kindly hearted woman and I'd tend you well.

CHRISTY [*piqued*]. Well I'm telling ⟨you⟩ you're building up your story the wrong road surely, and I'll be walking from you now, for it's not yourself I'm wanting but Pegeen beyond, and you'd do well to know that's not the voice to speak in to a man that's after splitting his poor father to the hasp upon his belt.

(5) *A further draft ('E'?) varies Christy's rejection of the Widow's offer:*

CHRISTY [*dancing with impatience to get away*]. I'm thinking herself has great consideration for my courage too, it's herself has first pick for my plighted hand. What would I say to her if I did turn to you when she was the first did warm and clothe me, and regard me right.

And the same draft emphasizes Christy's determination to be different from his fellow 'murderer':

CHRISTY. You were better so I'm thinking than holding out beside an ageing yellow divil for ten years and more!

WIDOW QUIN. It's true maybe for the single is lonesome and the double is lonesome, the way you'll see a single goat with its shins bled on its fetter with striving and lepping for to come unto its kind, and it coupleted them striving to part till each one of them will wear a bloody girdle in the socket of their necks.

(6) *A draft in Notebook 34 some time after draft 'E' (January 1906?) returns to the idea of the Widow's maturity and suggests further history:*

Scene [CHRISTY *and* WIDOW QUIN].

'Her maturity in contrast with Pegeen's fantasy (inc. story of wed to judge II b).'

WIDOW. Let you stop a short while and talk to myself. Two murderers the like of us should be great company!

CHRISTY. Didn't I hear them say it was the rust only did harm to him at all.

W. If it was there aren't many women did strike out with a pick and you'll find few only is the like of me [*she points from door*]—it's above in that little lonesome cot you see that I'm these seven years living alone [*she puts her hand on his shoulder*].

CHRISTY [*draws back*]. And you're lonesome living there?

WID. God knows what I am. There's many a time I do be sitting out there in the warm sun darning a stocking or stitching a shift and looking down on the village below where you'll see the people walking dancing dying—they're terrors for dying—and I heeding the divil a one and the divil a one heeding me.

CHRISTY. It's that way I was but I'm grand now.

W. Grand are you? You're a quiet looking young fellow, should have had great torment to rouse your spirits to a deed of blood.

CHRISTY. Torment surely. But I'll be grand now in this place with the kindness of young girls and all.

'Work queer attitude of girls in towards Widow using Pegeen's words in I.'

WIDOW. They think you're a great wonder fellow but they'll be wearying soon of that.

CH. Not a bit will they weary, there isn't many was ever heard of did the like of me and split down his father with one stroke to the hasp of his belt.

WIDOW. Sit down and tell me the real tale of your life. I'd think well to hear you talk simple sense to me for a while.

(7) *Finally Synge changed his mind about the scene, making the marginal note* 'Revise scene with Widow Quin so that it makes Christy in a boastful rampant mood reject the friendship she half offers him (observe her motif).' *And on the back of a draft of this scene which is pinned to TS. 'E' (24 May 1905) he wrote:* 'Make scene between exit Pegeen and entry of Old Mahon very short and buoyant. Then work in essential bits of Widow Quin into later dialogue with Christy—.' *With this new plan in mind he annotated an earlier version of the scene in Notebook 28:*

'Make scene a merry scuffle between widow and Christy she wanting to keep him to serve old man she has seen he wanting to get off to Pegeen, and she jeering at his eagerness, at last she lets him go and he darts to the door, then staggers back.
Quick sharp scene with Christy's jubilant note. No reflectiveness whatever, which is retained for final scene.'

W. Look at you dancing round like a tom cat smelling a fish!

CHRISTY. I am not then but the like of a man was after going from fire to the seat of Joy.

W.Q. Because of her?

CHRISTY. Because I'm known this day for a man with a mighty spirit in him and a flaming heart, and there'll ⟨be⟩ no woman from this day won't be looking kindly on me now—

WIDOW Q. You think a lot of women?

CH. And why wouldn't I?

WIDOW Q. I suppose you've known a power?

CH. There was Pegeen Mike and then the three you seen here at the while gone by!

WIDOW Q. Is it them only?

CHRISTY. Then a hardened widow with eleven children I was speaking of before.

'Make this scene quite short and direct—merely a statement of his hope and spirits.'

W.Q. You're looking now in great spirits and joy—

CH. It'd be queer if I wouldn't and I settled in this homely house after all my days walking the world!

W.Q. You're looking as if you were after growing I'm thinking since seen you at the fall of night.

(8) *Gradually he cut down the exchange, trying to retain the balance between the Widow's maturity and Christy's pride, as in the following remnant from draft 'I':*

CHRISTY. I'm little lost for company this day Widow Quin where I've the old and young paying their respects to me and bring clothes and feeding for my choice today. It's a companionable thing I'm seeing to slice down your father's skull.

WIDOW QUIN. You've grown mighty skittish since the fall of night.

CHRISTY. And why wouldn't I when I'm known in the end of time for a man with a mighty spirit in him and a gamey heart, the way there'll be no girl or woman from this out but will be looking kindly on me now.

WIDOW QUIN. Most females of the world is silly creatures Christy Mahon making their high-horsed romancing the way of Pegeen Mike, or a giggling gabbling set the like of the company I did find around you at the dawn of day. I'm telling you it isn't often you' find a gallant widow the like of me who has great knowledge and has killed her man.

CHRISTY [*breaking away from her*]. It's little I do need your likeness Widow Quin and I a man did with one blow slice his father to his breeches belt. And so God save you now *etc.*

b. *The transition scene following Old Mahon's appearance in Act II caused Synge further difficulty in retaining a balance between the Widow Quin and Christy (although a version about draft 'E' bears the marginal note 'Widow's scene'). This may have been the scene which first decided him to create the Widow Quin, for a marginal note to a early draft which still includes Sally Quin reads* 'Expand scene with Widow Porter. She advances to Christy—.'

From the earliest drafts the Widow appears more sympathetic, but at the same time attempting to control Christy's actions. It appears also that Synge at one time considered placing the 'second murder' in this act:

(1)

CHRISTY [*turning away*]. Didn't I hear her this day speaking my praises like a big wealthy noble maybe meeting a high horse would run in from winning a race and now she'll be scolding again like an old woman with a spavindy ass she'd have gibing on a hill, and I a fool from this day with the gallows gone from me and all the hope of love and marriage I had gained me now?

WIDOW QUIN. And you were making certain that she'd wed with you here?

CHRISTY. I was then, the way that I've a mind to follow him and strike him dead.

WIDOW QUIN. If you're so fiery you'd a right to strike him here, but it's only letting on you are. You wouldn't touch him at all.

CHRISTY [*working himself up*]. I wouldn't is it? Are you thinking I'd let the Heavens jilt me, and I with the strength in me to strike him lifeless on the sands below?

WIDOW QUIN. You'd make yourself a show of folly I'm telling you if you went to go assail him now.

CHRISTY. It's no lie maybe, but what'll I be doing if I've lost Pegeen?

(2) *A later version retains the Widow's 'loud surprise' at Christy's marriage hopes but eliminates her goading him into further action:*

CHRISTY. I was then, and it was the divil guided my hand I'm thinking to make myself a mortal hero for one day only, for what'll I be doing from this out, and I jilted by the Heavens to the end of time.

WIDOW QUIN [*with some bitterness*]. You'll be learning it's a plain world Christy Mahon, with short hours for romancing, and long hours to be pitying yourself and all. [*She comes over to him.*] And wasn't it a good right I had to be taking compassion on you at the fall of night when I seen you looking so simple and herself making you the miracle and pride of men?

CHRISTY [*despairingly*]. It was maybe.

(3) *An apparently later draft still retains the balance between the Widow's advance and Christy's folly, but reserves the Widow's bitterness for later:*

CHRISTY [*sinking on a chair in misery*]. And to think I'm lost surely, with the gallows gone from me and my great deeds and all the hope an glory have been spreading to me now.

WIDOW QUIN. If they are maybe now you'll win a widow's pit which is more than all for if young fools do seek romancing wonder for to make their joy, it's the deep and trusty spirits do ⟨be⟩ givin consolation to the broken-hearted and the poor of earth.

CHRISTY. Wasn't I well enough beyond and I used to being lonesom and a fool with all, and what did I want striking my father and mak ing myself gallous for one day only?

(4) *Originally Synge intended to show the Widow's compassion overcoming h self-interest. Draft 'F' reads:*

WIDOW QUIN [*stands up, hesitating*]. And you don't fancy givin heed to me at all?

CHRISTY [*going to her*]. It's Pegeen Mike I heed alone. It's Pegeen Mik I'm saying, and for the love of God Widow Quin tell me if I've lo her surely to the ends of time.

WIDOW QUIN. Why would I tell you?

CHRISTY. Have mercy on my torments this one day alone, and tell n have I lost her the way I'll be clawing the world as you'd see a sinn breaking his nails on the brassy pillars of the gate of hell.

WIDOW QUIN. Well it's a bitter world I'm thinking for poetry fellov is the like of you and I'll say this much to you Pegeen'll likely nev hear of the old fellow if you don't tell her yourself, for I've sent ⟨him walking where he'll not likely turn again.

CHRISTY [*with a ray of hope*]. And you'll not speak yourself is it?

WIDOW QUIN. I won't maybe for I'm pitying you now.

(5) *Dissatisfied, however, he wrote the marginal note* 'Make passionate appeal' *and in his next drafts he intensified both characters' speeches, as in this remnant from draft* 'I':

CHRISTY. Let you have pity on my lonesomeness and solitude of heart. Haven't you felt it your own self I'm saying, and you rising sleeping feasting fasting and you seeing nothing but yourself alone.

WIDOW QUIN [*with a touch of compassion*]. Well it's a hard world I'm thinking for poetry fellows is the like of you. But it's little good Pegeen will do you I'm thinking for them is born lonesome will go down lonesome to the bottom of the grave.

CHRISTY. Aid me for to win Pegeen, I'm saying and I will leave the rest and remnant to the will of God.

WIDOW QUIN [*turning back to him*]. Would you have the heart to go on this place play-acting you'd killed your father, if none knew he was running the world?

(6) *Finally Synge decided to harshen the Widow's character at the expense of her compassion, as in the following remnant from draft* 'K':

WIDOW QUIN [*bitterly*]. Wait now till you hear the great laugh there'll be when I tell your story to the lot of them that's coming now. There'll be sport now I'm telling you.

CHRISTY. Will you not have pity on me and you a woman is long years waking sleeping feasting fasting with yourself alone?

WIDOW QUIN [*coldly*]. What good's my pity when you're a man I'm thinking is born lonesome to go lonesome to the bottom of the grave.

CHRISTY. I am born for to wed Pegeen. Aid me for to win her and escape himself and I'll be asking God *etc.*

(7) *Draft* 'K' *remnants show one last attempt to retain the theme of lonely under-standing in the Widow Quin, while at the same time including the harsh* 'Rabelaisian' *tone:*

'I'm thinking it's a hard world maybe for poetry fellows is the like of you, are bred to win small pleasure from any two-legged bitch for all knows them is born lonesome will go lonesome to the bog-pit of the grave.'

2. *Act III, the Widow Quin, Old Mahon, and Christy:*

a. *After Old Mahon made his appearance in Act II, Synge built up his next appearance in Act III, again making use of the Widow Quin.*

(1) *They first romp together in draft 'F' (24 January 1906), after Philly and Jimmy have returned to the races:*

WIDOW QUIN [*coming in with jar of poteen*]. There was a run I thought there was a peeler looking up at me from the sports below. [*Sees* OLD MAHON.] Well what is it has brought you this way again?

OLD MAHON. I was near drownded following the way you did show me across the strands and by the time I was in it I seen the coasting ⟨steamer⟩ passing, I said to ⟨myself⟩ he's off on me now, and I turned back by the head of the bay.

WIDOW QUIN [*considering*]. You'd best not ⟨be⟩ dilly-dallying in this place there isn't a spot for the like of you to sleep and you'd need a long trudge to bring you to the town.

OLD MAHON. I'll stop now, if I sleep beyond with the pigs. I'm destroyed walking.

WIDOW QUIN. Then you'd do right to come up beyond to my own houseen, for you'll be moidered here with the turmoil when the sports is by.

OLD MAHON. Is it not yourself is the woman of the house.

WIDOW QUIN. Faith I'm not. Come on now and I'll show ⟨you⟩ where my own house ⟨is⟩ on the face of the hill.

OLD MAHON. Leave me easy when I'm saying I'll stop where I am.

WIDOW QUIN. There's a queer way to speak to a woman offering you company in her own house, and lodging for the night.

OLD MAHON. It's little I care for the like of you or lodging either.

WIDOW QUIN [*taking bottle of poteen from her pocket*]. Well you're a cranky fellow. But if you ⟨are⟩ itself you'd maybe think well to drink my health.

OLD MAHON [*putting out his hand for the bottle*]. Thank you kindly.

WIDOW QUIN. Rise up if you want it.

OLD MAHON. Give it here I'm saying.

WIDOW QUIN [*sitting down out of his reach and holding it out*]. Rise up I'm saying or I'll drink it all. [*She puts it to her mouth.*]

OLD MAHON [*getting up slowly*]. The divil brand your brows but you're the schemer. [*She stands up and holds out the glass to him he reaches out for it and she plucks it away from him and goes to door laughing.*]

WIDOW QUIN [*mocking him*]. The divil brand me indeed. Come on here if you want it. [*She looks quickly from door.*]

OLD MAHON. Give it here you'll maybe fool me again.

WIDOW QUIN [*stretching out towards him*]. Here take it. [*He grabs at it and she dodges him laughing loudly.*] Well aren't you a gamey old villain to be at your ⟨age⟩ romping with a ⟨widowed⟩ girl. Grab it again Mister.

OLD MAHON [*chuckling wicketly*]. You're a right one if its widow witch ᴏɪ wife you ⟨are⟩ or God knows what.

[CROWD *heard outside.*]

WIDOW QUIN. Here take it now. There's the crowd coming have your sip or I'll conceal it now.

CROWD [*cheering*]. He's the racer. Lift him up Philly. etc.

WIDOW QUIN [*with agitation*]. Here make haste will you.

[OLD MAHON *grabs at it again, she catches him by the wrist, whips him out of the door and she is seen running past window on L. pushing* OLD MAHON *before her. Crowd cheering Right all the time. Then crowd comes in nearly carrying* CHRISTY.]

(2) *Synge then decided to include the actual race, extending the scene between the Widow and Old Mahon, as indicated by the following rough sketch in Notebook 34:*

'W.Q. and Mahon. Mahon asks about young fellow who is making all the stir. W.Q. lies. He looks out and says he's very like. She says he's done so and so. He says, "that's not Christy".
Da Capo. Then they watch mule race from window, great excitement. "He's down he's up again. There⟨'s⟩ foam flying like seagulls in a wormy field." The Widow tries to inveigle him away, begins to

romp. Old Mahon thaws. "Old as I am there's many a woman would liefer have me this day than the Kings of England." She enters into humour of thing, he chases her. When she fails to get him ut by blandishment ⟨they⟩ battle. (strong *grotesque* climax leading .o lyric climax immediately of Pegeen and Christy)'

(3) *The following draft, a revision of TS. 'F', develops these ideas, extending the scene by including the above discussion before the race begins and emphasizing the element of the chase:*

WIDOW QUIN. There was a race. [*Great cheering far away.*] Look at them raising him up. They'll be bringing ⟨him⟩ here now and there won't be a spot for the two of us. Come on or you'll be deafened with their noise.

OLD MAHON [*going to fire*]. I'll stop and see them.

WIDOW QUIN. Is it stop and I asking you to go with me? Come. [*She pulls him.*]

OLD MAHON [*pulling back*]. I won't faith.

WIDOW QUIN. You will.

OLD MAHON. I won't.

WIDOW QUIN. Go on then [*she gives him a shove*], you're too old to have civility for girls at all.

OLD MAHON [*on the ground*]. Old as I am there's many girls would liefer have me than the slavish weeds of young lads you'd meet these days walking the world.

WIDOW QUIN [*jeering at him*]. Sooner have you is it? And you with a face on you like an old bullock you'd see at a post's head scratching his chin. [*Laughing again.*] It's beyond you were maybe cleaning out the dirtpits in the crazyhouse for females in the town of Cork?

OLD MAHON [*brightening up*]. I'm telling you if I live to four scores itself the women that will wash my corpse will be dropping tears down to see the like of me passed from the world.

WIDOW QUIN [*laughing derisively*]. You're thinking that. That the Lord in mercy may assist your head.

OLD MAHON [*going towards her*]. I am thinking it and you'll maybe think it too.

WIDOW QUIN [*getting behind table in mock fear*]. Keep off now. Keep off the time we're alone. . . . Aren't you a wrinkledy villain to go romping with a widowed girl?

OLD MAHON. It's little I care if it's widow wife or witch you are or God knows what.

WIDOW QUIN [*running to door*]. Well I'm going. [*With provocation.*] And I wouldn't have you come along with me if you went upon your two knees to ask my leave.

OLD MAHON. Maybe I'll go whether you'd have me or prevent me now.

WIDOW QUIN. If the people seen you following me what at all would they say? Come on so there's the crowd turning the road.

OLD MAHON. Well hasn't he a look of Christy I'll wait and see them I'm thinking.

WIDOW QUIN [*angrily*]. You're no use. [*She takes out a bottle of poteen.*] Here will you drink my health maybe before I go. [*She holds out bottle.*]

OLD MAHON [*holding out his hand*]. Faith I will.

WIDOW QUIN. Rise up if you want it.

OLD MAHON. Give it here.

WIDOW QUIN [*sitting down and drinking*]. Rise up or I'll maybe drink the whole of it.

OLD MAHON. The divil brand you. [*He goes over and reaches out for bottle but she pulls it away and retreats with it before him.*]

WIDOW QUIN [*holding it out again*]. Here take it. [*Noise heard.*] The crowd's coming. Take your sup or I'll conceal it now.

CROWD [*cheering*]. He's the racer. Bear him Philly.

WIDOW QUIN [*agitated*]. Take it will you. [*She is in door.*]

[OLD MAHON *reaches out for bottle, she catches him by the wrists, pulls him out of door and she is seen pushing him past window and off Right.*]

CROWD [*heard L. then at door*]. There you are now. Good jumper. Grand lepper. Darling boy.

(4) *Having developed the 'current' between the Widow and Old Mahon, Synge in the next draft, TS. 'G', decided to include a recognition scene, again exercising the Widow's ingenuity to prevent a premature meeting. (Draft 'H' is similar, except that Philly and Jimmy stay onstage and decide to remain quiet about Old Mahon for the time being; not until draft 'J' does Old Mahon's exit take its final form.)*

OLD MAHON. Flames but he's in. [*He breaks out into a cheer, then hesitates a moment.*] What the divil's that. Oh they're raising him. They're coming this way. [*With a roar of rage.*] It's Christy by the hairs of God. I'd know his way of spitting and he astride the moon. [*He jumps down and makes a rush out of door but* WIDOW QUIN *pulls him back.*]

WIDOW QUIN. Wait till I tell you. Stay quiet will you? Don't I tell you they're bringing him here?

OLD MAHON [*in a frightened whisper*]. What in the name of God has happened the world? Am I going cracked in my head. Cheering and triumphing and giving thanks to God! What is it you want holding me back. Let me go will you till I split his head.

WIDOW QUIN [*speaking volubly*]. Not a bit are you mad. He's not the same at all since he was quit of you, and he's pot-boy in this place a fine trading public-house with a licence and with poteen too. All say he's going to wed the daughter of ⟨the⟩ house itself so if you leave him quiet till he's wed you'll be able to get drunk every day and not pay a half-penny at all.

MAHON. That man marrying a monied girl? Is it mad yous are? Is it mad the whole of us are? Is it in a crazy house for females that I'm landed now?

WIDOW QUIN. Aren't ⟨you⟩ seeing what he's after doing here the way a silken lady might be proud this day to wed his like. It's yourself is crazy if you don't walk on quiet and let him wed her in peace the way you'll have a house for drink and shelter till the end of time.

OLD MAHON [*considering*]. Maybe it's right you are. Maybe if they knew we'd had a quarrel and they knew he'd raised his hand upon his father's head they'd pitch him out upon the road.

WIDOW QUIN [*laughing*]. That's what you're thinking is it? And they making much of him only because of his great story of the way he had you split unto the navel with a single clout.

OLD MAHON. Is that the truth? [*He begins to chuckle and then breaks into a roar of laughter and sits down on a chair.*] Me split to the navel is it, well I'll stay so and give my prayer and blessing to that playboy here.

WIDOW QUIN. You will not stay. Come on I'm telling you, it's safer so.

OLD MAHON [*with a roar of impatience*]. I will stay and let you not be meddling at all. What in the name of God do you want driving at me?

WIDOW QUIN [*looking out and coming back to him*]. Would you give them your blessing and you a filthy tramper with blood upon your head. They'll be making a solemn oath this day I've heard Christy say and if they set their eyes on you and you in that state of swinery and walking dirt, I'm thinking they won't have more to do with you unto the end of time.   'Clear her motive.'

OLD MAHON. I'm as good as any in this place. Don't be uneasy at ⟨me.⟩

WIDOW QUIN. You may be a fine old wicket warrior when you're washed and clean but you're looking frightful now.

OLD MAHON [*goes over to the glass and looks in*]. The divil is! Where at all could I wash my visage and get a clean old petticoat to swath my head?

WIDOW QUIN. Come on to my old houseen and I'll bind you if you will.

OLD MAHON. Come on so.

WIDOW QUIN. Make haste and lower your head. They're coming beyond. [*They lower their heads and run past window, crowd heard cheering.*]

b. *Again in earlier drafts the Widow Quin controlled the transition scene before Old Mahon's third entrance. Until draft 'G' Christy, goaded by the Widow Quin, demands that Pegeen swear an oath during which Old Mahon enters, as in the following scene from draft 'E' (May 1905):*

(1)

CHRISTY. It's now I'm mounted on the tide of luck and I'm fit to lift you with me I'm thinking for it's no common young lad would walk in darkness to a sleeping town and turn it to his glory at the dawn of day. So I'm thinking Pegeen Mike it's good contriving you'll be at to swear your oath unto me now. [*He lifts prayer book.*] Speak now with me. I swear this holy day by the grace and power of the Almighty God. . .

PEGEEN [*after him*]. I swear this day by the grace and power of the Almighty God . . .

CHRISTY. To wed this man. [*He stops.*] Go away you black walker of hell.

[OLD MAHON *makes a rush in at him from R. and knocks him down.*]

OLD MAHON. I've got you have I and you making blither-fools of all the walking world. [*He beats him.*]

(2) *Beside this draft Synge wrote 'expand', and in draft 'F' Old Mahon runs in pulling the Widow Quin after him, after Pegeen has completed her vow 'to wed with Christy Mahon and let come what will' and received the Crowd's congratulations.*

(3) *Still dissatisfied, however, Synge suggested a new situation on the back of the revised draft 'F':*

'Motive for Old Mahon's hiding to ensure his capture of Christy. What would W.Q. say to that? Work Mahon's astonishment as motive. Make him ask where he can hide instead of Widow Q. asking him to do so. More natural quoi?'

OLD MAHON *cries out in gable.*

CHRISTY [*his back to him*]. He's gone to Heaven in the latter end!

CROWD. What is it?

CHRISTY. It's the spirit of my murdered or my drownded pa!

CROWD. Where in the name of God?

CHRISTY. Above floating in the air. Oh isn't he a terror. Not a double death to fetter him at all.

[MAHON *comes people scatter.*]

(4) *About this time Synge considered altering Old Mahon's mood, and Notebook 34 develops both the idea of his hiding in the gable and his pleasure at the match:*

'Widow Quin puts him up at gable window to watch what is being said (at climax he ⟨speaks⟩ down on them).'

CHRISTY. It's my father⟨'s⟩ voice speaking down from Heaven. Who would have thought he⟨'d⟩ ever reach to there. . . .

'Michael James makes pseudo superfine speech and joins their hands. . . . They all collect in middle of floor in tight terrified group while Old Mahon is heard shouting round the house (like frightened sheep)'

ONE OF THE MEN. There's cursing for an angel of the air.
  He's the man who was split to the knob of his gullet, who was drowned in ⟨Belmullet⟩. Who was buried rotting in the earth— He's nine lives. He'll never die.
(*To be revived at end.*) Didn't I say he'd never die.

'Old Mahon (at middle entry) shakes hands with Michael James goes to kiss Pegeen. She hits him a clout, and then bursts out at Christy. He abuses his father then turns on him and all go into the pot.'

(5) *This idea is then transferred to draft 'G':*

OLD MAHON [*comes over and raises his hands above them*]. May God and Mary and St. Patrick bless you and increase you now, and it's proud and happy I am to set my eyes upon this shining day.

PEGEEN [*to* CHRISTY]. Who's that man?

MAHON. I'm his father God bless him, and I'll be your own father in a short while with the help of God and it's proud I'll be to see the like of you joined in marriage with the likes of me. [*He goes up to* PEGEEN *but she draws back from him.*]

By draft 'H', however, Synge returned to his original plan for Old Mahon's entrance as it appears in the final text.

c. *Not until draft 'J' does the Widow Quin cease to play an important role in the curtain scene. Up to draft 'F' the Widow rescues Christy; succeeding drafts have both father and son leaving with her, and in draft 'J' when Christy rejects both his father and the Widow, the father still leaves with her. The earliest drafts, however, definitely place the Widow on Christy's side, as in 'C':*

OLD F. Aren't you a poor good for nothing, and isn't it by the like of you the sins of the whole world are committed, and didn't the divil himself lay his mark on you the day you were born the way any man would lay a black mark on the thighs of a lamb?

CHRISTY [*hiding behind* HONOR BLAKE]. Oh for the love of Heaven will you step between us now?

GIRLS. And you the great tyrant to be wanting a woman's shawl to be shielding you now?

CHRISTY [*to the* WIDOW QUIN]. And yourself Widow Quin. Have pity on me this day for the love of God.

WIDOW QUIN [*coming down centre,* CHRISTY *at her side*]. Save you is it?

CHRISTY. Oh help and save me from the torment of the earth. Would you have me crying terrors to the name of God in the dawn and evening and the stillness of the night?

WIDOW QUIN. Can't you run off from him?

CHRISTY. Is it go off like a straying beggar walking from Union to Union with the frost white and hard to my feet? And I not knowing day or night when he'd catch up on my track?

WIDOW QUIN. Wouldn't be grand open days you'd have walking and strolling all ways viewing the world?

CHRISTY. And I lone man again after living one day in the praises of my kind?

WIDOW QUIN. Maybe you'd raise your hand on him and slay him surely and then you'd all men maybe praising you again?

OLD F. [*rushing up at her other hand*]. He'll not get that I'll swear this day to the holy Gods for I'll be wary of him from this day and keep terror in his eye.

WIDOW QUIN [*between them*]. Well you'll be queer company one for the other?

CHRISTY. Will you do nothing for me at all Widow Quin will you have no mercy on my soul?

WIDOW QUIN. Run off I'm saying surely a little supple fellow like you'd off from him easy and he'll not come up with you at all.

CHRISTY. Isn't a young rabbit running the hills as supple as sight, and yet you'd ⟨see⟩ an old weazel following on and following on till you'd hear the little divil starting to scream at the old one sucking his blood.

WIDOW QUIN. And what is it the like of me can do for you?

CHRISTY. You'd have a right to wed me I'm thinking and take me home to your house.

WIDOW QUIN. Do you ⟨think⟩ my wits is gone that when I was near hanged for getting shut of one man I'd go wedding anew?

CHRISTY. He wasn't the like of me maybe?

WIDOW. He'd more senses nor you.

CHRISTY. And will you do nothing at all.

WIDOW QUIN. What time would you take to get off away from him crossing the world?

CHRISTY. Two days or three I'm thinking for I'd be springing fearful with haste.

WIDOW QUIN. Off with you then and he'll not stir after you till Wednesday's noon.

CHRISTY. You'll hold him?

WIDOW QUIN. I will then.

CHRISTY. God Almighty save you.

[*He holds his breath for an instant then makes a bolt out of the door;* OLD FLAHERTY *tries to get after him but the* WIDOW QUIN *slips the spade crossways in the door. Then she catches hold of him and drags him back into the room. She ties him up and drives him out with dialogue.*]

III. RELATED PASSAGES IN NOTEBOOKS

(*Unless otherwise stated, the Oxford Prose edition is used.*)

A. *THE ARAN ISLANDS*

1. 'Another old man, the oldest on the island . . . often tells me about a Connaught man who killed his father with the blow of a spade when he was in a passion, and then fled to this island and threw himself on the mercy of some of the natives with whom he was said to be related. . . . This impulse to protect the criminal is universal in the west . . . due . . . more directly to the primitive feeling of these people . . . that a man will not do wrong unless he is under the influence of a passion which is as irresponsible as a storm on the sea', *p. 95*.

2. '"Bedad, noble person, I'm thinking it's soon you'll be getting married . . . a man who is not married is no better than an old jackass . . .; he eats a bit in this place and a bit in another place, but he has no home for himself; like an old jackass straying on the rocks"', *p. 121*.

3. 'Further on I had a long talk with a young man who is inquisitive about modern life, and I explained to him an elaborate trick or corner on the Stock Exchange that I heard of lately. . . . "Well", he said . . . "isn't it a great wonder to think that those rich men are as big rogues as ourselves"', *p. 175*.

B. *IN WICKLOW, WEST KERRY AND CONNEMARA*

1. '. . . "but now all this country is gone lonesome and bewildered, and there's no man knows what ails it"', '*The Oppression of the Hills*', *p. 210*.

2. '"The French do have two kinds of tobacco; one of them is called hay-tobacco" . . .', '*In West Kerry*', *p. 241*.

3. '. . . the little hostess . . . took off her apron, and fastened it up in the window as a blind . . .', '*In West Kerry*', *p. 249*.

4. '". . . and I humbly beg your pardon, might I ask your name? . . . Well, good night so," he said, "and may you have a good sleep your first night in this island"', '*In West Kerry*', *p. 250*.

5. 'One of the young men had been thrown from a car . . . and his face was still raw and bleeding and horrible to look at; but the young girls seemed to find romance in his condition, and several of them went over and sat in a group round him, stroking his arms and face', '*In West Kerry*', *p. 253*.

6. '"... that is called the Stooks of the Dead Women..."', '*In West Kerry*', *p. 264.*

7. '... blind beggars were kneeling on the pathway, praying with almost Oriental volubility for the souls of anyone who would throw them a coin. "May the Holy Immaculate Mother of Jesus Christ... intercede for you in the hour of need..."', '*In West Kerry*', *p. 265.*

8. 'The roulette man passed us first, unfolding his table and calling out at the top of his voice: "Come play me a game of timmun and tup...." The races had to be run between two tides while the sand was dry... and before we reached the strand the horses had been brought together, ridden by young men in many variations of jockey dress...', '*In West Kerry*', *p. 272.*

9. 'Here and there on my way I met old men with tail-coats of frieze, that are becoming so uncommon', '*In West Kerry*', *p. 280.*

10. 'Immediately she turned back towards me and began her thanks again, this time with extraordinary profusion...', '*From Galway to Gorumna*', *p. 287.*

11. 'It is not too much to say that one can hardly spend an hour in one of these Mayo crowds without being reminded in some way of the drain of people that has been and is still running from Ireland', '*The Small Town*', *p. 337.*

12. '... the steamer was put on a few years ago between Sligo and Belmullett', '*Possible Remedies*', *p. 340.*

c. *In Box File G, among the early drafts for* The Aran Islands, *omitted from the final text:*

'These people seem eager to believe in an imaginary punishment of an imaginary crime, yet none of them think of the real punishment of the real criminals who go out drunk in their curaghs and perish in the sound.'

D. *In Notebook 40, a fragment omitted from his description of the Blaskets in '*In West Kerry*':*

'One feels here too why the arts turn to the vices in cities because the virtues are debased but in places where the virtues have kept their garment of dignity the arts are virtuous and we have the little flowers of Assisi instead of Baudelaire and his Fleurs du Mal. That is why all of us who have any value delight in the slum and the company of the smuggler and the poteen maker and thief. The vices may be vulgar when they are put forward in the Rue de Rivoli but the penurious outdoors are always full of interest and dignity and freedom. The penurious charities are also perhaps dignified in themselves but in these countries that have nearly always a fat parson or priest leading them to perdition'

E. *On the cover of Notebook 41* (*August 1905*) (*see also 'In West Kerry', pp. 259–60*):

'It is told in Ballyferriter that a landlord's bailiff went out to the Blaskets some half century ago and that they tied a stone round his neck and threw him into the sea.'

F. *In Envelope 97, a page headed 'Sligo Notes':*

'a wee weak family, a kind of a stuttering fellow and he wasn't cowed at all but he wrought and he wrought till he was above on Ben Bulben—a horse beast.'

G. *In Notebook 28 interspersed with early notes and dialogue:*

'work out relations of outside types so as to make play in a sort ⟨of circle⟩

Types Old F. Old Michael James, group of girls and men Shawn Christy Pegeen and Widow Quin.

Shawn tall fair hair foolish young man

Christy small short and dark

Pegeen contented and goodfeathering but haughty and quick-tempered woman interested in her hope of marriage and ambitious in all ways hence her taking of Christy.

Widow (thirty dark) not gloomy but rather stiff in her relations with villagers very poor and very proud and very cynical (give her rich father in North that she will not write to because of her pride) (so indifferent that she has no ambition—hence her taking Christy)'

H. *In Notebook 32, a list of names; on a page between early drafts of Act III:*

'Cassidy Hennessy Doherty Curran Keane Timmons Kiernan Egan Daly Bailey Tandy Foley Doran Coonan MacCabe M'Mahon Flanagan M'Keown M'Dougal Hogan Kavanagh Hanna MacCoul Hannigan M'Grath Delany Maher MacDonagh Mooney MacKartney Toomey Lynch Fogarty Lonigan Leech M'Quilty Quirke Mac-Namara Leahy Kyle Mulroy'

IV. SYNGE'S PUBLIC DEFENCES OF
THE PLAYBOY OF THE WESTERN WORLD

A. The Playboy *was produced before the edition with Synge's Preface was published. For the first production on 26 January 1907, Synge wrote the following programme notes:*

In writing 'The Playboy of the Western World,' as in my other plays, I have used very few words that I have not heard among the country people, or spoken in my own childhood before I could read the newspapers. A certain number of the phrases I employ I have heard also among the fishermen of Kerry and Mayo, or from beggars nearer Dublin, and I am glad to acknowledge how much I owe, directly and indirectly, to the folk-imagination of these people. Nearly always when some friendly or angry critic tells me that such or such a phrase could not have been spoken by a peasant, he singles out some expression that I have heard, word for word, from some old woman or child, and the same is true also, to some extent, of the actions and incidents I work with. The central incident of the Playboy was suggested by an actual occurrence in the west.

★   ★   ★   ★

Fault has been found with the types of people that I usually present, so it may not be out of place to reprint the following paragraph from the Shanachie. 'In all the circumstances of this tramp life,' I wrote, after dealing with the vagrants of Wicklow, 'there is a certain wildness that gives it romance and a peculiar value for those who look at life in Ireland with an eye that is aware of the arts also. In all the healthy movements of art, variations from the ordinary types of manhood are made interesting for the ordinary man, and in this way only the higher arts are universal. Beside this art, however, founded on the variations which are a condition and effect of all vigorous life, there is another art—sometimes confounded with it—founded on the freak of nature, in itself a mere sign of atavism or disease. This latter art, which is occupied with the antics of the freak, is of interest only to the variations from ordinary minds, and, for this reason, is never universal. To be quite plain, the tramp in real life, Hamlet and Faust in the arts are variations, but the maniac in real life, and Des Esseintes and all his ugly crew in the arts, are freaks only.'

J. M. S.

The incident Synge refers to was probably not the Lynchehaun case but the story told to W. B. Yeats and Arthur Symons during their visit to Aran during the summer of

1896, recounted by Yeats in 'The Trembling of the Veil', Autobiographies, and 'J. M. Synge and the Ireland of his Time', Essays and Introductions, as well as by Synge in The Aran Islands. (*See Introduction.*)

B. *After the riots of the first production, an interview was published which quoted Synge as saying that the play was simply an 'extravaganza' and that he 'did not care a rap' for the public's reaction. Synge then published the following letter in the* Irish Times, *31 January 1907:*

As a rule the less a writer says about his own work the better, but as my views have been rather misunderstood in an interview which appeared in one of the evening papers, and was alluded to in your leader to-day, I would like to say a word or two to put myself right. The interview took place in conditions that made it nearly impossible for me—in spite of the patience and courtesy of the interviewer—to give a clear account of my views about the play, and the lines I followed in writing it. 'The Playboy of the Western World' is not a play with 'a purpose' in the modern sense of the word, but although parts of it are, or are meant to be, extravagant comedy, still a great deal more that is behind it, is perfectly serious when looked at in a certain light. That is often the case, I think, with comedy, and no one is quite sure to-day whether 'Shylock' and 'Alceste' should be played seriously or not. There are, it may be hinted, several sides to 'The Playboy'. 'Pat,' I am glad to notice, has seen some of them in his own way. There may be still others if anyone cares to look for them.

V. FIRST PRODUCTION

By the National Theatre Society Ltd. at the Abbey Theatre on Saturday, 26 January 1907, under the direction of W. G. Fay with the following cast:

CHRISTOPHER MAHON	W. G. Fay
OLD MAHON, his father, a squatter	A. Power
MICHAEL JAMES FLAHERTY (called MICHAEL JAMES), a publican	Arthur Sinclair
MARGARET FLAHERTY (called PEGEEN MIKE), his daughter	Maire O'Neill
SHAWN KEOGH, her second cousin, a young farmer	F. J. Fay
PHILLY CULLEN } small farmers	J. A. O'Rourke
JIMMY FARRELL }	J. M. Kerrigan

WIDOW QUIN		Sara Allgood
SARA TANSEY		Brigit O'Dempsey
SUSAN BRADY	village girls	Alice O'Sullivan
HONOR BLAKE		Mary Craig
PEASANTS		Harry Young
		U. Wright

APPENDIX C

DEIRDRE OF THE SORROWS: WORKSHEETS AND COMMENTARY

I. DESCRIPTION OF TEXTUAL SOURCES

(Unless otherwise stated, unpublished material is in the possession of the Synge Estate.)

A. *As Synge died before completing the play to his own satisfaction, no author's edition of the play exists.*

B. STANDARD EDITIONS

1. Deirdre of the Sorrows: A Play by John M. Synge (*Dundrum, Cuala Press, 1910*). *A limited edition of 250 copies. Wade's Bibliography of the Writings of W. B. Yeats states that the book was finished on May Eve, 1910 and published on 5 July 1910. A letter from Elizabeth Yeats to a subscriber (now in the possession of the University of Kansas Special Collections) states that the first proofs were just being corrected on 28 July 1909. The text for this edition was put together from the manuscripts by W. B. Yeats, Lady Gregory, and Molly Allgood (Maire O'Neill).*

2. Deirdre of the Sorrows: A Play by John M. Synge (*New York, printed for John Quinn, 1910*). *A limited edition for copyright purposes only of fifty copies, of which five are on vellum. Bound into some copies of this edition is the following note by John Quinn with a list of errata:* 'This edition of Deirdre of the Sorrows followed the Dublin edition printed at the Cuala Press, with many corrections in the punctuation and use of capitals and in three or four places in the spelling. After the book had been printed I compared it with Synge's MS. and found that the Dublin edition had various errors. I had all the copies of my edition except five on vellum and five on hand-made paper destroyed. I have had printed a new edition of fifty, which is a careful and faithful reproduction of Synge's MS. and gives as near as may be the punctuation indicated by him.

The corrections indicated below should be made in this edition.'

This second edition apparently never got beyond the proof stage:

a. *The Berg Collection, New York Public Library, has in its possession a copy of the first edition on vellum printed by Quinn, and the proof sheets of that first edition with manuscript corrections and alterations made by Vincent O'Sullivan and John Quinn.*

b. *The University of Texas Special Collections has in its possession the proof sheets of Quinn's projected second edition; this text is corrected according to the manuscript emendations in the proofs of the first edition and the list of errata bound in with the first edition, but these second proof sheets are in turn heavily annotated and corrected by*

Vincent O'Sullivan. At this stage Quinn evidently despaired of producing a satisfactory edition.

3. *In Volume II of* The Works of John M. Synge (*Dublin, Maunsel, 1910*). *In general this edition corresponds to the Cuala edition, but the few differences make it apparent that George Roberts of Maunsel and Company also had access to the manuscripts from the Estate before they were sold to John Quinn.*

C. EXTANT MANUSCRIPTS/TYPESCRIPTS

1. *In Box File F, an exercise book containing fifty-seven leaves of a translation made by Synge from* The Fate of the Children of Uisneach, *published by the Society for the Preservation of the Irish Language in Dublin in 1898 from a manuscript written about 1740 by Andrew MacCruitin of Corcomroe, County Clare* (*see Greene and Stephens,* J. M. Synge, *p. 307, n. 114*). *Aran, 1900 or 1901.*

2. *In Box File E, three pages of ink MS. on the back of final typescript draft of Act I of* The Well of the Saints. *Apparently the first version of the opening scene. October 1907 or earlier.*

3. *In Box File F, eleven manuscript fragments giving various scenarios for different acts. October 1907–January 1909.*

4. *In Notebook 42, one page of dialogue for Act II, the scene between Lavarcham and Naisi. 1907.*

5. *In the files of the Abbey Theatre, Dublin* (*typescript copy in the possession of the Synge Estate*), *a complete version of the play entitled* The Sons of Usnach: *Act I, TS. 'B'* (*1 November 1907*); *Act II, TS. 'F'* (*23 November 1907*); *Act III, TS. 'D'* (*10 November 1907*).

6. *In Notebook 46, eight pages in both ink and pencil of scenes for Acts I and II. January–April 1908?*

7. *In Item 50, one page in ink of Act III, scene between Deirdre, Naisi, and Conchubor, scribbled on the back of a letter from W. A. Henderson, Secretary of the Abbey Theatre, dated 28 August 1908. September 1908.*

8. *In Box File F, five envelopes of typescript pages and fragments, numbering more than 600 pages, almost all of them heavily emended, but not all drafts complete:*

> *Act I—TS. 'B'* (*1 November 1907*); *TS. 'C'* (*undated, mostly remnants*); *TS. 'E'* (*30 December 1907*); *TS. 'F'* (*10 January 1908*); *TS. 'H'* (*15 February 1908; from 'G', 6 February 1908*).

> *Act II—TS. 'B'* (*6 November 1907*); *TS. 'E'* (*14 November 1907*); *TS. 'F'* (*23 November 1907, but earlier than the 'F' version copied for the Abbey Theatre which corresponds to TS. 'G'*); *TS. 'G'* (*28 November 1907 and 6 December 1907*); *TS. 'H'* (*9 December 1907*); *TS. 'I'* (*11 and 12 December 1907*); *TS. 'J'* (*10 March, 1908*); *TS. 'K'* (*undated, August–October 1908?*); *TS. 'L'* (*21 November 1908*).

> *Act III* (*incorporating early drafts for Act IV which he discarded* (*8 November 1907*)—*TS. 'B'* (*5 November 1907, became 'C' without re-dating*); *TS. 'D'* (*10 November 1907*); *TS. 'E'* (*25 November 1907*); *TS. 'F'* (*25 November 1907*);

TS. 'G' (29 November 1907); TS. 'H' (17 March 1908); TS. 'I' (10 December 1908).

9. In the University of Texas Special Collections, the complete typescript draft sold to John Quinn by the Synge Estate as the final version of the play. This is the version on which the Cuala and Maunsel editions are based and which was used for the first production of the play at the Abbey Theatre. Ninety-four typescript pages with manuscript emendations by Synge, Yeats, Lady Gregory, John Quinn, and perhaps Harry Stephens, Synge's brother-in-law, and Maire O'Neill.

    Act I—TS. 'I' (7 March 1908).
    Act II—TS. 'O' (14 January 1909) plus pages 1–8 of TS. 'M' (30 November 1908) and pages 7, 10–12 of TS. 'N' (12 December 1908).
    Act III—TS. 'K' (1–5 January 1909; rewritten from TS. 'J', 18 December 1908).

10. In Notebook 47, three-quarters of the notebook devoted to scenes for Act II, with one scene from Act III. Late summer 1908, January 1909.

11. In Notebook 48, all but eight pages devoted to late drafts of Acts II and III. November 1908–January 1909.

II. DRAFT MANUSCRIPTS

A. Synge's method of rewriting entire scenes for each revision forced him in turn to re-examine the structure of the entire play. Many scenarios and discussions of motifs exist among his papers; doubtless many more were discarded as he went along. It is not always possible to date these various scenarios, but a rough idea can be gained of the order in which different ideas occurred to him and were in turn revised or rejected.

1. Two scenarios of the entire play exist, both fairly early before the appearance of Owen:

a. Possibly as early as November 1907.

Scenario Deirdre ! ! !

Act I Lavarcham House where D. has been put away by Conchubor. Old servant tells L. that C. is coming. They get ready D.'s needle work. He comes in looks at it. D. comes in shabby with furze sticks, and rather defies him. He goes. She hears a huntsman's horn, dresses herself magnificently. Thunder storm. She comes back, spins sings (left) women murmur (R). The sons of Usnach come in. Naisi goes to Deirdre in the end they go out both giving ominous curtain. (Ps) (Determination for love and life in spite of fate)

II   Scotland, woods. Dawn, the brothers go out to visit their trap. Lavarcham comes in to tell Deirdre the news and urge her to stay in Scotland. Is Naisi happy? He is. Would anything take him away? Ireland might. Brothers come back, Deirdre tries to make them swear they will not leave Scotland. Fergus' horn. Scene with him. Strong climax in which Deirdre is over-ruled. They all go out for Ireland. Curtain. (Ps) (Inevitable sweeping into current of life)

III At Dawn after the death of the Sons of Usnach. Grave being dug left. Deirdre alone. Conor comes. Final summing up and death of Deirdre (Rider-like)

Over the page Synge has written

Characters

Deirdre (very central and strong)
Naisi—
Lavarcham (wisdom)
Conor (Indifferent Life)

b. *Again fairly early, with Lavarcham acting as the catalyst in Act II.* (*The numbers appear to refer to the number of pages devoted to each scene.*)

Deirdre	
Old Woman Lavarcham current, where is she?	anxiety of fate

Ditto & Conchubor
     and Fergus
     current, where is she
	story and character

Ditto & Deirdre
     C. then eager, driving out of
     Conchubor
	Deirdre character

Deirdre & women
     short
—————————— } scene
women & Sons of U.
     strong	

Love scene Deirdre and Naisi	defiance of destiny welcome to destruction

Finale	with ominous note
She goes with them.	Lavarcham part important in this act.

II	
Lavarcham and Deirdre	statement of happiness
& Naisi	ditto he takes oath to
current oath	stay in Scotland for happiness etc.
	D & N 3 ominous merely
& Fergus	D & L 3 sparks to D.
They refuse to go	D & N & L 1 anxious
current refusal	Ditto & F 3 Naisi refuses
	D & N 3 Deirdre persuades N
Fergus goes to look	Ditto &
for A. and A.	F.A.A. 3 16 They go
	poetical love face what is to come
Deirdre & Naisi *centre*	she persuades him to go
they go	

III	
Deirdre	summing up
& Lav.	
Deirdre & Conchubor	defiance of life
she kills herself	poetical
Conchubor and Fergus	*Fateful*

2. Only one other suggestion for Act I exists outside the typescript drafts. On the back of page 4 of the revised TS. 'B' (probably mid-November 1907), Synge has scribbled:

Lavarcham tells Fergus that Old W. is an ally of N's and is trying to have Deirdre taken away. Motive for L & F scene.

3. Five suggested plans for Act II, four belonging to the October–November 1907 period, one perhaps as late as December 1908:

a. The following suggestions written in blue pencil on two sides of an undated separate page may precede the earliest existing draft of Act II.

Conchubor comes to Alban sees Naisi wants to get him, Naisi refuses and refuses to let him see Deirdre, Fergus goes to the brothers, Conchubor home. D. N. Fergus and brothers.

Begin L. and D. N	D. and Lav.	Lav & N & L
N. and D.	N. and D.	Deirdre D L
F. and N.	C. and N.	exit L
C. and N. and F.	C. and F.	—N & Fergus
C. and N.	F. and N. and D.	NF (confidential)
D. and N.	N. and D.	& D (profession)
	Finale	D & N

b. *On the back of the last page of an undated final scene to Act II, probably immediately following the above alternative plans.*

Possible motive—Naisi swears to remain in Scot. Here Fergus feels he has been hoodwinked by Lavarcham. Fergus enters—

c. *Scribbled in blue pencil on the back of page 4 of TS. 'B' (6 November 1906), conforming to the action in TS. 'G' (28 November 1907).*

D. dis. with Ainnle and Ardan. They go out	1
Lavarcham comes	
L. & Deirdre	3
& Naisi	2
& Fergus	3
Deirdre & N	4
Omnes	3

d. *On the back of page 7 of the revised TS. 'F', Act II (23 November 1907), evidently when Synge was still considering strengthening Ainnle's part.*

Fergus'	Lavarcham motif
They have been	Their life is so tolerable considering
so lucky they	her beauty and fate
should come	they should do nothing to disturb it.
to Emain to have	
full luck there	Ainnle
	ditto
	but priceless on account
	of this wisdom and
	glory of the woods.

e. *One page in Notebook 47, probably as late as December 1908.*

Act II	
Lavarcham & Deirdre	= emotional vein of C's message
	Deirdre swears she will stay
Deirdre and Ewon	irony. D decides to go.
Deirdre & Naisi	N. has seen Fergus and refuses. D.
	changes him
Naisi & L. and men	Fergus comes for adieu
& Deirdre	riot when N. will go
Deirdre	Brings peace again

4. *Five scenarios for Act III from the early versions of 1907 to what may be the final plan Synge had in mind:*

a. *At the bottom of a manuscript draft of Act II centre scene between Naisi and Deirdre, probably November 1907 or earlier.*

Scenario for III

Con. Have the messengers come from
Lavar. I have good news and bad etc.
Then Gel. tells of her beauty
Con. Send in the Sons of Usna
He tells the women to be ready. Enter D. and N. and A. and A.
She foresees what is to come and defics him
Then they close their swords around her and go out.
Conor pulls back curtain on left and calls out
   Kill the sons of Usnach!
Curtain

b. *On the back of page 22 of TS. 'F', Act III (25 November 1907). (Again, the numbers appear to refer to the number of pages devoted to each scene.)*

Con & Lavarcham & Owen ⎫	3
Deirdre and Naisi ⎭	3
Deirdre and Conor	2
Deirdre and Lav. ⎫	3
Deirdre and Con. ⎬	3
D. Con. Lav. and Fergus ⎭	3

c. *On the back of page 3 of TS. 'H', Act I (25 January 1908).*

Conor & L & S	3
Lav. & Sons D.	4
Sons D. & Con.	4
D. & L.	4
messenger	4
end	1
	20

d. *On the back of the last page of Act III, found pinned to TS. 'H' of Act I (25 January 1908), perhaps immediately following the above plan. (The repetition in numbering the scenes is probably not deliberate.)*

1 Lav. & Conchubor 2 (Soldier for transition)	
3 Deirdre and Naisi	(a) before finding grave (b) after finding grave
3 Deirdre and Naisi and Conchubor	
4 Deirdre and Naisi	(a) before quarrel (b) after quarrel
5 Deirdre and Conchubor 6 Deirdre and woman 7 Deirdre and Conchubor finale	

e. *In Notebook 48, perhaps as late as January 1909. It may be to this scenario that Synge is referring in his letter to Lady Gregory of 3 January 1909: 'I have done a great deal to Deirdre since I saw you,—chiefly in the way of strengthening motives ⟨motifs?⟩ and recasting the general scenario. . . .'*

III

Scene 1 Ow. C. L.C.	Introductory Passionate She pleads ⎰ current He decides ⎱ C's mood
+ men	(transition)
A.A.N.D.	Poetic fragment
N.D. (Naisi is alive to the horror of leaving her in Emain.)	Tragic Naisi strong exit passionate current events

D.C.	strange
D.	keen
L.D.	
C.D.	
C.D.F.OW. L.	Final summing up.
	Triumphant

B. *The three manuscript pages on the back of a typescript draft of Act I of* The Well of the Saints *appear to be the earliest version of the opening scene, written probably in October 1907 or earlier:*

Deirdre

[LAVARCHAM's *House, poorly matted.* LAVARCHAM *embroidering.* OLD WOMAN *comes in.*]

OLD NURSE. Conchubor is coming through the glen and Fergus along with him. It's here they're likely coming, and what will he say and herself abroad running on the hills.

LAVARCHAM [*anxiously*]. Is he close by?

OLD WOMAN. Crossing the stream.

LAVARCHAM. We've no time so, to tidy the house or a thing. When there's great trouble coming there's a swarm of worries all times hanging in the way.

OLD W. I see her now with furze sticks high up in the trees.

LAVARCHAM. And she'll be walking in all stained and dirty and he thinking she's learning the manner of a queen. There'll be sorrows on us this night surely. We'd best try and get him off before he'll see her at all.

[CONOR *and* FERGUS *come in.*]

CONOR. God save you.

LAVARCHAM *and* OLD WOMAN. God save you kindly.

CONCHUBOR. Where is Deirdre?

LAVARCHAM. Abroad some place picking flowers or walking in the hills.

CONCHUBOR. And she alone?

LAVARCHAM. Alone surely.

CONCHUB. You'd no call to send her out when there is a storm and thunder coming from the South and West.

LAVARCHAM. She is young and it's no light task handling her like, and if there is storm coming you⟨'d⟩ do well to be going forward to Emain Macha in place of loitering here and she maybe taking shelter with some old crony on the huts above Glen Demen.

CON. I've no dread of rain or thunder. What has she been stitching these days past?

LAVARCH. [*showing him embroidery*]. She has done these creatures Conchubor, and all say there isn't her match at fancying fine figures and throwing one colour on the other.

FERGUS [*looking also*]. It is queen's work surely, but I'd liefer see lighter fancies under the fingers of a girl so young as she is.

CONCH. There is someone [*listens*].

[DEIRDRE *comes in poorly dressed with a bundle of sticks.*]

CONCH. [*looking at her*]. Is this your learning of queen's ways?

DEIRDRE [*impatiently*]. I'm a girl and not queen. Why would you stop me doing what girls do?

c. *When Synge died, even though he had written at least fifteen full versions of Act II, he was still not satisfied with the structure of the middle act. Apart from the version of the final draft TS. 'O' (14 January 1909), where the emendations may simply be an attempt to leave extant a consistent action, he tried three other plans, each one involving drastic alterations in characterization and in turn affecting the other acts.*

1. His first idea seems to have been to broaden the characterization of Ainnle; this would explain the marriage ceremony at the end of Act I and the references to Ainnle's knowledge of the ways of 'wise men':

a. *Act II, TS. 'G' (28 November 1907), pp. 1–2.*

[AINNLE *is busy with tackle etc.* DEIRDRE *comes out of tent.*]

DEIRDRE. It is a bright day Ainnle. You are going to the woods?

AINNLE. Do you know ⟨what⟩ day we are this day?

DEIRDRE. Three weeks after Samhain.

AINNLE. And what day is that?

DEIRDRE. Tell me.

AINNLE. It is this day seven years we found you on Slieve Fuadh.

DEIRDRE [*counting for a moment on her fingers*]. It is, Ainnle, seven years are gone forever.

AINNLE. There have been strange things done in Alban and strange things done in Ireland, but this is the strangest, Deirdre, that myself and Ardan should be well pleased and we living bachelors and servants for yourself and Naisi.

DEIRDRE [*puzzled a little*]. Aren't we well pleased together, surely?

AINNLE. It's that is the great wonder. And I am often asking what is in yourself to make us satisfied and we vagrants only though we have our sway and riches.

DEIRDRE [*not very pleased with the subject*]. You'd have a right to go maybe and take a wife from the King of Alban.

AINNLE. Find me the match of yourself Deirdre, and I'll go surely, and if I don't find your match, it's the way I'll be a lonesome old fellow till my day is done.

DEIRDRE [*taking up a vessel*]. I'm going to the well Ainnle, Naisi is coming in a short while. [*She goes out.*]

AINNLE [*looking out on other side*]. There is Lavarcham coming. She can find them herself. [*He goes after* DEIRDRE.]

LAVARCHAM [*comes in muffled up in*

These pages are then crossed out by Synge and at the bottom of the second page he has written 'Bring Naisi on'.

b. *Act II, undated typescript (probably early December 1907), pp. 14b–15.*

FERGUS. Ainnle and Ardan will not come to Emain Macha.

LAVARCHAM [*triumphantly*]. There are none like these noble brothers for doing a wise thing together. When they're well off and easy, wouldn't they be great fools for to be travelling?

AINNLE. We'd be great fools if we went travelling from the best life is in the whole world. What would we get east or west we haven't here with Deirdre?

FERGUS. It's a poor thing to be pleased with a strange land, and a little tent, and it's a poor thing to see three who should be before others going to a ruin for a woman only.

AINNLE. It's a poor thing to see a man is passing for wise, and he mixing muck and jewels.

FERGUS. It's a poor thing bringing messages to those are away in their heads.

AINNLE [*to* NAISI]. Is it right we are Naisi not to heed him at all?

NAISI, [*slowly*]. I am going back with Fergus, and Deirdre is coming with me.

LAVARCHAM [*clasping her hands*]. Going back to Conchubor?

FERGUS [*greatly pleased*]. That is a wise choice Naisi, I thought well you were dreaming only.

NAISI. If I was thinking your thoughts or you mine who'd know what's wise or foolish.

FERGUS [*briskly*]. You'll be glad from this out you've done what was worthy of the sons of princes. I will go down and ready the curaghs and let you come after quickly, for the tide is turning below. [*He goes.*]

c. *Act II, TS. 'I' (11–12 December 1907), pp. 14–15.*

[FERGUS *goes.*]

AINNLE [*reproachfully*]. Isn't it a strange thing you'd run dangers for a whim only and take Deirdre back to Conchubor?

LAVARCHAM. It isn't Deirdre wishes it and it's a hard thing you'd go against her and she after laying aside a kingdom to come with you.

AINNLE. It's seven years myself and Ardan have been living bachelors and servants for yourself and Deirdre, and it's a hard thing you'd take her off to the man who is her king and sworn lover and who has hatred for yourself.

NAISI. I have done what Deirdre wishes—[*to* LAVARCHAM]—She is getting ready within. [*Pointing to tent.* LAVARCHAM *goes in.*]

AINNLE. If she asked for some girl's fancy you'd no call to.

NAISI [*meaningly*]. It was a light fancy she had surely.

AINNLE [*bending down before* NAISI]. Why is it she'd be going?

NAISI. She is in dread to see love burning out like a candle in its socket and a wind blowing.

AINNLE [*impetuously*]. Isn't Deirdre the like of the wind that is on the sea, and the wave on the shore, and the first plant in the summer and the moon ageing and brightening and the long lakes in the hills? What would she choose but to be growing forward like the whole face of the earth? Is it raving is upon the two of you who should be the lovers of the world forever?

NAISI [*sadly*]. What does the moon think of her ageing, or the storm of its falling away, or the golden flags and the broom and the snow of winter and the white thorns of May and they turning to muck only?

AINNLE [*surprised*]. It's that I was thinking many nights in the still woods Naisi, and I was saying to myself wasn't it great luck for yourself and Deirdre were beyond troubles and you shut up forever in the tower of deep love.

NAISI. Is there a·tower itself, but will crumble away, with one day rubbing on another?

AINNLE [*going back to his idea*]. Though there's crumbling none can get away from, yet it is a fool's choice to take Deirdre back to Conchubor and he eating up his heart with jealousy and hatred.

[DEIRDRE *comes out.*]

DEIRDRE. For seven years the sons of Usnach have not raised their voices in a quarrel.

Beside the direction for Deirdre's entrance Synge has written the word 'expand'.

d. *Act III, TS.* 'G' (*29 November 1907*), *p. 6.*

[*The three* SONS OF USNACH *and* DEIRDRE *come in together,* AINNLE *being the youngest is the least weary and most uneasy.*]

AINNLE [*looking round*]. It's a strange place he has put us camping our first night below Emain, and we come back as his friends?

ARDAN. It'd be best maybe we went on to Emain Macha with the sons of Fergus.

AINNLE. This is no place for a woman who was chosen for the queen of Ireland. I will go and ask the Red Branch house from Conchubor.

NAISI. If you are going it'd be best I went along with you, the three of ourselves are best all times together.

DEIRDRE [*with hidden timidity*]. Stay with me Naisi. It is not of Ainnle and Ardan that the king is jealous, and it would be best if they went to Conchubor and brought us news again. I've little will to go further till Fergus has come from the north.

AINNLE. We'll do that, and come again quickly. Come Ardan.

[*They go out.*]

Synge's hasty sketch of Act III in Notebook 48 (November 1908–January 1909) incorporates this scene and it could be that in his last drafts he had changed his mind about leaving Ainnle and Ardan out of the tent scene.

2. *On 30 April 1908 Synge went into hospital for another operation, and did no more work on* Deirdre of the Sorrows *until August. When he picked up the play again he once more tackled Act II, and by 29 August had become so discouraged that he wrote to Lady Gregory, 'I have been fiddling with Deirdre a little. I think I'll have to cut it down to two longish acts. The middle act in Scotland is impossible.' With this in mind he attempted to rescue the scene between Deirdre and Naisi by incorporating it into their speech together in Act III, as the following seven pages from Notebook 47 indicate:*

ACT II 7 [*exeunt A and A*]

DEIRDRE. I'm in dread Naisi though it was my will brought us out of Alban—What will it be for a poor thing if our life is put away this day, Naisi. It's that Lavarcham was dreading and Fergus when he left us on the mountain road.

NAISI. Leave troubling Deirdre. Fergus will be ⟨here⟩ in the dawn and with him to back us we are safe surely.

DEIRDRE. With the dawn it's you and I maybe will be journeying again or our blood and life maybe that will be running away. When the winter and the summer pass quickly what way would you and I Naisi have joy forever?

N. We'll have joy till age comes on us, Conchubor will be our friend from this out and we'll have great deeds to do in Emain.

D. It isn't to great deeds we're coming Naisi but to near troubles and the shortening of our days the time that they were bright and sunny, and isn't it a poor thing that I Deirdre could not hold you away.

N. [*surprised*].'Wasn't your wish brought us when you heard Fergus talking of the grey dawns and the lonesomeness of ourselves and we a long while banished away?

D. It's a long time we've had surely pressing the lips together, going up and down resting in our arms, Naisi, waking with the smell of June in the tops of the grasses, and listening to the birds in the branches that are highest—It's a long time we've had but the end has come surely.

N. That's low-voiced talking Deirdre when it's your gay words we're used to. What call had we journeying from Alban when it's only a booty to your mind?

D. We're after journeying as the thrushes fly out of the north and young birds fly out on a dark sea. We've grey hairs as our counsel Naisi and we did well coming to the life or death of the first men of Ulster. We did well journeying Naisi, and I'm well pleased we came forward in the winter the time the sun has a low place and the moon has her mastery in a dark sky, for it's you and I were well lodged the last days of our life where there was a light behind the clear trees and the berries on the thorns were a red wall.

N. If it's that dread you have we'd do well to go away into the woods of the East and forget Conchubor and Ainnle and Ardan for it's right to be away from all people when two lovers are awake only. Will we go Deirdre and be safe forever.

D. There is no safe place on the ridge of the world, and it's in the quiet woods I've seen them digging our grave Naisi throwing out the clay on leaves that are bright and withered.

N. I've little wish for Conchubor and you've a dread we'll go away and it's little we'll think of the grave clear nights when I have your cold cheek to my lips, and we resting in a little corner between the day-time and the long night.

DEIRDRE. It's this hour we're between the daytime and a night where there is sleep forever, and isn't it a better thing to be following on to a near death, than to be bending the head down and dragging with the feet, and seeing one day, a blight showing upon love where it is sweet and tender.

N. If it's a near death is coming what will be my trouble losing

3. *The character of Owen as he appears in the later drafts did not occur to Synge until he once more attempted Act II in the autumn of 1908. A messenger variously named 'Owen', 'Eoghan', and finally simply 'Captain' does appear in the November 1907 drafts of the opening scene of Act III, but a more appropriate prototype would be another messenger named 'Gelban' with whom in TS. 'B' (5 November 1907) Conchubor has been drinking, and who is described by the Old Woman as 'the man has ill-will to Naisi'. By TS. 'D' (10 November 1907) it is Eoghan who is 'sworn to hatred of the Sons of Usnach'.*

a. *The first indication of the later Owen (also spelt 'Ewon') occurs in a revised version of TS. 'J', Act II (August 1908?), where he appears as one of Fergus's company. The following speech is retained in TS. 'K' (Autumn 1908?):*

AINNLE. You did well refusing, Naisi. We will not go with Fergus.

OWEN. There's wisdom. Now Ardan double that.

ARDAN. Why would we go when we're well off in Alban, and there's no one is the match for Deirdre for keeping spirits in a company is far away by itself.

HORSEBOYS. We'll stay with Deirdre always.

FERGUS. I'll be going forward for the turning tide, and it'll be a poor story I'll have to tell the kings in Emain.

NAISI. It will not Fergus. We are going back when the tide turns, I and Deirdre with yourself.

OWEN [*triumphantly*]. Didn't I say in seven years the best were weary.

FERGUS. That's the talk of fools and ~~prophets~~ horseboys. But there is no wise man but will be glad you've done the thing was worthy of yourselves and Deirdre.

AINNLE. What has turned your head? Why will you take Deirdre back to Conchubor?

This scene is again revised on a typescript page identified only as (b), *which corresponds in form to TS. 'I'* (12 December 1907). *The Sons of Usnach are still emphasized:*

LAVARCHAM. It isn't Deirdre wishes it ~~in her backmost mind~~. And it's a poor thing you'd take her off to Emain when she left a kingdom to go with you.

AINNLE. It's seven years myself and Ardan have been servants and bachelors for ~~yourself and~~ Deirdre, and we'll stop her going to Conchubor who loves her and has hatred for yourself.

NAISI. I have done what Deirdre wishes and has chosen.

AINNLE. If she wishes what is crazy you've no call to. We will not have her go to Emain.

ARDAN. We'll not Naisi, and our horse-boys will stand with us.

FERGUS. Do not quarrel when I've come bringing messages of peace from Ulster.

OWEN. Be dutiful ~~brothers~~ the two of you.

ARDAN. We will not obey Conchubor.

NAISI. I and Deirdre have chosen. . . . We will go back with Fergus.

MEN. We will not go back. . . . We'll burn your curaghs by the sea.

Notebook 47 contains a snatch of dialogue which implies that at a much later date (*November 1908*) *Synge was still contemplating using both Ainnle and Owen as contrasting figures:*

AINNLE. It's the like of that talk you'll hear from tinkers prophets horseboys and their like—

OWEN. ——

b. *Synge next developed the scene between Owen and Deirdre, which arrived at its final form by TS. 'L'* (21 November 1908). *Five versions occur in Notebook 47, two in TS. 'M'* (*December 1908 and perhaps later*), *and one in Notebook 48* (*possibly as late as January 1909*).

i. *Five pages in Notebook 47 suggest that his first idea was to make Owen Fergus's messenger:*

Deirdre and Ewon

II scene II

DEIRDRE. You have come with Fergus?

E. I have—he's gone to Naisi and his brothers—we saw them hunting above by the streams. Who told you we had come.

DEIRDRE. Lavarcham told me. You should have had a good passage this night on the sea.

EWON. We had—It's a wonder Conchubor didn't come along with us. He's such a rage to set eyes on the lot of you again. They're building up bonfires along the shore to set a blaze to when we see you coming again.

DEIRDRE. Those that are too hasty do waste their labour.

EW. And those do be delaying waste their lives—Are you coming with Fergus?

DEIRDRE. The message is to Naisi.

EWON. You'd best come, Deirdre. You're seven years this place and I'm thinking by this time you'll have been asking yourself was your beauty gone when you seen Naisi looking on you with a cold wondering eye.

DEIRDRE. What's made you think it.

EWON. There was a lady in Tara and she used to go out every day into the road from till she'd see a stranger look on her with joy. Her own man had no eye left for her, she'd say, till she was doubting her senses when she saw her⟨self⟩ in a glass.

DEIRDRE [*sadly*]. And she was long married?

EWON. A long weary time—three months it was and months with it. You'd do best coming to Emain.

DEIRDRE. What is ⟨Conchubor⟩ doing?

EWON. Stretching his belly and losing his hair. Do you know why my father isn't bald or fat?

DEIRDRE [*shakes her head*].

EWON. Because Naisi killed him. Did they never tell you that?

DEIRDRE. Never.

EWON. I'd have thought in seven years they'd have been shaking their brain for a thing to tell. They must know it was a shabby trick when all said.

[DEIRDRE *moves away from him.*]

EWON [*laughing*]. You'd do best not to be huffy—It's likely you'll hear queer stories from this day.

DEIRDRE. If you've come to talk me over for the journey to Ireland you're not doing it well.

EWON. I'm not talking you over. I'd as lief you stayed here another quarter if you wish—the longer you stay the sooner you'll weary, and when you're weary of himself then's the day for another.

DEIRDRE. The world should be a simple pleasant place for a man's a rogue and liar.

EWON. It's that you're thinking [*he goes after her*]. Ah Deirdre isn't a hard thing the world's not pleasant at all.

~~LAVARCHAM~~

ii. *Almost immediately Synge decided to emphasize the element of madness in the character of Owen and give him an identity separate from Fergus. The following scene is written from the other end of Notebook 47.*

OWEN. I've found you alone! The gods be praised. I've been three weeks waiting in the bogs below, getting ague and asthma, and now I've talked with the boatmen brought Fergus and I've run up to warn you.

DEIR. You're kind Owen.

O. I'm more than kind. If you go to Emain you'll lose Naisi and I'll lose yourself.

D. People only lose the things they have.

O. They can the things they hope to have. Don't go to Emain.

DEIR. Naisi will decide with Fergus.

O. You'd do well to let Naisi and his brothers go with Fergus—without yourself there's no danger for their lives in Emain, and let you come off with me who had a father killed by Naisi that⟨'s⟩ a fair bargain.

iii. *This motif is then developed in a passage written on the pages opposite the first draft of the scene between Deirdre and Owen in Notebook 47.*

E. I've found ⟨you⟩ alone is it? And I after loafing around two weeks in the wet muck of the bogs till I've ague and asthma, and water in my guts. Have you a cake.

DEIRD. [*gives him cake*]. What brought you from Ulster?

E. The full moon squeezing the crack I have in the crown of my brain. Was there ever a man pewked out the inside of himself crossing the sea after a woman that wasn't away in his head? Answer that when you've given me something to drink.

DEIRDRE. It should be a long while since you have been in Emain where there's civility in speech with queens—

E. It is long surely—three long weeks I've been singing to water hens and bull frogs below in the bog. I'm as cross as a weazel I tell you, and when the breath's short civility goes first—as gold and good rugs when there's storm at sea.

D. What is it you wish?

E. I⟨'ll⟩ tell you when I'm full within. You're seven years with Naisi, and after seven you're tired of him as he of you both of each other— Stop your mouth—There was a queen in Tara had to go out on the road every day till she'd meet a stranger. Before that she thought ⟨she⟩ was cracked the same as me for when she looked in the glass she thought she was a great wonder, but her king couldn't see it and they three weeks married. And you're seven years [*whistles*]! Listen! Do you know why my father's not as mad as I am?

DEIRDRE [*shakes her head*].

EWON. Because Naisi killed him. Now I'm come to see will you run off with me now you're tired of Naisi?

DEIRDRE [*almost amused*]. The world should be a simple pleasant place when a man's a rogue and liar.

EW. I'm a rich man. You⟨'d⟩ best come off with me. Who's the crowd above?

DEIRDRE. It is Fergus and his sons have come with messages to take us back to Emain.

EWON. And I'd no word of that. You're going is it?

D. The message is to Naisi.

E. I'd a right to say you were tired. Take your choice stay and rot and see Naisi getting harder in the eyes or go back to Conchubor with his swelled up belly and his polished crown.

EWON. Listen to me. Conchubor⟨'s⟩ an old man with his two eyes falling down his face. Naisi should be stale I'm thinking and you'd do best choosing me. I'm great company and I've great knowledge how to please your like.

D. You've little knowledge I'm thinking of my like at all.

E. You won't have me?

D. No.

E. You'll stay here.

D. If Naisi wishes.

EWON. That'll be great sport for the two of you, getting flatter every day. Naisi'll be growing a body on him like Conchubor and ⟨thirsting?⟩ and you'll be shrivelling up to a bit of a stick. It'll be great sport to look on yourself one day with your arms and your two legs, with a hoop in your back and your nose scraping your chin, and you thinking you'd small sport only in the time for sport.

D. That's strange talking for a man's in love.

EWON. I tell the truth there's shame and pity in my heart I tell you when I see your like your wasting away it's a pitiful thing when any'd let life slip and it a little short space only. I'm cracked maybe, but I've a kind pitiful mind. There's Lavarcham coming again—Would you credit my father was sitting in a bed of grass and heather kissing that one under the ear, and the twilight coming and a little bird looking downward from the top of a tree. Would you believe that I ask you and he an old skeleton and she a scarecrow with two legs in place of one.

LAV. Naisi's coming down through the wood.

EWON. He is? I'm going. I wouldn't be one too many in this place they should have great talk and whispering and they only seven short years hanging on their necks. Come. [*He takes* LAVARCHAM *by the arm*.] Come I'm saying. I'll find Fergus and we'll talk of talk. [*They go*.]

L. Go yourself. I have a word for Deirdre. [*He goes*.]

LAV. What's he said?

D. Trash and love and nonsense and great talk of the old age will come upon us all.

L. There's great wit and wisdom many'll say, with those have swapped decency for a cold and bloody eye.

D.

iv. *Having built up the character of Owen, Synge then apparently decided to alter the structure of the entire act; the following outline and scene from Notebook 47 were written after the above versions, but before 30 November 1908.*

II. I.?

NAISI [*calls to* DEIRDRE]. This evening we'll go to Glen da Ruadh I am going up the hill to Ainnle and Ardan, let you pack our things together.

D. I will Naisi. [*He goes*.] [DEIRDRE *brings out things and begins packing and folding*.]

Enter OWEN. It's three weeks I've been seeking to find you and not a bit could I. Then scene with Owen. Scene with Lavarcham. Scene with Naisi.

OWEN. I've found you alone and I three weeks loafing and waiting in the wet muck of the bogs till I've ague and asthma, and watery guts. Have you a cake

DEIRDRE [*gives him cake*]. What brought you from Ulster?

OWEN. The full moon squeezing the crack I have in the crown of my brain. Who'd go on the cold sea, pewking his heart out for a woman and he not away in his head?

D. It should be a long while since you've been in Emain, where men are civil in their speech with queens.

OWEN. It's a long time—a score of days I'm singing to waterhens and badger on the rim of the bog. I'm as cross this day as a weazel and when the breath's short civility goes over like gold bags in a storm at sea. Three weeks is a great while and seven years—it's seven years this day you've been with Naisi. A stone post would get an ague and it thinking on the like.

D. You've come seven times in seven years and I don't know what you've gained.

v. *Later in Notebook 47 Synge decided to emphasize the parallel between Owen and Naisi by making them confront each other.*

End of scene D. and Owen

OWEN. ⟨When⟩ a man's ⟨blood⟩ does get cool he's jealous jealous of stars and moon, jealous of his ass and dog and jealous of the sun and wind. [*He comes very near her.*] If I had you, and I saw myself beside you the way I'm sitting now there'd be a new story for the writers to set in their books. There he is. The gods save and bless you Naisi. Let you not be jealous it's of that we were talking but I've got the cold shoulder. I'm going. Let you not be jealous. Let you not be jealous, Naisi, a fine man like you! [*He goes.*]

NAISI. What brought that man to you?

DEIRDRE. You had a right to ask him. It's little I know of his mind.

NAISI. He's here a long while?

DEIR. A good space. Three weeks he's waited in the hogs he says to see me alone. He says if he was you he'd be jealous of himself. Isn't it a pitiful ⟨thing⟩ to rouse the love I have for quiet oaks you'll see the windy skies through when I'll lose them at the day of death, and isn't a pitiful ⟨thing⟩ great lovers do meet hard sorrow in the end.

NAISI [*coming to her side*]. I've been with Fergus and Lavarcham. I've sent word to Conchubor we'll stay in Alban always.

DEIRDRE. You were in great haste with a judgement is a life or death to us—we four that were so happy.

NAISI. Would you have us go with Fergus?

DEIRDRE. Wasn't it this night I saw a red cloud over the greenness of Ireland, and three birds coming with drops of honey in their mouths to take our blood away from us?

NAISI. Then fold our rugs Deirdre. Leave troubling on Fergus or Owen and this night we'll go to Glen da Ruadh when the salmon will be running with the tide, etc.

vi. *But although the current of madness was sufficiently developed in the Notebook 47 drafts, Synge was still not satisfied with his use of Owen as a character. On the back of a discarded typescript he scribbled the following suggestions:* 'Deirdre gets angrily excited against Owen and sends him out with a vehement speech. Then Naisi and Fergus come in. Naisi runs over Fergus' arguments, Deirdre implores Fergus to leave them alone. Fergus says old age brings peace and he'd have peace he goes. Then scene as before Deirdre and Naisi.'

Notebook 48 emphasizes Owen's role as Conchubor's messenger, in a passage which may have been written as late as January 1909:

ow. Then take your choice—stay here and rot with Naisi or go to Conchubor in Emain. Con⟨chubor⟩ has a swelling belly on him and his two eyes falling downward from his shiny crown. Naisi should be stale and weary—Did ever you think there are others left walking the world—the like of myself that would liefer be bleaching in a bog-hole than living onwards without some touch of kindness from yourself today.

D. Are there no women like yourself to be your friends in Emain?

O. There are none like yourself Deirdre and it's I'm after sitting up seven years and I so lonesome I'd squeeze kisses on a cur-dog's nose.

DEIRD. You're talking queer things. What is it brought you into Alban and what is it you're seeking now?

O. Two things brought me to see yourself I have a love for, and Naisi that I hate forever and the gold Conchubor gave me to bring him news of the two of you in Alban—Now answer are you going this night with Fergus—

vii. *Finally, after he had apparently decided to work Owen into Act I, Synge tried to strengthen this scene even further; the greatly reworked TS. 'M' (dated 30 November 1908) indicates how he planned to use Owen in the first act also:*

OWEN [*very sharply*]. I'll tell you how to make a silly world. Stay here and rot with Naisi or go to Conchubor in Emain. [*Leaning forward.*] Conchubor's a swelling belly, and his eyes falling downward from his shiny crown. Naisi should be stale and weary, yet there are many roads, Deirdre [*he goes towards her*], and there are those have great knowledge how to please your like.

DEIRDRE [*coldly*]. I'm thinking you've little knowledge of my like at all.

OWEN [*going to her, more wildly*]. And have you knowledge of the way I'd liefer be bleaching in a bog-hole than living on without a touch of kindness from your eyes and voice? Do you know what that is? That's Conchubor's knife he cut your logs with on Slieve Fuadh. I stole it after, for it's a cold thing to be so lonesome you'd squeeze kisses on a cur dog's nose, and you missing your chances seeing others walking . . . or sitting . . . in the place you'd choose.

DEIRDRE [*interested*]. And are there no women like yourself in Emain?

OWEN [*vehemently*]. There are none like you Deirdre . . . and it's for that there's neither man or woman is the like of me. . . . Give me a little ring or necklace, the way I can have a thing to twist between my fingers and I going the road. You've ⟨a⟩ store of jewels, Deirdre, and I hear their voices in the trees.

DEIRDRE [*hesitates, then gives him a ring*].

OWEN. The gods reward you. Are you going west this night with Fergus?

DEIRDRE [*stiffly again*]. I will be where Naisi chooses.

There is a large question mark in the margin beside these last passages, and on the back of the preceding typescript page Synge scribbled yet another version:

of my like at all.

OWEN [*throwing himself at her feet*]. Though I play the fool I'm no fool Deirdre, saving I'd liefer be bleaching in a bog hole, than living onward without a touch ⟨of⟩ kindness from your eyes and voice. It's a cold thing missing your chances from Inishmaan to the plain of Meath and you so lonesome you're ready to squeeze kisses on a cur dog's nose. . . .

Give me a little ring you have, or a necklace or a brooch itself. Give ⟨me⟩ something I can twist between my finger⟨s⟩ and I going the road. You've ⟨a⟩ store of jewels surely.

DEIRDRE [*gives him something doubtfully looking round to see that no one sees them.*]

OW. Take my word now and stay away from Emain.

DEIR. [*stiffly*]. I will be where Naisi choose.

OWEN [*roughly*]. Naisi Naisi is it.

TS. '*O*' *originally contained the following speech which conforms to this action by Owen:*

NAISI [*giving* DEIRDRE *her ring*]. He was always a thief and rogue, and he'd stolen your ring. [DEIRDRE *takes it quietly*.]

c. *At one time during the last three months Synge considered placing Owen's death scene in Act III.*

i. *An undated typescript fragment of the scene between Deirdre and Naisi after Conchubor has left them seems to be the first attempt to introduce Owen into the final act:*

NAISI. It would be a good thing if all was done.

DEIRDRE. It would Naisi . . . I went and looked on Owen in the trees. Death should be a troubled nasty thing no matter who may die.

ii. *A later passage in Notebook 47 appears to be the first draft of the contemplated death scene:*

OWEN. I'll be with them. I've thought more on Deirdre than the pack of you, and I'll be with ⟨them⟩ this night in the grave.

FERGUS. Keep back we'll have no noisy talker stretched beside them when their rest has come.

CON. Get back among your men.

OWEN. It's of dead men that you're king tonight. [*Falls in the darkness.*]

OLD W. He's dead Conchubor he'd weak wits the gods forgive him.

FERGUS. Four white bodies have their grave together. etc.

iii. *Later still Synge expanded this scene in a typescript fragment:*

have done this night in Emain.

OWEN [*in a whisper*]. I'll be with them. I've thought more of Deirdre than ⟨the⟩ pack of you. I'll be friends with Naisi ~~this night~~ in the grave.

FERGUS [*stopping him*]. Keep back we'll have no noisy talker ~~in that grave tonight~~.

CON. ~~Get back among~~ Go to my men.

OWEN. It's of dead men you're king tonight. [*Crying behind.*] Dead men, dead men. Men died for Deirdre's beauty keep me company tonight.

LAV. He's dead Conchubor. He's split his heart.

FERGUS. It's in this grave four white bodies are laid down together, four clear lights are quenched in Ireland—[*throws his sword into the grave*] —There is my sword that could not shield you etc. etc.

III. RELATED PASSAGES IN NOTEBOOKS

A. *Although there exists in an exercise book in Box File F Synge's own translation while on Aran in 1900 or 1901 of* The Fate of the Children of Uisneach *from the Irish text of Andrew MacCruitin, there is no further evidence that he used this as the basis for his dramatization of the story six years later. On the other hand, he had urged Molly Allgood in November 1906 to read Lady Gregory's translation of the story in her* Cuchulain of Muirthemne *and had previously referred to the saga in three articles:*

1. '*La Vieille Littérature Irlandaise*', L'Européen (*Paris*), 15 March 1902, p. 11.

2. '*An Epic of Ulster*', The Speaker (*London*), 7 June 1902, pp. 284–5. (*A review of Lady Gregory's* Cuchulain of Muirthemne.)

3. '*A Translation of Irish Romance*', Manchester Guardian, 28 December 1905 (*A review of A. H. Leahy's* Heroic Romances of Ireland. vol. i.) '*Irish Heroic Romance*', *Manchester Guardian*, 6 March 1906, (*vol ii*).

B. *In Notebook 33, the following draft of an essay written presumably after his review of Leahy's* Heroic Romances *turned his mind once more to the story of Deirdre:*

Historical or Peasant Drama   18/3/07

The moment the sense of historical truth awoke in Europe, historical fiction became impossible. For a time it seemed otherwise. Antiquarian writers, fools now exploded. Old writers (Elizabethan Louis XIV) saw historical personages as living contemporaries. Now it is impossible to use our own language or feeling with perfect sincerity for personages we know to have been different from ourselves. Hence Hist. Fiction insincere. It is possible to use a national tradition a century or more old which is still alive in the soul of the people see Walter Scott. But any one who is familiar with Elizabethan writings will not tolerate Kenil-worth or Westward Ho. Promessi Sposi (?) To us now *as readers* the old literature itself is so priceless we look with disgust at imitations of it. As creators? It is impossible to use a legend ⟨such⟩ as Faust which from the outset defies historical reality—in the making up of an absolutely modern work. ⟨That⟩ is only to be done possibly in verse, as our modern spoken prose cannot be put into the mouths of antique persons. On stage this is so most of all. In thinking over the poems of the last century that one reads with most pleasure how many are historical? Browning, Rossetti. For my own part I only care for personal lyrical modern poetry and little of that, but I am possibly exceptional. That is why lyrical poetry is now the only poetry. The real world is mostly unpoetical, fiction even in poetry is not totally sincere hence failure of modern poetry. This is to be taken with all reserve, there is always the poet's dream which makes itself a sort of world. When it is kept a dream is this possible on the stage? I think not. Maeterlinck, Pelleas and Meli-sande? Is the drama—as a beautiful thing a lost art? The drama of swords is. Few of us except soldiers have seen swords in use, to drag them out on the stage is babyish. They are so rustic for us with the association of pseudo-antique fiction and drama. For the present the only possible beauty in drama is peasant drama, for the future we must await the making of life beautiful again before we can have beautiful drama. You cannot gather grapes of chimney pots.

IV. FIRST PRODUCTION

By the Irish Players under the direction of Maire O'Neill at the Abbey Theatre, Dublin, on 13 January 1910 with the following cast:

LAVARCHAM	Sara Allgood
OLD WOMAN	Eileen O'Doherty
OWEN	J. A. O'Rourke
CONCHUBOR	Arthur Sinclair
FERGUS	Sydney J. Morgan
DEIRDRE	Maire O'Neill
NAISI	Fred O'Donovan
BROTHERS OF NAISI:	
AINNLE	J. M. Kerrigan
ARDAN	John Carrick
TWO SOLDIERS	Ambrose Power, Harry Young

The costumes were designed by Charles Ricketts and the setting was designed by Robert Gregory. A special prelude was composed by John Larchet.

J. M. Synge died in 1909 and *The Works of John M. Synge* was published in four volumes by Maunsel & Co., Dublin, in 1910. Since then the canon of his work has remained largely unaltered. Nevertheless, much unpublished material exists, including notebooks, poems, early drafts of the plays, and fragments of poetic drama, and this has now been thoroughly explored in order to create this definitive edition, not only collecting together all that is of significance in Synge's printed and in his unprinted work, but also, by a careful use of workshee and early drafts, indicating much of the process of creation. The *Collected Wor* is under the general editorship of Professor Robin Skelton, of the University of Victoria, British Columbia. The first volume contains his edition of Synge's poems and translations, the second assembles all Synge's prose writings of any merit or interest, edited by the late Dr. Alan Price, of The Queen's University, Belfast.

The third and fourth volumes are devoted to Synge's plays, edited by Professor Ann Saddlemyer, of Victoria College, University of Toronto. The fir of these volumes contains texts of *Riders to the Sea, The Shadow of the Glen,* and *The Well of the Saints,* and of the originally little known *When the Moon Has Set,* with appendixes analysing the drafts of each play and giving details of first productions. In addition the volume contains much unpublished material, scenarios, dialogues, and fragments, discovered among Synge's notebooks.

This volume provides definitive texts of *The Tinker's Wedding, The Playb of the Western World,* and *Deirdre of the Sorrows.* For all these three plays recently discovered manuscript and notebook material has involved a certain amount of textual alteration; an examination of the long-lost final typescript of *The Playboy of the Western World* has provided many clues to the author's intentions, while comparison of the various drafts of *Deirdre of the Sorrows* wit the typescript given by the executors to Yeats and Lady Gregory has enabled Dr. Saddlemyer to determine the extent of posthumous collaboration.

Synge re-wrote his plays many times; one act of *The Playboy* ran to at lea: fifteen full drafts, not counting numerous internal alterations. By examining eac available draft of every play, the editor has been able to provide not only a final text of each play as close as possible to the dramatist's version, but in her accompanying notes almost a variorum study of significant passages. Appendix record the growth of each play from the original scenario through many drafts to the final text, and include discarded scenes which throw new light on the playwright's creative process. Details of first productions and a comprehensive description of all the manuscript sources are also included. The introduction traces the history of each play, quoting extensively from Synge's unpublished correspondence and notebooks to record the dramatist's attitude to his own work in the making, and to set each play against the broader background of the Abbey Theatre.

In searching out the material for this edition, Dr. Saddlemyer has made us of public and private collections in both Ireland and the United States.

Cover picture : 'The Playboy' by Jack B. Yeats, reproduced by kind permissio of Michael B. Yeats and Anne Yeats.

Colin Smythe Ltd., Gerrards Cross, Buckinghamshire
0–86140–137–9 Hbk and 0–86140–061–2 Pbk

The Catholic University of America Press, Washington, D.C.
0–8132–0569–7 Hbk and 0–8132–0568–9 Pbk